HINTON

AGGRESSION AND BEHAVIOR CHANGE

AGGRESSION AND BEHAVIOR CHANGE

Biological and Social Processes

edited by
Seymour Feshbach
Adam Frączek

PRAEGER

PRAEGER SPECIAL STUDIES • PRAEGER SCIENTIFIC

Library of Congress Cataloging in Publication Data

Main entry under title:

Aggression and behavior change.

   Includes bibliographical references and index.
   1.   Aggressiveness (Psychology)--Physiological aspects.
2.   Aggressiveness (Psychology)--Social aspects.
3.   Behavior modification.   I.   Feshbach, Seymour.
II.   Frączek, Adam.
BF575.A3A5   152.5   79-17934
ISBN 0-03-052446-6

Published in 1979 by Praeger Publishers
A Division of Holt, Rinehart and Winston/CBS, Inc.
383 Madison Avenue, New York, New York 10017 U.S.A.

9 038 987654321

Printed in the United States of America

PREFACE

This volume is based on a conference held in Warsaw, Poland. We are deeply grateful for the hospitality and facilities provided by the Polish Academy of Sciences and the travel assistance rendered by the International Research and Exchanges Board. The support provided by both of these groups made the conference possible.

The stimulus for the conference on psychological factors and issues entailed in changing aggressive behavior arose in connection with a several-month visit by Prof. Adam Frączek to the psychology laboratory at UCLA. One major research program under way at the time was addressed to the effects of inhibiting and modifying aggression upon other personality components—notably sexual responsiveness. A second research activity, at that time in its preliminary stages, involved a joint project with Prof. Norma Feshbach addressed to the effects of empathy and fantasy training upon aggression in elementary-school-age children. Given this research context, plans for a conference at which alternative approaches to the modification of aggression could be examined evolved quite naturally.

The decision to hold the conference in Warsaw was in part influenced by Professor Frączek's association with the Polish Academy of Sciences and by its interest in sponsoring the conference. However, a more important factor was the desirability of psychologists in the United States and other Western countries becoming more familiar with the research of East European psychologists in the setting in which they carry out their work. There appears to be a much closer relationship between basic research and its application in Poland than is the case in the United States. It was also revealing that while the material resources available to the Polish psychologists in the form of equipment, space, secretarial support, and other areas are quite limited, the personnel resources in the form of bright, well-read, intellectually involved, and stimulating graduate students are quite impressive. The presence of students at the conference contributed to its success.

In addition, besides the authors of the papers in this volume, there were a number of psychologists in attendance who contributed importantly to the discussions and conference proceedings. Among them were Dr. S. A. Barnett of Australia; Drs. B. Buda, M. Kun, and I. Munnich of Hungary; Drs. T. Arzelas, T. Karylowski, M. Kofta, M. Kosewski, Maria Susulowska, and Maria Zebrowska of Poland; and Drs. V. Derlega, P. Mussen, A. Pepitone, D. Rimm, and R. D. Singer of the United States. Unfortunately, for the sake of brevity and because of the structural organization of this volume, we have not included their helpful and incisive comments. However, they are to some extent reflected in the concluding chapter. It is our hope that the volume resulting from this conference will provide a useful theoretical perspective from which to examine various alternatives for modifying aggressive behavior and, further, will foster the development of programs that will reduce the incidence of destructive aggressive behavior that is still too prevalent in contemporary society.

CONTENTS

LIST OF TABLES

LIST OF FIGURES

Figure   Page

AGGRESSION AND BEHAVIOR CHANGE

1

CHANGING AGGRESSION:
THE NEED AND THE APPROACH

Seymour Feshbach and
Adam Frączek

A recurrent and omnipresent contemporary theme is the problem of human violence and aggression. It is a theme that permeates our films, our literature, our political life, and, in many instances, our daily lives. In the United States alone, there have been two major national inquiries in less than a decade addressed to problems of aggression: the Surgeon General's Scientific Advisory Committee on Television and Social Behavior in 1971 and the National Commission on the Causes and Prevention of Violence in 1970. This social concern has been stimulated by an apparent increase in crimes of violence by groups that are attempting to bring about major social and political changes, and by the ever-present specter of war—either its imminence or its actuality; and there is a covert, nagging anxiety that we do not have much time left to solve the problems of human aggression. The characterization of the modern era as the "Age of Anxiety" might be more aptly, if less elegantly, altered to the "Age of Anxiety about Violence."

The community's concern with the threat of human violence has been met by a surfeit of volumes directly concerned with the problems of violence and aggression. These books, written by experts and pseudoexperts, offer a mélange of information and assertions about aggression that is difficult to digest. When Robert Ardrey writes of man's descent from a killer ape, is that science, pseudoscience, or mere speculation? When the eminent ethologist Konrad Lorenz sees *Homo sapiens* in the image of our species's animal ancestors, is that more or less valid than emphasizing those features of experience that are unique to human beings—for example, understanding human aggressive behavior in terms of human values, culture, and economics? Does Sigmund Freud's view of aggression as a manifestation of an innate, biological urge provide a superior guide to the understanding of aggression and its more extreme form, violence, than the theoretical concepts of B. F. Skinner, who sees aggression in the same context that he sees other important human behaviors—namely, as a behavior that is acquired because it is systematically rewarded or reinforced?

How we view the antecedents of aggression has, of course, direct implication for how we go about the task of modifying aggression. In this volume we shall consider physiological, psychological, and social mechanisms that are implicated in both the evocation-maintenance and regulation-reduction of aggression. We shall also focus on the modification of aggression in children, although the analyses and data presented will not be restricted to them. There are a number of reasons for emphasizing the modification of aggression in children, within the context of a more general analysis of aggressive behavior.

A contributing factor to public concern over the threat of violence has been the participation of young people in acts of extreme aggression and destruction. In the United States there is increasing anxiety over vandalism, juvenile assaults and use of lethal weapons, and the decreasing age at which homicides are committed. There is also broad public and scientific interest in the reasons for this upsurge in juvenile violence and—most especially—in the solution. An area of particular concern has been the effects of mass communication, particularly of exposure to the depiction of violence on television.

Aggression in children also merits special attention because of the developmental continuity in patterns of aggressive behaviors. Given the evidence that adult aggressive behaviors are related to the degree of aggression displayed in a child, and the likelihood that aggressive tendencies are more readily modified at a younger than at an older age, it would seem appropriate to devote particular attention to the alternatives to aggressive behavior patterns before the child attains maturity.

The label "aggression," whether applied to responses of the child or of the adult, embraces a diverse set of behaviors ranging from teasing and hostile remarks to playful jostling and physical assault. It includes dreams of violence and acts of violence; it refers to behaviors that are socially normative, sometimes even socially idealized, and to behaviors that are viewed as antisocial, criminal acts. In the case of animals, it may denote ritualized "threat" displays, circumscribed dominance-related interactions, and highly destructive attack behaviors. Given the variety and complexity of phenomena that fall under the heading of aggression, one can anticipate that diverse and conflicting alternatives will be proposed with regard to its management.

At the same time, no attempt was made to arrive at a consensus on a definition of aggression, a task that could have consumed all of the efforts of the conference participants. Rather, participants addressed issues of aggression in terms of the particular behaviors with which they were most concerned and of the particular theoretical perspective that had guided their research. It remained, then, for the conferees and the editors to delineate areas of consensus and of disagreement, and to determine whether apparent theoretical differences resulted from definitional ambiguities or reflected genuine theoretical alternative analyses of similar empirical phenomena. Most often, the approaches presented in the papers in this volume tend to complement rather than conflict with each other. Taken together, they provide a multidimensional framework for conceptualizing and implementing procedures for modifying aggressive behaviors.

The set of papers by Elzbieta Fonberg, José Delgado, and Kirsti Lagerspetz is addressed to biological aspects of aggressive behavior, particularly neurophysiological mechanisms implicated in aggressive acts. Through the use of refined brain stimulation, brain lesion, and behavioral genetic techniques, these investigators clarify the role of specific brain structures and neurochemical processes in the evocation and inhibition of aggression. They also examine in some detail the interplay between biological and learning mechanisms in the developmental regulation of aggressive behavior patterns.

In reviewing these papers, one might well consider several questions that extend beyond the theoretical and empirical merits of the particular studies reported. One such question is the implication of these findings for human aggression. To what extent do the neural and genetic mechanisms observed in animal studies apply to human beings? In what way do these animal studies contribute to an understanding of the aggression that takes place between people? Assuming some generality and parallelism of mechanisms, another, more difficult question arises as to "appropriateness" of the systematic use of these biological procedures for the regulation of aggression at the human level. Here we encounter some thorny social, ethical, and even political issues. In order to deal with them, a reasoned and explicit identification of the specific aggressive behaviors to be modified and the mediating mechanisms becomes imperative. It is of interest that these papers demonstrate that even at the physiological level, one can distinguish functionally distinct categories of aggressive behavior.

The next group of papers is concerned with the modification and control of aggression through behavioral mechanisms. It is evident from these analyses that at the psychological level, the roots and determinants of aggressive behaviors are differently interpreted and that the processes and structures believed to be involved in the regulation of aggressive actions vary markedly, depending upon the particular theoretical model involved. The papers by G. R. Patterson and Leonard D. Eron, focusing on social learning processes in the modification of aggression, form one subset within this group. The emphasis here is on the pattern of stimuli and reinforcers instigating and maintaining aggressive versus alternative responses to provocative stimulus situations. However, social learning theorists have become increasingly attentive to cognitive mediating mechanisms, and consequently the gap between these behavioral approaches and the more "dynamic" models that follow is less sharp than has hitherto been the case.

The papers by Frączek and Janusz Reykowski fall into the latter category. In dynamic approaches to aggression, greater attention is given to sources of conflict, to emotional and motivational factors that are believed to underlie and give rise to the aggressive act. At the same time, these emotional and motivational processes are seen as intimately connected to cognitive parameters. Thus, the emotional instigation of aggression is usually dependent upon the cognitive appraisal of certain stimulus situations as threatening, malevolent, or injurious. Also, the role of cognitive processes in the regulation of aggression is not limited to appraisal and the evocation of response alternatives to or interferences with aggression. Certain cognitive structures, notably those associated with consciousness, and especially the ability to verbalize one's emotions and anticipate the outcome of one's behavior, are important factors in aggression and its control.

The complexity of aggression and its management in humans as compared with other organisms is further reflected in the extent to which aggressive behavior is influenced by social norms and parameters. Social and cultural factors are addressed in the papers by Marvin Wolfgang and Marek Kosewski and, to some extent, by Sepp Schindler. All three papers share a common concern with social deviance and with aggressive behavior sufficiently deviant to fall into a category of criminal activity. The role of sociocultural determinants in influencing aggression, criminal and otherwise, is broad and varied, and may be approached from two complementary perspectives. One, a sociohistorical perspective, traces changes in customs, value systems, and goals from generation to generation, linking these changes to political, socioeconomic, and other historically pertinent dimensions. A second perspective from which to examine social factors is that of the specific social milieu in which the instigation, maintenance, and alteration of aggressive acts take place. Particularly important here is an examination of the role of small social groups in regulating aggressive behavior. All three papers are written largely from the second perspective, investigating characteristics of an aggressive subculture that facilitates delinquency, of a prison subculture that fosters aggression, and of a therapeutic orientation and environmental changes that reduce delinquency and aggression. Ultimately, the insights provided by each of these perspectives need to be integrated theoretically and empirically, demonstrating, for example, how socioeconomic changes modify the norms of an aggressive subculture and how the latter changes are reflected in changes in aggressive behaviors.

The presentations up to this point have concerned themselves with factors stimulating and maintaining aggressive behavior and with changing aggression through alteration of the aggressive response—through biochemical intervention and electrical stimulation, through modifications of parentally administered reinforcers, and through changing the social milieu. One can, however, approach the problem of changing aggression by examining the factors involved in the development of prosocial behaviors and the psychological mechanisms regulating prosocial actions. The papers by Norma Feshbach and Lea Pitkänen-Pulkkinen are concerned with precisely such issues. In shifting attention to prosocial behaviors as a means of altering aggressive response patterns, we find another significant dimension that distinguishes the regulation of animal aggression from the regulation of human aggression.

For most animal species, the response to conflict or to noxious and threatening stimuli can be adequately described by a "fight-flight" model. The organism responds with attack to a threat or with an avoidant, escape reaction. The animal's territory is violated and it responds with an aggressive display or, if the invader is clearly superior in strength, may run away. Competition for food and sexual activity elicits analogous response alternatives: fighting for a dominant position or acceptance of a subordinate role. There is a wider array of responses to threat and competition available to humans than attack and retreat. Humans have the capacity for assuming the roles of others and perceiving conflict situations from the vantage points of others as well as from their own. Humans have the capacity to develop compromise and cooperative solutions, and to behave in accordance with moral standards that may or may not conflict with self-interest. Given these considerations, aggressive, destructive behaviors may be seen not only as a consequence of strong instigations and a defect in inhibitory, avoidance responses but also as a reflection of weak prosocial responses and the failure to develop strong nonpersonal social goals and values. It is possible, then, by focusing on the development of prosocial behaviors, to bring about significant changes in aggression without attempting direct modification of aggressive responses.

The concluding chapter, by Seymour Feshbach, compares the various alternative approaches to the changing of aggressions, examining points of consensus and possible areas of contention. Gaps in our knowledge are noted and directions for research that appear promising are discussed. At the same time, in addition to the comparative examination of scientific theory and data pertinent to the modification of aggression, pragmatic and ethical issues and dilemmas are considered.

We know, in advance of the presentation of these alternative approaches to the modification of aggression, that we will not emerge with a simple panacea or with a set of accepted, scientifically based prescriptions for the reduction of human violence and aggression. We can further anticipate that many issues will remain unresolved and that many questions of importance for the understanding and control of aggression will not be dealt with. However, we do believe that this effort to specify, explicitly and critically, insights into the dynamics and management of aggression that are derived from physiological, psychological, and behavioral research will be of substantial scientific value. It will also, one hopes, have some social and practical value, contributing, even if only in a very small way, to contemporary efforts to reduce the hatred, violence, and aggressive interactions that beset so many modern societies.

2

PHYSIOLOGICAL MECHANISMS OF EMOTIONAL AND INSTRUMENTAL AGGRESSION

Elzbieta Fonberg

INTRODUCTION

When we talk about aggression, it is assumed that we mean aggressive behavior (that is, offense and attack). It is also assumed that the main basis for aggressive behavior is a certain emotional state. But is this always so? And if so, is this emotional state always the same in different forms of aggression?

Aggressive behavior is composed of certain behavioral patterns directed toward certain goals: prey, another aggressor, or any object. For the complete act of aggression, the coordination of various integrative neural mechanisms is indispensable: perception of an object and its identification as enemy (threat) or prey; emotional-motivational arousal; ability to pattern, mediate, and perform specific, adequate behavioral acts. The neural mechanisms underlying the aggressive behavior are, therefore, not simple ones. They involve the coordinated integration of various brain systems. First, to arouse the emotional state of rage, anger, or hatred, the activation and coordination of the subcortical structures mediating emotions is necessary; then this emotional aggression should be directed toward a certain object, which must be recognized and identified as the proper object of aggression. Moreover, an evaluation of the efficacy of the attack must be carried out prior to the attack. Therefore, the activation of specific perceiving and analyzing (discriminating) brain areas is essential in directed aggression.

This work was partly supported by the U.S. Department of Health, Education, and Welfare under PL-480, Foreign Research Agreement, no. 05.001.0.a.283A, and Polish Academy of Sciences Grant no. 10.4.1.01.4.1.

I am greatly indebted to Mrs. Kurzaj for her technical assistance.

The direction of certain behavioral motor patterns, either learned or innate, and their performance in a manner suitable for the object (that is, activation of various levels of the motor system) is also important. Before the efficient attack starts, the typical external signs of aggression appear: mimicry, vocalization, and motor reactions preparatory to the act of aggression that are dependent on mechanisms other than voluntary movements. We should also include in this list various autonomic reactions that, besides the symptoms common to all instances of sympathetic mobilization, involve traits specific to rage. Therefore, the brain systems governing the autonomic central and peripheral mechanisms are activated. These neural structures may be involved in various forms of aggression to different degrees and in different combinations. Even from superficial observations it is evident that there are various categories of aggressive behavior that depend on differences in degree and content of motivational components.

There are several classifications of aggressive behavior. The most important is K. E. Moyer's (1971). He proposed eight categories: predatory aggression, intermale aggression, fear-induced aggression (which, according to Moyer, involves both a threatening agent and the blocking of an escape route), irritable aggression (which is enhanced by frustration and any stressor), territorial defense (provoked by an intruder), maternal aggression (which occurs in the presence of both the young and a threat), instrumental aggression, and sex-related aggression.

This classification is very important, and one of the most inclusive. However, in my opinion, in order to analyze differences in basic mechanisms of various forms of aggressive behavior, it seems useful to divide aggression into two main categories: emotional and instrumental. Emotional aggression may be either primary or secondary. The former is evoked by the increasing excitation of rage and anger "centers," whereas the latter depends on primary activation of the other motivational systems, such as the defensive, the sexual, or the alimentary. Most of Moyer's categories belong to the latter class. In some sense all these examples of aggression are instrumental, because aggressive behavior with its display of rage subserves other motivations; and behavioral patterns of aggression are used as an instrumental act to get food, defend territory, or win in the sexual contest. But, on the other hand, they are not purely instrumental, since they are based on emotional states and involve innate patterns of behavior.

Pure emotional aggression, without any reinforcement except the feedback from aggressive behavior, would be on one end of this wide range of "aggressions," and purely instrumental aggression without any sign of emotion would be on the opposite end. These extremes are artificial concepts, and in the pure form they do not exist in natural behavior. But they are probably based on two different mechanisms, and this division therefore seems to be a fruitful and promising attempt to analyze the mechanisms implicated in aggressive behavior and to manipulate that behavior. The difference between these two classes of aggression consists in different stimuli adequate for evoking aggression, and in the kind of reinforcement.

FIGURE 2.1

Emotional and Instrumental Aggression

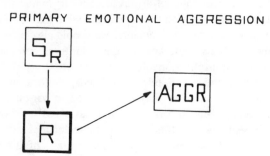

Stimulus-evoking rage (S_R) excites rage system (R) within the brain, which produces aggressive behavior (Aggr).

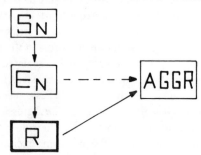

Stimulus (S_N), specific for particular form of aggression, evokes excitation of that specific emotional-motivational system (E_N). This secondarily produces excitation of the rage system (R), and evokes aggressive behavior (Aggr).

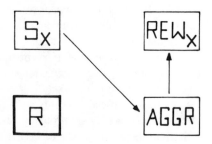

Any stimulus (S_X) may evoke aggressive behavior (Aggr) if it receives any reward (Rew_X). The excitation of rage is not important in this case.

Source: Zagrodzka and Fonberg 1975, 1977.

Figure 2.1 represents an attempt to demonstrate the differences in the mechanisms of emotional and instrumental aggression. In primary emotional aggression, the main neural basis consists of an excitation of the "rage system" within the brain. This evokes aggressive behavior, and the feedback from its performance serves as the reinforcement. In secondary emotional aggression, the source of aggressive behavior is the excitation of other emotional-motivational systems that in consequence activate "rage." In this instance aggression is reinforced by rewards specific to each kind of aggression (such as avoidance of danger or getting food).

In pure instrumental aggression, excitation of the emotional rage centers is omitted from the neural chain; the motivation to perform the instrumental aggression is to obtain a particular reward, which may be different in each case.

These schemes are simplistic and may evoke controversy. In particular, in secondary emotional aggression it is merely hypothetical that aggressive behavior is mediated through the rage-aggression system in the brain and not directly by the specific emotional mechanisms independent of rage.

REINFORCEMENT IN AGGRESSION

Instrumental Aggression

The mechanisms of reinforcement in instrumental aggression seem to be simple. The definition of instrumental behavior is based on the law of effect; performance of an instrumental act serves to get the reward. This reward may be of any kind, and therefore general, well-known rules of instrumental conditioning should apply to retraining or extinction of aggression. Thus, the aggressive behavior should be relatively easy to extinguish if the reinforcement is removed. In reality it is not so simple. It may happen that in the process of learning and performing the instrumental aggressive act, the subject acquires the emotions of rage and hatred or aversion toward the attacked object or class of objects, and/or starts to like aggressive actions as such because they lead to rewards.

Consequently, there is a real question as to whether there is purely instrumental aggression without any emotional components. These emotions, acquired during active aggression, may persist and be the basis of further aggressive behavior in spite of the lack of reward or even if the behavior is punished. This may be one factor contributing to the commonly observed tendency to recidivism. On the other hand, we know that murderers who kill people for money may seem completely emotionless or only feel some tension. It is easy to detect the differences between homicide performed by someone who hated the victim for a long time and homicide performed by a hired murderer who has been paid for this instrumental aggressive act. But these are human examples. It is more difficult to find cases of purely instrumental aggression in animals in nature (that is, not especially trained by man). For example, the dog may be trained to attack certain kinds of people or to hunt certain animals, and receive a reward only for these particular aggressive acts. However, such training may also be based on emotional aggression that is extinguished in the course of training for some subjects and enhanced for others. And even if, at a later point, emotional arousal is no longer involved for a well-trained dog, we cannot consider its aggression as purely instrumental.

A quite separate problem is that the animal may be taught to display or to inhibit emotionally based aggression. It is possible to increase aggressive responses triggered by every kind of motivation if they are rewarded. We may call it "instrumental aggression," but in my judgment this category should be distinguished from pure instrumental aggression (see also Feshbach 1964). In Chapter 4 of this volume, Kirsti Lagerspetz reports success in increasing aggressiveness in nonaggressive strains of mice and in decreasing it in aggressive ones. T. J. Stachnik et al. (1966) were able to provoke the rat to attack not only other rats but also monkeys and cats, by reinforcing such behavior through stimulation of the pleasure center in the brain. There are other examples of the enhancement or decrease of aggressive tendencies by learning.

Secondary Emotional Aggression

Aggressive acts that subserve other drives and emotions are reinforced by different biological rewards, and therefore the mechanisms of their reinforcement appear to be relatively simple. According to Asratyan (personal communication), aggressive behavior is always reinforced by positive biological rewards: food, sex, and other biological incentives that serve for preservation of the individual and of the species. In my opinion, this class of aggression, although the most common in nature, is only secondarily based on aggressive mechanisms (see Figure 2.2).

Let us consider one particular case from the wide range of this category of behavior: predatory behavior. It may be a good model for at least some kinds of human aggression. According to several authors, human civilization, or at least its next higher step started when *Homo sapiens* turned from fructivore to hunter (see Montagu and discussion of his paper 1974). A hunter was more likely to survive and transfer genes. Hunting also led to the invention of arms, which were later used against the human species. (Aggression toward human mates is based on different mechanisms.) In carnivores, hunting behavior is, at least partly, dependent on the alimentary mechanisms, since in nature it serves to supply food for the predator. Satiation suppresses or diminishes predatory aggression. For example, the satiated lion will not attack the antelope that quietly grazes in its vicinity. Also, in my experiments on cats with J. Zagrodzka (1975, 1977), it was shown that fully satiated cats very rarely attacked the mouse, and never

FIGURE 2.2

Secondary Emotional Aggression

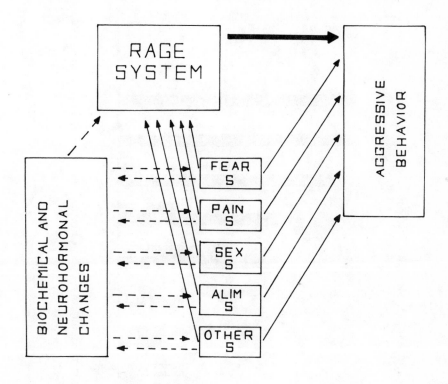

This scheme attempts to show how activation of different motivational systems secondarily excites the rage system, which in consequence evokes aggressive behavior. At the same time the arousal of any particular system is both enhanced by biochemical turnover and produces its changes. This also may increase the excitation of the "rage system." It is also possible that aggressive behavior may sometimes be provoked directly by excitation of specific motivational systems without producing rage.

Source: Zagrodzka and Fonberg 1975, 1977.

FIGURE 2.3

Predatory Behavior of Cats Before and After Lesions of Ventromedial Amygdala

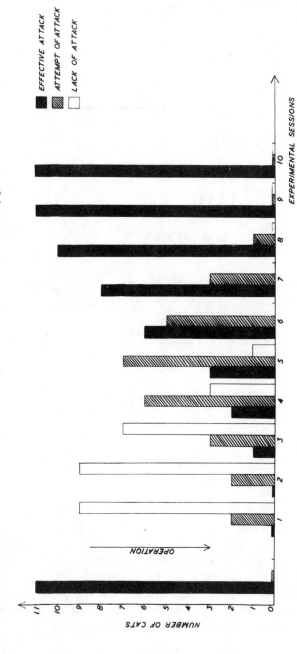

Bars denote number of cats within the group that attacked or did not attack the mouse during each experimental session (two sessions per week).

Source: Zagrodzka and Fonberg 1977.

FIGURE 2.4

Effect of Lesions of Ventromedial Amygdala on Food Intake of Cats

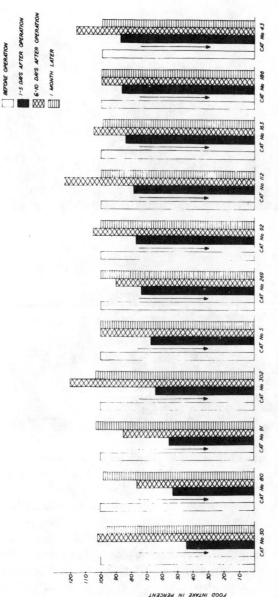

Each bar represents mean food intake one–five days, six–ten days, and one month after operation, as percent of the preoperative level. Arrows denote operation.

Source: Zagrodzka and Fonberg 1977.

FIGURE 2.5

Predatory Behavior of a Cat Before and After Lesions of Ventromedial Amygdala

ate it if they did attack. On the other hand, food deprivation does not intensify predatory behavior. Moreover, we found clear evidence that there are separate neural mechanisms for food intake and predatory behavior.

We performed experiments on cats that were preoperatively defined as good predators. After lesions of the ventromedial amygdala, predatory activity against mice was greatly reduced for several weeks (see Figure 2.3), whereas the food intake was diminished for only a few days (see Figure 2.4). Before the operation the cats chose the living mouse if it was presented simultaneously with a bowl of food, but after the operation they consumed meat from the bowl, ignoring the mouse (see Figure 2.5). Therefore the lack of the predatory response was not produced by a decrease in hunger, nor was it caused by the impairment of instrumental mechanisms as such, because another series of experiments

Before the operation (left) the cat devours the mouse, ignoring the bowl of food. After the operation (right) the cat is indifferent to the mouse, preferring the food in the bowl.

Source: Zagrodzka and Fonberg 1977.

showed that the instrumental response of pressing a bar to an acoustic Conditioned Signal for food reinforcement was not disturbed in these cats after lesions of the amygdala (Fonberg and Zagrodzka 1977). On the other hand, lesions of the dorsolateral amygdala produced prolonged hypophagia and disturbances in conditioned instrumental performance but did not abolish the hunting, killing, or eating of the mouse. Moreover, lesions of the lateral hypothalamus (Fonberg, Serduchenko, and Brudnias in preparation) did not change interest in mice and attacking them, but completely abolished consumption of the prey. All these experiments indicate that the mechanisms of predatory and alimentary behaviors are separate. The reward—eating the prey—seems not to be essential in predatory behavior. Consequently, we cannot consider the predatory aggressive act as instrumentally subserving the alimentary goal.

Predatory attack, to a great extent, depends on innate patterns of behavior. The proof for this assertion is that cats tested as nonpredators (that is, they did not have the opportunity to learn predatory behavior) exhibit adequate, precise responses of stalking and killing a rat during stimulation of certain spots within the hypothalamus (Flynn 1967, 1974; Flynn et al. 1970). Also, W. W. Roberts and E. H. Berquist (1968) showed that cats raised in isolation, without opportunity to attack, display very effective attack during brain stimulation. On the other hand, according to R. R. Hutchinson and W. W. Renfrew (1966), predatory attack is a learned form of behavior that is reinforced by food acquisition. P. Karli (1956) and Karli et al. (1972) showed that a nonkiller rat will starve to death when put in a cage with a living mouse, because it will not hunt it. But it is possible to teach the nonpredatory rat (Moyer 1971) or cat (Zagrodzka and Fonberg unpublished observations) to use the mouse as a ready food, which step by step provokes it to start the predatory attack. According to Moyer, such a rat will kill the mouse not by the typical bite on the neck, but by biting its tail or belly.

It seems, therefore, that some components of the predatory attack are instrumental while others are innate (see also Myer and White 1965). J. P. Flynn (1967) and Flynn et al. (1970) have shown that there are different brain sites where both attack and eating are found and others where only pure predatory attack is located. M. Wasman and J. P. Flynn (1962) showed that during stimulation of "stalking attack" points, a hungry cat will leave a bowl of food and attack a rat even if the stimulation is stopped before it starts to consume the rat. From these experiments, as well as from the experiments of Zagrodzka and Fonberg described above, it is clear that in predatory behavior, reinforcement is not analogous to food reward. Similar conclusions were made by W. W. Roberts and H. O. Kiess (1964), who also found that during stimulation of "rage attack" points, cats are able to learn to go to the arm of a Y-maze where they are rewarded by attack of a rat. From all these studies it follows that in predatory attack the mechanisms and the character of reward are different from those of the alimentary system.

We have assumed that in our cats with ventromedial amygdala lesions, attack and play behavior with the mouse lost their rewarding values, and that this may at least partly have caused the decrease in predatory behavior. If we accept such possible reward mechanisms, the predatory behavior will be closer to pure emotional than to instrumental aggression. We also noticed that the cats with amygdala lesions lost their social dominance in the mouse-killing competition. Tested in pairs before the operation, they showed a definite social hierarchy. After the operation on the ventromedial and the dorsolateral amygdala, and recovery of their predatory behavior, the formerly dominant cats, when tested in a group, did not even approach the mouse in the presence of another cat (even the least dominant cat in the preoperatively tested hierarchy). This behavior changed that of the previously submissive, nonoperated cat. It became more and more self-confident, sometimes playing with the mouse directly in front of the operated cat (Zagrodzka and Fonberg 1977).

I have purposely discussed predatory aggression more extensively because of the complexity of its motivational basis, which shows that it is distinguishable from both pure rage aggression and instrumental aggression. I am aware that my choice may evoke some differing opinions.

S. A. Barnett (1969) has strongly objected to reference to predatory behavior as "aggression." Also, B. W. Robinson (1971), B. E. Eleftheriou and J. P. Scott (1971), R. Plotnik et al. (1971), and others have expressed the view that predatory behavior is based on mechanisms different from those of any kind of aggression. In my opinion it is also different from pure emotional, as well as pure instrumental, aggression; but it is an aggressive behavior, and therefore I have classified it within the category of secondary emotional aggression. It fits with the commonly accepted definition of aggression. Moreover, the other kinds of secondary aggression also have motivational bases different from pure emotional and pure instrumental aggression, as well as from each other. I suppose that some categories of human aggression may involve components similar to those of predatory aggression. The experiments of Zagrodzka and Fonberg, as well as those of other authors, described above, demonstrate that predatory attack is based partially on alimentary mechanisms, but that it differs basically from behavior reinforced by food. In addition, it involves other emotional and social components.

Similarly, human aggressive behavior is often motivated not only by the desire to obtain a definite reward, but also by the desire to increase self-esteem through social dominance. Moreover, aggressive display itself furnishes rewards similar to any play. It would prolong my paper enormously to describe other examples of secondary emotional aggression, such as fear-induced, sex-dependent, or intermale aggression. The last, in my opinion, is the closest to pure emotional aggression, and I will refer to it when discussing the reinforcement of emotional aggression. I believe that all these aggressions are based on similar mechanisms: primary excitation of specific motivational-emotional circuits that secondarily excite the "rage circuit" and thus lead to aggressive behavior (see Figure 2.2).

Pure Emotional Aggression

The problem of reinforcement in pure emotional aggression is both controversial and important. Primary emotional aggression—pure aggressive motives, neither linked to other motives nor subserving them, and also not leading to any rewards besides the aggressive display itself—seems almost unreal and impossible to detect. But, on the other hand, understanding of such pure mechanisms of aggression may be very important to elucidate the overexaggerated, impulsive, "aimless," "inadequate" human aggressive behaviors. The examples of aggression evoked by primary excitation of the rage-emotional circuit (see Figure 2.1) that

are convenient for experimental studies are excitation produced by direct electrical or chemical stimulation of brain centers, spontaneous excitation of these
centers by pathological brain activity (epileptic afterdischarges or neurohormonal
disturbances), and neurotic or post-frustrative aggression. All of these are in some
sense abnormal.

Let us first consider the aggression produced by stimulation of brain
centers of rage (see section "Brain Structures Involved in Aggression"). Rage and
aggression have been clarified by several authors as parts of the aversive system.
R. W. Hunsperger (1959) and J. L. Brown et al. (1969) reported that rage culmi-
nated in flight during hypothalamic stimulation. R. Plotnik, D. Mir, and J. M. R.
Delgado (1971) and Delgado et al. (1968) found that stimulation of most brain
points that produced attack simultaneously caused aversive behavior. It is well-
known that pain or other unpleasant stimulation may produce rage and attack in
both decorticate and intact animals. Normal cats or rats shocked through the
paw or tail attack rats (Ulrich, Wolff, and Azrin 1964; Adams and Flynn 1966).
These results, as well as many similar ones, were the basis for the assumption
that attack, in particular affective attack, is the response to aversive stimuli. If it
were always true, then stimulation of brain centers that evoke rage might be used
as negative reinforcement for avoidance training. In my experiments on dogs
(Fonberg 1963a, b, 1966, 1967), in an attempt to elucidate the motivational
basis of aggression, I compared the elaboration of the instrumental avoidance
responses reinforced by the cerebral stimulation of three different points that
evoke three patterns, all presumably belonging to the aversive system: fear-flight,
defense, and rage-aggression. I must explain what I mean by these three categories, which, as I found in experiments with brain stimulation, are distinct
from each other. Fear responses consisted of attempts to flee, chaotic motility,
whining, screaming, frightened looks, and absence of biting or barking. Defense
responses consisted of similar symptoms of fear, but were connected with biting
in attempts to escape and sometimes with barking and growling. Rage responses
consisted of a very definite symptom pattern always appearing in the same
sequence: low growling, pupillary dilation, and exophthalmos, showing the
teeth with retraction of the lip angles, then movement forward with an attempt
to bite and loud barks and growls.

The instrumental response of a bar press to an acoustic CSi in order to
avoid brain stimulation was easily taught as a response to the stimulation of
"fear points," much more slowly as a response to stimulation of "defense
points," and was established in only one dog as a response to the stimulation
of "rage points" (Figure 2.6). It must be stressed that in the latter dog the tip
of the electrode was localized in the lower part of the "rage circuit," in the
midbrain. In all remaining dogs they were in the medial hypothalamus. In
another dog the electrode was dislocated in the course of experiments; and
when stimulation started also to evoke fear, avoidance was quickly established.
The inability to elaborate the instrumental response to avoid stimulation of
hypothalamic points evoking rage indicates that the state of rage (excitation of

the centers of aggression) cannot be considered as aversive. We repeated these experiments on other dogs, and always obtained similar results.

The classically conditioned rage responses also were not observed during avoidance training to stimulation of rage points. Although during stimulation of fear and defense points, after several trials of CS presentation, the dogs reacted to CS by fear or defense, the CS reinforced by stimulation of the rage point did not evoke the typical pattern of rage before stimulation started. Similar observations on the classical conditioning of rage reactions have been reported by T. H. Oniani (personal communication), Delgado (1969), and Plotnik et al. (1971). On the other hand, pain-induced fighting behavior may be conditioned to a preceding signal (Delgado 1963; Ulrich et al. 1964; cited in Ulrich and Symannek 1969). But these last responses are probably based on the aversive rather than the rage-aggression system. We noticed that the threshold for evoking rage responses in our dogs decreased in the course of experiments with brain stimulation (Fonberg unpublished), and the dogs did not resist going to the experimental chamber. In results similar to ours, other authors have shown that the state of pure emotional rage is not aversive (Nakao 1958; Robinson 1971; Robinson et al. 1969; Flynn et al. 1970).

If rage were always unpleasant, aggression might be explained by drive-reduction theory; that is, an unpleasant drive is reduced by energy expenditure through an external aggressive act or inhibited by the feedback from this act. But we have already provided evidence that aggression is not aversive. On the contrary, there is some evidence that it might be rewarding. A. A. Perachio and M. Alexander (1974) found that the same sites of the brain that produce attack are self-rewarding. N. H. Azrin et al. (1965) showed that monkeys, when shocked, will learn the instrumental responses that expose an object (tail) they can attack. This might somehow be explained by drive reduction. However, pigeons will also learn to peck a key, which action is "rewarded" by the exposure of another bird to attack (Azrin 1964; Azrin et al. 1964).

Intermale fighting is the closest example of pure emotional aggression in natural conditions. Kirsti Lagerspetz (1969; see also Ch. 4), in laboratory studies, has found that a mouse will cross an electrified grid "in order to" attack another mouse. She assumed that aggressive behavior itself may have "reward value." But what is the character of this reward? It may be hypothesized that feedback from aggressive actions is rewarding. This feedback may produce the biochemical changes that lead to restoration of the homeostasis disturbed by arousal of rage; and this restoration may be rewarding. According to W. Wyrwicka (1972), any improvement—what she calls "better being"—is the basis for reinforcement. But it should be stressed that the effectiveness of aggression also plays an important role from both behavioral and biochemical points of view. Quick restoration of homeostasis occurs only in victorious subjects. Also, the aggressiveness of nonaggressive subjects may be increased by victories, and inhibited in aggressive subjects by failures, in fights (see Ch. 4). We do not know whether these last procedures involved mainly emotional or instrumental mechanisms.

FIGURE 2.6

Avoidance Training: "Fear," "Defense," and "Rage" Points

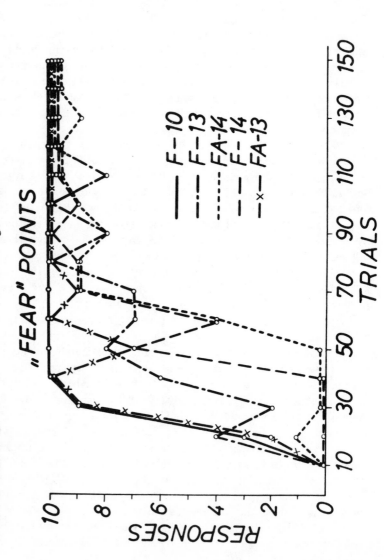

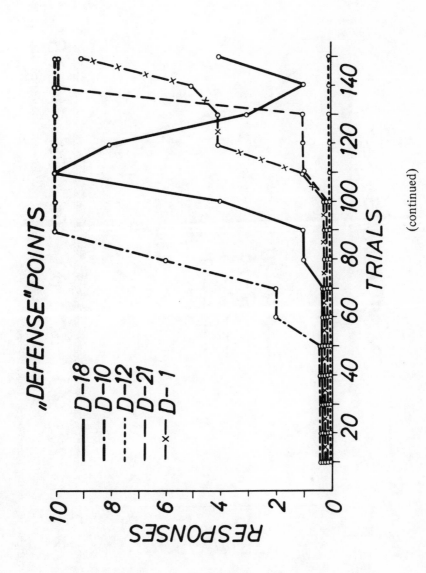

"DEFENSE" POINTS

D—18
D—10
D—12
D—21
D— 1

RESPONSES

TRIALS

(continued)

FIGURE 2.6 (continued)

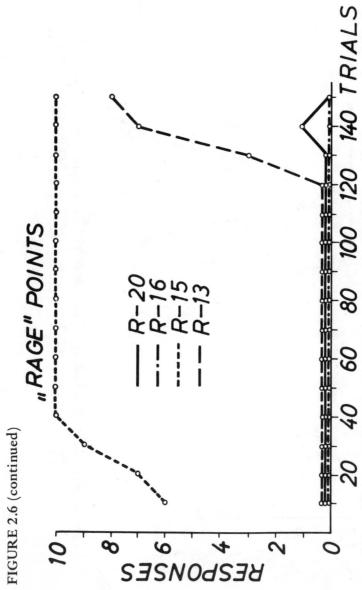

Elaboration of avoidance training (bar pressing) to CSi reinforced by electrical stimulation of brain areas that elicited fear-flight, fear-defense, and rage-attack responses.

Source: Fonberg 1963a, b, 1966, 1967.

FIGURE 2.7

Avoidance Reactions in the Neurotic State

a) Normal State

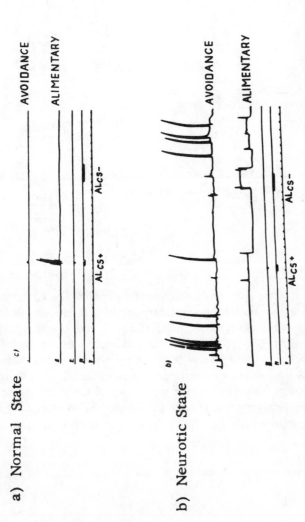

b) Neurotic State

Spontaneous manifestations of avoidance responses in neurotic states. In the normal state the dog performs the instrumental alimentary reaction to AL_{CS+} only. In the neurotic state the alimentary performance is disturbed and the dog exhibits numerous avoidance responses.

Source: Drawn from kymographs of experimental sessions of Fonberg and Flynn 1963.

FIGURE 2.8

Normal and Neurotic States

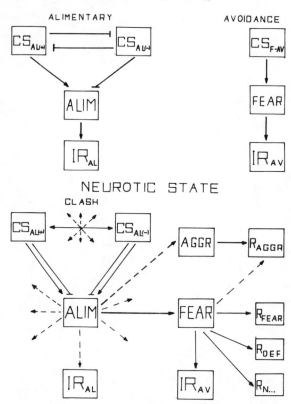

In the normal state the positive alimentary stimulus—CS_{AL+} (reinforced by food)—evoked excitation of the alimentary center and adequate instrumental response—IR_{AL}—whereas negative stimulus—$CS_{AL(-)}$—not reinforced, evoked its inhibition. Similarly, CS_{F-AV} (stimulus for avoidance) activated the fear center, which led to avoidance performance—IR_{AV}. In the neurotic state a clash between CS_{AL+} and $CS_{AL(-)}$ produced chaotic activation of subcortical structures and, among other things, activated the fear system, which led to spontaneous manifestation of avoidance response (Fonberg 1958), as well as other defensive reactions. Similar mechanisms may activate the aggressive system and lead to aggressive reactions.

Source: Constructed by the author.

Just as it is difficult to exclude the emotional components in pure instrumental aggression, so it is difficult to exclude learning in pure emotional aggression. From the numerous experiments of H. F. Harlow and his co-workers(1959, 1965) on infant monkeys and wide observations on children, we know that the ability to perceive and exhibit emotions is learned.

Plotnik et al. (1971) and Delgado (1963, 1965, 1969a, b) have shown that brain stimulation evokes behavioral aggression in the form defined by previous social-emotional relations. The dominant monkey, during stimulation of cerebral "rage points," attacked the submissive monkey, but subordinates did not attack the "boss." In my experiments on brain stimulation in dogs, the dog during stimulation attacked the unknown person with ferocity; but even if it displayed the same rage symptoms in the presence of the friend-experimenter, it would rather attack any other object in its vicinity. If the experimenter waved a stick near the dog, the dog would bite the stick but not the experimenter's hand. This may mean that eliciting the negative emotion of pure rage did not affect the positive emotion previously acquired toward the experimenter. Such a mechanism, involving the interference of two emotions, may have great importance in manipulating aggressive behavior.

The mechanisms of reinforcement may be similar in neurotic or post-frustration aggression to those in other kinds of emotional aggression. The changes in neurochemical turnover and either the increase of free norepinephrine or the depletion of monoamines (aggressive behavior in depressive patients) may create the physiological background for aggressive behavior. We may suppose that various aggressive reactions, both muscular and autonomic, as well as the feedback from aggressive display itself, help to reestablish, at least partly, the disturbed neurohumoral homeostasis, and that this "better state" (improved even slightly) may serve as a reinforcement. We have obtained evidence that inner states (for example, changed level of nutrients in the blood) may be used as conditioned stimuli and as reinforcement.

The mechanism of the origin of the aggressive behavior that appears in the neurotic state may be similar to the mechanism of fear reactions manifested in neurosis. These mechanisms were investigated in my experiments on dogs (Fonberg 1956, 1958, 1960, 1971). We observed that in a neurotic state produced by the conflict of stimuli apart from fear-inducing factors (for instance, produced by the "clash" between two alimentary stimuli, reinforced and not reinforced by food), previously learned instrumental avoidance responses spontaneously reappear, although neither shock, nor CSi used for avoidance training, nor any other noxious stimuli are present (see Figure 2.7). This fact, as I assumed, might be explained by the activation of a subcortical "fear circuit" (see Figure 2.8).

It may be hypothesized that the "rage circuit" might be activated in a similar way. Avoidance responses are one way of coping with frustration; aggression may be another one; and the basis for both may be the state of increased nervous activity produced by conflict. This increase, being chaotic and unspecifically directed, may lead to activation of subcortical brain systems of fear and/or rage. In my experiments on dogs, avoidance activity, while not helping to solve a difficult task, did produce a decrease of other neurotic symptoms. As I supposed, it acted as a "buffer," channeling the pathological overexcitation. A similar assumption that the performance of any motor act diminishes a neurotic state was made by N. R. F. Maier (1949) concerning the role of fixation in frustrated rats, by H. S. Liddell (1953) on the origin of neurosis in goats, and by many other experimenters and clinicians.

The physiological mechanisms of post-frustration or neurotic aggressive reactions may have a neurohormonal basis similar to the fear-avoidance response activation of the adrenergic system or, rather, to several basic disturbances in various monoamine turnovers. It is well-known that depression does not exclude aggression and that fits of aggressive behavior are often observed in neurotic patients, as well as in experimentally induced neurosis in dogs (Fonberg 1958, 1971, 1976a, 1976b), which possibly reflects the shifts in neurohumoral balance.

NEUROPHYSIOLOGICAL MECHANISMS OF AGGRESSIVE BEHAVIOR

Brain Structures Involved in Aggression

It is well documented that aggressive behavior depends on the activity of various brain structures. Beginning with W. R. Hess (1928), who, with unanesthetized animals, evoked the aggressive-defensive responses through electrodes implanted in the hypothalamus, the latter structure was commonly considered the main emotional center for rage and aggression. The hypothalamus also constitutes the main center for various autonomic responses, and is closely connected, through relations with the hypophysis, with the neurohormonal regulation of aggression.

Since the work of Hess, the experiments of many others have supported the dominant role of the hypothalamus in rage and attack (Flynn et al. 1962, 1967, 1970, 1974; Fonberg 1963a, b, 1965, 1966, 1967; Hess and Brügger 1943; Kling and Hutt 1958; Nakao 1958; Masserman 1943; Romaniuk 1965; Wheatly 1944; Yasukochi 1960). Several other structures also were found to play a role in mediating aggressive behavior. Among them the most important seem to be the amygdala and the midbrain, which, as shown by A. Fernández de Molina and R. W. Hunsperger (1959, 1962), form the successive levels of the aversive system. Flynn (1967, 1974) and Flynn et al. (1970) have carried out excellent reviews of the brain mechanisms involved in aggression and have demonstrated the different roles that particular structures play in the various motor, sensory, and affective components of the aggressive act. The very important fact was observed that within the hypothalamus there are distinct points at which stimulation produces two different forms of attack: affective and quiet attack (Wasman and Flynn 1962; Flynn 1967). In these two forms the behavioral patterns are different. Affective attack involves more vocalization (hissing, growling) and autonomic components than quiet or stalking attack. The cat typically uses its paw to attack the rat, whereas the stalking attack is more quiet and ends with the killing of the rat by precise biting on the neck. This may indicate that there are separate mechanisms of predatory (which is at least partly instrumental) and emotional aggression.

Flynn et al. (1970) have shown that there are separate cerebral points at which stimulation evokes attack of rat and others at which stimulation evokes attack of the experimenter. M. F. MacDonnel and J. P. Flynn (1966, 1968) investigated the sensory mechanisms of attack. They compared the hypothalamic attack with the attack evoked by thalamic stimulation. Thalamic attack has fewer autonomic components. If the rat is not seen by the cat during thalamic stimulation, the cat does not search for it, as it does when the hypothalamus is stimulated. This may indicate that thalamic attack is less emotional and that it depends, more than the hypothalamic attack, on sensory (visual) stimuli. On the other hand, hypothalamic attack involves more locomotor components. It was also shown by MacDonnel and Flynn (1966) that the reflex from the trigeminal nerve is important in an effective attack. A blind cat, even during thalamic stimulation, will attack a rat if its mouth touches the rat. After section of the trigeminal nerve (its sensory part), this attack is abolished.

The mesencephalic level, as shown by D. B. Adams and J. P. Flynn (1966), M. H. Sheard and J. P. Flynn (1967), Plotnik et al. (1971), R. J. Bandler et al. (1972), A. Zanchetti et al (1972), and others, is also an important structure mediating aggressive behavior. This level probably involves the effectory mechanisms of patterning attack responses.

Another structure that, as shown by many authors, plays a very important role in aggression, is the amygdala (Kling and Hutt 1958; Rosvold et al. 1954; Karli 1956; Schreiner and Kling 1956; Woods 1956; Shealy and Peele 1957; Alonso de Florida and Delgado 1958; Ursin 1960; Summers and Kaebler 1962; Karli and Vergnes 1964; Kling 1972; Kaada 1972). In their experiments on cats, Zagrodzka and Fonberg (1975,1977) have shown that very small, precise lesions of medial and cortical nuclei produce a loss of predatory behavior (see Figure 2.9). Similarly, Karli et al. (1969, 1972) reported a loss of mouse-killing behavior in rats after dorsomedial amygdala lesions. Impairment of predatory behavior, in our amygdalar cats, probably is caused at least partly by loss of rewarding properties of the emotional component of play with a mouse and reward from attack itself. Thus, again, emotional mechanisms seem to be an important factor in the predatory attack. The amygdala plays a role in evaluating stimuli according to their biological values and rewarding or aversive properties. Its importance in emotions is accepted by various authors. The development and progressive differentiation of the amygdalar nuclei in phylogenetic evolution, in comparison with the hypothalamus (which is more or less similarly complex in higher mammals and in men), suggest that the amygdala may also play an important role in the regulation of higher, specifically human, emotions.

FIGURE 2.9

Localization of Ventromedial Amygdalar Lesions

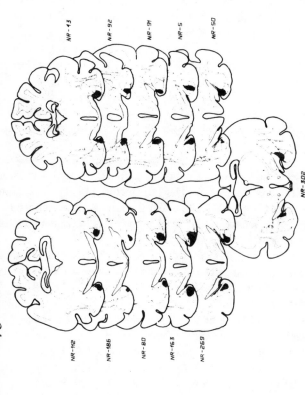

Schematic reconstructions of the localization of lesions of the ventromedial amygdala, which produced loss of predatory attack in cats.

Source: Zagrodzka and Fonberg 1975, 1977.

Our recent experiments with Flynn (in preparation) have furnished results that may be interpreted in different ways. During stimulation of the centro-medial amygdalar area, we produced in two cats the display of rage and various components characteristic of an affective attack—without directed attack. The cats showed all autonomic (piloerection, pupillary dilation, and so on) and motor components of the attack, described previously by other authors during stimulation of the amygdala (Fernández de Molina and Hunsperger 1962; Shealy and Peele 1957; Hilton and Zbrozyna 1963). Then the cats started to walk with heads low, claws unsheathed, and legs bent as if preparing for attack. At the same time they hissed and growled. However, when the rat was presented, they did not attack it, even if it was put close to their noses. Interestingly, the rat perceived the cat's behavior as threatening, as indicated by its reactions. It ran ahead of the circling cat and jumped up with each hiss or growl of the "predator."

It is possible that stimulation of the amygdala evoked purely emotional components of aggression, without engaging the instrumental mechanisms indispensable for effective attack, and in this respect it might be compared with the pure affective display evoked by M. Wasman and J. P. Flynn (1962) during stimulation of certain hypothalamic points. On the other hand, it may be assumed that lack of rat-killing attempts indicates that the stimulation evoked "sham rage," that is, purely effectory motor and autonomic patterns of aggression that, being "sham," were not influenced by the external stimulus (rat). However, we observed that during stimulation the cat reacted to auditory stimuli and to movement of the experimenter. These experiments are too limited to permit any definite conclusions, and further studies are required for full elucidation of the role of the amygdala in aggression.

There is no doubt that aggressive behavior evoked by hypothalamic stimulation has all the properties of the normal response under natural conditions. I will not repeat the substantial information furnished by Flynn in his elegant experiments and reviewed in his papers (Flynn 1967, 1974; Wasman and Flynn 1962; Levison and Flynn 1965; Flynn et al. 1970). Other authors who have studied centrally evoked aggressive behavior are of a similar opinion. The spectacular work of Delgado on monkeys (1964, 1965, 1967, see also Ch. 3), in particular the evidence that social conditions modify the behavior during brain stimulation, furnish another demonstration that brain stimulation is equivalent to normal excitation of brain structures. For example, Delgado showed that during stimulation of the brain sites that consistently evoked aggression, the monkey was able to control its aggressive behavior so that the submissive one would not attack the dominant animal but the dominant one would attack any monkeys from the colony (Delgado 1963; Plotnik et al. 1971). Perachio and Alexander (1974) and Robinson (1971) also found that stimulation of the hypothalamus had a long-lasting effect on a social group of rhesus monkeys; but in contrast with Delgado, these authors observed changes in the social hierarchy produced by stimulation (see also Robinson, Alexander, and Bowne 1969). The possibility of controlling behavior during brain stimulation indicates the presence of instrumental components even in this kind of aggression that otherwise should be classified as purely emotional.

All these experiments demonstrate that brain stimulation produces a state analogous with the normal state of aggression.

Electrophysiological Correlates of Aggressive Behavior

Relatively few experiments have attempted to ascertain the electrophysiological correlates of brain activity in aggressive behavior. Nevertheless, they give evidence of the role of limbic structures (in particular the amygdala, hypothalamus, and midbrain) in aggression. For example, in rats, during spontaneous attacks upon mice, the amplitude and frequency of hippocampal theta rhythm increases (Vergnes and Karli 1968). J. F. De France and R. R. Hutchinson (1972) reported desynchronization of spontaneous electrical activity recorded in the amygdala and hippocampus before and after nose-biting evoked by restraint in squirrel monkeys. D. B. Adams (1968) recorded activity of some units of the midbrain central gray matter as well as in the hypothalamus during affective defense, and Lesse (1957) and M. Sawa and J. M. R. Delgado (1963) observed arousal of amygdalar EEG during emotional reactions. J. O'Keeffe and H. Bouma (1969) reported that certain neurons in the cat's amygdala respond only to the sight or sound of mouse or bird, which may correspond to sensory components of predatory aggression.

There are several electrophysiological findings consistent with the hypothesized dichotomy (Fonberg 1963a, b, 1968) of the amygdalar functions—that is, the medial being excitatory and the lateral, inhibitory (Kreindler and Steriade 1963; Dreifuss 1972; Murphy 1972; Oomura et al. 1970; Oniani et al. 1968). The electrophysiological data support behavioral findings concerning the amygdalar-hypothalamic relations and explain the mechanisms of the inhibitory role of the lateral amygdala in aggression (see Chapter 4). The electrophysiological correlates do not, however, indicate what kind of behavior is inhibited or excited. Since the amygdalar dichotomy also applies to other kinds of behavior (for example, alimentary; see Fonberg 1974), we do not know how much the electrophysiological correlates are valid specifically for aggressive behavior.

It is worthwhile to stress once more that amygdalar neurons have a very low threshold for epileptic discharges and that this is widely assumed to be a principal neurological basis of pathological aggressive behavior in humans.

Biochemical and Neurohumoral Factors in Aggressive Behavior

In the preceding paragraphs I tried to show that there are different behavioral and neural mechanisms mediating aggressive behavior, depending upon the motivation of the aggressive act. The neurohumoral regulation of different kinds of aggression is not uniform. The functional significance of the brain mono-amines in affecting aggressive behavior varies, depending upon whether aggression is provoked by shock, sexual rivalry, predation, or some other factor. Also, the level of various substances and their turnover is different in different forms of aggression.

Several autonomic changes accompanying an affective form of attack reflect the arousal of the sympathetic system (piloerection, pupillary dilation, increase of heart rate and blood pressure). These autonomic components, which to some extent are present in all categories of aggressive behavior, are the most evident in emotional aggression. The sympathetic mobilization observed in aggression suggests that adrenergic substances may play an important role in aggressive behavior. However, injection of adrenaline and noradrenaline into the brain does not enhance aggression. Some authors reported that, on the contrary, aggressive behavior is produced by acetylcholine (Allikmets and Lapin 1967; Vahing et al. 1971; Bandler 1970; Karli et al. 1972; Burov and Kurochkin 1972), whereas norepinephrine or amphetamine may inhibit attack (Sheard 1967; Karli et al. 1969; Leaf et al. 1969). On the other hand, amphetamine in large doses may evoke aggression (Sabelli and Giardina 1973).

According to P. Karli et al. (1972), monoamine depletion causes increased aggressiveness. However, the recent catecholamine hypothesis suggests that norepinephrine and dopamine play an excitatory role in aggressive behavior, whereas serotonine suppresses the activity of amygdalar neurons (Sabelli and Giardina 1973; Straughan and Legge 1965; Eidelberg et al. 1967). Karli et al. (1969, 1972) succeeded in inducing mouse-killing in rats by para-chloro-phenyl-alanine, which blocks the endogenous synthesis of serotonine. Lagerspetz (1969) showed that the level of norepinephrine is higher and the level of serotonine is lower in the brain of hereditarily aggressive strains of mice than in nonaggressive strains. On the other hand, some other authors have reported different results (see Welch and Welch 1969, 1971). The role of dopamine in aggression has also been discussed by several authors. B. Bernard and R. Paolino (1975) found that an aggressive strain of mice had higher dopamine utilization. According to A. S. Welch and B. L. Welch (1971), in long-lasting stress, the level of norepinephrine, as well as of dopamine and serotonine, decreases. But, in the initial period of fighting, the level of monoamines is elevated, as a rule, reflecting increased brain activity. On the other hand, an increase in catecholamines has been shown to produce greater irritability and aggressiveness in mice and rats (Everett 1968; Randrup and Munkvad 1969).

The discrepancies between the results of various investigations may be due to the different forms of attack used as dependent measures of aggression. F. Hoffmeister and W. Wuttke (1969) have shown that defensive-aggressive behavior in cats, a paw attack analog to the affective attack of Flynn, has pharmacological features different from those of a biting attack. For example, metamphetamine abolishes a biting attack, but may enhance a defensive-aggressive one. And chlorodiazepoxide, which inhibits defensive-aggressive attack, does not influence intermale fighting. But in the mouse, metamphetamine may even enhance defensive-aggressive behavior, whereas chlorodiazepoxide abolishes it as it does in the cat.

There is evidence that predatory aggression is based on biochemical mechanisms that are separate from those mediating pain-induced and sex-dependent fighting. Several authors have stressed the basic role of male sex hormones in aggression. According to A. A. Perachio and M. Alexander (1974), after fighting, the plasma testosterone level increases; they assume that the increase may be produced by neuroendocrine reflex via hypothalamichypophysial mechanisms. There is also other evidence for the role of hormones in aggression (Fredericson 1950; Seward 1945; Levine et al. 1972). F. H. Bronson and C. Desjardins (1971) have presented an extensive amount of data concerning the role of male hormones in aggression. They show that testosterone level not only influences the motivation to fight, but also affects the ontogenetic formation of the brain structures that control aggression. The absence of testosterone in the critical developmental period of the growing organism diminishes the tendency to fight in adult subjects. It is known that castration reduces aggression (Bronson and Desjardins 1971), but does it reduce all kinds of aggression? For example, shock-induced attack is androgen-dependent, but frog-killing by the rat is not. Karli et al. (1969, 1972) have shown that castration does not affect the killing of mice by the rat, and the administration of testosterone to nonkiller rats does not produce a tendency to kill.

It may be assumed that increase of testosterone affects only those kinds of aggression that are based on activation of sex-dependent behavior: intermale fighting, sex-rivalry fights, and maternal aggression. According to E. Endröczi et al. (1958), maternal aggression in the rat may be deactivated and reactivated by androgen and hydrocorticosterone, respectively. From the experiments of A. I. Leshner et al. (1975) it follows that it is not the quantitative level of pituitary-adrenocortical hormones that is decisive in aggressive behavior but, rather, the optimum level. Mice with either very low or very high levels of these hormones exhibited a tendency to avoid attack.

During fighting, neurohormonal changes occur in adrenocorticosteroids, adrenal glucosteroids, the luteinizing hormone, thyreotropin, and others (Bronson and Desjardins 1971). All these changes persist beyond the fight, and may have severe physiological consequences. It should be stressed that these neurohumoral changes are very prolonged in defeated animals. In victorious animals, in contrast, normal homeostasis is quickly restored. These findings may be the basis for understanding the rewarding properties of successful fights. During a fight the level of monoamines increases, then decreases. In defeated animals (which applies also to cases of frustration produced by other factors) the disturbances in neurohumoral balance are long-lasting and may lead to hypertension, hypertrophy of the heart muscle, and even to sudden death without signs of severe injuries received during the fight (Henry et al. 1972).

Very interesting results were obtained in the experiments of B. E. Eleftheriou (1971), who investigated changes in ribonucleic acid (RNA) during fighting. Long fights at first produced an increase of RNA in the hypothalamus and amygdala; but later, especially in defeated animals, the level of RNA diminished. This decrease may be caused by the increased need for RNA in stress and defeat. Intensive turnover during fighting that surpasses the biological capability may exhaust the RNA. Also, the increase of the adrenocorticosteroids during fighting may produce enhanced activity of ribonuclease, an enzyme that destroys RNA. This latter factor may be the cause of the low level of RNA observed after fighting. It is pertinent to note that a long-term decreased level of RNA in defeated animals may produce negative consequences, including the impairment of memory, learning, and other mental abilities. Inhibition of the effectory part of aggression—that is, suppression of the overt aggressive act, without influencing the emotional and neurohumoral mechanisms—may have physiological consequences similar to those of defeat.

I have referred to only a few facts from the extensive literature on the effect of biochemical and neurohumoral factors in aggression. They indicate that various forms of aggressive behavior have different biochemical mechanisms as their basis. The diffuse biochemical and neurohumoral changes are probably less evident in pure instrumental aggression, than in the other categories, and their disturbances have the least influence on the intensity of this form of aggression. In secondary emotional aggression, neurohumoral mechanisms are different in fear-induced, irritative, sex-dependent, and predatory behavior. In pure emotional aggression the role of free epinephrine and other monoamines may be important. But the results of various authors are conflicting, and show either inhibitory or excitatory effects of free norepinephrine on aggression. I shall not discuss, at this point, the possible differences in the mechanisms of synaptic transmission in various forms of aggression, since there are no experimentally adequate data for such speculations.

Aggression in Humans

There is strong evidence that similar brain structures mediate aggressive behavior in humans and in animals. Experiments of R. G. Heath (1960), Heath and W. A. Mickle (1972), V. H. Mark and F. R. Ervin (1970), H. E. King (1961), and D. A. Treffert (1964) have demonstrated that stimulation of hypothalamic and amygdalar areas produces aggressive behavior and subjective feelings of rage and aversive irritation. Therefore, we should not ignore the possibility that the brain contains the mechanisms that are the basis for aggression. Also, neurochemical and humoral changes may increase or diminish aggressive tendencies in humans in a way similar to that in animals. The problem arises as to how it is possible to "tame our nature" and how much of contemporary aggression is learned and enhanced by our culture. How strong are the innate tendencies of aggression in humans? By being nonaggressive shall we be denying our nature?

Ashley Montagu (1974), in contrast with Konrad Lorenz (1963), states that most primitive tribes are not aggressive, but friendly and affectionate. As examples he cites the Tasaday, a newly discovered society on the island of Mindanao in the Philippines, and describes the nonaggressive, cooperative life of other primitive societies (Eskimos, Pygmies, Australian aborigines). Even in more aggressive primitive tribes, before fighting starts, there are many preparatory and warning signals and quarrels that, as among animals, often prevent murderous fights. If innate tendencies can be so readily modified, it must be supposed that most of human aggression is acquired by instrumental learning, as part of our culture. The Tasaday may have "genes" for aggression similar to ours, but they have never learned the behavioral patterns of aggression, just as some nonpredatory cats never use their innate aggressive abilities. However, it is possible that there are also some hereditary differences in aggressive tendencies. We know that some primitive tribes are more aggressive than others. The differences also might be related to the kind of nutrients and their procurement. For example, the Masai, who have an almost exclusively protein diet (milk, blood, and meat) are more aggressive than vegetarian tribes. But until the effects of these possible variables have been investigated systematically, it would seem appropriate to be very cautious about references to "hereditary tendencies."

Moreover, we cannot exclude the role of learning in aggression, a factor that seems to be predominant in humans. Native aggressive tendencies are enhanced in those societies in which the individual is rewarded for an aggressive behavior. Montagu (1974) stressed that among the Tasadays aggression is condemned (children have little opportunity to observe and copy examples of aggressive behavior in adults). In addition, in my opinion, most primitive societies are able to manipulate emotions and act efficiently on the emotional level of aggression, and not only on its verbal and instrumental components, as we attempt to do in our culture. We verbally condemn aggression; but at the same time, by a variety of means, we stimulate and enhance aggressive emotions, delight in perceiving acts of aggression (criminal stories) in films and television, and expose an attractive model of brutal heroes. But what are the roots of these tendencies in our culture? Are they innate, or learned in the process of social competition for survival and gain? Is it through an increase of aggressiveness that the white man gained dominance over other races?

Another problem is the cause of enhanced aggressiveness in an individual subject. Although it is well-known that there are differences in aggressiveness among various strains of mice, rats, dogs, and other animals, as well as more prominent differences between aggressive and nonaggressive species, we know very little about the role of different neuronal or biochemical organization of individual subjects. There are many biochemical and neurohumoral characteristics of the individual, in both learned and innate behavior, that may influence aggressiveness in normal subjects. Some pathological mechanisms are relatively well-known. Apart from chromosomal abnormalities and other pathological genetic changes, increase of aggressiveness may be produced by epileptic after-discharges or even by an innate low threshold for epileptic-like spikes in certain brain areas. It has been reported that 14/second and 6/second spikes in EEG result in aggression, fire-setting, murder, sexual assault, and violence (Schwade and Geiger 1960). Violent outbursts of anger and uncontrollable murderous behavior may be triggered by almost any stimulus in epileptics (Gloor 1957). Amygdalar neurons have, in general, a very low threshold and high excitability; and it is known that this structure plays an important role in both excitatory and inhibitory mechanisms of aggression. Several authors have reported that stimulation of the amygdala produces aggression in humans (King 1961; Sem-Jacobsen 1960; Sweet et al. 1969). Mark and Erwin (1970) and Delgado et al. (1968) were able not only to evoke aggression by stimulation of the medial part of the amygdala, but also to inhibit aggressiveness in epileptic patients by stimulation of the lateral amygdalar part.

The question arises as to whether stimulation produces an attack only in those persons who are aggressive because of a malfunction of the brain (epileptic seizures). There is some evidence that rage and attack may be evoked by amygdalar stimulation in nonepileptic patients (Reeves and Plum 1969). The assumption that pathological activity of the amygdala is the cause of aggression is the basis for the increasing tendency to treat aggressive patients surgically. H. Narabayashi (1972) and V. Balasubramaniam and B. Ramamurthi (1970), by ablation of the amygdala, abolished aggressive behavior in difficult children and other aggressive patients. Similarly, K. Vaernet and A. J. Madsen (1970), Heimburger et al. (1966), and E. Mempel (1975) obtained a decrease or total abolition of aggressive behavior in humans through amygdalar damage. Lesions of the posterior hypothalamus (Sano et al. 1966), temporal lobe (Pool 1949), dorsomedial thalamus (Spiegel et al. 1951), anterior cingulum (Ballantine et al. 1967; Le Beau 1952), and substantia innominata (Knight 1972) have also been reported as successful in eliminating aggression. The efficacy of abolishing aggressive behavior by lesion of various limbic structures, in my opinion, indicates an emotional, and not an instrumental, basis for this kind of aggression. The fact that aggressive behavior in humans is mediated by the activity of certain brain structures, and may be abolished by their lesion, can lead to some dangerous suggestions. Recently some investigators proposed the performance of extensive experiments on human volunteers and prisoners, entailing the determination of the brain "centers of aggression" in hyperaggressive subjects even without any signs of a pathological EEG. At this point the problem was changed from a scientific to an ethical issue. The protests that this proposal evoked in the United States and other countries are understandable.

INHIBITION OF AGGRESSION

The preceding paragraph gives some idea of one means used to inhibit aggression in humans. It may be done by destroying the brain structures that, when excited, stimulate aggressive behavior. The attempts to treat human aggression in this manner were based on experiments on animals. Lesions of the structures crucial for the motivational-emotional bases of aggression have been shown to be effective in abolishing aggressive behavior. For example, it was found that hypothalamic damage abolishes mouse-killing in the rat (Karli et al. 1969) and in the cat (Wolgin et al. 1976). Lesions of the medial or central amygdala produce similar, but even more pronounced and specific, effects (Zagrodzka and Fonberg 1975, 1977; Karli et al. 1969). By impairing the sensory or motor components of the aggressive behavior patterns, it is also possible to diminish or abolish attack. It was mentioned above that visual or tactile deprivation (Flynn et al. 1970) may prevent some forms of attack. On the other hand, Karli (1961) and Karli et al. (1969) found that mouse-killing behavior of the rat persists in the combined absence of olfactory, visual, and auditory sensations, and that olfactory deprivation may even enhance killing.

Another way to suppress aggression is to excite structures that play an inhibitory role. Inhibition of aggression may be produced by different mechanisms and act on different brain levels. There are different brain areas that play a role in inhibiting attack behavior. First, we should take into account the neocortical inhibition that is the basis of all psychological methods for manipulating aggression. Evidence for cortical influences is increased aggressiveness in decorticated animals (cortical inhibition probably plays the most important role in instrumental aggression). However, neocortical inhibition presumably acts directly on the effector level, inhibiting overt aggressive behavior. In this case the central and peripheral physiological changes produced by the activity of the subcortical system of aggression, and not expended in overt activity, may accumulate and have future consequences in the form of sudden outbursts of aggression or in the development of psychosomatic disturbances (hypertension, heart attack, stomach ulcers). Second, neocortical inhibition may suppress the perception of emotion. This may lead to acts for which the motivation is not experienced introspectively by the subjects (who may be convinced that their aggressive acts are performed for highly idealistic and purposeful reasons) while all other physiological changes characteristic of emotional aggression may persist. According to J. C. Nemiah (1972), the lack of perception and verbalization of emotions is the main cause of psychosomatic illness. He has observed that such persons are characterized by "emotional flatness."

Inhibition of the effectory or sensory components of aggression may derive not only from the cortical level. M. F. McDonnel and J. P. Flynn (1966) have demonstrated the role of sensory mechanisms in attack. In his spectacular experiments Delgado (1969b) showed that by stimulating the head of the nucleus caudatus, it is possible to inhibit an attacking bull and an aggressive "boss" in a monkey colony. Stimulation of the caudate nucleus, which is part of the extrapyramidal system, probably acts on the effector level of attack. On the other hand, Delgado (1969a) and Plotnik et al. (1971) reported that monkeys repeatedly stimulated in inhibitory areas become less aggressive in general, which points to either a lasting emotional effect or the learning of inhibition of instrumental aggression. By acting on the effector level, I do not mean the inhibition of muscle responses as such, but influences exerted on structures patterning or predisposing an aggressive act. On the other hand, the stimulation of the caudate nucleus may also act by an inhibitory loop on both the cortex and inhibitory influences from the frontal lobes operating through the caudate nucleus.

Inhibition of aggression also may be produced by counteracting influences from the antagonistic systems. R. G. Heath (1972) observed the transfer from rage to happiness and euphoria by stimulation of the septum in humans. This stimulation was rewarding, as he showed in other experiments.

There is other evidence of the antagonism between the reward and aversive systems but, as mentioned above, not all kinds of aggression belong to the aversive system. On the other hand, several experiments have shown that pain or other aversive stimuli may inhibit aggressive behavior. Predatory attack may be suppressed by punishment of the attack response (Myer 1968; Azrin et al. 1964, 1965; Azrin 1964). This procedure, however, is not always efficient, because the aversive stimulus itself may produce attack. Although the overt response may be inhibited, pain-induced excitation of the aversive system may produce an increase in emotional rage. In animal colonies dominance is obviously built up on the basis of punishment of aggression displayed by a submissive subject toward a stronger one. We do not know, however, whether social dominance acts by inhibiting the emotion of rage. I doubt that this is the case, since, as is often observed, the subordinate attacked by the "boss" will attack another subject lower in the hierarchy, thereby expressing emotional aggressiveness. These kinds of observations indicate that only overt aggression toward the dominant animal was inhibited, not the emotional basis for it. All the above procedures seem, therefore, to act mainly on the overt effector mechanisms of aggression.

Positive or negative relations between fear-pain and attack may depend on the category of aggression. Fear is probably antagonistic to predatory attack, but facilitates some other kind of attack (pain-induced, irritative, intermale). Our experiments with Flynn (Fonberg and Flynn 1962, 1963) have shown that stimulation of fear points may interfere with attack. These experiments were designed so that a cat with electrodes implanted in the "fear" and "attack" areas was placed in the middle compartment of a four-compartment cage (see Figure 2.10) a few seconds after the onset of brain stimulation. All three doors from the remaining compartments were opened simultaneously. The cat was trained to go to the left compartment in order to terminate "fear" and to go to the right one to attack the rat. The fourth compartment served as a control. The two separate responses to stimulation of different points in the brain were easily taught, and the cat regularly moved toward the appropriate compartment.

FIGURE 2.10

The Choice Cage

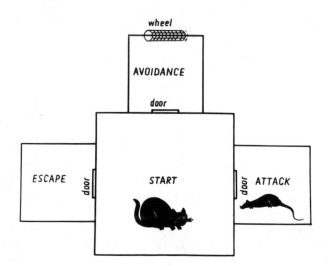

Schematic presentation of the four-compartment cage designed for the experiments on the relation between "fear-flight" and "rage-attack" responses to the stimulation of various brain sites.

Source: Fonberg and Flynn 1963.

Only stimulation of fear points was aversive. In the crucial experiment both sites in the brain were stimulated simultaneously. This procedure, in the beginning, blocked both responses. The cat was sitting in the middle compartment and only turned its head to the right or left, as if hesitating where to go. After several sessions it started to jump between both compartments and, if it attacked the rat, it was a paw attack and not a biting attack. Simultaneous stimulation of both points was more aversive than that of each separately, which may be a reflection of the central conflict.

During previous sessions, even if fear points were stimulated many times, the cat was quiet, often asleep, between trials. Now, in between trials it was upset, unquiet, meowing, and trying to escape through the roof of the cage.

FIGURE 2.11

Effect of Simultaneous Stimulation of "Fear" and "Rage" Brain Points in Cats

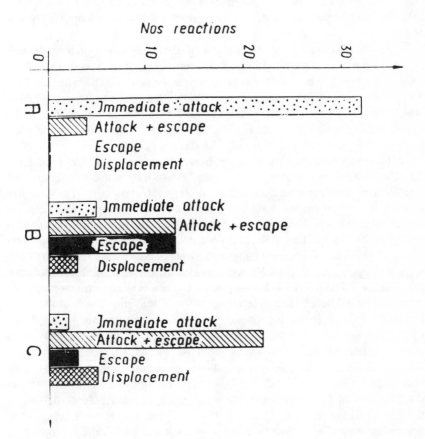

Bars represent the correct effective attack on the rat during single stimulation of the "rage-attack" point (A), simultaneous stimulation of the "rage-attack" and "fear-flight" points (B), and single stimulation of the "rage-attack" point (C). Displacement means that the cat goes to the control (avoidance) compartment and occasionally turns the wheel there. The long-lasting disturbing effect of double stimulation (B) indicates similarities with the "conflict" mechanisms in neurotic states.

Source: Fonberg and Flynn 1963.

Several times it went to the control compartment and pressed the lever there, a behavior that had previously been trained as an avoidance response to tail shock (see Figure 2.11). The cat was easily trained to prefer one compartment if the "conflict" stimulation was discontinued in that compartment. These experiments point to the antagonism between fear-flight and rage-attack. However, such antagonism may concern only the stalking attack. Other categories of aggressive behavior, such as pain-induced, may be provoked rather than inhibited by pain or fear.

Another example of counteraction of the antagonistic brain systems in aggressive behavior is provided by the experiments of M. B. Sterman and C. D. Clemente (1962). They observed sleep waves (synchronization) in the EEG during stimulation of the preoptic area. Stimulation of the same area inhibited attack. Perachio and Alexander (1974) found that stimulation of the anterior hypothalamus, which produces gagging and vomiting, also inhibits aggression— probably the result of interaction with the alimentary system.

The most important mechanism, however, seems to be inhibition acting directly on the emotional centers, which, as we may suppose, changes their activity and suppresses rage by acting on its emotional origin. The amygdala seems to be one of the most important structures in this respect. Stimulation of the lateral amygdala, which Delgado and I (Fonberg and Delgado 1961) demonstrated to have inhibitory influences on alimentary responses, later was shown by me (1963a) to inhibit fear in dogs and by M. O. Egger and J. P. Flynn (1963) to inhibit aggression in cats. My experiments on the role of the amygdala in inhibiting fear demonstrated that amygdalar influences act on the emotional, not the instrumental, level. In dogs (Fonberg 1963a, 1968) stimulation of the lateral amygdala, applied during teaching of instrumental performance to avoid foot shock, did not affect instrumental responses to the CSi, but suppressed all signs of fear (whining, screaming, attempts to escape, and intertrial responses that are, as we know from other experiments, good indicators of intensity of the state of fear) (see Figure 2.12). Similar results—inhibition of fear—were obtained if stimulation of the lateral amygdala was applied, during avoidance training, to the hypothalamic fear area (Fonberg 1963b). These experiments indicate that the mechanisms of instrumental and emotional responses based on fear are separate. It may be assumed that inhibition of aggression by amygdalar stimulation is based on similar mechanisms—that is, that it produces inhibition of emotion.

Attack may be also suppressed by stimulation of several other limbic structures—the dorsal hippocampus, midbrain R.F., and thalamic midline nuclei (Flynn 1974; Sheard and Flynn 1967), whereas Karli et al. (1969, 1972) found that lesions of the frontal lobe and dorsomedial thalamus may evoke aggressiveness. Inhibition of aggression was also produced by stimulation of several other structures, such as the periventricular preoptic area and the diagonal band of Broca (MacDonnel and Flynn 1968; Inselman and Flynn 1972). A. Siegel et al. (1972) found that stimulation of the medial preperiform cortex has an inhibitory effect, and Siegel and D. Skog (1970) produced inhibition of attack by septal

FIGURE 2.12

Effect of Amygdalar Stimulation on Fear and Avoidance

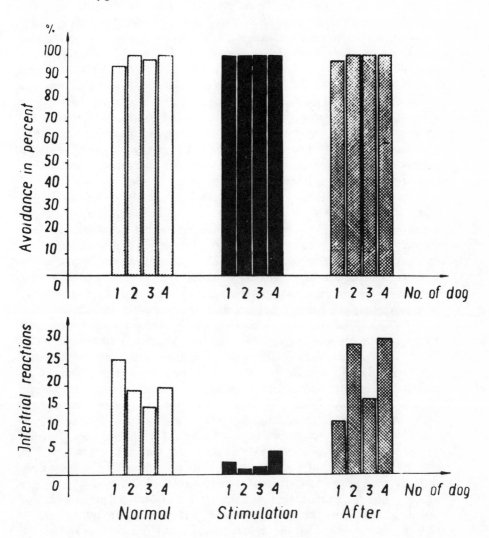

The effect of stimulation of the basolateral amygdala in dogs on the avoidance performance and general fear reaction (upper tier) reflected in the number of intertrial responses (lower tier). Note that amygdalar stimulation inhibits only the intertrial responses, whereas the instrumental avoidance performance is slightly improved.

Source: Fonberg 1963a.

41

stimulation. On the other hand, several authors found an increase of aggression and irritability after a septal lesion.

From this brief description it follows that inhibition of aggression may be mediated by different cerebral levels. Most of these areas belong to the limbic system. In my opinion, inhibition of the emotional "background" of aggressiveness should be the most important and effective mechanism for controlling aggression. Experimentally, such inhibition was produced by brain stimulation of inhibitory limbic areas, but in normal life it should be done by psychological and sociological means. As I have previously suggested, in our culture we are accustomed to acting on the cognitive and effector levels of aggression, which often is not very efficient. We act by persuasion and punishment; but we do not know how to change the emotional basis, except secondarily. Primitive cultures, by various means, including magic ceremonies but chiefly by a social-emotional attitude adequate to the stage of development, can act efficiently on the basic emotional mechanisms. Inhibition of aggression, to be effective, must be carried out at certain optimal stages of life. F. Eclancher et al. (1975) have shown that if, in the early stage of life (a few days after birth), the central nucleus of the amygdala in a rat is damaged, later in adult life the rat is not able to inhibit aggression. And B. E. Ginsburg (1972) has demonstrated that there is a certain critical period of development when the wild wolf can be tamed. This tameness, however, is dependent upon counteracting overt aggression. If the wolf is tranquilized by chlorpromazine or other drugs, and does not have the opportunity to display aggression, taming is not successful.

It is not possible to enumerate, in this limited space, all physiological methods that have been employed to diminish aggression. Sedatives and neuroleptics are administered as standard practice in psychiatric clinics for the treatment of agitated psychotic patients and in everyday therapy. The results, however, are sometimes puzzling. Tranquilizers such as Librium may increase aggression (Lion and Penna 1974). As noted earlier, the administration of tricyclic antidepressants to depressed dogs evoked aggressiveness. We are not sure whether certain drugs act on the basic mechanisms of aggression or only diminish general activity as such. Some authors have described a favorable effect of anticonvulsant treatment on aggression, which may indicate that in those cases the aggressive behavior was produced by pathological brain activity. Neurosurgeons who are enthusiastic about the method of brain lesions have claimed that drug therapy may be as dangerous as, if not more dangerous than, psychosurgery. The abuse of drugs may also produce irreversible emotional and personality changes.

GENERAL CONCLUSIONS

In the present paper aggressive behavior has been tentatively divided into emotional and instrumental categories, and an attempt has been made to ascertain whether these two categories are based on different mechanisms. This division may be important in determining our approach to reducing various kinds of aggressive behavior. The analysis of different classes of aggression showed, however, that both pure emotional and pure instrumental aggression are highly artificial models, and are found in nature only in exceptional circumstances. In almost every kind of aggressive behavior, emotional and instrumental components are present, but in different degrees. The relation of these components and the kind of reinforcements adequate for each specific aggression may play a fundamental role in learning, relearning, and inhibiting of aggression. As shown above, the excitation of emotional centers is almost always present and plays a decisive role in aggression. Therefore, it would be very important to develop our ability to act on the emotional level of aggression, not by surgical or drug treatment, but through social and psychological manipulations.

In my judgment, inhibition of aggression on a cognitive-intellectual level or on an effector level can, in certain circumstances, be efficient at least temporarily; but this inhibition, as well as the inhibition of subjective feelings (or, rather, their perception and identification as incentives for aggression) does not influence the basic emotional-motivational mechanisms of aggression. These, although suppressed at the moment, may have distant repercussions through the building up of subconscious excitation of the rage circuit that may later result in explosive behavior or, at the least, may further psychosomatic disorders. The problem arises as to the methods by which it would be possible to act on an emotional level.

I would suggest implementation and evaluation of the following methods for the diminution of aggression:

1. One of the bases of increased aggressiveness in society is, I would argue, a decrease, in comparison with earlier cultures, of the positive emotions and their rank in the social hierarchy. Therefore, from early childhood we should try to develop multiform positive emotions toward people, nature, and culture, and inhibit aggression not by punishment but by reward and the counteracting influence of the positive emotions. I imagine, for example, that children's cruelty toward animals may be more efficiently inhibited by exciting love and sympathy toward animals than by either punishment of cruel actions or verbal persuasion. This is a very difficult task in our civilization, in which television, films, and everyday life offer attractive models of aggressive behavior to follow. Also, in real life the personality of the cold, efficient, and aggressive subject, what K. Dąbrowski (1976) called the "little psychopath," is socially reinforced rather than the warm, truth-seeking, sensitive personality. The latter is often considered to be conflicted, since such a person does not like to conform to injustice and, in some sense, in special circumstances becomes aggressive. This raises the problem of whether there are "good" aggressions, and whether lack of aggressive behavior does not mean excessive conformity. I again emphasize my opinion that we should work to inhibit not aggressive behavior itself, but its

emotional bases. We should study the means by which our more primitive ancestors were able to manipulate emotions.

2. We should try to exclude all stimuli that may evoke pain-induced or irritable aggression. These types of aggression are created by unnatural institutional organization in the life of civilized people, and by an increasing number of aversive stimuli that are products of our civilization (for example, noise).

3. I have shown above that there are neural mechanisms that mediate aggressive behavior and that they are present in the human brain. We may disapprove of these mechanisms, but we cannot ignore their existence. Therefore, we should create the possibility of exhibiting safe pseudo-aggressive actions as "buffers" for innate aggressive tendencies.

4. A quite different approach is to treat the diseases causing aggressiveness sufficiently early. I am, however, against extensive experimentation and brain lesions in aggressive patients. Although these studies supply very interesting results and enlarge our knowledge about the function of the brain, the perspective they foster might be very dangerous. Humanity is not yet prepared to have in its hands such dangerous means for changing the personality and influencing emotions and actions. We have already had a sad experience to show how scientific discoveries may be used against humanity. And even if these means would serve only to improve human behavior, there remains the ethical problem of how far one can go, and who will establish our rights in this respect and justify limits.

REFERENCES

Adams, D. B. 1968. *Archivio italiano di biologia* 106:243–69.

———, and J. P. Flynn. 1966. *Journal of the Experimental Analysis of Behavior* 9:401–08.

Allikmets, L. H., and J. M. R. Delgado. 1968. *Archives internationales de pharmacodynamie et de théorie* 175:170–78.

Allikmets, L. H., and I. P. Lapin. 1967. *International Journal of Neuropharmacology* 6:99–108.

Alonso de Florida, F., and J. M. R. Delgado. 1958. *American Journal of Physiology* 193:223–29.

Azrin, N. H. 1964. "Aggression." Paper read at American Psychological Association meeting, Los Angeles. Cited in Moyer 1971.

———, R. R. Hutchinson, and R. D. Sallery. 1964. *Journal of the Experimental Analysis of Behavior* 7:223.

Azrin, N. H., R. R. Hutchinson, and R. J. McLaughlin. 1965. *Journal of the Experimental Analysis of Behavior* 8:171–80.

Balasubramaniam, V., and B. Ramamurthi. 1970. *Confinia neurologica* 32:367–73.

Ballantine, T. H., W. L. Cassidy, N. B. Flanagan, and R. Marino. 1967. *Journal of Neurosurgery* 26:488–95.

Bandler, R. J. 1970. *Brain Research* 20:409–24.

———, C. C. Chi, and J. P. Flynn. 1971. *Science* 177:363–66.

Barnett, S. A. 1969. In *Aggressive Behavior*, ed. S. Garattini and E. B. Sigg, pp. 3–14. Amsterdam: Excerpta Medica.

Bernard, B., and R. Paolina. 1975. *Physiology and Behavior* 14:201–06.

Bronson, F. H., and C. Desjardins. 1971. In *The Physiology of Aggression and Defeat*, ed. B. E. Eleftheriou and J. P. Scott, pp. 43–64. New York: Plenum Press.

Brown, J. L., R. W. Hunsperger, and H. E. Rosvold. 1969. *Experimental Brain Research* 8:130–49.

Burov, Y. V., and I. G. Kurochkin. 1971. *Zhurnal vysshei nervnoi deyatel'nosti* 22:1311–13.

Dąbrowski, K. 1974. In *Two Attitudes*. Warsaw: P.T.H.P.-Wiedza Powszechna. Also in *Personality and Its Formation by Positive Disintegration*. Warsaw: P.T.H.P.-Wiedza Powszechna. Both in Polish.

De France, J. F., and R. R. Hutchinson. 1972. *Physiology and Behavior* 9:83–88.

Delgado, J. M. R. 1963. *Science* 141:161–63.

———. 1964. *International Review of Neurobiology* 6:349–449.

———. 1965. *American Zoologist* 5:642.

———. 1967. "Aggression and Defense: Neural Mechanisms and Social Patterns." *UCLA Forum Med. Sci.* 7:171–93.

———. 1969a. In *Aggressive Behavior*, ed. S. Garattini and E. B. Sigg, pp. 109–19. Amsterdam: Excerpta Medica.

———. 1969b. *Physiological Control of the Mind: Toward a Psychocivilized Society*. New York: Harper and Row.

———, W. Mark, W. H. Sweet, F. R. Erwin, G. Weiss, G. Bach y Rita, and K. Hagiwara. 1968. *Journal of Nervous and Mental Diseases* 147:329–40.

Dreifuss, J. J. 1972. In *The Neurobiology of the Amygdala*, ed. B. E. Eleftheriou, pp. 295–318. New York: Plenum Press.

Eclancher, F., P. Schmitt, and P. Karli. 1975. *Physiology and Behavior* 14:277–83.

Egger, M. D., and J. P. Flynn. 1963. *Journal of Neurophysiology* 26:705–20.

Eidelberg, E., G. P. Goldstein, and L. Deza. 1967. *Experimental Brain Research* 4:73–80.

Eleftheriou, B. E. 1971. In *The Physiology of Aggression and Defeat*, ed. B. E. Eleftheriou and J. P. Scott, pp. 65–90. New York: Plenum Press.

———, and J. P. Scott. 1971. In *The Physiology of Aggression and Defeat*, ed. B. E. Eleftheriou and J. P. Scott, pp. 1–11. New York: Plenum Press.

Endröczi, E., K. Lissak, and G. Telegdy. 1958. *Acta physilogica Academiae scientiarum hungaricae* 14:353–57.

Everett, G. M. 1968. Paper read at I. Symposium on Aggressive Behavior, Milan. Cited in Moyer 1971.

Fernández de Molina, A., and R. W. Hunsperger. 1959. *Journal of Physiology* 145:251–65.

———. 1962. *Journal of Physiology* 160:200–13.

Feshbach, S. 1964. *Psychological Review* 71:257–72.

Flynn, J. P. 1967. In *Neurophysiology and Emotion*, ed. D. C. Glass, pp. 40–60. New York: Rockefeller University Press.

———. 1974. In *The Neurophysiology of Aggression*, ed. R. E. Whalen. New York: Plenum Press.

———, H. Vanegas, W. Foote, and S. Edwards. 1970. In *The Neural Control of Behavior*, ed. R. E. Whalen, R. F. Thompson, M. Verzano, and M. Edinberger, pp. 135–73. New York: Academic Press.

Fonberg, E. 1956. *Bull. Soc. Lodz* class III, 7:1–8.

———. 1958. *Acta neurobiologiae experimentalis* 18:89–116.

———. 1960. In *Central and Peripheral Mechanisms of Motor Reflexes*, ed. Soviet Academy of Sciences. Moscow. In Russian.

———. 1963a. *Acta neurobiologiae experimentalis* 23:171–80.

———. 1963b. *Bulletin de l'Académie polonaise des sciences* class II, 11:47–49.

———. 1965. *Bulletin de l'Académie polonaise des sciences* class II, 13:429–32.

———. 1966. In *Central and Peripheral Mechanisms of Motor Reactions in Animals*, pp. 255–62. Moscow: Nauka. In Russian.

———. 1967. *Acta neurobiologiae experimentalis* 27:303–18.

———. 1968. *Progress in Brain Research* 22:275–81.

———. 1971. *Neuroses.* Warsaw: Wiedza Powszechna. In Polish.

———. 1972. In *Physiology, Emotion and Psychosomatic Illness*, ed. R. Porter and J. Knight, pp. 131–61. Amsterdam: Excerpta Medica.

———. 1974. *Acta neurobiologiae experimentalis* 34:435–66.

———. 1976a. In *Hunger: Basic Mechanisms and Clinical Implications*, ed. D. Novin, W. Wyrwicka, and G. Bray, pp. 61–75. New York: Raven Press.

———. 1976b. *Acta neurobiologiae experimentalis* 36:710–11.

———, and J. M. R. Delgado. 1961. *Journal of Neurophysiology* 24:651–64.

Fonberg, E., and J. P. Flynn. 1962. In *Proceedings of the XXII International Congress of the Physiological Sciences, Leiden.*

———. 1963. In *Proceedings of the IX Congress of the Polish Physiological Association.* In Polish.

Fonberg, E., M. Gołębiewska, S. Kasicki, R. Korczyński, and J. Zagrodzka. 1974. In *Proceedings of the XXVI International Congress of the Physiological Sciences.* New Delhi.

Fredericson, E. 1950. *Journal of Psychology* 29:89–100.

Ginsburg, B. E. 1972. In *Physiology, Emotion and Psychosomatic Illness*, ed. R. Porter and J. Knight, pp. 163–74. Amsterdam: Excerpta Medica.

Gloor, P. 1957. *Archives of Neurology and Psychiatry* (New York) 77:247–58.

Harlow, H. F., and M. K. Harlow. 1965. In *Behavior of Nonhuman Primates*, ed. A. M. Schrier, H. P. Harlow, and F. Stollnitz, pp. 287–334. New York: Academic Press.

Harlow, H. F., and R. R. Zimmerman. 1959. *Science* 130:421–32.

Heath, R. G. 1972. *Journal of Nervous and Mental Diseases* 154:3–18.

———, and W. A. Mickle. 1960. In *Electrical Studies on the Unanesthetized Brain*, ed. E. R. Ramey and D. S. O'Doherty, pp. 214–48. New York: P. B. Hoeber.

Heimburger, R. F., C. C. Whitlock, and J. E. Kalsbeck. 1966. *Journal of the American Medical Association* 198:741–45. Cited in Valenstein 1973.

Henry, J. P., D. L. Ely, and P. M. Stevens. 1972. In *Physiology, Emotion and Psychosomatic Illness*, ed. R. Porter and J. Knight, pp. 225–46. Amsterdam: Excerpta Medica.

Hess, W. R. 1928. "Stammganglia Reizversuche." *Berichte über die gesamte Physiologie und experimentelle Pharmakologie* 42:554–55.

———, and M. Brügger. 1943. *Helvetica physiologica et pharmacologica acta* 1:33–52.

Hilton, S. M., and A. W. Zbrozyna. 1963. *Journal of Physiology* (London) 165:160–73.

Hoffmeister, F., and W. Wuttke. 1969. In *Aggressive Behavior*, ed. S. Garattini and E. B. Sigg, pp. 273–80. Amsterdam: Excerpta Medica.

Horovitz, Z. P., and R. Leaf. 1967. In *Neuropsychopharmacology*, ed. H. Brill, J. O. Cole, P. Deniker, H. Hippius, and P. B. Bradley, p. 1042. Amsterdam: Excerpta Medica.

Hunsperger, R. W. 1959. *J. Neurochirurgie* 5:207–23.

Hutchinson, R. R., and J. W. Renfrew. 1966. *Journal of Comparative and Physiological Psychology* 61:360–67.

Inselman, B. R., and J. P. Flynn. 1972. *Brain Research* 42:73–87.

Kaada, B. R. 1972. In *The Neurobiology of the Amygdala*, ed. B. E. Eleftheriou, pp. 205–81. New York: Plenum Press.

Karli, P. 1956. *Behavior* 10:81–103.

———. 1961. *Comptes rendus des séances de la Société de biologie* 155:644–46.

———, and M. Vergnes. 1964. *Comptes rendus des séances de la Société de biologie* 158:650–53.

———, and F. Didiergeogres. 1969. In *Aggressive Behavior*, ed. S. Garattini and E. B. Sigg, pp. 47–55. Amsterdam: Excerpta Medica.

Karli, P., M. Vergnes, F. Eclancher, P. Schmitt, and J. P. Chaurand. 1972. In *The Neurobiology of the Amygdala*, ed. B. E. Eleftheriou, pp. 553–80. New York: Plenum Press.

King, H. E. 1961. In *Electrical Stimulation of the Brain*, ed. D. E. Sheer, pp. 477–86. Austin: University of Texas Press.

Kling, A. 1972. In *The Neurobiology of the Amygdala*, ed. B. E. Eleftheriou, pp. 511–36. New York: Plenum Press.

——, and P. Hutt. 1958. *Archives of Neurology and Psychiatry* (New York) 79:511–17.

Knight, G. G. 1972. In *Psychosurgery*, ed. E. Hitchcock, L. Laitinen, and K. Vaernet, pp. 267–77. Springfield, Ill.: C. C. Thomas. Cited in Valenstein 1973.

Kreindler, A., and M. Steriade. 1963. *Electroencephalography and Clinical Neurophysiology* 15:811–26.

Lagerspetz, K. 1969. In *Aggressive Behavior*, ed. S. Garattini and E. B. Sigg, pp. 77–85. Amsterdam: Excerpta Medica.

Leaf, R. C., L. Lerner, and Z. P. Horovitz. 1969. In *Aggressive Behavior*, ed. S. Garattini and E. B. Sigg, pp. 120–31. Amsterdam: Excerpta Medica.

Le Beau, J. 1952. *Acta psychiatrica et neurologica scandinavica* 27:305–16.

Leshner, A. I., J. A. Meyer, and W. A. Walker. 1975. *Physiology and Behavior* 15:689–93.

Lesse, H. 1957. *Federation Proceedings. Federation of American Societies for Experimental Biology* 16, pt. I:79.

Lesse, S. 1957. In *Experimental Psychopathology*, ed. P. H. Hoch and J. Zubin, pp. 246–54. New York: Grune and Stratton.

Levine, S., L. Goldman, and G. D. Coover. 1972. In *Physiology, Emotion and Psychosomatic Illness*, ed. R. Porter and J. Knight, pp. 281–97. Amsterdam: Excerpta Medica.

Levison, P. K., and J. P. Flynn. 1965. *Animal Behaviour* 15:217–20.

Liddell, H. S. 1953. *Annals of the New York Academy of Sciences* 56:164–70.

Lion, J. R., and M. Penna. 1974. In *The Neuropsychology of Aggression*, ed. R. W. Whalen, pp. 165–82. New York: Plenum Press.

Lorenz, K. 1963. *Das sogenannte Böse: Zur Naturgeschichte der Aggression.* Vienna: Dr. G. Berotha-Shoelen Verlag.

MacDonnel, M. F., and J. P. Flynn. 1966. *Animal Behaviour* 14:339–405.

———. 1968. *Animal Behaviour* 31:185–202.

Maier, N. R. F. 1949. *Frustration.* New York: McGraw-Hill.

Mark, V. H., and F. R. Ervin. 1970. *Violence and the Brain.* New York: Harper and Row.

Masserman, J. H. 1943. *Behavior and Neurosis.* Chicago: University of Chicago Press.

Mempel, E. 1975. *Neurologia, neurochirurgia i psychiatria polska* 5:81–86.

Montagu, A. 1974. In *The Neuropsychology of Aggression*, ed. R. E. Whalen, 12:1–33. New York: Plenum Press.

Moyer, K. E. 1971. In *The Physiology of Aggression and Defeat*, ed. B. E. Eleftheriou and J. P. Scott, pp. 223–64. New York: Plenum Press.

Murphy, J. T. 1972. In *The Neurobiology of the Amygdala*, ed. B. E. Eleftheriou, pp. 371–96. New York: Plenum Press.

Myer, J. S. 1968. *Journal of Comparative and Physiological Psychology* 66:17–21.

———, and R. T. White. 1965. *Animal Behaviour* 13:430–33.

Nakao, H. 1958. *American Journal of Physiology* 194:411–18.

Narabayashi, H. 1972. In *The Neurobiology of the Amygdala*, ed. B. E. Eleftheriou, pp. 459–83. New York: Plenum Press.

Nemiah, J. C. 1972. In *Physiology, Emotion and Psychosomatic Illness*, ed. R. Porter and J. Knight, pp. 15–31. Amsterdam: Excerpta Medica.

O'Keefe, J., and H. Bouma. 1969. *Experimental Neurology* 23:384–98.

Oniani, T. H., and T. L. Naneishvili. 1968. In *Problems of the Physiology of the Hypothalamus*, pp. 89–99. Kiev: University of Kiev Press.

Oomura, Y., T. Ono, and H. Ooyama. 1970. *Nature* 228:1108–10.

Perachio, A. A., and M. Alexander. 1974. In *The Neuropsychology of Aggression*, ed. R. E. Whalen, 12:65–84. New York: Plenum Press.

Plotnik, R., D. Mir, and J. M. R. Delgado. 1971. In *The Physiology of Aggression and Defeat*, ed. B. E. Eleftheriou and J. P. Scott, pp. 143–221. New York: Plenum Press.

Pool, J. L. 1949. "Topectomy." *Proceedings of the Royal Society of Medicine* 42, supps. 1–3. Cited in Valenstein 1973.

Randrup, A., and I. Munkvad. 1969. In *Aggressive Behavior*, ed. S. Garattini and E. B. Sigg, pp. 228–35. Amsterdam: Excerpta Medica.

Reeves, A. G., and F. Plum. 1969. *Archives of Neurology* 20: 616–24.

Roberts, W. R., and E. H. Berquist. 1968. *Journal of Comparative and Physiological Psychology* 66:590–95.

Roberts, W. W., and H. O. Kiess. 1964. *Journal of Comparative and Physiological Psychology* 58:187–93.

Robinson, B. W. 1971. "Summary and Overview." In *The Physiology of Aggression and Defeat*, ed. B. E. Eleftheriou and J. P. Scott, pp. 291–305. New York: Plenum Press.

———, M. Alexander, and G. Bowne. 1969. *Physiology and Behavior* 4:749–52.

Romaniuk, A. 1965. *Acta biologiae experimentalis* 25:177–86.

Rosvold, H. E., A. F. Mirsky, and K. H. Pribam. 1954. *Journal of Comparative and Physiological Psychology* 47:173–78.

Sabelli, H. C., and W. J. Giardina. 1973. In *Chemical Modulation of Brain Function*, ed. H. C. Sabelli, pp. 223–59. New York: Raven Press.

Sano, K., K. Yoshioka, M. Ogashiwa, B. Ishijima, and C. Ohye. 1966. *Confinia neurologica* 27:164–67.

Sawa, M., and J. M. R. Delgado. 1963. *Electroencephalography and Clinical Neurophysiology* 15:637–50.

Schreiner, L. H., and A. Kling. 1956. *American Journal of Physiology* 184:486–90.

Schwade, E. D., and S. C. Geiger. 1960. *Diseases of the Nervous System* 21:616–20.

Sem-Jacobsen, C. W., and A. Torkildsen. 1960. In *Electrical Studies on the Unanesthetized Brain*, ed. E. E. Ramey and D. S. O'Doherty, pp. 275–87. New York: P. B. Hoeber.

Seward, J. P. 1945. *Journal of Comparative and Physiological Psychology* 38: 175–97.

Shealy, C. N., and T. L. Peele. 1957. *Journal of Neurophysiology* 20:125–39.

Sheard, M. H. 1967. *Brain Research* 5:331–38.

———, and J. P. Flynn. 1967. *Brain Research* 4:324–33.

Siegel, A., and D. Skog. 1970. *Brain Research* 23:371–80.

Siegel, A., R. Bandler, and J. P. Flynn. 1972. *Brain Behav. Evol.* 6:542–55.

Spiegel, E. A., H. T. Wycis, H. Freed, and C. Orchnik. 1951. *American Journal of Psychiatry* 108:426–32.

Stachnik, T. J., R. E. Ulrich, and J. H. Mabry. 1966. *Psychonomic Science* 5: 101–02.

Stein, L. 1962. In *First International Hahnemann Symposium on Psychosomatic Medicine*, ch. 36.

———. 1964. In *The Role of Pleasure in Behavior*, ed. R. G. Heath, pp. 113–39. New York: Harper and Row.

———. 1969. In *Reinforcement and Behavior*, ed. J. T. Tapp, pp. 328–55. New York: Academic Press.

Sterman, M. B., and C. D. Clemente. 1962. *Experimental Neurology* 6:103–17.

Straughan, D. W., and K. T. Legge. 1965. *Journal of Pharmacy and Pharmacology* 17:675–77.

Summers, T. B., and W. W. Kaebler. 1962. *American Journal of Physiology* 203: 1117–19.

Sweet, W. H., F. Ervin, and V. H. Mark. 1969. In *Aggressive Behavior*, ed. S. Garattini and E. B. Sigg, pp. 336–52. Amsterdam: Excerpta Medica.

Treffert, D. A. 1964. *American Journal of Psychiatry* 120:765–71.

Ulrich, R. E., and B. Symannek. 1969. In *Aggressive Behavior*, ed. S. Garattini and E. B. Sigg, pp. 59–69. Amsterdam: Excerpta Medica.

Ulrich, R. E., P. C. Wolff, and N. H. Azrin. 1964. *Animal Behaviour* 12:14–15.

Ursin, H. 1960. *Acta psychiatrica et neurologica scandinavica* 35:378–96.

Vaernet, K., and A. Madsen. 1970. *Journal of Neurology, Neurosurgery and Psychiatry* 33:858–63. Cited in Valenstein 1973.

Vahing, V. A., L. S. Mahilane, and L. H. Allikmets. 1971. *Zhurnal vysshei nervnoi deyatel'nosti* 21:551–58.

Valenstein, E. S. 1973. *Brain Control*. New York: John Wiley.

Vergnes, M., and P. Karli. 1968. *Comptes rendus des séances de la Société de biologie* 162:555–58.

Wasman, M., and J. P. Flynn. 1962. *Archives of Neurology* 6:220–27.

Welch, A. S., and B. L. Welch. 1971. In *The Physiology of Aggression and Defeat*, ed. B. E. Eleftheriou and J. P. Scott, pp. 91–142. New York: Plenum Press.

Welch, B. L., and A. S. Welch. 1969. In *Aggressive Behavior*, ed. S. Garattini and E. B. Sigg, pp. 188–202. Amsterdam: Excerpta Medica.

Wheatly, M. D. 1944. *Archives of Neurology and Psychiatry* (New York) 52: 296–316.

Wolgin, D. L., J. Cytawa, and P. Teitelbaum. 1976. In *Hunger: Basic Mechanisms and Clinical Implication*, ed. D. Novin, W. Wyrwicka, and B. Bray, pp. 179–91. New York: Raven Press.

Woods, J. W. 1956. *Nature* 178:869.

Wyrwicka, W. 1972. *The Mechanisms of Conditioned Behavior*. Springfield, Ill.: C. C. Thomas.

Yasukochi, G. 1960. *Folio psychiatrica et neurologica japonica* 14:260–67.

Zagrodzka, J., and E. Fonberg. 1975. Proceedings from the *XIII Congress of the Physiological Association*, held in Gdańsk, p. 431. In Polish.

———. 1977. *Acta neurobiologiae experimentalis* 37:131–36.

Zanchetti, A., B. Baccelli, G. Mancia, and G. D. Ellison. 1972. In *Physiology, Emotion and Psychosomatic Illness*, ed. R. Porter and J. Knight, pp. 201–23. Amsterdam: Excerpta Medica.

3

NEUROPHYSIOLOGICAL MECHANISMS OF AGGRESSIVE BEHAVIOR

José M. R. Delgado

Aggressive behavior is a very complex phenomenon that, according to K. E. Moyer (1968) and S. N. Pradhan (1975), may be classified as predatory, intermale, fear-induced, irritable, territorial, maternal, and instrumental. Other forms of more typically human aggression may be cited, such as violence related to social maladaptation and alienation; mental disturbances with aggressive manifestations; technological violence, in which intellectual effort, scientific knowledge, and individual skills are applied for destructive purposes, often without personal, emotional involvement—for example, the designers, manufacturers, directors, and users of weapons of war; cruelty "for kicks," perhaps the most disturbing form of human violence, with detachment from the attacked subject, and terrorism to impose political aims, with total disregard for the victims; and unintentional violence, including the destructive side effects of human activities that are harmful not by purposeful design but by chance or poor planning, such as automobile accidents (the great killer of mechanized humanity) and industrial destruction of the ecological system.

Although causality, neurological mechanisms, and manifestations may be different in each of the above forms of violence, the following conditions are shared by all of them. First, some information from the environment must reach the individual through sensory inputs. Second, this information will necessarily be transduced into electrical and neurochemical codes in order to be transported into the central nervous system. Third, in all cases interpretation of sensory messages and their evaluation as fearful, threatening, or appeasing requires a frame of reference in order to compare present perception with past

This research was supported in part by the National Institute "Ramón y Cajal" and the March Foundation, Madrid, Spain.

experience. Without this referential past, it is not possible to understand the present. For example, a newborn baby cannot be concerned about insulting words or social injustice. The frame of reference is a personal characteristic stored in individual memory. Fourth, the interpretation of reality will activate preestablished mechanisms to trigger emotional reactions, conscious perceptions, and behavioral responses. Fifth, behavioral activity will depend to a great extent on previously learned ideokinetic formulas and on individually acquired motor skills, modulated by immediate feedback from sensory perceptions.

This neurobiological conception of violence is rather different from the usual sociological approach, which analyzes mainly the environmental sources of conflict; it also differs from the psychological and psychiatric views, which emphasize genetic and cultural determinants. Certainly we must recognize the role of ideological antagonisms and the fact that poverty, social injustice, territoriality, and other factors may induce violent behavior; but they should not be considered the only basic triggers of aggression, when in reality they are merely concomitant elements.

We may ask whether the treatment of cardiac patients could have advanced without knowledge of the anatomy and physiology of the heart; if the airplane could have been invented without knowledge of physics and mathematics; and if individual and social violence can be understood and prevented without knowing the intracerebral mechanisms involved. The neurological study of aggression should be given the same importance as the analysis of its social, economic, and cultural aspects.

The consequence of this conception, which gives equivalent importance to environmental factors and intracerebral mechanisms, is that a program for the prevention of violence should recognize the multifactor causality involved and that prophylaxis should therefore be directed to the environment, to society, to the individual, and to the brain. Experimental studies in animals, preferably in primates, will allow the investigation of anatomical and physiological factors involved in behavior in general and aggression in particular.

EXPERIMENTAL INVESTIGATION OF AGGRESSION

The experimental study of behavior is possible because of the recurrence of typical patterns that can be observed, identified, recorded, and analyzed in time and space. Objective description of behavior in terms of muscles and movements is not practical because of the complexity and variability of the phenomena. For this reason it is preferable to use available behavioral terminology. For example, one monkey chasing another may display a great variety of postures and movements that would be difficult to describe in temporal-spatial sequences of muscle activation, while using the term "chase" and giving details of the interactions between the animals allows this behavior to be easily identified and quantified.

In behavioral experimentation we should not attribute to animals emotional feelings that are unverifiable anthropomorphic interpretations. The observation of an animal cannot reveal whether it is frightened or furious; we merely see a display of manifestations. The classical studies of W. R. Hess (1957) described the "affective-defense reaction" based on spitting, growling, piloerection, and retraction of the ears. W. R. Ingram and J. R. Knott (1960) defined rage reaction as "dilation of the pupils, piloerection, urination, flattening of the ears, hissing, and attack." A. Fernández de Molina and R. W. Hunsperger (1959) emphasized the aspects of growling, hissing, shrieking, and flight. A problem in these studies is that it was not clear which elements were essential and which were accessory for the identification of the offensive-defensive reaction. Also, it was difficult to evaluate whether the electrically evoked rage was "real"—that is, similar to the reactions spontaneously observed in natural conflicts.

Pupillary dilation cannot be considered specific to aggression because it can be evoked in the absence of offensive displays by electrical stimulation of the inferior part of the lateral hypothalamus and other cerebral areas, and attacks may be elicited without pupillary changes. The same is true for piloerection, flattening of the ears, and other signs of the offensive-defensive pattern.

In studies by J. M. R. Delgado (1964) "true" rage in the cat was identified by the following elements: typical display oriented toward another cat; attack with well-oriented blows directed against other cats, which reacted with appropriate offensive-defensive pattern; attack against friendly experimenters; learning of instrumental responses to stop brain stimulation, thus demonstrating the negative reinforcing properties of the experiment. In contrast, "false" rage may be characterized as display similar to true rage but lacking the aggressive direction against control animals, which often do not react defensively, showing that they do not identify the display of the stimulated animal as threatening; lack of defensive pattern and retaliation when the stimulated animal is attacked by a control cat; no aggression against friendly human observers; and no instrumental learning.

Some of the data obtained in animals may be applicable to human beings; but some results probably have more limited value, and for their interpretation the following considerations may be pertinent.

Predatory aggression in mammals is to a great extent learned, and is not necessarily related to hunger or feeding (Karli et al. 1969; Polisky 1975). In the cat the responses of attacking, killing, and feeding seem to be supported by different anatomical and physiological mechanisms (Flynn 1967; Flynn et al. 1970). Human beings were predators when hunting was necessary for survival, but in modern times food is usually purchased in the market. It is improbable that the hypothalamic representation of predatory attack demonstrated in the cat should be present in humans.

Expression of aggression and submission is different in rats, cats, monkeys, and humans. For example, the threatening gesture of biting its own hand and the appeasing act of presenting the genitalia are typical monkey behavior without parallel in the cat. The complexity and variety of hostility, including sensory triggers, perceptual feelings, and expressive acts, are far richer in humans than in animals. Mechanisms therefore should be not only richer but also different, and great caution should be used before generalizing the results of animal experimentation to humans.

GENETIC AND ENVIRONMENTAL DETERMINANTS

It is well-known that, at birth, the human brain is very immature and functionally inferior to that of animals. For example, a newborn cat is able to walk and in a few weeks has acquired many skills, while the human baby needs months before taking its first step. This initial animal superiority is related to greater genetic determination of behavior, with a preponderance of instincts and automatisms, and limits the possibilities of adapting to a changing environment. The fact that human babies must learn to walk, talk, think, and behave provides the bases for human superiority, because in a few years the child may profit from centuries of cultural evolution. According to several authors (Ardrey 1966; Dart 1959; Lorenz 1966; Morris 1967; Storr 1968; Tinbergen 1968), an animalistic aggressive, killing instinct has persevered in humans through genetic determination. Violence and war are the inescapable consequences of hereditary tendencies, and our only hope is to minimize disaster.

There is scientific evidence, however, favoring the opposite view (see Montagu 1976). We should accept the tragic reality of human violence, and also recognize the fact that our initial brain organization is genetically determined. One of the distinctive qualities of the human brain, however, with respect to the brains of lower animals, is the high degree of immaturity at birth and great dependence on sensory inputs and information to direct individual development. The environment, through experience, learning, and conditioning, shapes many of the anatomical, chemical, and functional characteristics of the individual brain. Through genetic factors a new brain starts the construction of neurons, pathways, transmitters, and connections. A huge number of possibilities are opened, but not fulfilled. The codes of information, the system of values, the frame of reference concerning sensory perceptions, the axis to evaluate threats, the formulas for motor activity and aggressive performance are not genetically determined, but must be learned. Even the use of language, one of the most typical human qualities, requires a process of learning. Each of us has the capability to learn any existent language, but in practice we usually speak only one or very few. In a similar way we have the capability to learn the use of deadly weapons or to become skilled in karate, but most people do not develop these abilities. When children's aggressive behavior is strongly discouraged by the prevailing culture—for example, among the Amish or the Zuñi Indians—then peaceful societies develop.

If the human baby needs to learn the most elementary motility, including apprehension of objects and walking, it is logical to suppose that the more complex activities required for fighting must also be learned. Basically (genetically) human beings are not born killing predators or naked apes. Neither are they born loving brothers or charming angels. At this time their brains do not possess established mechanisms for cruelty, hostility, or aggression. Understanding of reality, intelligence, purposeful behavior, and other functional properties of the central nervous system have not yet appeared. Good and evil have no meaning in the very immature brain. The system of values and the motor skills are not transmitted by genes, and must be acquired by individual experience, through messages received by sensory receptors. The obvious consequence is that the brain, in its structure, function, and reactivity, will be shaped by information reaching each individual. The providers of this information are therefore the main determinants of behavior, within the biological limits and the possibilities of the genetic set.

PRIORITIES, MEANING, AND AUTOMATISMS

The many millions of neurons in the brain are firing nearly continuously, day and night, with reciprocal excitatory and inhibitory influences moving through multichannel loops of extraordinary complexity. Most of this activity is unnoticed because the main pathways of the central nervous system have limited functional capacity, and systems of priorities are required to organize the traffic of a relatively small number of messages selected from millions of neuronal spikes.

The environment is also sending a barrage of stimuli to our sensory receptors, which must filter out, select, and code a very small percentage of the available data. For example, the process of reading a book has strict spatiotemporal limitations: usually we visually scan a small group of words, following the horizontal lines from left to right and from top to bottom. This technique may be reversed in Arabic or Oriental languages, but it is always linear and temporal because the visual system, including eyes and brain, lacks the capacity for instantaneous sensing of the details of large areas. This spatiotemporal limitation is related to the anatomy and physiology of neurological mechanisms, but the functional characteristic of linearity may be related to the cultural invention of the written word, which has been decisive in the adaptation of cerebral mechanisms for sensing and understanding. This is a good example of how culture may shape cerebral physiology.

All sensations, including optic, acoustic, and tactile, require the establishment of priorities. The choice may be related to "drives," "emotions," or "intellectual reasoning." For example, a hungry person will be more sensitive to alimentary cues, while another person, absorbed in an interesting book, may forget that it is lunch time and not hear the call to the meal.

Sensory priorities, filtering out as "noise" the information that is not considered relevant at the moment, have a parallel in motor priorities. Purposeful and organized behavioral responses require a precise temporal-spatial correlation of many muscles for the maintenance of a postural tonus and for the performance of motor sequences with well-controlled strength, speed, direction, and coordination. We must choose specific groups of muscles and determined patterns of performance in order to walk, eat, play the piano, or fight. With a few exceptions the systems of priorities for sensing and acting are not inborn, but acquired through personal experience. Also, we must learn the meaning of symbols through a slow process of repetitive experiences in order to acquire frames of reference to be stored in the brain. To understand a word, we must compare the present sensory experience with the codes learned in the past. Through symbols we re-create a past experience, giving meaning to present perceptions.

Our sensory receptors provide cues for behavioral responses, but the mechanisms to release aggression—or any other pattern—are not in the environment; rather, they are in the depth of the individual brain. The cues must be decoded by the individual, and therefore to the present perception other elements are added from previous experience, including significance and emotionality. If understanding or experience is lacking, the cue is ineffective. For example, a burglar assumed to be a peaceful neighbor will not seem frightening. Guns pose no threat for inexperienced natives. Geographic representations have no meaning for primitive people. Identification of meaning, which is essential in aggressive behavior, must be learned, and therefore depends on individual experience.

Another aspect to be considered is that the processes of understanding the environment, making reactive decisions, and performing hostile activities require great speed and efficiency, which are incompatible with the relatively slow process of intellectual evaluation of many intervening factors. The initial process of learning a skill is slow and tedious; but with practice motor performance can become speedy and efficient. Fast action must be free of doubt. If we start considering the many possible ways to react, or the strength, velocity, and amplitude of each contracting muscle, the movements will be clumsy. It is well-known that most of our daily activities are highly automatic, from reaction to the alarm clock, to dressing, eating, driving to work, on-the-job operation of machinery, participation in athletics, returning home, reacting to friends and to family, and saying good night. Our thinking mechanisms are far slower than our already learned, automatic responses. Preexisting mechanisms may be triggered in a similar way by sensory cues, by volition, or even by electrical stimulation of the brain (Delgado 1969). After being triggered, the many details of muscle adjustments and motor coordination do not depend on conscious evaluation. Thinking also has a high degree of automatism. We may select a subject by a volitional effort; but then the ideas, words, images, and their associations will flow "spontaneously, by themselves," and only from time to time do we search consciously, thereby slowing the entire process, to find a particular word or concept.

Fighting is a highly automatic act, and opponents usually do not think how they are going to use their bodies, limbs, and mouths, reacting automatically

FIGURE 3.1

Stimulated Aggression in Gibbons

Aggressive behavior induced by radio stimulation of the central gray in gibbons. Fighting lasted beyond the stimulation periods, and attacks were well-oriented, skillful, and ferocious.

Source: Delgado 1967.

to the changes in position of their adversary and using motor formulas established by past experience. This need for training is the rationale behind schools for self-defense.

Experiments in brain stimulation have demonstrated the existence of behavioral fragments that may be triggered by electricity. In our studies monkeys and gibbons stimulated in the central gray (see Figure 3.1) abruptly moved from peaceful behavior to ferocious attacks. Motor performance was well coordinated, and specific targets were selected (usually a lower-ranking animal with which there was a previous history of conflict). Chasing, grabbing, hitting, pulling, and biting proceeded at a fast pace, and the stimulated attacking animal adapted its strategies according to the jumps and evading actions of the other. To explain the complicated organization of attacks, the well-directed aim of hostility, and adequate reaction to sensory cues for the specific purpose of inflicting punishment on an adversary presupposes the existence of automatic mechanisms. Electrical stimulation of the brain does not carry specific messages; and the simplicity of a train of pulses does not correspond to the variety of evoked responses, unless we accept that stimulation is only a trigger of an already formed pattern of response.

At the onset of central gray stimulation, nothing had been changed in the environment or in the social attitude of the colony. The effect of brain stimulation was to modify the interpretation of sensory cues; optic perception of a subordinate monkey, which was neutral just before stimulation, now provided the orienting feedback to launch an attack. Perception of the previously neutral subject was modified, becoming a fighting target under the influence of brain stimulation. Interpretation of reality—of the environment—was therefore altered in a specific way by excitation of a specific brain area. These findings suggest that the function of some cerebral areas may be essential for the decoding of information and for the emotional orientation of responses. These areas can probably be triggered in a similar way by physiological, sensory inputs (territoriality, feeding, mating), by electrical stimulation, and by chemical disturbances.

HIERARCHICAL MODULATION OF AGGRESSIVENESS

The increase of aggressive behavior evoked by electrical stimulation of specific areas of the brain has a remarkable reliability. Experiments in monkeys have been repeated for five seconds every minute, for one hour, with similar results in different animals and on different days. Electrical stimulation of the motor cortex also evoked reliable results; but in this case the response was blind, automatic, and nonadaptive. On the contrary, electrically evoked complex behavior in general, and aggression in particular, is influenced by the processing of available information from the environment that may increase or decrease the responses. This fact indicates that electrical stimulation may interact with normal inputs, supporting the physiological quality of the electrically triggered mechanisms, and that the final output (behavioral performance) is the result of many interacting factors that may neutralize each other.

These considerations are supported by the experimental hierarchical modification of evoked aggressiveness (see Delgado 1967). Experiments were performed with a female monkey placed in three different colonies of four animals. In the first group (A) she ranked the lowest (4), in group B she ranked 3, and in group C she ranked 2. The monkey was always radio-stimulated in the same point (the nucleus ventralis posterior lateralis of the thalamus) with the same intensity (cathodal, 100 hertz, 0.5 millisecond of pulse duration, 0.3 milliampere),

TABLE 3.1

Aggressive Behavior in Different Colonies of Monkeys where the Same Stimulated Animal Had Different Hierarchical Status

Group	Rank of the stimulated monkey	Aggressive acts of the stimulated monkey	Aggressive acts of other colony animals against stimulated monkey
A	4	8	20
B	3	41	17
C	2	84	0

Source: Delgado 1967.

for five seconds per minute for one hour, repeated on two different days. The number of aggressive acts recorded per session (threats and attacks) were totaled, and are presented in Table 3.1. In Group A brain stimulation increased the hostility of the rest of the colony, whereas in group C, where the monkey ranked second, none of the other animals performed aggressive acts and the stimulated monkey attacked other animals 84 times. These findings indicate that the hierarchical position of an animal is a decisive factor modulating the effects of electrically evoked aggressive behavior.

This hypothesis was supported by another study in which one monkey was stimulated in the same aversive cerebral point (in the nucleus corporis geniculati medialis) with identical parameters (100 hertz, 1.0 milliampere, 0.1 second), the only variable being the animal's changing hierarchical rank. When the test monkey was paired with a submissive animal, this stimulation evoked threatening and attacking, whereas in the presence of a dominant partner, the test monkey reacted to stimulation only by grimacing and showing submissive behavior. Therefore both dominant and submissive responses could be obtained following aversive stimulation, depending on the monkey's social rank (Plotnik et al. 1970).

The importance of social status has also been confirmed in pharmacological studies, in which mobility and spontaneous behavior of rhesus monkeys receiving diazepam were evaluated with the animals alone or paired with a dominant or submissive partner (Delgado et al. 1976). Results demonstrated that some behavioral categories were significantly modified, depending on the social situation of the test animal. Administration of 0.1-0.3 milligrams of diazepam per kilogram of body weight had significant effects on the behavioral profile of submissive monkeys, decreasing the hostility of the dominant, nondrugged partner. Administration of higher doses (3.0–10.0 milligrams per kilogram) diminished mobility of the test animal when alone or dominant, and especially when submissive.

SUMMARY

Causality, neurological mechanisms, and behavioral manifestations may be different in various forms of aggressive behavior; but some elements are shared by all forms of violence, including the necessity of sensory inputs, the coding and decoding of information according to acquired frames of reference, and the activation of preestablished patterns of response.

Understanding and prevention of violence requires a simultaneous study of its social, cultural, and economic aspects, at the same time as investigation of its neurological mechanisms. Part of the latter information may be obtained through animal experimentation, preferably in nonhuman primates. Feline predatory behavior has no equivalent in humans, and therefore its hypothalamic representation probably does not exist in the human brain.

Codes of information, frames of reference for sensory perception, access to recall to evaluate threats, and formulas for aggressive performance are not established genetically; they must be learned individually. We are born with the capacity to learn aggressive behavior, but not with established patterns of violence. Mechanisms for fighting, which are acquired by individual experience, may be triggered in a similar way by sensory cues, volition, and electrical stimulation of specific cerebral areas.

In monkeys aggressive responses may be modified by changing the hierarchical position of the stimulated animal, indicating the physiological quality of the neurological mechanisms electrically activated.

REFERENCES

Ardrey, Robert. 1966. *The Territorial Imperative*. New York: Atheneum.

Dart, R. 1959. *Adventures with the Missing Link*. New York: Harper and Row.

Delgado, J. M. R. 1952. "Hidden Motor Cortex of the Cat." *American Journal of Physiology* 170:673–81.

———. 1964. "Free Behavior and Brain Stimulation." *International Review of Neurobiology* 6:349–449.

———. 1967. "Social Rank and Radio-Stimulated Aggressiveness in Monkeys." *Journal of Nervous and Mental Diseases* 144:383–90.

———. 1969. *Physical Control of the Mind: Toward a Psychocivilized Society*. New York: Harper and Row.

————, C. Grau, J. M. Delgado-García, and J. M. Rodero. 1976. "Effects of Diazepam Related to Social Hierarchy in Rhesus Monkeys." *Neuropharmacology* 15:409–14.

Fernández de Molina, A., and R. W. Hunsperger. 1959. "Central Representation of Affective Reactions in Forebrain and Brain Stem: Electrical Stimulation of Amygdala, Tria Terminalis, and Adjacent Structures." *Journal of Physiology* 145:251–65.

Flynn, J. P. 1967. "The Neural Basis of Aggression in Cats." In *Neurophysiology and Emotion*, ed. D. C. Glass, pp. 40–60. New York: Rockefeller University Press.

————, H. Vanegas, W. Foote, and S. Edwards. 1970. "Neural Mechanisms Involved in a Cat's Attack on a Rat." In *Neural Control of Behavior*, ed. R. E. Whalen, R. F. Thompson, M. Verzeano, and N. F. Weinberger, pp. 135–73. New York: Academic Press.

Hess, W. R. 1957. *The Functional Organization of the Diencephalon*. New York: Grune and Stratton.

Ingram, W. R., and J. R. Knott. 1960. "Exploration of the Roles of the Upper Brainstem and Basal Forebrain in Animal Behavior." In *Mental Retardation*, ed. P. W. Bowman and H. V. Mautner, pp. 112–28. New York: Grune and Stratton.

Karli, P., M. Vergnes, and F. Didiergeorges. 1969. "Rat-Mouse Interspecific Aggressive Behaviour and Its Manipulation by Brain Ablation and by Brain Stimulation." In *Aggressive Behavior*, ed. S. Garattini and E. B. Sigg, pp. 47–55. Amsterdam: Excerpta Medica.

Lorenz, Konrad. 1966. *On Aggression*. New York: Harcourt, Brace and World.

Montagu, Ashley. 1976. *The Nature of Human Aggression*. New York: Oxford University Press.

Morris, Desmond. 1967. *The Naked Ape*. New York: McGraw-Hill.

Moyer, K. E. 1968. "Kinds of Aggression and Their Physiological Basis." *Communications Behavioral Biology* A, 2:65–87.

Plotnik, R., D. Mir, and J. M. R. Delgado. 1970. "Aggression, Noxiousness and Brain Stimulation in Unrestrained Rhesus Monkeys." In *Physiology of Aggression and Defeat*, ed. B. F. Eleftheriou, pp. 143–221. New York: Plenum Press.

Polisky, R. H. 1975. "Hunger, Prey Feeding, and Predatory Aggression." *Behav. Biol.* 13:81–93.

Pradhan, S. N. 1975. "Aggression and Central Neurotransmitters." *International Review of Neurobiology* 18:213–62.

Storr, A. 1968. *Human Aggression*. New York: Atheneum.

Tinbergen, N. 1968. "On War and Peace in Animals and Man." *Science* 160:411–18.

4

MODIFICATION OF AGGRESSIVENESS IN MICE

Kirsti Lagerspetz

In recent times, changing the level of aggressiveness has received much interest. For instance, it has been shown that human aggressive behavior can be modified by social learning experiences.

The study of animal behavior can be seen as a way to a better understanding of the roots of human psychology. In the hope of contributing something to the understanding of the nature of aggression, this chapter will review some experiments on the modification of aggressiveness in mice. I shall mostly discuss my own studies performed in the Department of Psychology, Åbo Akademi (the Swedish University of Turku), Finland. I shall also refer to some other studies.

Animals with different levels of aggressiveness can be obtained through three main methods: manipulating the genetic makeup of the animals, manipulating the environment (resulting in the learning of aggressiveness or nonagressiveness), and physiological and pharmacological techniques. In my experiments with mice I have used all these methods. I shall present some experiments on the heredity of aggressiveness, on the learning of aggression and nonaggression by different procedures, and on the influence of androgens and of alcohol on aggressiveness in mice.

EXPERIMENTS ON THE HEREDITY OF AGGRESSION

The hereditary determination of aggressiveness is, for obvious reasons, difficult if not impossible to investigate in humans. Thus animal experiments are a very useful tool in this field. Rodents have mostly been used as the experimental animals in psychogenetic studies. The literature on the genetic determination of aggressiveness has been reviewed by Kirsti Lagerspetz and Kari Lagerspetz (1974).

The heredity of aggressiveness has been studied by many researchers through comparisons of different strains of the same species. There are often differences in aggressiveness between the strains. Aggressive or nonaggressive animals can thus be obtained simply by taking animals from strains that are known to be aggressive or nonaggressive. Unfortunately, the strains usually differ in respect to other characteristics as well. Thus, when taking an animal from a highly aggressive strain and comparing it with animals of a less aggressive strain, you will also get differences, for instance, in metabolism, size, fur color, general activity, and learning capacity. Some of these properties might be inherited together with aggressiveness, while others might not.

Strain comparisons have, however, been used quite extensively in psychogenetic research. For instance, matings between strains have been used as the basis for estimation of numbers of genes responsible for a behavior trait. In a study by B. E. Eleftheriou, D. W. Bailey, and V. H. Denenberg (1974), it was suggested that two loci are involved in the determination of aggressiveness.

To obtain animals that differ only in aggressiveness and not in other traits as well, selective breeding for aggressiveness within a strain must be used. In each generation the animals have to be specially selected for matings on the basis of their aggressiveness. The lines thus obtained will also differ in some characteristics other than aggressiveness. These are traits that either depend upon the same pleiotropic genes or are inherited through genes linked with genes determining aggressiveness. Selectively bred lines thus offer an opportunity to study correlations of aggressiveness with other traits (Lagerspetz 1964, pp. 115-16).

In the Department of Psychology at Turun Yliopisto, and since 1970 at Åbo Akademi, Turku, Finland, selective breeding of mice for aggressiveness (TA strain) and for nonaggressiveness (TNA strain) has been made for 26 generations. Starting from a Swiss albino mouse stock with a relatively normal distribution for aggressiveness, the most aggressive and least aggressive males were selected for matings. Since the individual variation of aggressiveness in females was slight and their level of aggressiveness was very low, they were selected on the basis of their brothers' aggression scores. The males were selected on the basis of their behavior toward nonaggressive standard opponents (see Lagerspetz 1964).

The difference in aggressiveness between the lines was already significant in the second generation of selection (S_2) (Lagerspetz 1961, 1964). At present we have generation S_{26}. Figure 4.1 shows distributions of aggression scores in some of the selectively bred generations.

At present an investigation is in progress about the possible estimation of the number of genes involved in the determination of aggressiveness. When TA and TNA strains were crossed, the aggressiveness distributions of F_1 were intermediate (see Figure 4.2). This was expected on the basis of previous studies (such as Scott 1958). Since behavioral traits are rarely dichotomous, but continuously variable in expression, at least two loci must be involved in their hereditary determination.

Selective breeding thus is a means to obtain highly aggressive and nonaggressive animals. This selective breeding experiment demonstrated the existence of a hereditary effect upon aggressiveness.

FIGURE 4.1

Aggression Scale Scores, First Three Generations

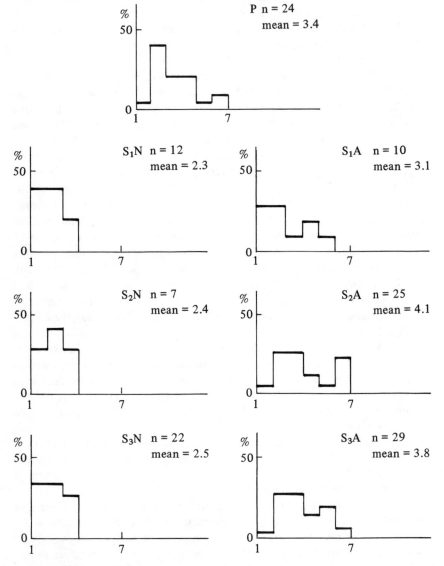

The distributions of aggression scale scores in the first three generations of selection for aggressiveness (A) and nonaggressiveness (N). The scale ranges from 1 (lowest) to 7 (highest aggression).

Source: Lagerspetz 1964.

FIGURE 4.2

Aggression Scale Scores, Twenty-Third Generation

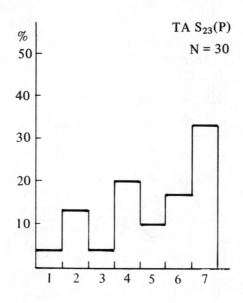

TA S$_{23}$(P)
N = 30

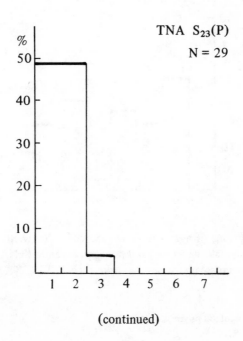

TNA S$_{23}$(P)
N = 29

(continued)

FIGURE 4.2 (continued)

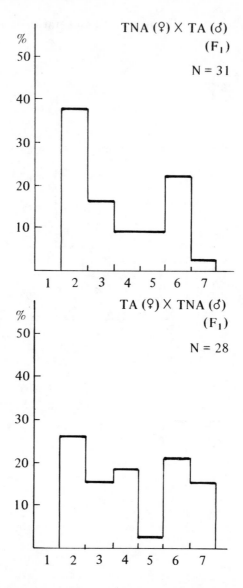

The distributions of aggression scale scores in the twenty-third generation of selection for aggressiveness (TA) and nonaggressiveness (TNA), and in the first generation (F₁) of crosses between the strains TNA (♀) X TA (♂) and TA (♀) X TNA (♂).

Source: Lagerspetz in progress.

It can be argued, however, that the social contacts with a mother of a given strain may account for the differences in aggressiveness found between the offspring of the two strains. In order to investigate this possibility, we made cross-fostering experiments in the seventh generation of selection (Lagerspetz and Wuorinen 1965). The offspring of the aggressive strain were transferred immediately after birth to be nursed by mothers of the nonaggressive strain, and vice versa. When the offspring were tested as adults, the animals derived from the aggressive strain showed significantly more aggression than the subjects from the nonaggressive strain, regardless of the strain of the foster mother.

We observed the nursing behavior of the mothers, and found some differences. These could not, however, mask the genetically controlled variation achieved through selective breeding.

The animals of these selectively bred strains can also profitably be used to study the interaction of heredity and environment on the development of aggressiveness. If we know that newborn animals have a genetic disposition for high or low aggressiveness, we can, by varying the conditions of their environment, obtain information about the possibilities and limits of hereditary and environmental effects.

THE SOCIAL ENVIRONMENT AS A MODIFIER OF AGGRESSIVENESS

Learning of Aggression and Nonaggression

Learning of aggression and nonaggression in the two strains is an example of the interaction of genotype and environment in the formation of aggressiveness.

There have been many studies showing that aggressive behavior of animals can be influenced by learning. For instance, it has been repeatedly shown that victories in fights increase the level of aggressiveness, whereas defeats have the contrary effect (for example, Ginsburg and Allee 1942). The effects of victories and defeats were investigated using animals of the TA and TNA strains.

It was found that defeats decreased the aggressiveness of the aggressive strain to the level of complete nonaggression in five consecutive confrontations with a highly aggressive "fighter" opponent (Lagerspetz 1964). The aggressiveness of the TNA strain could be enhanced through victories, but not to such an extent as the aggressiveness of the TA animals could be inhibited.

The original level of aggressiveness that had been found in the animals when they were kept in separate cages was restored within three weeks after the termination of the experiments. Thus, although the effects of victories and defeats on the aggressiveness were quite remarkable, they were only transitory.

Living in isolation is, of course, unnatural for animals. In normal circumstances they are continuously exposed to social influences, and might have experiences of winning or losing fights, or both. The genetic variance of aggressiveness thus cannot be observed. The phenotypic aggressiveness is a product of both heredity and environment. Our experiments showed, however, that even hereditarily extreme aggressiveness can be modified.

Aggression as a Reward

Increase in aggressiveness resulting from victories over another animal shows that aggressiveness can be learned. Psychological studies have shown that learning requires some kind of reward. However, when training animals to high aggression through victories in fights, no other reward is needed than the aggressive behavior itself.

We investigated the "reward value" of fighting by experiments with preference and obstruction boxes. In the preference experiments we interrupted the fights of two males and transferred the partner to another compartment, where the experimental animal could go and resume the fight. In the fights in which the experimental animal was either victorious over or equally matched with its opponent, it was significantly more eager to resume contact with the opponent than in fights in which the subject was defeated or when no fight occurred (Lagerspetz 1964). (See Table 4.1.)

TABLE 4.1

Times of Latency until Resumption of Fighting, after Interruptions, Various Situations

Situation	Mean (sec)	σ (sec)	N
Aggressive situation; subject victorious	31.5	42.2	14
Aggressive situation; subject and opponent equal	31.5	34.9	10
Aggressive situation; opponent victorious	95.0	141.2	28
Nonaggressive situation	94.8	137.0	16

Source: Lagerspetz 1964, p. 100.

In the experiments with the obstruction apparatus, the experimental subjects had to go over an electric grid to reach a goal box where the opponent was placed. When the animals were males of the aggressive strain, which always fought with their opponents, the willingness to cross the grid could be taken as a measure of the strength of the aggressive tendency. For half of the animals, the opponent was first placed in the entrance compartment, where the subject started a fight. After a few seconds the animals were separated, and the opponent was transferred to the goal box. These subjects crossed the grid more rapidly and more often in the same time unit than did the animals without this first encounter. The latter did not do better than animals in the control group. This result can be interpreted so that aggression is rewarding for animals that are in an aggressive state. Under this condition aggression can motivate behavior.

This "warm-up effect" has been observed by others, including Tellegen et al. (1969), and in another study by Thornberg and Lagerspetz (in preparation). In this study we repeated these results with aggression and, in addition, performed similar experiments with other drives. The facilitating effect of the "warm-up" procedure was found to influence crossing latencies in sexual behavior, hunger, and thirst. It seems that these drive-type behaviors function more effectively as motivators when they have first been started than in an unstimulated state.

Punishment of Aggression

It has been repeatedly shown that aggression, like any other behavior, can be suppressed by punishment (for example, Ulrich et al. 1968). Predatory aggression can be suppressed in the same manner (Baenninger 1970).

Electric shocks have been used as the punishment for aggression. Another method is to use defeats in fights, as we did in the experiments in which the animals of the aggressive strain were conditioned to low aggressiveness.

When the behavior to be suppressed by punishment is aggression, the function of the punishing stimulation is complicated. Noxious stimulation (electric shocks and attacks by an opponent) is at the same time the type of stimulation that evokes aggression in animals. In some experiments by Lagerspetz and R. Portin (1968) attacks by an opponent were simulated by movement of a bottle brush in the cage of the animals. This caused fighting behavior. Electric shocks also are commonly known to stimulate attacking behavior (Ulrich et al. 1968).

The dual effect of noxious stimulation—as a stimulus of aggression and as a punishment for it—was also seen in the trials when the aggressive animals were trained to nonaggression (see Figure 4.3). When first confronted with their opponents, they showed a considerably higher aggression than previously. The new aggressive partner stimulated or "released" the aggression of the subjects through its attacks. In the second trial of the series of confrontations with the aggressive opponent, a sudden drop in the aggressiveness of the subjects was already seen. Even though the subject reacted with aggression to the attacks of

FIGURE 4.3

Effects of Victories and Defeats on Mean Aggression Scores

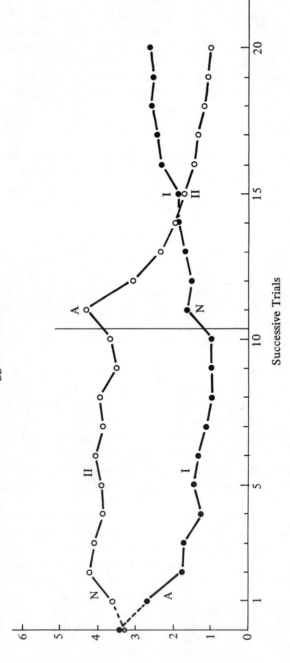

Group I (black dots): 21 animals first allowed to fight with more aggressive partners (A) and, subsequently, with less aggressive partners (N). Group II (open circles): 21 animals first allowed to fight with less aggressive partners (N) and then with more aggressive partners (A).

Source: Lagerspetz 1964, p. 62.

74

the opponent during the fight, a subsequent test showed that the noxious stimulation had suppressed the animal's aggressiveness.

The immediate and long-range effects of punishment on agression—first an increase and later a decrease of aggression—have been taken up by some authors on human aggressiveness, such as A. H. Buss (1961). This question has also been touched upon in discussions on education and on behavior therapy, some writers emphasizing that punishment for aggression only leads to more aggression, and others claiming that aggression, like any other behavior, can be decreased by aversive stimulation.

Sexual Experiences

In experiments made by Kirsti Lagerspetz and Sirkka Hautojärvi (1967) and Hautojärvi and Lagerspetz (1968), a clear negative transfer effect of sexual experiences on aggressiveness in male mice was found. The animals used in these experiments were socially naïve, in that they had lived in isolation since weaning. As adults they were put together with a female in estrus on seven successive days, so that they learned sexual behavior. This learning of sexual behavior significantly decreased their aggressive behavior in a subsequent encounter with a male. The decrease in aggressiveness was comparable with the decrease produced by defeats inflicted by the aggressive fighters (Lagerspetz and Hautojärvi 1967).

The reverse relationship also held: high aggressiveness induced by repeated victories over another male was found to significantly decrease the sexual behavior of the inexperienced males. However, defeats in fights did not affect the sexual behavior. The suppression of aggression thus seemed to be specific, and was not generalized to blocking sexual behavior (Hautojärvi and Lagerspetz 1968).

In writings on dynamic psychology and psychiatry it is often assumed that inhibition of one drive generalizes to inhibition of other drives as well. At least in these experiments this clearly was not the case. On the other hand, reinforcement of aggression through victorious fights did impair sexual behavior.

It seems that sexual activity and aggression are to some extent alternative modes of social behavior that can be selectively learned and reinforced. When only one of these is learned, it is used in all social encounters.

As previously stated, the animals in these experiments were socially naïve. Later, when they had the opportunity to engage in both sexual activity and aggression, the mutually inhibiting effect disappeared.

Social Isolation

The animals of our TA and TNA strains are habitually raised in separate cages after weaning, that is, from the age of three weeks. Thus they do not have any social contacts other than those provided deliberately through the training

TABLE 4.2

Percentages of Male TA and TNA Mice Showing Aggressive Behavior after Different Periods in Isolation, Nineteenth Generation

Time in isolation (weeks)	TA Strain				TNA Strain			
	Tail Rattling	Biting	Biting to Blood	N	Tail Rattling	Biting	Biting to Blood	N
0	0	0	0	38	0	0	0	50
1	32	32	0	28	0	0	0	39
2	50	39	4	28	8	5	0	39
3	40	36	4	28	8	8	0	39
6	57	50	14	28	5	5	0	39
8	59	52	4	28	8	5	0	39

Source: Lagerspetz and Lagerspetz 1971, p. 245.

and test trials. This implies that the variation in aggressiveness—for instance, the difference between the strains—can be seen as genetically determined.

Social isolation is, however, known to enhance the level of aggressiveness in most animals. The increase is so regular and of such an amount that isolation is commonly used as a method of inducing aggressiveness in, for instance, pharmacological experiments.

In fact, it is only after some period of isolation that the difference in aggressiveness between the TA and TNA strains becomes observable. When reared together, the animals of the TA strain do not show much aggression. Table 4.2 shows the development of aggression after one, two, and three weeks of isolation in the two strains. A clear interaction of strain and isolation is seen.

The reason why isolation increases, and caging together decreases, the aggressiveness in rodents has been speculated upon by several authors. For instance, it has been suggested (Welch and Welch 1969) that the lack of environmental stimulation may produce supersensitivity to stimuli because of stimulus deprivation. A plausible explanation for the increase of aggressiveness in isolation could, however, be that when isolated, the animals do not receive punishment from their cage mates (Lagerspetz 1971; Lagerspetz and Lagerspetz 1971). When the animals are caged together, each receives some punishment from its cage mates for its aggressive attempts. This keeps the aggressiveness low. In isolation the nonfighting behavior is extinguished and aggressiveness reappears.

In accordance with this is the observation that the vigor of fighting, at least in mice and rats, decreases in successive fights. It is true that animals can be trained to be highly aggressive by successive victories over another animals. The opponents in this training are specially chosen and trained to submissiveness, so that the victorious animals do not get any punishment from them. However, in ordinary fights, partners are more or less equally matched. Even the victor gets some punishment for its aggression. This punishment inhibits its aggression during the next encounter.

This nonpunishment theory of the increase of aggression in social isolation has been substantiated by several experiments. For instance, in a study by J. N. Crawley, Schleidt and J. F. Contrera (1975), male mice reared in isolation and those reared with females (which usually do not fight) both showed high fighting frequencies, compared with males raised with other males.

This explanation implies, first, that without punishment, aggressiveness has a tendency to arise spontaneously. Aggressiveness thus has, in this respect, a drivelike tendency. Second, it implies that aggressiveness does not rise infinitely, but only to the level that is "originally" typical for the individual, as a result either of genotypic constitution or of very early learning. All animals are thus thought to have an individual basic level of aggressiveness attained only in isolation or under conditions in which the animal does not receive punishment for aggressive reactions.

SOME PHYSIOLOGICAL EFFECTS ON
THE LEVEL OF AGGRESSIVENESS

Females and Androgen Treatment

The specific aggressiveness level typical for each individual can obviously be a result of the animal's genetic structure, or of early or prenatal influences, which can be either social of physiological. In mice the females usually are very nonaggressive. I mentioned that even the females of the TA strain show virtually no aggression. Isolation also does not enhance their level of aggression to any remarkable degree (unpublished observation).

It has been shown, however, that administration of androgens either neonatally or both neonatally and in adulthood (Bronson and Desjardins 1970; Edwards 1971) or in adulthood only (Brain and Evans 1975) enhances the level of aggressiveness in females.

Female mice of the strains selectively bred for aggressiveness (TA) and nonaggressiveness (TNA) were injected with testosterone propionate at the age of two days and as adults, or were injected as adults only. Control animals received solvent oil. The females that had received both testosterone propionate treatments displayed as much or as little aggression as males of the same strain—that is, the females from the TA strain became aggressive, whereas those of the TNA strain did not. This implies that the expression of aggressiveness depends on the presence of androgen in the animals, and not on the genetic structure per se. Presence of androgens, however, depends normally on the presence of the male sex chromosome.

Alcohol and Aggressiveness

In humans, alcohol is commonly known to increase violence and aggression. On the psychological level this has been accounted for by two types of theories (Bennett, Buss, and Carpenter 1969): disinhibition—alcohol lowers the learned inhibitions against aggression; "direct" enhancement—alcohol enhances aggression through some mechanism other than disinhibition.

In order to find out which of these two hypotheses is valid (if either is), we performed experiments in which we tested the effect of alcohol on the aggressiveness of two types of nonaggressive animals: males of the TNA strain and those of the TA strain whose aggressiveness had been inhibited by defeats. If alcohol has a nonspecific aggression-enhancing effect, the aggressiveness of both types of animals would be expected to rise. On the other hand, if the possible aggression-heightening effect of alcohol depends on the lessening of inhibitions, the aggression level of TA animals trained to nonaggression would increase, whereas the aggressiveness of the TNA animals would remain unaltered under the influence of alcohol. Alcohol was injected intraperitoneally in a

10 percent solution in physiological saline. Two dosages were used, 1.0 gram per kilogram of body weight and 1.5 grams per kilogram. As control 0.9 percent sodium chloride solution was injected in an amount comparable with the alcohol solution, in proportion to the body weight of the animal.

Unfortunately, the results of alcohol treatment did not show any aggression-enhancing effect whatsoever. On the contrary, aggression was most common in the "normal" tests between the experiments and in the tests with sodium chloride injections. The experiments were repeated three times with almost the same design. The results did not give support to either of the two hypotheses: alcohol was not found generally to increase the aggression level of the animals, and it also was not found to remove or diminish inhibitions acquired through learning.

If alcohol had a very clear-cut pharmacological effect on aggressiveness, it would certainly be observed even in lower mammals. When trying to find explanations for the increase of violence under the influence of alcohol, undoubtedly observed in humans, the reasons should be sought on more complicated levels typical of humans.

SUMMARY AND CONCLUSIONS

What can we infer from the results reviewed, in regard to the general theory of aggression? The results show a few things that might be of interest.

It is difficult at present to state the implications for human aggression research of the finding that each individual seems to have its own genetically determined maximum level of aggressiveness. There certainly are individual hereditary differences in aggressiveness. These variations, however, are powerfully masked by social experiences. In mice, isolation and training in fighting increase aggressiveness, and punishment and sexual activity decrease it. In humans, the factors that modify aggression certainly are various, and the modification functions on a more complicated level.

A factor that is found to be powerful in inducing aggression in some individuals does not do it in others. Most animals of the TNA strain do not become aggressive in isolation, nor do females. The aggressiveness of the females can, however, be increased to the level corresponding to that of the males of similar genotype, through neonatal and adult androgen treatment.

I think it is wiser not to pay too much attention to the difference in aggressiveness between the sexes in mice. It might be a species-specific phenomenon. Of course, it is not impossible that there is a corresponding difference in humans. In animals, however, the aggression level is susceptible to learning. It obviously is even more so in humans, since learning plays a greater part in the development of their behavior.

Aggressiveness could be learned and unlearned by the animals through rewards and punishments. The level attained by the individual animal was partly determined by the genetic makeup: animals of the TNA strain could not be trained to a very high level of aggression, but those of the TA strain could be trained to complete nonaggression.

The finding that inhibition of aggressiveness did not result in inhibition of sexuality contradicts the results of S. Feshbach and Y. Jaffe (Feshbach 1971) on humans. These authors found that experimentally induced inhibition of aggression in male college students resulted in a decrease on a subsequent measure of sexual arousal. We do not know whether this discrepancy of results reflects a genuine difference between animal and human motivation, or is dependent on the fact that the human experiments concerned situational reactions, whereas in the animal experiments the results of one week's daily punishment for aggression were observed.

The experiments on the learning of aggressiveness showed that no other reward except the opportunity to display aggression was needed to reinforce aggression and increase it through learning. Preference experiments and experiments with an obstruction box also indicated that aggression was rewarding for the animals, provided they were in a state of aggression arousal. Punishment reduced the level of aggressiveness, although at first it functioned as a stimulus for aggression.

I suggested that the rise of aggressiveness in isolation can be accounted for by absence of punishment. To my knowledge, the evidence from experiments performed by others on isolation and social experiences in mice and rats substantiates this view. (In humans, which are much more complicated, the meaning of isolation is of course quite different, and need not be considered here. The equivalent of isolation in mice might be some other state for humans, both phenomenally and behaviorally—for instance, primarily a state without punishment for aggressive reactions.)

The spontaneous return of aggressiveness in an organism that is not punished for it, the reward properties of aggression, and the hereditary determination of aggressiveness level suggest a primary motive or a behavior motivated by an instinct. On the other hand, that aggressiveness can be completely although temporarily inhibited; that learning has a very marked effect on aggressiveness; and that aggression functions as a reward only when an aggression state has first been evoked by a previous fight suggest that aggressiveness is a behavior pattern that can be changed like any other behavior.

It seems that the picture of aggressiveness obtained from these studies with mice fits reasonably well with most contemporary human studies. The modifiability of aggressiveness by learning, for instance, is common in both approaches. The spontaneous recovery of aggressiveness in the absence of punishment and the rewarding properties of the possibility to display aggression for provoked individuals, so clearly found in these animals, may deserve some consideration.

On a simple, more "physiological" level, it is possible to think that even humans have their hereditarily determined individual level of aggressiveness.

We must remember, however, that aggressiveness itself is not such a relatively simple and unitary variable in humans as it is in mice, but a result of many social, situational, and personality factors or interactions of factors. Even in mice, though, aggressiveness could be very much modified and even completely masked by social and other learning experiences.

REFERENCES

Baenninger, R. 1970. "Suppression of Interspecies Aggression in the Rat by Several Aversive Training Procedures." *Journal of Comparative and Physiological Psychology* 70:382–88.

Bennett, R. M., A. H. Buss, and J. A. Carpenter. 1969. "Alcohol and Human Physical Aggression." *Quarterly Journal of Studies of Alcohol* 30:870–76.

Brain, P. F., and C. M. Evans. 1975. "Attempts to Influence Fighting and Threat Behaviors in Adult Isolated Female CFW Mice in Standard Opponent Aggression Tests Using Injected and Subcutaneously Implanted Androgens." *Physiology and Behavior* 14:551–56.

Bronson, F. H., and C. Desjardins. 1970. "Neonatal Androgen Administration and Adult Aggressiveness in Female Mice." *Gen. Comp. Endocrinol.* 15:320–25.

Buss, A. H. 1961. *The Psychology of Aggression.* New York: John Wiley.

Crawley, J. N., W. M. Schleidt, and J. F. Contrera. 1975. "Does Social Environment Decrease Propensity to Fight in Male Mice?" *Behavioral Biology* 15:73–83.

DeGhett, V. J. 1975. "A Factor Influencing Aggression in Adult Mice: Witnessing Aggression When Young." *Behavioral Biology* 13:291–300.

Edwards, D. A. 1971. "Neonatal Administration of Androstenedione, Testosterone or Testosterone Propionate: Effects on Ovulation, Sexual Receptivity and Aggressive Behavior in Female Mice." *Physiology and Behavior* 6:223–28.

Eleftheriou, B. E., D. W. Bailey, and V. H. Denenberg. 1974. "Genetic Analysis of Fighting Behavior in Mice." *Physiology and Behavior* 13:773–77.

Feshbach, S. 1971. "Dynamics and Morality of Violence and Aggression: Some Psychological Considerations." *American Psychologist* 26:281–91.

Ginsburg, B., and W. C. Allee. 1942. "Some Effects of Conditioning on Social Dominance and Subordination in Inbred Strains of Mice." *Physiological Zoology* 15:485–506.

Hautojärvi, S., and K. M. J. Lagerspetz. 1968. "The Effects of Socially Induced Aggressiveness or Nonaggressiveness on the Sexual Behaviour of Inexperienced Male Mice." *Scandinavian Journal of Psychology* 9:45–49.

Lagerspetz, K. M. J. 1961. "Genetic and Social Causes of Aggressive Behaviour in Mice." *Scandinavian Journal of Psychology* 2:167–73.

———. 1964. "Studies on the Aggressive Behaviour of Mice." *Annales Academiae scientiarum fenniae* ser. B, 131:1–131.

———. 1971. "Learning and Suppression of Aggressiveness in Animal Experiments: A Reinterpretation." *Reports from the Institute of Psychology, University of Turku* 35:1–19.

———, and S. Hautojärvi. 1967. "The Effect of Prior Aggressive or Sexual Arousal on Subsequent Aggressive or Sexual Reactions in Male Mice." *Scandinavian Journal of Psychology* 8:1–6.

Lagerspetz, K. M. J., and K. Y. H. Lagerspetz. 1971. "Changes in the Level of Aggressiveness of Mice as Results of Isolation, Learning, and Selective Breeding." *Scandinavian Journal of Psychology* 12:241–48.

———. 1974. "Genetic Determination of Aggressive Behavior." In *Behavioural Genetics*, ed. I. H. F. van Abeelen, pp. 321–46. Amsterdam: North Holland.

———. 1975. "The Expression of the Genes of Aggressiveness in Mice: The Effect of Androgen on Aggression and Sexual Behaviour in Females." *Aggressive Behavior* 1:291–96.

Lagerspetz, K. M. J., and R. Portin. 1968. "Simulation of Cues Eliciting Aggressive Responses in Mice at Two Age Levels." *Journal of Genetic Psychology* 113:53–63.

Lagerspetz, K. M. J., and Kauko Wuorinen. 1965. "A Cross Fostering Experiment with Mice, Selectively Bred for Aggressiveness and Non-aggressiveness." *Reports from the Institute of Psychology, University of Turku* 17:1–9.

Scott, J. P. 1958. *Aggression.* Chicago: University of Chicago Press.

Tellegen, A., J. M. Horn, and R. Legrand. "Opportunity for Aggression as a Reinforcer in Mice." *Psychonomic Science* 14:104–05.

Ulrich, R. E., M. Wolfe, and S. Dulaney. 1968. "Punishment of Shock-Induced Aggression." Kalamazoo: Western Michigan University (mimeographed).

Welch, B. L., and A. S. Welch. 1969. "Aggression and the Biogenic Amine Neurohumors." In *Aggressive Behavior*, ed. S. Garattini and E. B. Sigg, pp. 188–202. Amsterdam: Excerpta Medica.

5

TREATMENT FOR CHILDREN
WITH CONDUCT PROBLEMS:
A REVIEW OF OUTCOME STUDIES

Gerald R. Patterson

The research literature shows that many children with conduct problems do not outgrow them. On the contrary, both the delinquent and the antisocial components of conduct problems seem to have long-term implications for later adjustment as an adolescent or adult. Even at the turn of the century, the mental health movement was aware of the necessity to cope with these problems. At that time the child guidance movement emphasized the necessity of treating these children. By 1932 there were 232 child guidance clinics in operation (Rhodes and Gibbons 1972). About a half to two-thirds of the problems for which children were referred concerned conduct. More recently, the treatment of these problems has also become a primary focus for the social learning emphasis upon parent training. The present report reviews the published literature relating to the efficacy of these attempts to treat the out-of-control child.

CHILDREN WHO ACT OUT

H. C. Quay (1972) reviewed the numerous factor-analytic studies of various kinds of data describing children's behavior. Whether based upon parent report, child report, symptoms, teachers' ratings, or observed behavior, the resulting structures showed a surprising consistency in identifying two uncorrelated factors, both describing children who act out. One related to social aggressiveness, and included disobedience, fighting, temper tantrums, bossiness, and irritability. The other, socialized delinquency, included stealing, truancy, and staying out late at night.

G. R. Patterson (1978b) analyzed the problems presented by parents of out-of-control children referred for treatment. The Guttman scalogram for

The review was supported by grant MH 25548 from NIMH, Section on Crime and Delinquency.

children who steal showed transitive progression for poor peer relations, lying, stealing, and fire-setting. The reproducibility coefficient (RQ) of .94 showed that the progression consistently held across children such that most all fire-setters also stole, lied, and had poor peer relations. A replication study also included wandering and produced the progression: defy, lie, wander, steal, set fire. The RQ was again .94.

The scalogram analyses for the socially aggressive children produced the following progression: difficult to control, fight with siblings, temper tantrums, extremely high observed rate of coercive behavior. The RQ, however, was a borderline .80, although the replication sample showed a more acceptable .88.

The analysis by J. B. Reid and A. F. C. J. Hendriks (1973) showed significant differences in observed rates of aversive behavior among samples of non-problem boys and samples referred for socially aggressive and socialized delinquent problems. Mothers and their socially aggressive sons were the most aversive, and mothers and sons from the matched nonproblem families were the least aversive. On the other hand, the mothers and their sons referred for stealing showed the least amount of positive interaction; mothers and their nonproblem sons showed the most. Reid concluded that families of children who steal showed weak, distant social ties.

A study by Patterson (1978c) compared the MMPI self-report questionnaires for mothers of boys referred for stealing and of boys referred as social aggressors. The significant differences in base-line scores suggested that mothers of children who steal described themselves in the same way as do adolescent delinquents. Mothers of socially aggressive boys, on the other hand, described themselves as more anxious, depressed, angry, and isolated. Following supervised training in child management, there were significant improvements in the way in which the mothers described themselves.

Observation data in the homes of socially aggressive and nonproblem boys showed that deviant children engaged in coercive behaviors at significantly higher rates than did their matched, nonproblem compatriots (Delfini, Bernal, and Rosen 1976; Patterson 1976). Observation data had also shown that mothers and older siblings from these families were significantly more coercive than were their compatriots from nonproblem families (Patterson 1976). The general picture that emerges is that the socially aggressive child resides in an aversive system. It seems highly probable that such a child makes a significant contribution to the continued disruption of this system. Be that as it may, at least a third of the child's coercive responses are a reaction to aversive intrusions by other family members, that is, counterattacks (Patterson 1978a). Given such an intrusion, the coercive responses "pay off" significantly more, about 40 percent of the time. The general findings suggest that negative reinforcement may be a key mechanism for supporting high-rate coercive child behaviors—that is, aversive antecedent → coercive response → termination of aversive intrusion. Presumably, prosocial outcomes constitute positive reinforcers for the bulk of the child's coercive behaviors.

The child with conduct problems tends to have problems in more than one setting. Of 27 boys labeled "acting out" by community referral sources, 14 were thought to have problems adjusting to the classroom (Patterson 1974a). Roughly 50 percent were thought to be disruptive in the classroom and/or retarded in academic skills. These findings are in agreement with those from the study by S. M. Johnson, O. D. Bolstad, and G. Lobitz (1976). In their study, of 15 acting-out children referred for treatment because of difficulties in the home, 50 percent were observed to be deviant in the classroom. Conversely, of 12 children referred because of severe classroom problems, 45 percent were also observed to be deviant in the home. A study by M. E. Bernal, L. F. Delfini, J. A. North, and S. L. Kreutzer (1976) obtained much lower values (30 percent and 14 percent, respectively) when observing much younger children.*

These findings suggest that children who are coercive in one setting will be coercive in other settings. In one sense, one might consider social aggression to be a trait. L. H. Robins' (1974) review of epidemiological studies noted that the data from M. Rutter, J. Tizard, and K. Whitmore (1970) showed that as high as 6 percent of the boys aged 10 to 12 years might appropriately be labeled as antisocial. This set of problems also accounted for over two-thirds of the referrals of boys to child guidance clinics.

There seems to be a growing belief in the clinical literature that these problems are transitory phenomena. For example, a much-cited study by M. Shepherd, A. M. Oppenheim, and S. Mitchell (1966) matched families referred for treatment with nonreferred families who reported having the same kinds of problems with their children. A two-year follow-up interview showed few differences in adjustment for the untreated and the clinic families. It should be noted, however, that court-referred cases—the most extreme acting-out children—were carefully excluded from the analyses. Furthermore, there are several studies that show that mothers of problem children are biased to overestimate positive changes in their children (Clement and Milne 1967; Walter and Gilmore 1973). In both studies, observation data showed no changes in behavior even though parents' ratings showed improvement. In the latter, 66 percent of the mothers' global ratings showed improvement even though their own daily telephone

---

*All three studies found zero-order correlations in observed rates of deviant behavior across the two settings. It is assumed that a child trained to be out of control at home will have a higher probability of displaying out-of-control behaviors in the classroom. However, the observed classroom rates will vary from one year to the next, depending upon the kind of teacher the child has. For example, the interaction of laissez-faire teacher and coercive child would produce very high performance rates for that child in that year. It is assumed that the "teacher" structure variable accounts for a large portion of the across-subject variance, and thus initiates a low-order positive correlation that one might expect from the discussion above.

Data from Patterson (1978b) showed that given coercive behaviors that occur in both settings (such as tease, yell, hit) are under the control of different kinds of social stimuli.

report data showed the children were getting (slightly) worse. It is of interest to note that this is almost exactly the improvement rate obtained in the study by Shepherd et al. (1966) and the figure for waiting-list control groups reviewed by E. E. Levitt (1971).

Given that one uses data other than mothers' interview data, there is substantial evidence for the stability of acting-out behaviors over time. In his extensive review of longitudinal studies, D. Olweus (1976b) summarized observation data of two- and three-year-olds in nursery school settings. He showed correlations in the range of .70-.79 over six-month intervals, and in the .50-.70 range for one-year intervals. Several studies of children in elementary grades showed stability in peer sociometrics over one-year to three-year periods. The uncorrected stability correlations for the aggression scores ranged from .55 to .82. L. D. Eron, L. O. Walder, and M. Lefkowitz (1974) found a stability correlation of .38 ($p < .001$) for peer sociometric scores on aggression. The first measure for the 211 boys was obtained in grade 3, and the next in grade 13. It is reasonable to assume that most of the variance would be accounted for by the scores at the extreme—for instance, boys extremely aggressive in grade 3. The writer assumes that such children employed their coercive skills so effectively that they produce stable environmental reactions that, in turn, ensure the child will be labeled "aggressive" by peers ten years later. The data from Eron et al. (1974) were reanalyzed to test this hypothesis. Table 5.1 summarizes the findings. About a third of the boys identified as extremely aggressive in grade 3 were identified in the same percentile range ten years later. Almost all those identified as extreme in grade 3 were perceived as above average in aggression ten years later.

TABLE 5.1

Stability of Status as Aggressor over Ten-Year Interval

Peer Sociometric Aggressive Score, Grade 3	Ten Years Later, Percent		
	≥ Same Percentile	False Negative	≥ Median for Grade 13
≥ 95th percentile	38.5	70	100
≥ 90th percentile	32.0	62	88
≥ 85th percentile	32.3	63	79

Source: Evan et al., 1974.

The finding of false negative (the child will not be extremely aggressive in grade 13) showed that roughly two-thirds at the extreme in grade 13 had not been perceived as extreme in grade 3. However, most of those identified as extreme in grade 13 had been perceived at or above the median for aggression in grade 3. It seems, then, that children at the extremes in grade 13 were not novices to the art of coercion at earlier ages.

If one were to conceptualize a prevention program in grade 3 that would involve all of the children for a (future) ninety-fifth percentile in grade 13, one would have to treat almost everyone (98 percent). If one wished to include 86 percent of the future extremes, it would still be necessary to treat 106 third-grade boys. If one took into account father presence-absence, socioeconomic status, number of siblings, and the fact that a child was identified at the ninety-fifth percentile in two consecutive years (on peer sociometrics), then doubtless the efficiency of such prevention programs could be much improved.

A carefully designed study by J. C. Gersten, T. S. Langner, J. G. Eisenberg, O. Simcha-Fagan, and E. D. McCarthy (1976) sampled a cross section of 732 children and adolescents 5 to 18 years of age. The mothers of these children were reinterviewed five years later. Factor analyses of these data produced three factors relating to out-of-control behaviors. The average test/retest correlation for the five-year period for fighting was .50; for delinquency, .44; for conflict with siblings, .48; and for conflict with parents, .49. The rates for these behaviors tended to increase or remain constant, in contrast with more neurotic behaviors, which tended both to be less stable and to decrease in mean level over time.

The general findings attest to the stability of both social aggressive and delinquent behavior over three- to five-year periods, and some stability in extremes for up to ten years. The next question concerns the possibility of predicting delinquent behaviors of adolescents from these earlier adjustments in the classroom and home—that is, do early patterns of social aggression or delinquency relate to later adjustment? Probably the best-known study of this type was the series by S. and E. Glueck (1972). Their analyses of variables from interviews with parents suggested dramatic correlations between out-of-control behavior at ages five and six, and adolescent delinquency. Their omission of all false-positive errors provided spurious estimates of predictive efficiency. There are, in addition, other procedural problems that cast doubt on their findings (Kahn 1965). The literature cited by R. J. Lundman and F. R. Scarpitti (1978) showed their overall prediction rate to be 84 percent, less than the base rate for delinquency.

In 1955 and 1960 studies appeared that showed significant correlations between teachers' ratings of classroom conduct and delinquency in the community (Kvaraceus 1955; Havighurst, Bowman, Liddle, Matthews, and Pierce 1960). Since that time other studies have shown that teachers' ratings can be used to make moderately efficient predictions of delinquency over a four-year span (Hathaway and Monachesi 1963; Feldhusen, Thurston, and Benning 1970; Weiner and Gallistet 1961). The findings of these studies were partially attenuated by the fact that some of the boys were 10 to 17 years of age when the studies began, and could, therefore, have already been adjudicated delinquents.

In two follow-up studies of large samples of third- and fourth-grade children, teachers could identify behaviors that related to seriousness of later adolescent delinquency (Douglas 1966; West and Farrington 1973). Similarly, in a longitudinal study beginning in kindergarten, consistent behavioral differences were found between children who were later identified as delinquents and those who were not (Conger and Miller 1966). In the study by Eron et al. (1974), three times as many boys from the upper as compared to the other quartiles on aggression in the third grade committed police offenses during the ensuing ten years. Rather well controlled studies, such as that by S. Dinitz, F. Scarpitti, and W. C. Reckless (1962), suggest the predictive utility of teachers' ratings for older children.

Although weaker in design, there are data from three retrospective studies that show that an out-of-control style of dealing with the social environment has dire implications for later adult adjustment. Morris (1956) followed up 71 children who had earlier been characterized as having "conduct disorders," including "extremely aggressive" ratings. The follow-up data showed that as young adults, 18 percent were psychotic and 10 percent had criminal records. In fact, only about 21 percent were characterized as "adjusted." This dismal picture was corroborated in a 30-year follow-up study by N. L. Robins (1966), in which 406 antisocial children in an outpatient clinic were studied together with a group of matched controls. The data indicated that 39 percent of the aggressive children were diagnosed as psychotic in adulthood; 6 percent of the controls were similarly diagnosed. Only 15 percent of the aggressive males were considered well-adjusted adults, in contrast with 52 percent of the controls. As adults, 44 percent of the males were arrested for major crimes, versus 3 percent of the male controls; they also had marginal employment records and were more likely to rear antisocial children. Similar evidence was provided by M. Pritchard and P. Graham (1966) in a retrospective follow-up study of 71 adults in a psychiatric hospital who had been seen as children.

Studies by J. Block (1971) cited in Olweus (1976b) establish a significant correlation between aggression among high school students and aggression among middle-aged adults. Similarly, the 14-year follow-up study by West and Farrington (1973) showed that 14 percent of aggressive nine-year-olds would become violent delinquents. This is in contrast with the base rate of 4.5 percent for the rest of the sample. In fact, 48.1 percent of the violent adolescent delinquents had been rated as aggressive at age nine. It might be noted in passing that Robins (1974) showed that none of the adult psychopathics he studied had begun their careers after the age of 18 years.

In his careful review of 12 longitudinal studies, Olweus (1976b) found an average stability correlation of .63 with an average time interval of 5.7 years. Taken together, the studies suggest that by the age of four or five, extremely coercive children have acquired a stable mode of dealing with others (cf. Gersten et al. 1976). It is unlikely that they will "outgrow" this pattern. If effective treatment exists, it could well be applied at an early age.

From the standpoint of economy of prevention effort, the question arises as to which out-of-control child is most likely to end up in a correctional institution. K. Polk's (1975) follow-up data showed that only 4 percent of grade 14 boys followed into adulthood were institutionalized. Such a low base rate does not provide a promising lead if one is considering the possibility of prevention.

Turning the question around, one might ask, "Which acting-out child is most likely to become the chronic offender in later adolescence and adulthood?" The study by Polk (1975) showed that 73 percent of the boys who committed a police offense before and after grade 14 went on to commit further offenses as young adults. The massive follow-up study by M. E. Wolfgang, Robert M. Figlio, and T. Sellin (1973) showed that 54 percent of police offenses were committed by only 18 percent of the adolescent offenders. Given one offense, the probability was .52 that they would commit a second; given a second, the probability was .65 of committing a third; and given a third, probability was .72 of committing a fourth. These studies are not definitive, but they strongly suggest that the young boy who has committed three or more offenses is definitely at risk from society's point of view.

A follow-up study of out-of-control preadolescent boys by D. R. Moore, P. Chamberlain, and L. H. Mukai (1978) showed that over three-fourths of preadolescent boys who stole later committed a police offense. It seems, then, that high rates of stealing in the elementary grades may be precursors of later police offenses. This group may constitute a sample of children who are genuinely at risk, and thus merit the attention of prevention programs.

TREATMENT OUTSIDE THE COMMUNITY

The decision to institutionalize reflects two possible perceptions about treating out-of-control children: the community must be protected from these children as long as possible, or the institutional regime will produce changes within the child such that, when returned to the community, that child will be able to adjust adequately. Given the second viewpoint, a reasonable assessment of the efficacy of institutional treatment for acting-out children would require the following design:

1. Random assignment of deviant children to institutional and noninstitutional treatment
2. Pre- and post-treatment multiple criteria assessment showing changes in the child's behavior while on campus
3. Multiple criteria measures demonstrating the child's adjustment in the community following return. These should include institutionalization and police offense rates over at least a two-year period. The two-year follow-up is perhaps an arbitrary decision. It was chosen because this interval seems to be a critical one in the community treatment studies to be reviewed later
4. Data specifying the cost.

To the writer's knowledge, no studies using random assignment have been done. For this reason no definitive conclusions can be reached about this type of treatment. The data from D. L. Fixsen, E. L. Phillips, and M. M. Wolf (1973) for Kansas reformatories in 1971 showed an estimated cost of $9,500 per child. L. T. Empey and M. L. Ericksen (1972) estimated a cost of $2,015 for treatment over an average of nine and one-half months. The recidivism rates (child reinstitutionalized) for correctional institutions are usually within the 50 percent to 60 percent range, although rates for some institutions may go as high as 75 percent during the first year (Burchard 1976).

The longitudinal study by Wolfgang et al. (1973) compared two groups of boys having comparable numbers of police offenses. The analyses showed that sending adolescents to institutions was associated with increases in the probability of future offenses and, in keeping with the obvious confounds in those analyses, were duly noted by the authors. Even so, the results are highly suggestive. For current reviews of this literature by experts in the field, see Lundman and Scarpitti (1978). An observation study by R. E. Buehler, G. R. Patterson, and F. M. Furness (1966) of peer group and staff interactions in a correctional setting showed a massive preponderance of positive consequences for delinquent-type behaviors. This, in turn, suggested a teaching machine-like efficiency for training in these behaviors in institutional treatment. Perhaps this related in turn to the iatrogenic treatment effect.

There is only one study known to the writer that carefully documents changes in the behavior during residential treatment. In this study the techniques described by R. Redl and J. Wineman (1952) were applied to extremely aggressive boys in a residential treatment setting. Observation data showed that the behavior of the boys changed significantly in the treatment setting (Raush 1965; Raush, Deltman, and Taylor 1959). However, a clinical follow-up showed that the effects were lost a short time after the boys returned to their homes (Redl and Wineman 1952).

The advent of social learning approaches to correctional institutions in the late 1960s was met with great expectations. Frequent monitoring of the child, use of token economy, daily consequences, and a heavy emphasis upon remediating academic skills were the hallmarks of these approaches. The CASE project was an exemplar of this approach (Cohen and Filipczak 1971). Within a short time other equally well documented programs were under way: the Intensive Training Program (ITP) (Burchard 1967; Burchard and Barrera 1972), the Youth Center Research Project (Jesness, DeRisis, McCormick, and Quedge 1972), and the PACE program, Kennedy Youth Center (Karachi, Schmidt, and Cairor 1972). Burchard (1976) has prepared a detailed description of several of these programs together with their outcome data.

One means of evaluating these programs is to analyze their success in reducing police contact when the children are returned to the community. Some community-based treatment programs reviewed later showed significant effects that, however, were invariably lost between the first and second follow-up years. It is assumed, then, that a program should demonstrate its increased effectiveness relative to the comparison procedure beyond the two-year follow-up point. Follow-up studies were available for three of the four major token economy programs. The proportion of boys reinstitutionalized one and two years following treatment is summarized in Table 5.2.

During the first year of follow-up, most of these studies claimed a modest treatment effect of 6 percent to 48 percent when compared with local recidivism rates. Given the loss of over one-fourth of the subjects in one study (CASE) and the lack of random assignment to traditional institutional treatment, one does not know how to interpret even claims for these short-term effects. The CASE program claimed the greatest success at one year; but by the second follow-up year, its data showed no difference. Comparable data are not yet available from the other studies. However, in general the findings have a ringing consistency. All claim that the treatment procedures produced significant changes in social and academic behavior while the child was on campus. One year later these improvements are only minimally reflected in changes in the child's community adjustment. Indeed, the most parsimonious statement is that the programs had no impact on later adjustment. If one accepts a figure of roughly $9,000 per year per child, it would suggest that these unproven social experiments are costly to society; certainly there is good reason to believe they are costly to the child.

It seems that behavior modifiers have been successful in producing changes in adjustment to the correctional institutions, but have been no more successful than earlier investigators in programming for generalization from successful institutional treatment to community adjustment. It is conceivable that a residential milieu could provide even more intensive treatment, and this could have a lasting impact. Younger acting-out children and finer-grained measures of outcome would further enhance this possibility. R. G. Wahler, R. Berland, and G. Leske (1975) evaluated residential treatment for 30 boys aged 5–18. The boys received an average of 400 hours of professional time while involved in various token economy programs. Both observation and daily teacher report data showed significant changes in the children's institutional adjustment. Immediately upon return to the community, the observation data showed modest gains, but parent and teacher ratings reflected little change. Within a year 40 percent of the boys had returned to institutional care, 57 percent had court contacts, and 82 percent required additional intervention.

The general tenor of these findings leads one to look for other approaches to treatment that, it is hoped, will be less costly to society and to the child, and will produce a more lasting impact upon the child's adjustment to the community.

TABLE 5.2

Follow-up Data for Institutional Treatment

Treatment Program	Random Assignment	Percent Subjects Recidivists			
		First-Year Follow-up		Second-year Follow-up	
		Treatment Group	Comparison Group	Treatment Group	Comparison Group
CASE	no	27%*	62.5% subjects transferred out of treatment 75% National Training School	no difference at third year	
Youth Center	yes; partial	31.9%	31.4 transactional treatment 46% California Youth Authority	n.a.	n.a.
ITP	no	25%–35%	n.a.	n.a.	
KYC	no	27%	33% other state institutions	44%	n.a.

*Burchard (1976) points out that 25 percent of the treated subjects were "lost."

n.a. = not available.

Sources: Cohen and Filipczak 1971; Jesness et al. 1972; Burchard 1976; Karachi et al. 1972.

COMMUNITY-BASED TREATMENT

In some respects the social learning and sociological viewpoints agree in their general formulation about treatment for the acting-out child. Both would assume that the problem does not lie within the child; rather, it lies in the interaction of the child and the social environment. From the social learning viewpoint, one must examine each major setting—home and school—to determine the sense in which each fosters and maintains acting-out behaviors. In each setting the treatment agents are those persons whose reactions elicit and reinforce the deviant behavior. On the other hand, the child brings to these settings certain deficiencies (academic and social skills) and certain habitual modes of interacting that set up the social environment. For persistent treatment effects, both the child and the environment must be reprogrammed. While perhaps in agreement on this general viewpoint, the traditional sociological and contemporary social learning approaches differ in the means by which one brings about these changes.

Since as far back as the early 1950s, large-scale, well-designed studies have been conducted to evaluate treatment outcomes for out-of-control children. There are at least four such studies, all of which employed random assignment to treated and nontreated groups and follow-up procedures. In varying degrees each study employed counseling with the child and parents, casework with the social agencies and family, and recreational outlets. Some of the more recent efforts included remediation for academic, social, and work skills. All arrived at the same conclusion.

The classic study was the Cambridge-Somerville study (Powers and Witmer 1951). Young children identified as delinquency-prone were randomly assigned to an experimental and a comparison group. The boys in the treated group received counseling; their families were contacted at least once a month. Many boys also received remedial training for academic deficiencies. Most of them were also involved in local boys' clubs and summer camp experiences. The median length of time for treatment was four years, with a range of two to eight years. At the end of treatment about two-thirds of the counselors indicated that the boys had been helped; 50 percent of the boys agreed with them. Eight of the ten counselors felt the experiment had been a success.

As shown in Table 5.3, during follow-up, 29.5 percent of the boys in the treated group had made at least one court appearance, and 28.3 percent in the comparison group. J. McCord's (1976) follow-up of these children as adults successfully located 94 percent of the original sample—a landmark achievement in its own right. Her data showed that as adults, the treated group evidenced significantly high rates of alcoholism, psychiatric illness, and criminal records. This finding is even more surprising in light of the fact that as adults many of the treated subjects emphasized the importance of this treatment experience. A similar well-designed, large-scale study with high-risk girls showed no difference between treated and nontreated girls (Meyer et al. 1965).

TABLE 5.3

Summary of Outcomes for Comparative Studies

Study	Term of Treatment	Termination		Follow-up		
		Treated Group	Comparative Group	Interval	Treated Group	Comparative Group
Cambridge-Somerville Study	4 years	325	325		29.5% court appearance	28.3% court appearance
Vocational High Study	3 years	200	200			
Inner City Study	5 months median 75 hours contact	51	44	3 years	47% police contact	47% police contact dropout school grades
Atlantic St. Center Project	mean 75 hours	26	26	1 year	51% police contact	53% police contact
Lane County Study	3 years	95		no differences in grades or police offenses		
Provo Experiment	4–7 months	75 48% arrests	80 68% arrests 138 institution**	1 year 2 years 3 years 4 years	.55 arrests .97 arrests 1.24 arrests 1.32 arrests	.70 arrests .93 arrests 1.01 arrests 1.42 arrests

*See other studies that employed random assignment to experimental and comparative groupings. The Atlantic St. Center study employed matched groupings.

**This group not randomly assigned.

Sources: Powers and Witmer 1951; Meyer et al. 1965; Reckless and Dinitz 1972; Berleman and Steinburn 1967; Polk 1967; Empey and Ericksen 1972.

One reasonable criticism of these studies is that the fact of such a large-scale effort precluded intensive casework contacts. There may also have been a lack of coordination among all community agencies. Considerable advances had been made in casework techniques since the 1930s, when the Cambridge-Somerville Project took place. The study by W. Reckless and J. Dinitz (1972) employed small case loads (17 cases), weekly group sessions, special classes in the school, and family counseling. These treated cases were chosen from a select group of high-risk, inner-city youths from the seventh grade. As summarized in Table 5.3, the three-year follow-up data showed no effect on any major variable such as police offenses, school grades, or dropout rates. It is interesting to note that both the teachers and the treated children perceived significant changes resulting from the treatment.

The Atlantic Street Center Project was also designed to provide intensive treatment for high-risk children in grades 6 through 9. The average of 75 hours of contact attests to the fact that the study fulfilled this requirement (Berleman and Steinburn 1967). The data showed a marginal decrease in disruption at school, but this effect disappeared during follow-up. At follow-up the police offense data showed no difference between comparison groups.

The final studies focused upon high-risk children living in nonmetropolitan areas (Polk 1967). A major focus was upon altering the regression in the school and remediation for academic skills. The data showed no changes in grades significantly different from changes for the nontreated controls. As another component, intensive work was carried out with a subsample of 82 multiproblem families. The emphasis was upon extensive group therapy. As the data in Table 5.3 show, there were no changes in grades or in delinquent behavior for this group.

The Provo Experiment is probably one of the best-designed and best-documented studies in the literature (Empey and Ericksen 1972). The boys were multiple offenders, aged 14–18, randomly assigned to either traditional probation or to the experimental procedure. The latter consisted of daily intensive group interaction with work for pay as a reward. The cost of the treatment was estimated to be $609 per child. During treatment the mean number of arrests was .58 for the experimental and 1.28 for the comparison group. The seriousness of the offenses also declined. The follow-up data in Table 5.3 show that these effects were lost during the second year of follow-up. It should be noted, however, that during the four-year period the rates of incarceration were only 3 percent for the experimental and 19 percent for the comparison group. If this were replicated, it would constitute a major finding.

SOCIAL LEARNING APPROACHES

The social learning and sociology approaches might agree in their emphasis upon teaching social skills (academic, social, job) to enhance the child's ability to produce positive reinforcers from the environment. They might also agree with the necessity for involving parents and other family members in an effective treatment program. They would, however, be likely to disagree on what should be taught to the family. Casework approaches typically provide assistance in the use of community services and exploration of emotional conflicts. The social learning approach would more likely stress parental involvement in tracking child behavior, negotiating agreements with the child, and providing consequences for deviant behaviors (Patterson, Reid, Jones, and Conger 1975). Both approaches would emphasize training in problem-solving and communication skills. The social learning approach assumes, however, that the latter are necessary but not sufficient conditions for reducing children's out-of-control behaviors. From that viewpoint, the additional necessary component is for the parent to provide an aversive consequence for social aggression or delinquent behavior. It is assumed that without change of the latter sort, there will be no significant reduction in a high rate of out-of-control behaviors. The former relate to whether or not these changes will persist. Data to be reviewed in this section relate to these assumptions.

Such a stance implies that parents (adults) of both problem and nonproblem children must monitor and provide consequences for out-of-control behaviors until the child leaves the home. This is obviously a far cry from the notion of an early internalization of moral knowledge that effectively guides behavior through life, such as that of L. Kohlberg (1969). If one assumes that sanctions for deviancy are necessary, then one must also assume the need to monitor and track the child's adolescent behavior. It is assumed by the writer that the parent is in the position of being the most effective agent for the dual role of monitoring and punishing deviant behavior. In settings in which parents are not present, the responsibility may be delegated to the teacher. However, this requires a careful coordination between school and home. Many parents of acting-out children seem unable or unwilling to engage in this process. As noted in the review by Robins (1974), these parents tend to be uncooperative for even such simple commitments as appearing for an interview, let alone participating in parent training programs. Perhaps for this reason, many therapists have opted for the halfway house concept. Based within the community, the staff of the halfway house takes over the function of parent and coordinates information and consequences relating to the child's adjustment within the home and the community.

The initial efforts to use this approach seemed to meet with success, and led to its enthusiastic endorsement as a humane alternative to traditional institutionalization. Perhaps the best-known was the High Field experiment described by A. H. Weeks (1962). A critique of these earlier, poorly designed efforts showed that the effect on later recidivism rates was negligible (Pearl 1963).

Beginning in the late 1960s, the Achievement Place studies emanating from the University of Kansas represented the most intensive analyses of process variables in the entire field. At this point there are dozens of such community-sponsored treatment programs scattered about the country. Each consists of a pair of highly trained teaching parents and six to eight adolescents, some of whom are adjudicated delinquents.

The house parents receive several weeks of intensive training in the use of token economies, self-government meetings, working with community agencies, and monitoring classroom problems (Phillips, Phillips, Fixsen, and Wolf 1971). Following placement, they return for further intensive training. The procedures are described in such detail (Phillips, Phillips, Fixsen, and Wolf 1972) as to facilitate the replication studies now under way.

While in residence the boys are involved in regular school programs and at propitious times are returned to their families for weekends. As they gradually return to their homes, their parents receive a small amount of training and supervision in extending the token economy program from the halfway house to the family. While in residence, the boys are trained via a token economy in an impressive variety of social skills, including study skills, articulation, neatness, self-report, participating in family conferences, punctuality, room cleanliness, and how to talk to would-be employers (and to police). The efficacy of each of these programs within the halfway house has been carefully investigated in over 40 single-subject (replicated) experiments. The findings were summarized in a careful review by J. D. Burchard (1976).

The crucial question concerns the follow-up effects of this relatively expensive treatment. The average stay was 12–15 months, at a cost of about $4,100 per child. K. A. Kirigin (1976) has prepared an interim report for the first 28 boys treated at the original Achievement Place. The institutionalization and police data were presented for the first year following treatment of these children and of 16 children treated at comparison halfway houses. At one year follow-up, both the Achievement Place and the comparison showed about two offenses per subject. There were no differences between treatments. In one year both groups have made substantial returns to base-line offense rates. One suspects that at two-year follow-up the return could be complete. The finding of no difference in police offense rate was also obtained by R. R. Jones (1978) in a nationwide study comparing Achievement Place models with traditional halfway houses.

It is important to note for these preliminary findings that random assignment was not reported for either the Kirigin or the Jones study. It is also quite possible that data for untreated children would show significant increases in police offenses over those treated in either traditional or Achievement Place model halfway houses. To the writer's knowledge, there are at this time no studies available that employ a random assignment design for comparison of probation, halfway house, Achievement Place, and institutionalization models. However, at the very least the halfway house may represent a less expensive mode for reducing community pressure to "do something" rather than, say, institutionalization.

PARENT TRAINING

One might characterize the early halcyon period from the mid-1960s to the 1970s as the "whoopee phase" in the development of parent training procedures. The investigators working with oppositional and aggressive children and parents were employing observation data as criteria and N = 1 designs of varying degrees of sophistication (Bernal, Duryee, Pruett, and Burns 1969; Hanf 1968; Hawkins, Peterson, Schweid, and Bijou 1966; Johnson and Brown 1969; Patterson and Brodsky 1966; Patterson, McNeal, Hawkins, and Phelps 1967; Wahler, Winkle, Peterson, and Morrison 1965; Zeilberger, Sampen, and Sloane 1968).

Some investigators quickly moved on to work with larger samples. R. Tharp and R. Wetzel (1969) treated a large number of families, all referred because of acting-out problems. However, many tended to be rather mild problems; none of the children were on probation with the juvenile court. No follow-up data were provided, and much of the data on the outcomes of specific programs were lost. Of 92 cases treated, 90 percent were rated by parents and therapists as improved. A methodological study by J. Schelle (1974) examined the parent questionnaire used by Tharp and Wetzel. As in the Tharp and Wetzel study, the parents were asked to rate school attendance. The correlation between these ratings and actual school records of attendance was -.20 (n.s.). Many of the methodological problems raised by this pioneering study continue to plague current efforts.

R. Stuart (1969) also began a series of studies. The first showed that family interactions of delinquents were more negative than interactions of nondelinquents. In the next study (Stuart and Tripodi 1971) 79 children were treated. The children were essentially from middle-class families; only 13 had prior court contacts. The amount of professional time invested ranged from 13 hours for one group to 30 hours for the other. Plans were made to collect follow-up data. However, none were presented. One would hope that the preliminary report will be supplemented by a more intensive analysis including the follow-up data. The therapists worked with the parents and with the school. The criterion data consisted of parent attitudes, child self-report, school attendance, and grades. This major effort also employed an interesting design involving random assignment to three different time-limited treatment groups: 15 days (receiving 13 hours of time); 45 days (over 16 hours); and 90 days (over 30 hours). Because the data were not presented for base line and termination, it is difficult to determine whether significant changes occurred.

OREGON SOCIAL LEARNING CENTER STUDIES

The Oregon Social Learning Center (OSLC) studies, like the others cited above, began in the mid-1960s with a series of single case studies (Patterson and Brodsky 1966; Patterson, McNeal, Hawkins, and Phelps 1967; Patterson and Reid 1970). These, in turn, led to a pilot study in which six consecutive referrals were treated (Patterson, Ray, and Shaw 1968). An observation code was developed to assess changes in family interaction data (Reid 1978). The 29-category code described sequential interactions. Fourteen of the categories describe noxious behaviors; summing across them provides a measure of rate (per minute) of deviant behavior for problem child, parents, or siblings. The families were referred for treatment by community agencies because one or more members were thought to be out of control. The data in Table 5.4 summarize the findings for changes from base line to termination and through follow-up, the amount of treatment time involved, changes in sibling behavior, and demographic variables. The data from this one measure show that each case made progress. The treatment effects also seemed to persist over the relatively brief follow-up periods of 4 to 13 months. Presumably, this latter effect occurred because the family as a system was altered—that is, the mutual reinforcement contingencies were changed in some unspecified manner. The data from the siblings showed a rather modest alteration in their rates of deviant behavior for two of four families. These pilot data were encouraging.

In the first single-case studies the experimenters were the change agents. However, it quickly became apparent that when studies were done in this way, the changes would not persist. In fact, it seemed necessary to change or reprogram the entire system. In the study by Patterson, Ray, and Shaw (1968) it became obvious that the parents, siblings, and teachers must become the primary change agents. This point was also emphasized in the work of Tharp and Wetzel (1969). Second, it became apparent that successful treatment in the home did not generalize to problems occurring in the classroom (Skinrud 1972). This required the development of two clinical techniques: one for reprogramming family interactions and the other for altering peer and teacher reactions.

Following the 1968 pilot studies, the parent training procedures were "standardized" and taught to a new group of therapists. The procedures were outlined by G. R. Patterson, J. A. Cobb, and R. S. Ray (1973), and were applied to 27 cases treated through 1972. The training now included, first, teaching the parents social learning language and family management concepts found in programmed texts prepared for that purpose (Patterson 1971; Patterson and Gullion 1968). A clinical study by B. L. Baker and L. J. Herfesty (1974) showed that parents of retarded children who read a manual were as successful in changing child behavior as were those parents who also received group training. Patterson (1975) showed significant decreases in observed rates of deviant child behavior immediately following parents' reading *Living with Children*. In a more carefully controlled study, O. Christensen (1976) showed comparable effects that were significantly greater than those obtained for a nontreatment control group. The follow-up data showed, however, that such effects may be short-lived even for the middle-class sample used by Christensen. The parents then learned to carefully define, track, and record a series of targeted deviant and/or prosocial child behaviors. They were monitored frequently by telephone during this and all

TABLE 5.4

Observed Changes in Behavior of the Pilot Sample

| | | | | Demographic Data | | | Mean Rate Deviant Behavior per Minute | | | | | |
| | | | | | | | For Target Person | | | For Siblings | | |
Family Number	Setting of Treatment	Age of Problem Child	Father Absent/ Present	Parent Occupation	Referral Symptoms	Setting	Base Line	Termination	Follow-up	Base Line	Termination	Hours of Treatment
1	home	4	absent	welfare	hyperactivity, negativism, temper, stealing	home (child)	.51	.22	moved	.18	.02	9.8
2	home	6	present	unskilled worker	extreme negativism, fighting with sibs, noncompliance	home (child)	.20	Lost	.06 (6 mos.)	.20	.13	12.6
3	home	11	present	librarian	bizarre, psychosomatic symptoms, facial tic, fire-setting	home (child)	.59	.09	.05 (8 mos.)	.01	.02	46.7
4	home	10	absent	welfare	crying, enuresis, lying, stealing	home (mother)	.75	.12	.20 (11 mos.)	—	—	29.0
5	home, school	8	present	professor	underachieving, aggression to peers, arguing, isolation	school (child)	2.53	.60	.90 (4 mos.)	—	—	16.0
6	home, school	10	present	engineer	underachievement, non-compliance, arguing	home, school (child)	1.20 2.78	.60 1.00	.41 (13 mos.) 1.27 (8 mos.)	.18	.09	16.0 32.0

Source: Patterson, Ray, and Shaw 1968.

all other stages of training. They were then assigned to a parent training group, where modeling and role-playing procedures were used to illustrate appropriate use of positive and aversive consequences. Fourth, they learned how to construct contracts that specified contingencies for a list of problem behaviors occurring at home and/or at school. Where necessary, training sessions were also conducted in the home, with the experimenters modeling the desired parenting skills.

Beginning in 1972, the new sample consisted of many nonmotivated parents whose children stole frequently. This led to the introduction of a deposit or breakage fee. The studies by H. A. Peine and B. Munro (1973) showed that paying the parents increased their rates of being on time, attendance, and carrying out assignments. The effect seemed clearly significant for families of lower socioeconomic status, but partially vitiated when working with middle-class families. S. M. Eyberg and S. M. Johnson (1974) found that monetary contingencies affected task completion, but not attendance, for a sample of middle-class families referred because of mildly out-of-control children. M. J. Fleischman (1978) randomly assigned parents of acting-out children to a salaried or nonsalaried parenting group receiving training in child management skills. Parenting salary contingencies significantly increased parental cooperation and also reduced dropout rates. The effect was particularly dramatic for the families of lower socioeconomic status.

In addition to parenting salaries and breakage fees for some families, there was a new emphasis upon including the child in all negotiating sessions. The new contracts often made provision for the child to change the behavior of the parent or of a sibling. The details of these clinical procedures are presented in the clinical manual by Patterson, Reid, Jones, and Conger (1975).

These relatively standardized procedures were applied to three clinical samples. The first consisted of 27 consecutive referrals of boys with severe conduct problems (Patterson 1974a, 1974b; 1975). The second sample was 32 boys and girls referred because of high rates of stealing (Reid, Rivera, and Lorber 1978). The third sample was a replication consisting of 26 children referred for severe conduct problems (M. Fleischman 1978b). The demographic data for these samples are summarized in Table 5.5. The referred children tended to be preadolescent boys with out-of-control problems of long standing. Only the last two samples accepted girls as subjects. Relative to the Eugene, Oregon, community, the lower socioeconomic levels were overrepresented in the treated samples.

The dropout rates for the base-line period were 23 percent, 27 percent, and 18 percent. These figures did not include families who contacted the project but did not agree to a base-line study. Also, no information is available about those families prescreened by community agents and judged inappropriate for this approach. Under these limitations no information can be provided that specifies the proportion of families in the community that can be helped. These pretreatment dropout rates compare favorably with data for other social learning approaches to family training—for instance, 56 percent for Eyberg and Johnson

TABLE 5.5

Demographic Information for Three Treated Samples

Variable	1972 Conduct Problem Sample	1975 Stealer Sample	1977 Replication Sample
Number of families referred	35	45	34
Number of families treated	27	28	26
Sex of referred child	All male	24 males 4 females	19 males 7 females
Age of referred child	mean 8.7 years range 5–13	mean 9.3 years range 5–14	mean 7.38 years range 3–12
Number of siblings	mean 2.44 range 1–5	mean 2.1 range 0–7	mean 1.64 range 0–4
Number of families with father absent	8		10
Socioeconomic level*	mean 4.5	mean 5.70	mean 4.39
Dropouts during baseline	8	12	6
Dropouts prior to five weeks' treatment	0	5	7
Dropouts after five weeks' treatment	6	6	5
Partial follow-up	21	18	in process
12-month follow-up	16		
In process	0		

*Based on system provided by A. Hollingshead and F. Redlich (1958), with class 1 denoting higher executive or professional; class 4, clerical; and class 7, unskilled laborer.
Sources: Patterson 1974a, 1974b, 1975; Reid 1978; Fleischman 1978.

(1974) and 58 percent for S. Johnson and A. Christensen (1976). The comparable rate for traditional therapies cited in the D. H. Olson (1976) review was 30 percent.

Of those who began treatment at the OSLC, the proportions terminating before the therapist considered them ready were 22 percent, 21 percent, and 46 percent. With the exception of the figure for the replication study, these figures are in general agreement with the comparable figure of 29 percent for the Eyberg and Johnson (1974) study, 14 percent for B. Martin (1977), and 38 percent in the programmatic study of families having lower socioeconomic status by Martha Bernal (1978). In the Oregon Research Institute (ORI) evaluation, all families who received five or more weeks of treatment were included in the analyses of the outcome. As noted by other reviewers, the comparable dropout rates for traditional therapies have been in the 40 percent to 60 percent range (Graziano and Fink 1973). In his review of traditional therapies, Olson (1976) noted a range of from 25 percent dropout for filial therapy to as high as 70 percent for some psychotherapies. As often as not, those cases who dropped out during treatment were not included when estimating success rates. Olson (1976) cited one author who claimed that in his study, only 7 percent of the original referrals remained for the full course of therapy. Including families receiving incomplete training in outcome evaluation should provide a conservative estimate of efficacy of treatment. At this juncture such a conservative stance would seem desirable.

Outcome Studies

Successful training in child management must be demonstrated at many different levels. First, it should be demonstrated that the specific child behaviors for which the parents received training and supervision significantly changed from base line to termination. Given that, then the parents should apply the child management procedures to the wide spectrum of out-of-control behaviors that characterize both problem child and siblings. Significant changes here should be measured both by outside observers and by parents. Given these generalized applications, one would expect reductions in coercive behaviors among all family members, together with significant shifts in parent perceptions of the child and of themselves. There should also be changes in the way that the family members react to the child's coercive behaviors. Given changes in level of deviancy and in family process, this would lead one to expect extended follow-up data to show significant persistence of treatment effects.

For all samples the evaluations were based upon a minimum two-week base line (four weeks for the sample of children who steal), systematic probes at four to five weeks of treatment, and termination. A probe consists of data collected on at least two consecutive days, including 20 minutes in each session for the problem child. Probes were also carried out at regular intervals over the 12 months following treatment.

FIGURE 5.1

Changes in Targeted Behaviors for Two Samples

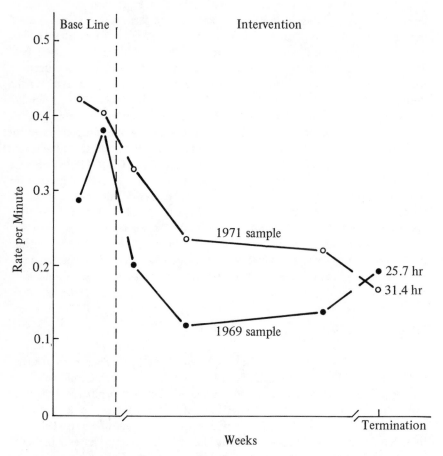

Source: Patterson and Reid 1973.

During the intake interview, each family selected from one to seven or more behaviors that were also sampled by the observation code system. The sum of these scores constituted a targeted deviant score. These data were collected in six to ten base-line sessions in the home after four weeks, eight weeks, and at termination of treatment.

The pretargeted and posttargeted deviant scores were calculated for the first 13 cases from the 1972 sample (Patterson et al. 1973). The *F* value of 4.31 was significant at the .05 level. The next 11 cases constituted the replication sample (Patterson and Reid 1973). The results are summarized in Figure 5.1.

A later analysis of the entire 27 cases for this study showed that the parents significantly changed the targeted behaviors during their supervised training, and that these effects persisted during the 12-month follow-up period (Patterson 1974b).*

The clinical utility of such parent training procedures rests upon the extent to which the parents generalize their child management skills to include a wider range of problem behaviors for the target child. The Total Aversive Behavior (TAB) score summarizes the rates for 14 coercive behaviors including, of course, the "targeted" categories already discussed. The test/retest correlation for this TAB score for the first and second weeks of base line was .78 ($df = 26; p < .01$). Studies reviewed in Reid (1978) demonstrate its validity in differentiating between normal and deviant samples as well as in covarying with other measures of child deviancy.

It was predicted that there would be significant reductions in TAB scores from base line to termination for both the 1972 sample and the 1977 replication. The majority of children who steal have been shown to be relatively noncoercive in their family interactions (Reid and Hendriks 1973). Therefore, it would be assumed that the TAB score at base line would be lower than that of the samples of mixed conduct problems. For children who steal, the treatment effect would be less marked. Figure 5.2 summarizes the scores for the three samples. Data are included for all cases receiving five or more weeks of training.

For the two studies involving a heterogeneous sample of social aggressors and children who steal, the outcome data were surprisingly consistent. The replication by Fleischman (1978b) used a newly trained staff of therapists and observers. It also employed the additions to treatment (breakage fee, parent salary, school contracts) described in Patterson et al. (1975). These changes might have been expected to increase the efficiency of the replication treatment. However, Fleischman and his group had also adopted a more educational stance, which meant that they spent little time trying to motivate resistant or unengaged parents. This may explain the fact that they lost many more clients in the first weeks of treatment. For the 1972 sample a comparison among total deviant (TD) scores over base line and three treatment probes produced an F value of

---

*If one used data collected by parents to measure changes in targeted behavior, the results are even more striking. The data from four studies showed that over 90 percent of the families were successful in decreasing these problem behaviors (Patterson et al. 1973; Johnson and Eyberg 1975; Johnson and Christensen 1976; Tharp and Wetzer 1969; Fleischman 1978b).

In considering the problem, the question arises of what happened to those behaviors not specifically targeted. In Patterson (1974b) such an analysis showed changes in these nontargeted behaviors. However, the t of 1.61 ($df = 26; p < .07$, one-tailed test) was of borderline significance. This analysis must be carried out again with the new samples. The finding suggests the necessity for programming greater generalization into the training procedures.

FIGURE 5.2

Changes in Problem Children's Total Aversive Behavior Score in Home

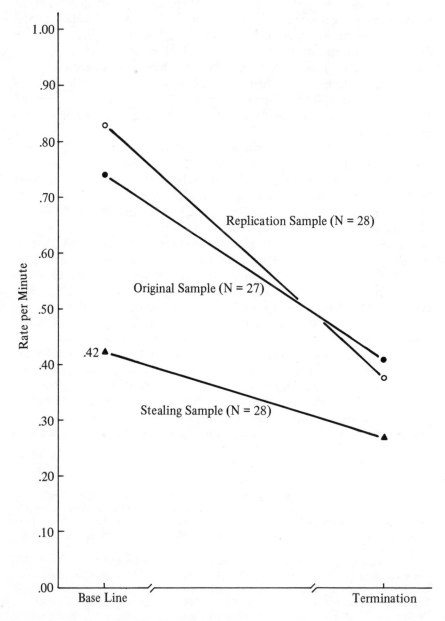

Source: Constructed by the author.

5.15 ($p < .01; df = 3.78$). For the replication study the comparison of base line with termination produced a t for correlated means of 2.79 ($df = 18; p < .001$, one-tailed test). In both studies 67 percent of the subjects showed a less than 30 percent drop from base line. As expected from the earlier study by Reid and Hendriks (1973), the rate of coercive behaviors for stealers was close to the normal range (.27) at base line and showed only a nonsignificant reduction at termination.

It had become apparent even during the pilot study that some out-of-control behaviors could not be efficiently sampled by observation codes. Half the children were referred because they were thought to lie, steal, set fires, and run away. Many of them were not socially aggressive. Therefore, it was necessary to devise a means for measuring low-base-rate events.

For the second criterion, the parents were asked during the intake interview whether or not each behavior from a list of "symptoms" (Patterson et al. 1975) was of sufficient concern for them to wish to change it. For the 1972 sample these data were collected on each occasion that the observers went to the home during base line, treatment, and follow-up. The parents were asked to indicate the occurrence, or nonoccurrence, of each of these events during that day for the time up to, and including, the observation session. In the 1975 and 1976 studies the data were collected by daily telephone calls. To determine the test/retest reliability, the mean proportion of parent daily report (PDR) symptoms for the first week of base line was correlated with the comparable score for the second week of base line. The Pearson product-moment correlation (uncorrected) was .60 ($df = 16; p < .01$). A comparison of reports given by mothers and fathers showed a correlation of .83 ($df = 25; p < .01$). In a study by Patterson (1974a), the mean PDR frequency for base line correlated .69 ($df = 14$; $p < .01$) with the total deviant scores obtained from the base line observations. A comparable correlation of .46 ($df = 21; p < .02$) was obtained by Fleischman (1978b) for the replication sample, and in the study by Reid et al. (1978), where the correlation was .58 ($df = 31; p < .001$). In that there is some overlap in categories of coercive measures, these correlations are not unexpected. S. Waksman (1978) examined six coercive traits measured by the PDR and observation procedures. The analysis showed significant convergence for three of the traits (whining, destructive behavior, and crying). The trait of whining also met the criteria for discriminative validity. The PDR score samples both low-base-rate problems and a select sample of higher-rate coercive behaviors.

The score was not developed until the 1972 study was nearly half completed; and through a misunderstanding, it was not used until the replication study was well under way. For this reason the samples are smaller than expected for those two studies. The data for all three samples are summarized in Figure 5.3.

For the 1972 sample the F value for the Analysis Variance (ANOVA) for repeated measures comparing base line was 15.85 ($df = 1.16; p < .01$). Approximately two-thirds of the boys showed reductions of less than 30 percent from base line (Patterson 1974a). The comparable value for the 1976 replication study

FIGURE 5.3

Changes in Parent Daily Report of Symptom Occurrence

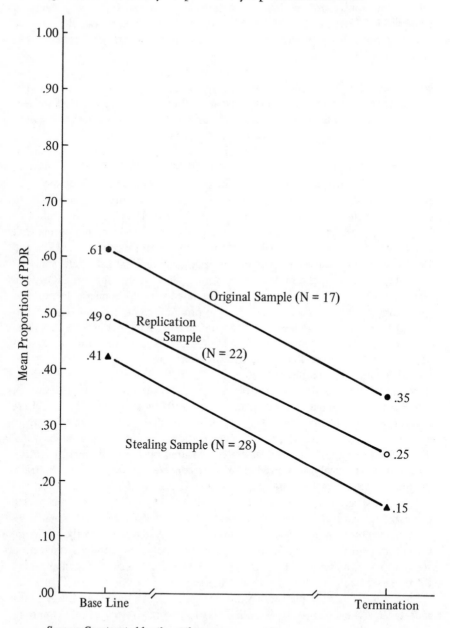

Source: Constructed by the author.

was a *t* for correlated means of 4.20 (*df* = 26; *p* < .001, one-tailed test) (Fleischman 1978b). The average number of problem behaviors tracked by parents during base line was 3.57. As shown in Figure 5.3, about half these problems occurred on any given day. For the samples of children who steal, the *t* value was 5.70 (*df* = 22; *p* < .0001) (Reid et al. 1978).

The data from the three samples offer strong support for the hypothesis that changes occur in a wide spectrum of deviant child behaviors.

What Is Success in Treatment?

Given that two or more outcome criteria are employed, how does one decide what is a "success" or a "failure"? In the original study both TAB and PDR criteria showed that 67 percent of the subjects dropped at least 30 percent from base-line levels. However, from a subset of this sample, parent global ratings (Patterson and Reid 1973) of improvement showed a success rate of 100 percent. While one naturally wishes to believe the latter figure, our clinical impression is that it is an exaggerated index of success.

Different success rates for different criteria have been noted by other investigators (Eyberg and Johnson 1974; Johnson and Christensen 1976). In general it seems that the success rates increase as one moves from molecular measures (TAB score, PDR score) to measures of parent attitude to global measures of change. Table 5.6 summarizes some findings that suggested the hypothesis just presented.

What the writer would choose to call hard data (observation and PDR) show success rates ranging from 38 percent to 78 percent for the five studies. Data from parents' perception or attitudes gave a range of 81 percent to 89 percent success.* Data from parent global ratings showed a range of 90 percent to

---

*Johnson's group has also consistently found changes in parental attitudes (Eyberg and Johnson 1974; Christensen 1976). However, three treatment studies employed no treatment control or placebo groups in which parents were asked to provide global estimates of improvement (Clement and Milne 1967; Walter and Gilmore 1973). All showed improvement in parent perceptions of the problem child. In two, their global perceptions of the child implied improvement when, in fact, other criterion measures showed no change (Clement and Milne 1967) or a nonsignificant trend toward greater deviancy (Walter and Gilmore 1973). These preliminary findings suggest that parents of problem children are biased to perceive improvements when changes have not occurred in the children's behavior. This assumption is buttressed by the findings from Schelle's (1974) study, which showed that over 40 percent of the parents perceived improvements in school attendance when, in fact, the school records showed less attendance following treatment.

The question of parent bias in global ratings will be considered again. At this point, however, it seems clear that parents' perceptions of the child become more positive during or following their successful applications of child management skills.

TABLE 5.6

Success Rates by Different Criteria (percent)

| | | Criterion Measures | | | | | |
| | | Observer Data | | | Parent Data | | |
Treated Sample	N	Targeted Deviant Score[a]	Total Deviant Score[a]	PDR Score[a]	Becker	Attitude	Global Rating of Improvement
Johnson and Eyberg (1975)	22	48	41	–	89[b]	81	not analyzed
Johnson and Christensen (1976)	14	38	43	–	87[c]	81	not analyzed
Patterson (1974a, 1974b)	27	75	67	67	87[c]	not analyzed	100[d]
Fleischman (1978b)	26	not analyzed	78	78	not analyzed	not analyzed	90
Reid et al. (1978)	28	not analyzed	52	74	not analyzed	not analyzed	not analyzed

[a]As an arbitrary rule, success was defined as ≥ 30 percent reduction from base line.

[b]Johnson used a sum for three of the Becker factors: relaxed disposition, aggression, and conduct problems.

[c]From Patterson et al. (1973), N = 13. Pre/post ratings on conduct problems and aggression. To qualify, a child had to be rated by the mother as showing improvement on each of the three factors.

[d]From Patterson and Reid (1973), N = 11, and from Walter and Gilmore (1973), N = 12.

Source: Compiled by the author.

100 percent. In lieu of the data demonstrating the differential implications that these variables have for later adjustment in the community (a project in progress), the writer proposes that success be defined as a reduction from base line to "normal" limits for two or more hard measures—for instance, the TAB score and PDR in the case of socially aggressive children, or PDR score alone in the case of children who steal, set fires, or are truant.* These changes might be thought to be necessary but not sufficient—for instance, they must also be accompanied by changes in the family system. This would include changes in variables measuring family process, parent attitudes, and perception. These variables will be reviewed later.

As an alternative, Johnson and Christensen (1976) and Johnson and Eyberg (1975) suggest an equal weighting of all these variables in assigning the labels of success and failure. Cases showing positive changes in half of the criteria are identified as a "success." S. B. Gordon (1975) sharply criticized this equal weighting of what he termed "hard" and "soft" data—a concern, incidentally, shared by this writer. Indeed, it seems that the therapist can preselect a criterion to match the hoped-for level of success. To look good, one need only select the traditional measure of parent/therapist global ratings on improvement (Levitt 1971). As shown in Table 5.6, in two small studies using global ratings, 100 percent of the parents felt the child had improved. Other investigators have produced comparable success rates using global ratings (Walter and Gilmore 1973). H. Cohen et al. (1974) obtained 80 percent success in their parent training groups using global ratings as a criterion. Certainly such ratings must be viewed as a necessary outcome for successful rating. It does seem, however, to have the validity required in order to constitute its status in the traditional literature as a sufficient condition for labeling treatment as successful.

Changes in Process

The claim that the treatment reprograms a family requires data showing changes in the relevant interactional process. This is particularly true if one hopes to demonstrate (and understand) persistence of effects over time. In keeping with the social learning formulation, the process changes one would expect to

---

*The mean total deviant score for the matched normal sample of 27 nonproblem boys was .277 (Patterson 1974). Setting .450 responses per minute as a decision point for normal/deviant gave a false negative error of 15 percent—that is, children who were labeled normal but performed greater than .450. For the 1972 sample of conduct problem children, half were referred for low-base-rate problems. Forty-one percent of that sample would be identified as false positives—for instance, referred as problem children but observed to perform at less than .449 of TD. The comparable figure from Fleischman's (1978b) study was 26 percent. The normative data for PDR scores are only now becoming available.

occur would be, first of all, decreases in rates of aversive behaviors by siblings and mothers. These changes would imply that the system was less aversive for the problem child. For the time being, fathers are not implicated because of the analyses showing that fathers of problem children are essentially no different from fathers of nonproblem children (Patterson 1976, 1978c; Reid and Hendriks 1973). Second would be changes in consequences provided by parents: the training program emphasizes increases in positive consequences for prosocial behavior and decreases for deviant behavior. G. Sallows (1973) showed that parents of problem children were more likely to provide positive consequences for deviant behaviors than were parents of normal children; the parents were also more likely to punish prosocial behavior. Therefore, a second concomitant of training would be a reduction in punishment for prosocial behaviors. After training, the parents should be more effective in their use of punishment to suppress coercive child behaviors. Previous research showed that aggressive children tend not to respond to "garden variety" punishment (Patterson 1976). At termination there should be an increase in positive feelings among family members. They should no longer respond in such a way as to maintain the child's coercive sequence (STET). There should be increased self-esteem expressed by the mother and the problem child.

The findings relating to changes in process have been reviewed in Patterson and Fleischman (1978) and Patterson (1978a). The findings showed a decrease in the rates of aversive behavior for siblings and for mothers. As might be expected, there were also significantly fewer attacks with which the problem child must cope. The parents provided fewer positive consequences for deviant behavior. The family in general had learned to respond in such a way that the problem child's coercive sequences tended to be short ones, rather than the more extended ones that characterized the child's interactions at base line. As might be expected, these changes in familial reaction were accompanied by fewer coercive changes; those that did occur tended to be short. When punished for being coercive, the child tended to stop. In fact, the likelihood was now in the normal range.

The mothers and fathers perceived the problem child in a more positive way, particularly on those scales measuring perception of tenseness, aggression, conduct problems, and academic skills. In fact, the mothers' global ratings showed that the entire family functioned better, and they felt more positive toward the problem child. Pre/post comparisons of mothers' MMPI questionnaires showed significant changes for the better on a number of the scales.

The findings support the idea that supervised training in family management skills not only alters the deviant behavior of the problem child but also produces changes in related family processes.

Follow-up Studies

The recent reviews of parent training studies emphasize the relative absence of follow-up data (Tavormina 1974; Forehand and Atkeson 1976). In fact, some writers assert that it is a logical fallacy to expect treatment effects to persist.

As noted earlier in the discussion, the writer assumes that persistence of treatment effects will occur if the system is altered—that is, if it becomes generally less aversive and less reinforcing for coercive responses. Given that the techniques of parent management reduce the aversive behaviors of problem child and siblings, reinforcement should provide for the future performance of the skills. For example, when the coercive behaviors again increase in rate, a reapplication of the child management techniques should again reduce their occurrence. The mechanism for the support of these skills is then negative reinforcement. Its relevance to maintenance of treatment effect is detailed in the report by Patterson and Fleischman (1978).

In the pilot studies, follow-up data were available for four families (Patterson et al. 1968). All four showed the expected persistence. Following this, 114 families with children between the ages of 3 and 12 were referred for out-of-control behaviors. About half this sample were also characterized by out-of-control behavior in the classroom or academic retardation. For 49 percent of these children, their high rates of aggressive, coercive behaviors were readily observable in the home, using the naturalistic observation code system previously described. These children were labeled as socially aggressive; about half of this subgroup also stole, were truant, or set fires. Of the remaining referrals, about 20 percent were not socially aggressive, but were truant, stole, and set fires. The rest of the sample consisted of children with only classroom problems (about 11 percent), minor problems in the home, or children who were normal but falsely labeled as deviant by parents (about 11 percent).

Of the 114 cases studied, 17 percent dropped out during base-line study. Of the 86 who received treatment, 35 dropped out during the 12-month follow-up study; 8 more are participating, but have not completed the entire study. In the report by Patterson and Fleischman (1978), complete observation data for base-line, termination, fourth-, eighth-, and twefth-month follow-up data are available for 50 families. The data showed a mean score of .57 at base line and .26 at termination. The latter was well within the range for normal children. The comparison of base line with termination and the follow-up probes showed a significant reduction ($F = 8.42; df = 3.159, p < .001$). During base line, 42 percent of this mixed sample (children who steal and are socially aggressive) had a total deviant (TD) score within the normal range at base line; 76 percent were within that range by termination. At the twelve-month probe 84 percent were observed to function within the normal range. The data provide clear support for the hypothesis that the problem children were less coercive after treatment, and that the changes persisted.

Complete data were available for 33 families. The base-line-to-termination comparisons showed comparable reductions in occurrence of the referral problems that were of concern to them. The ANOVA for repeated measures produced an F value of 26.89 ($df = 3.84; p < .001$). During base line 18 percent of the

TABLE 5.7

Follow-up Parent Daily Report Data: Two Studies

	Mean PDR		Follow-up	
Study	Base Line	Termination	Six Months	One Year
Christophersen (1975, 1976)				
Parent training	58% (116)	24% (13)		18% (10)
Nondirective	64% (10)	41% (9)		30% (8)
Martin (1977)				
Parent training	1.25 hrs. (28)	40 (28)	.41 (28) at 6 months	
Bibliotherapy	94 hrs. (15)	88 (15)	not available	
Alexander and Parsons (1973)				
Family inter- vention	none given	none given*	26% recidivism (46)	
Client-centered	none given	none given	47% recidivism (19)	
No treatment	none given	none given	50% recidivism (10)	
Eclectic treatment	none given	none given	73% recidivism (11)	

*An earlier analysis suggested that the pretreatment recidivism rates may have been comparable for the three groups. Alexander and Parsons (1973) did demonstrate significant changes from base line to termination in "silence," "variance of talk time," and "frequency of interruptions." The follow-up intervals ranged from 6 to 18 months.

Source: Alexander and Parsons, 1973.

treated subjects were within the normal range. At termination 76 percent were within the normal range. At the 12-month follow-up probe, 82 percent were within the normal range. The two measures converge in showing that 12 months after training, over three-quarters of the families were functioning within the normal range.

These effects are in keeping with those obtained by studies under way in other settings. The report by B. Martin (1977) showed a persistence of treatment effects over a six-month interval.

The study involved 42 essentially middle-class families with children aged 6 to 11 who volunteered for treatment. A median of five sessions was sufficient to teach the family negotiating and contracting skills. The families were randomly assigned to one of two experimental or bibliotherapy control groups who simply read a how-to-do-it manual. The PDR data are summarized in Table 5.7 for child problems. The mean number of problems per day was obtained by taking an average across two experimental groups and two broad classes of deviant child behavior. The comparisons made by Martin (1977) showed significant differences between the treated and the bibliotherapy groups.

R. G. Wahler and D. Moore (1969) reported follow-up data for two small samples in which each child received over 100 hours of professional time. The one-year follow-up showed all the change measures (observation data, achievement data, teacher and parent ratings) maintained and/or improved for children (N = 8) treated in the essentially middle-class neighborhood. However, the inner-city sample of acting-out preadolescents (N = 5) maintained their academic skills, but essentially returned to base line for social behaviors.

Extensive follow-up studies have been carried out by Steve Johnson at the University of Oregon. The first study by Johnson and Christensen (1976) showed significant changes in targeted deviant scores (observation data) from a mean of 115.9 responses at base line to 79.9 at termination. However, the change in TD score was not significant. At eight-month follow-up, there was a return to base line in both measures. Their data did show changes in "softer" measures involving parent attitudes and perceptions that persisted through follow-up. However, the fact that the change in TD scores was nonsignificant for such a large sample (N = 22) would indicate that the treatment itself was of limited effectiveness, and therefore less likely to show persistence of effects. The study by S. Ferber, S. M. Keeley, and K. M. Shemberg (1974) also employed time-limited treatment (eight weeks) and graduate student therapists. They used the same code system as Johnson and the OSLC studies. Their targeted deviant scores showed that only one case in five was "successful" (less than 30 percent drop from base line). Like Johnson, they failed to find any treatment effect at follow-up.

In the studies by E. R. Christophersen, J. Barnard, D. Ford, and M. Wolf (1976) and by Christophersen (1976), 25 families referred for treatment were randomly assigned to parent training or nondirective treatments. The former required a mean of 30 hours of professional time; the average age of the child was six years. The PDR data for base line, termination, and follow-up are summarized in Table 5.7. The figures in parentheses refer to the sample size. No statistical analyses are available, but the trends suggest that both modes of treatment produce changes that persist over a one-year period. The data, however, are difficult to interpret, in that base line and termination means are not presented separately for the cases who have completed follow-up. A nontreated control group was not provided.

Alexander and Parsons (1973) used a broad-based combination of family therapy plus social learning concepts in a time-limited treatment. Eighty-six families were referred for treatment by the juvenile court. These were generally first offenses and essentially middle-class, relatively intact families. The families were randomly assigned to either family treatment or one of several comparison groups. The follow-up interval of from 6 to 18 months revealed differences among the recidivism rates, as shown by the chi-square value of 10.25, to be significant at the .02 level. Given a more adequate design (base line to follow-up comparison) and an extension of the follow-up to two and three years, this study would meet the standards necessary to establish a treatment of delinquent children as being successful.

In summary, those studies that demonstrated treatment effects generally showed persistence of treatment effects on the same variables. The measures employed ranged from observation, STET daily report, and parent perception to police contacts. The time intervals ranged from 6 to 18 months. In some instances the follow-up effects were demonstrated on multiple criteria, and for various age groups from six through adolescence. The interesting exception to this trend lies in the small sample of inner-city families treated and followed up by R. G. Wahler (1975). It may be that the current procedures are appropriate only for blue-collar families, families on welfare (OSLC studies), and middle-class families. However, the extremely disrupted family that lives in such destructive environments as extreme poverty or a ghetto may not be able to perform these skills for the extended interval required.

Comparison Studies

In the six comparison studies known to the writer, random assignment was made to social-learning-oriented family training and one or more of the following comparison groups: nondirective counseling (Alexander and Parsons 1973; Christophersen 1976; Christophersen et al. 1976); reading parent training manuals (Martin 1977; Christensen 1976); waiting-list control (Alexander and Parsons 1973; Patterson and Wiltz 1974); eclectic treatments (Alexander and Parsons 1973). Leaderless group discussion was employed by H. I. Walter and S. K. Gilmore (1973).

Since some of these studies are currently in progress, it is perhaps somewhat premature to speak of conclusions. However, some trends do seem noticeable. For example, both studies that employed nondirective comparison groups happened to be working with families of young children (six to seven years old). Bernal (1978) reports that the out-of-control children assigned to this treatment group showed some improvement on the pre/postobservation comparisons. In this vein the data in Table 5.7 from Christophersen et al. (1976) showed a 36 percent improvement from base line on the PDR measure. It is interesting to note that a comparable shift was not obtained by Alexander and Parsons (1973), who worked with older children.

The study by Patterson (1975) showed a 20 percent drop from base line for the children, as measured by PDR following their parents' reading *Living with Children* (Patterson and Gullion 1968). In a study employing a comparison design, Christensen (1976) found a drop of 33.6 percent. The PDR measure employed was similar to that used in the OSLC studies. It might be noted that the five-week follow-up showed that the effect was probably short-lived; the mean drop from base line at that time was 12.9 percent. Martin (1977) obtained only a 6 percent drop from base line for a group reading a comparable manual. However, the range of 6 percent to 33 percent improvement for such groups suggests a need to take this into consideration when estimating the size of the sample required to produce significant differences for more intensive parent training groups.

While the third comparison group, the waiting-list control, looks more promising, most of the studies employing it used relatively short time intervals. Even so, the fact that many studies have used treatment intervals as brief as eight to twelve weeks makes these data relevant.

The placebo and waiting-list control studies support the notion that spontaneous remission does not occur over the relatively short span of four to five weeks. The placebo study by Walter and Gilmore (1973) showed that simply being involved in "some" kind of treatment that produced high expectancy for change was not sufficient to produce changes in child behavior. As noted earlier, this condition did produce changes in parent global perceptions: 67 percent thought their children improved. The longer time intervals employed by Reid et al. (1978) also show no changes in either observation or PDR criteria. While this is reassuring, it constitutes only a minimal coverage for many studies (such as OSLC) that employ time intervals considerably in excess of eight weeks. However, as the data stand, they suggest that the waiting-list control may provide the most powerful basis for evaluating family intervention outcomes.

CLASSROOM INTERVENTION

Clinical experience in working with aggressive children quickly suggested that there was little correlation across home and school settings in observed rates or kinds of behavior for other than the most extreme cases. S. Wolff (1967) found little overlap among children identified as problems at home and those identified as problems in the classroom. Similarly, G. R. Patterson, J. A. Cobb, and R. S. Ray (1972), M. E. Bernal et al. (1976), S. M. Johnson et al. (1976), and H. M. Walker, S. M. Johnson, and H. Hops (1975) found a zero-order correlation for observed rates of inappropriate behavior in the home and classroom for samples of aggressive boys. These correlational findings showed no consistency in the ordinal rankings on aggressiveness for these relatively homogeneous samples of problem children. However, their general status as deviant-aggressive might very well hold across settings. For example, of 21 boys actually shown to have conduct-behavior problems in the home, 52 percent were also shown to have significant social and/or academic problems in the classroom (Patterson 1976). Johnson et al. (1976) also observed the classroom behavior of a small sample of children identified as having conduct problems at home. Observation data showed that 50 percent were deviant in their classroom behavior. Forty-five percent of the children referred for conduct problems in the classroom were also shown to be deviant in their interactions with their families.

Clinical experience and empirical data quickly converged in demonstrating that there is also a lack of generalization for treatment effects from the home to the classroom, or the converse (Johnson, Bolstad, and Lobitz 1976; Wahler

1969). The exigencies of the phenomenon itself dictated that successful community-based treatment of aggressive children would have to make provisions for treatment tailored to altering both the classroom and the home environment.

The general format that developed during the mid-1960s was the token economy tailored for either a special class of aggressive children (Martin, Burkholder, Rosenthal, Tharp, and Thorne 1968; O'Leary and Becker 1966; Quay, Sprague, Werry, and McQueen 1967; Walker, Mattson, and Buckley 1968) or a more clinical approach to the individual child in that child's classroom (Patterson, Shaw, and Ebner 1969). In either approach, later development in the treatment focused upon both social adjustment and, if necessary, remediation of academic skills.

As might be expected, the commitment to high rates of disruptive classroom behaviors is associated with lower achievement-test scores (Cobb 1972; Cobb and Hops 1972). Experience shows that identified aggressive children receive lower grades, and score lower on achievement tests. They also tend to be rejected by their peers. As might be expected from observation studies, children labeled as out of control did, in fact, display significantly higher rates of disruptive behavior than did peers from the same classroom (Bernal et al. 1976; Patterson, Cobb, and Ray 1972). Presumably, outcome evaluations would provide data relevant to changes in rates of observed disruptive behavior, achievement, and sociometric status.

On the face of it, it seems economical to place the school's antisocial children into a single classroom and spare the teacher and peers of their former classrooms. It would also seem less costly than tracking each child in the original classroom. Hill Walker and his colleagues H. Hops and C. Greenwood at the Center at Oregon for Research in the Behavioral Education of the Handicapped have carried out the most careful work on this problem. The data showed dramatic treatment effects (Walker et al. 1968) even when applied to the school district's most obstreperous children. H. C. Quay, J. P. Glavin, F. R. Annesley, and J. S. Werry (1972) showed similar effects, but no generalization of treatment, when the child was returned to the regular classroom. Even in his earliest studies, Walker had anticipated the problem of generalization by also training the teacher to whom the child would be returned following treatment in the special classroom (Walker et al. 1968). In doing so, his observation at three-month follow-up showed that four children maintained adequate levels of appropriate behavior and two did not. In a replication and extension, two groups were treated in the token-culture classroom. One group was returned to regular classroom teachers trained in these procedures, and the members of the other group to untrained teachers. At four months, all five in the first group had maintained adequate gains, while in the second group only one of four was at such a level. Walker's next study used larger samples and compared three different modes for maximizing generalization: training the teacher, putting token culture in the regular classroom, reprogramming the peer groups. While the peer reprogramming and token-culture procedures cost an average of five and eight hours, respectively, they produced significantly greater maintenance effects than the control or teacher training groups at the second-month follow-up.

The studies of special classrooms suggest that two months may be sufficient to produce dramatic changes in each member of a small group (six or less) of antisocial boys. The preliminary studies also suggest that procedures may be developed that will provide for generalization back to the regular classroom. More extended follow-up and comparison studies are needed, but this seems to be a promising approach, particularly for the most extreme cases that can no longer be tolerated in their home rooms.

An alternative is to treat the aggressive child in the regular classroom by training the teacher and/or introducing a new treatment agent (Kent, O'Leary, Daniel, Diament, and Dietz 1974; Patterson and Brodsky 1966). Whether one chooses to train the teacher depends on how motivated the teacher is to learn the procedures and to perform them. Given interest, it would seem reasonable to train the teacher as a treatment agent. H. Hops, H. Walker, and S. Hutton (1973) have a detailed program providing such training. The clinical experience of the writer has shown that many teachers seem unmotivated for any procedure but that of removing the child from the classroom. However, contracting procedures seem to have a special utility in this context. They specify consequences earned for the peer group or at home for the child's successful performance in the classroom. Some of the more recent work involves negotiations between family and school such that parents provide the primary consequences (Patterson et al. 1975). The virtue of the latter procedure is that it requires only a moment of teacher time and the major response cost is incurred by the parents.

In a report by Patterson (1974a), the classroom observation showed a baseline mean of 58 percent appropriate behavior for a sample of 14 problem children. After an average of 28.6 hours of training, the mean was 77 percent appropriate. The t for correlated means of 4.15 (df = 13; $p <$ .001) was highly significant. During the three- to six-month follow-up, three families had moved and one refused to cooperate. For the remaining eleven cases, nine had scores about 70 percent—within the normal range. G. G. Hett (1972) replicated these procedures, using a comparative design. The control group showed no improvement during treatment or during the two-month follow-up. The experimental group used only a classroom manager, but none of the newer contracting procedures. The abbreviated treatment produced significant effects, although at two months there had been a partial return to base line.

Clearly, the foregoing studies' small sample size and two- to six-month follow-up intervals are insufficient to the task. However, the studies by Wahler (1976) remedy both deficiencies. His data showed significant maintenance of intervention when parents, teachers, and classroom manager coordinated their efforts. This major study was carried out in two separate communities. In one, 70 percent of the treated families were on welfare and 90 percent were single-parent families. The comparable figures for the other community were zero and 20 percent, respectively. The token economies in the classroom were coordinated with parents' providing consequences for both prosocial and deviant behaviors occurring at school. Pre/post multiple-criterion measures (observation, teacher ratings) showed significant treatment effects. One-year follow-up showed that the treatment gains were sustained and increased for children from the more middle-class community; the average cost of treatment had been 105 hours of professional time. While the other sample had received an average of 150 hours of treatment, the follow-up data looked much worse. Their gains in academic skills were sustained, which replicated the R. N. Kent et al. (1974) findings for a nine-month follow-up. However, the children's noncompliant behaviors and the teachers' negative evaluations of the children had returned to base-line levels. This latter effect was also noted by Kent et al. for their follow-up. While the latter limited their treatment efforts to approximately 17 hours, one wonders if their sample was not also drawn from lower socioeconomic levels. The demographic data are not provided in their study.

In summary, there seem to be some preliminary data that suggest that classroom intervention is feasible, and that the results will persist; no data exist that demonstrate the long-range impact of such programs upon adolescent adjudicated delinquency; only a single case can be offered showing altered sociometric status as the result of classroom intervention (Drabman and Lahey 1974); and training the child to adjust produces significant increases in achievement test scores. Provisions for programmed remedial instruction plus adjustment training produce significant increases in achievement test scores, as related by Walker et al. (1968, 1975). These increases in academic skills are significantly greater than those of problem children receiving no treatment and classroom regimes (Kent et al. 1974; Quay et al. 1972).

SUMMARY

The review of the literature for the treatment of antisocial children suggests the following tentative conclusions:

1. Children identified by observation data, peer sociometrics, or teachers' ratings as socially aggressive tended to be stable in the performance of these behaviors over time. Presumably, although the specific topography may change, the more extreme cases do not outgrow coercion as a style of interacting with adults and peers.

2. Children identified as coercive in the home have about a 50 percent chance of being similarly identified in the classroom. The converse is also true for those referred for disruptive classroom behaviors. The base rate for being so labeled in either setting is probably less than .10.

3. In that sense, coercion may be viewed as a trait that is relatively stable over time and across these two settings.

4. Coercive children tend to come from coercive families.

5. Socially aggressive children and children who steal come from different kinds of families. Both are different from families of nonproblem children.

6. Young preadolescent children who steal at high rates have a probability of from .4 to .5 of committing a police offense in two years. Socially aggressive children do not exceed the base rates for nonproblem children.

7. Several programs have demonstrated that institutions may provide treatment programs that significantly decrease deviant and increase prosocial/academic behaviors. These significant effects do not persist over a year following discharge.

8. Six large-scale, well-designed studies have shown that traditional casework therapy for the child and the parents has not been effective in reducing police offenses two years after treatment.

9. Contemporary social learning approaches to community-based halfway houses are being evaluated by appropriate follow-up designs.

10. Outcome studies of social learning approaches to families of antisocial children are under way in Oregon, Tennessee, North Carolina, Kansas, Colorado, and British Columbia. Within-site replications have been successful in several groups. It should be noted, however, that two investigators have failed to obtain significant treatment. At present, the reason for the failures are not understood. Treatment produces significant changes in the family as well as in the problem child.

REFERENCES

Alexander, J. R., and B. V. Parsons. 1973. "Short-Term Behavioral Intervention with Delinquent Families: Impact on Family Process and Recidivism." *Journal of Abnormal Psychology* 81, no. 3:219–25.

Baker, B. L., and L. J. Herfesty. 1974. "The READ Project: Teaching Manuals for Parents of Retarded Children." Paper presented at the Conference on Early Intervention for High Risk Infants, University of North Carolina.

Berlemen, W. C., and T. W. Steinburn. 1967. *The Execution and Evaluation of a Delinquency Prevention Program*. Seattle: Atlantic Street Center. Also in *Social Problems* 14:413–23.

Bernal, M. 1978. Personal communication.

———, L. F. Delfini, J. A. North, and S. L. Kreutzer. 1976. "Comparison of Boys' Behavior in Homes and Classrooms." In *Behavior Modification and Families*, ed. E. Mash, L. Handy, and L. A. Hamerlynck, pp. 204–27. New York: Brunner/Mazell.

Bernal, M., J. Duryee, H. Pruett, and B. Burns. 1968. "Behavior Modification and the BRAT Syndrome." *Journal of Consulting and Clinical Psychology* 32:447–55.

Block, J. 1971. *Lives Through Time*. Berkeley: Coty Bancroft.

Buehler, R. E., G. R. Patterson, and F. M. Furness. 1966. "The Reinforcement of Behavior in Institutional Settings." *Behavior Research and Therapy* 4:157–67.

Burchard, J. D. 1967. "Systematic Socialization: A Programmed Environment for the Habituation of Anti-Social Retardates." *Psychological Record* 17: 461–76.

———. 1976. "Behavior Modification and Juvenile Delinquency." In *Handbook of Behavior Modification and Behavior Therapy*, ed. H. Leitenberg, pp. 405–52. Englewood Cliffs, N.J.: Prentice-Hall.

———, and F. Barrera. 1972. "An Analysis of Time Out and Response Cost in a Programmed Environment." *Journal of Applied Behavior Analysis* 5:271–82.

Christensen, O. 1976. "Cost Effectiveness in Family Behavior Therapy." Ph.D. dissertation, University of Oregon.

Christophersen, E. R. 1975. "Outcomes for Parent Training in Families of Delinquent Children." Paper presented at the Association for the Advancement of Behavior Therapy convention, New York.

———, J. Barnard, D. Ford, and M. Wolf. 1976. "The Family Training Program: Improving Parent/Child Interaction Patterns." In *Behavior Modification and Families*, II, *Applications and Developments*, ed. L. A. Hamerlynck, L. C. Handy, and E. J. Mash. New York: Brunner/Mazell.

Clement, B. W., and D. C. Milne. 1967. "Group Play Therapy and Tangible Reinforcers Used to Modify the Behavior of Eight-Year-Old Boys." *Behavior Research and Therapy* 5:301–12.

Cobb, J. A. 1972. "The Relationship of Discrete Classroom Behaviors to Fourth-Grade Academic Achievement." *Journal of Educational Psychology* 63, no. 1:74–80.

———, and H. Hops. 1972. "Effects of Academic Survival Skill Training on Low-Achieving First Graders." *Journal of Educational Research*.

Cohen, H., and J. Filipczak. 1971. *A New Learning Environment*. San Francisco: Jossey-Bass.

———, J. Boren, J. Hoding, R. Storm, R. Bishop, and J. Breiling. 1974. *Academic and Social Behavior Change in a Public School Setting*. Final progress report 1RO1 MH44431 (April).

Conger, J. J., and W. C. Miller. *Personality, Social Class and Delinquency*. New York: John Wiley.

Delfini, L. F., M. Bernal, and P. Rosen. 1976. "Comparison of Deviant and Normal Boys in Home Settings." In *Behavior Modification and Families*, ed. L. A. Hamerlynck, L. C. Handy, and E. J. Mash, pp. 228–48. New York: Brunner/Mazell.

Dinitz, S., F. Scarpitti, and W. C. Reckless. 1962. "Delinquency Vulnerability: A Cross-Group and Longitudinal Analysis." *American Sociological Review* 27:515–17.

Douglas, J. W. B. 1966. "The School Progress of Nervous and Troublesome Children." *British Journal of Psychiatry* 112:1115–16.

Drabman, R. S., and B. B. Lahey. 1974. "Feedback in Classroom Behavior Modification: Effects on the Target and Her Classmates." *Journal of Applied Behavior Analysis* 7:591–98.

Empey, L. T., and M. L. Ericksen. 1972. *The Provo Experiment*. Lexington, Mass.: Lexington Books.

Eron, L. D., L. O. Walder, and M. Lefkowitz. 1974. "The Convergence of Laboratory and Field Studies of the Development of Aggression." In *Determinants and Origins of Aggressive Behavior*, ed. J. DeWit and W. Hartup, pp. 347–80. The Hague: Mouton.

Eyberg, S. M., and S. M. Johnson. 1974. "Multiple Assessment of Behavior Modification with Families: Effects of Contingency Contracting and Order of Treated Problems." *Journal of Consulting and Clinical Psychology* 42, no. 4:594–606.

Feldhusen, J. F., J. R. Thurston, and J. J. Benning. 1970. "Aggressive Classroom Behavior and School Achievement." *Journal of Special Education* 4, no. 4: 431–39.

Ferber, H., S. M. Keeley, and K. M. Shemberg. 1974. "Training Parents in Behavior Modification: Outcome of and Problems Encountered in a Program After Patterson's Work." *Behavior Therapy* 5:415–19.

Fixsen, D. L., E. L. Phillips, and M. M. Wolf. 1973. "Achievement Place: Experiments in Self-Government with Pre-adolescents." *Journal of Applied Behavior Analysis* 6:31–47.

Fleischman, M. J. 1978. "A Replication of Patterson's Model of Treatment of Conduct Problem Children." Unpublished manuscript. Available from OSLC.

———. In press. "The Effects of a Parenting Salary and Family SES in the Social Learning Treatment of Aggressive Children." *Behavior Therapy*.

Forehand, R., and B. Atkeson. 1976. "Generality of Treatment Effects with Parents as Therapists: A Review of Assessment and Implementation Procedures." *Behavior Therapy*.

Gersten, J. C., T. S. Langner, J. G. Eisenberg, O. Simcha-Fagan, and E. D. McCarthy. 1976. "Stability and Change in Types of Behavior Disturbance of Children and Adolescents." *Journal of Abnormal Child Psychology* 4: 111–27.

Glueck, S., and E. Glueck. 1972. *Identification of Pre-delinquents*. New York: Intercontinental Medical Book Corp.

Gordon, S. B. 1975. "Multiple Assessment of Behavior Modification with Families." *Journal of Consulting and Clinical Psychology* 43:917–19.

Graziano, A. M., and R. S. Fink. 1973. "Secondary Effects in Mental Health Treatment." *Journal of Consulting and Clinical Psychology* 40, no. 3: 356–64.

Hanf, C. 1968. "Modification of Mother-Child Controlling Behavior During Mother-Child Interaction in Standardized Laboratory Situations." Paper presented at regional meeting of Association for the Advancement of Behavior Therapy, Olympia, Wash.

Hathaway, S. R., and E. Monachesi. 1963. *Adolescent Personality and Behavior*. Minneapolis: University of Minnesota Press.

Havighurst, R. J., P. H. Bowman, G. P. Liddle, C. V. Matthews, and J. V. Pierce. 1960. *Growing up in River City*. New York: John Wiley.

Hawkins, R. P., R. F. Peterson, E. Schweid, and S. W. Bijou. 1966. "Behavior Therapy in the Home: Amelioration of Problem Parent-Child Relations with the Parent in a Therapeutic Role." *Journal of Experimental Child Psychology* 4:99–107.

Hett, G. G. 1972. "The Modification and Maintenance of Attending Behavior for Second, Third, and Fourth Grade Children." Ph.D. dissertation, University of Oregon.

Hollingshead, A. B., and F. C. Redlich. 1958. *Social Class and Mental Illness*. New York: John Wiley.

Hops, H., H. Walker, and S. Hutton. 1973. "CLASS Program for Acting-out Children: Contingencies for Learning Academic and Social Skills." Center at Oregon for Research in the Behavioral Education of the Handicapped, Eugene: University of Oregon. Mimeographed.

Jesness, C. F., W. J. DeRisis, P. M. McCormick, and R. F. Quedge. 1972. *The Youth Center Research Project*. Sacramento: American Justice Institute.

Johnson, S. M., O. D. Bolstad, and G. Lobitz. 1976. "Generalization and Contrast Phenomena in Behavior Modification with Children." In *Behavior Modification and Families*, ed. L. A. Hamerlynck, L. C. Handy, and E. J. Mash, pp. 160–88. New York: Brunner/Mazell.

Johnson, S. M., and A. Christensen. 1976. "Multiple Criterion Follow-up Behavior Modification." Book in preparation.

Johnson, S. M., and R. A. Brown. 1969. "Producing Behavior Change in Parents of Disturbed Children." *Journal of Child Psychology and Psychiatry* 10: 107–21.

Johnson, S. M., and S. Eyberg. 1975. "Evaluating Outcome Data: A Reply to Gordon." *Journal of Consulting and Clinical Psychology* 43:917–19.

Jones, R. R. 1978. "Helping Youth in Trouble: An Evaluation of the Family Teaching Model." Paper presented at meeting of Association for the Advancement of Behavior Therapy, Chicago.

Kahn, A. J. 1965. "The Case of the Premature Claims, Public Policy, and Delinquency Prediction." *Crime and Delinquency* 11:217–28.

Karachi, L., A. Schmidt, and H. Cairor. 1972. "Follow-up of Kennedy Youth Center Releases." Kennedy Youth Center.

Kent, R. N., K. D. O'Leary, K. Daniel, C. Diament, and A. Dietz. 1974. "Expectation Biases in Observational Evaluation of Therapeutic Change." *Journal of Consulting and Clinical Psychology* 42, no. 6:774–80.

Kirigin, K. A. 1976. "Achievement Place: The Researchers' Perspective." Paper presented at American Psychological Association convention, Washington, D.C.

Kohlberg, L. 1969. "Stage and Sequence: The Cognitive Development Approach to Socialization." In *Handbook of Socialization Theory and Research*, ed. D. A. Goslin. Chicago: Rand McNally.

Kvaraceus, W. C. 1955. "Teacher's Checklist for Identifying Potential Delinquents." *Journal of Education* 17:21–22.

Levitt, E. E. 1971. "Research on Psychotherapy with Children." In *Handbook of Psychotherapy and Behavior Change*, ed. A. E. Bergin and S. L. Garfield, pp. 474–94. New York: John Wiley.

Lundman, R. J., and F. R. Scarpitti. 1978. "Delinquency Prevention: Recommendation for Future Projects." *Crime and Delinquency* 24:207–20.

Martin, B. 1977. "Brief Family Intervention: The Effectiveness and the Importance of Including the Father." *Journal of Consulting and Clinical Psychology* 45, no. 6:1002–10.

Martin, M., R. Burkholder, T. L. Rosenthal, R. G. Tharp, and G. L. Thorne. 1968. "Programming Behavior Change and Reintegration into the School Milieu of Extreme Adolescent Deviates." *Behavior Research and Therapy* 6:371–83.

Martin, S., S. M. Johnson, S. Johansson, and G. Wahl. 1976. "The Comparability of Behavioral Data in Laboratory and Natural Settings." In *Behavior Modification and Families*, ed. L. A. Hamerlynck, L. C. Handy, and E. J. Mash, pp. 189–203. New York: Brunner/Mazell.

McCord, J. 1976. "A Thirty-Year Follow-up of Treatment Effects." Paper presented at the American Association of Psychiatric Services for Children, San Francisco.

Meyer, H. J., E. F. Borgatta, and W. C. Jones. 1965. *Girls at Vocational High: An Experiment in Social Work Intervention.* New York: Russell Sage Foundation.

Moore, D. R., P. Chamberlain, and L. H. Mukai. 1978. "Later Community Adjustments of Children Who Steal." Manuscript submitted for publication.

Morris, H. H. 1956. "Aggressive Behavior Disorders in Children: A Follow-up Study." *American Journal of Psychiatry* 112:991–97.

O'Leary, K. D., and W. C. Becker. 1966. "Behavior Modification of an Adjustment Class: A Token Reinforcement Program." *University of Illinois Review* (Sept.).

Olson, D. H. 1976. "Treating Relationships: Trends and Overview." In *Treating Relationships*, ed. D. H. Olson, pp. 3–20. Lake Mills, Iowa: Graphic Publication Co.

Olweus, D. 1976a. "Aggression and Peer Acceptance in Preadolescent Boys: Two Short-Term Longitudinal Studies of Ratings." Paper presented at the biennial meeting of the International Society for Research on Aggression, Paris.

———. 1976b. "Longitudinal Studies of Aggressive Reaction Patterns: A Review." Paper presented at XXI International Congress of Psychology, Paris.

Patterson, G. R. 1971. *Families: Applications of Social Learning to Family Life*. Champaign, Ill.: Research Press.

———. 1974a. "Interventions for Boys with Conduct Problems: Multiple Settings, Treatments, and Criteria." *Journal of Consulting and Clinical Psychology* 42:471–81.

———. 1974b. "Retraining of Aggressive Boys by Their Parents: Review of Recent Literature and Follow-up Evaluations." In "Symposium on the Seriously Disturbed Preschool Child," ed. F. Lowy. *Canadian Psychiatric Association Journal* 19:142–61.

———. 1975. "Multiple Evaluations of a Parent Training Program." In *Applications of Behavior Modification*, ed. T. Thomson and W. S. Dockens III, pp. 299–322. New York: Academic Press.

———. 1976. "The Aggressive Child: Victim and Architect of a Coercive System." In *Behavior Modification and Families*, I, *Theory and Research*, ed. L. A. Hamerlynck, L. C. Handy, and E. J. Mash, pp. 367–76. New York: Brunner/Mazell.

———. 1978a. "Contexts and Reactions: An Interactional Approach." Book in preparation.

———. 1978b. "An Interactional Approach to Coercive Family Processes." Book in preparation.

———. 1978c. "Mothers: The Unacknowledged Victims." Manuscript submitted for publication.

———, and G. Brodsky. 1966. "A Behavior Modification Programme for a Child with Multiple Problem Behaviors." *Journal of Child Psychology and Psychiatry* 7:277–95.

Patterson, G. R., J. A. Cobb, and R. S. Ray. 1972. "Direct Intervention in the Classroom: A Set of Procedures for the Aggressive Child." In *Implementing Behavioral Programs for Schools and Clinics*, ed. F. W. Clark, D. R. Evans, and L. A. Hamerlynck. Champaign, Ill.: Research Press.

———. 1973. "A Social Engineering Technology for Retraining the Families of Aggressive Boys." In *Issues and Trends in Behavior Therapy*, ed. H. E. Adams and I. P. Unikel, pp. 139–224. Springfield, Ill.: Charles C. Thomas.

Patterson, G. R., and M. J. Fleischman. 1979. "Maintenance of Treatment Effects: Some Considerations Concerning Family Systems and Follow-up Data." *Behavior Therapy* 10:168–85.

Patterson, G. R., and M. E. Gullion. 1968. *Living with Children: New Methods for Parents and Teachers*. Champaign, Ill.: Research Press.

Patterson, G. R., S. McNeal, N. Hawkins, and R. Phelps. 1967. "Reprogramming the Social Environment." *Journal of Child Psychology and Psychiatry* 8:181–94.

Patterson, G. R., R. S. Ray, and D. A. Shaw. 1968. "Direct Intervention in Families of Deviant Children." *Oregon Research Institute Bulletin* 8, no. 9.

Patterson, G. R., and J. B. Reid. 1970. "Reciprocity and Coercion: Two Facets of Social Systems." In *Behavior Modification in Clinical Psychology*, ed. C. Neuringer and L. L. Michael, pp. 133–77. New York: Appleton-Century-Crofts.

———. 1973. "Intervention for Families of Aggressive Boys: A Replication Study." *Behavior Research and Therapy* 11:383–94.

———, R. R. Jones, and R. E. Conger. 1975. *A Social Learning Approach to Family Intervention*, I, *Families with Aggressive Children*. Eugene, Ore.: Castalia.

Patterson, G. R., D. A. Shaw, and M. Ebner. 1969. "Teachers, Peers, and Parents as Agents of Change in the Classroom." In *Modifying Deviant Social Behaviors in Various Classroom Settings*, ed. F. A. M. Benson. Eugene: University of Oregon, No. 1. 13–47.

Pearl, A. 1963. "The High Field's Program: A Critique and Evaluation." In *Mental Health of the Poor*, ed. F. Riessman, J. Cohen, and A. Pearl, pp. 481–85. Glencoe, Ill.: Free Press.

Peine, H. A., and B. Munro. 1973. "Behavioral Management of Parent Training Programs." Paper presented at Rocky Mountain Psychological Association convention, Las Vegas.

Phillips, E. L., E. A. Phillips, D. L. Fixsen, and M. Wolf. 1971. "Achievement Place: Modification of the Behavior of Pre-delinquent Boys Within a Token Economy." *Journal of Applied Behavior Analysis* 4:45–59.

———. 1972. *The Teaching-Family Handbook*. Lawrence: University of Kansas Printing Service.

Polk, K. 1967. *Lane County Youth Project: Final Report*. Washington, D.C.: U.S. Department of Health, Education, and Welfare, Office of Juvenile Delinquency and Youth Development.

———. 1975. *Teenage Delinquency in Small Town America*. Research Report 5. Washington, D.C.: Center for Studies of Crime and Delinquency, National Institute of Mental Health.

Powers, E., and H. Witmer. 1951. *An Experiment in the Prevention of Delinquency.* New York: Columbia University Press.

Pritchard, M., and P. Graham. 1966. "An Investigation of a Group of Patients Who Have Attended Both the Child and Adult Departments of the Same Psychiatric Hospital." *British Journal of Psychiatry* 112:603–13.

Quay, H. C. 1972. "Patterns of Aggression, Withdrawal, and Immaturity." In *Psychopathological Disorders of Childhood*, ed. H. C. Quay and J. S. Werry. New York: John Wiley.

————, J. P. Glavin, F. R. Annesley, and J. S. Werry. 1972. "The Modification of Problem Behavior and Academic Achievement in a Resource Room." *Journal of School Psychology* 10:187–98.

Quay, H. C., R. L. Sprague, J. S. Werry, and M. M. McQueen. 1967. "Conditioning Visual Orientation of Conduct Problem Children in the Classroom." *Journal of Experimental Child Psychology* 5:512–17.

Raush, H. L. 1965. "Interaction Sequences." *Journal of Personality and Social Psychology* 2:487–99.

————, A. T. Deltman, and T. J. Taylor. 1959. "The Interpersonal Behavior Among Children in Residential Treatment." *Journal of Abnormal Social Psychology* 58:9–26.

Reckless, W., and J. Dinitz. 1972. *The Prevention of Juvenile Delinquency.* Columbus: Ohio State University Press.

Redl, R., and J. Wineman. 1952. *Control from Within.* New York: Free Press.

Reid, J. B., ed. 1978. *A Social Learning Approach to Family Intervention*, II, *Observation in Home Settings.* Eugene: Castalia Press.

————, and A. F. C. J. Hendriks. 1973. "A Preliminary Analysis of the Effectiveness of Direct Home Intervention for Treatment of Predelinquent Boys Who Steal." In *Behavior Therapy: Methodology, Concepts and Practices*, ed. L. A. Hamerlynck, L. C. Handy, and E. J. Mash, pp. 209–20. Champaign, Ill.: Research Press.

Reid, J. B., G. Rivera, and R. Lorber. 1978. "A Social Learning Approach to Outpatient Treatment of Children Who Steal." Manuscript submitted for publication.

Rhodes, W. C., and S. Gibbins. 1972. "Community Programming for the Behaviorally Deviant Child." In *Psychopathological Disorders of Childhood*, ed. H. C. Quay and J. S. Werry. New York: John Wiley.

Robins, L. H. 1974. "Antisocial Behavior Disturbances of Childhood: Prevalence, Prognosis, and Prospects." In *The Child and His Family: Of Children at Psychiatric Risk*, ed. E. J. Anthony and C. Coupernik. New York: John Wiley.

Robins, N. L. 1966. *Deviant Children Grown-up: A Sociological and Psychiatric Study of Sociopathic Personality*. Baltimore: Williams and Wilkins.

Rutter, M., J. Tizard, and K. Whitmore. 1970. *Education, Health, and Behavior*. New York: John Wiley.

Sallows. G. 1973. "Responsiveness of Deviant and Normal Children to Naturally Occurring Parental Consequences." Paper presented at Midwestern Psychological Association convention, Chicago.

Schelle, J. 1974. "A Brief Report on Invalidity of Parent Evaluations of Behavior Change." *Journal of Applied Behavior Analysis* 7:341–43.

Shepherd, M., A. M. Oppenheim, and S. Mitchell. 1966. "Childhood Behavior Disorders of the Child-Guidance Clinic: An Epidemiological Study." *Journal of Child Psychology and Psychiatry* 7, no. 1:39–52.

Skinrud, K. 1972. "Generalization of Treatment Effects from Home to School." *Oregon Research Institute Bulletin*.

Stuart, R. 1969. "Assessment and Change of the Communication Patterns of Juvenile Delinquents and Their Parents." Paper presented at meeting of the Association for the Advancement of Behavior Therapy, Washington, D.C.

———, and T. Tripodi. 1971. "Experimental Evolution of Three Time Constrained Behavioral Treatments for Predelinquents and Delinquents." Paper presented at meeting of Association for the Advancement of Behavior Therapy, Washington, D.C.

Tavormina, J. B. 1974. "Basic Models of Parent Counseling: A Critical Review." *Psychological Bulletin* 81, no. 11: 827–35.

Tharp, R., and R. Wetzel. 1969. *Behavior Modification in the Natural Environment*. New York: Academic Press.

Wahler, R. G. 1969. "Setting Generality: Some Specific and General Effects of Child Behavior Therapy." *Journal of Applied Behavior Analysis* 2, no. 4: 239–46.

———. 1975. "Some Structural Aspects of Deviant Child Behavior." *Journal of Applied Behavior Analysis* 8:27–42.

———. 1976. "Generalization Processes in Child Behavior Change." Nashville, Tenn.: HEW grant application.

———, R. Berland, and G. Leske. 1975. "Environmental Boundaries in Behavior Modification: Problems in Residential Treatment of Children." Nashville, Tenn.: Paper presented at annual conference at Otter Crest.

Wahler, R. G., and D. Moore. 1975. "School-Home Behavior Change Procedures in a 'High Risk' Community." Paper presented at Association for the Advancement of Behavior Therapy convention, San Francisco.

Wahler, R. G., G. H. Winkle, R. F. Peterson, and D. C. Morrison. 1965. "Mothers as Behavior Therapists for Their Own Children." *Behavior Research and Therapy* 3:113-24.

Waksman, S. 1978. "An Empirical Investigation of Campbell and Fiske's Multi-state, Multimetrics Using Social Learning Measures." *Journal of Abnormal Child Psychology* 6:1-10.

Walker, H. M., S. M. Johnson, and H. Hops. 1975. "Generalization and Maintenance of Classroom Treatment Effects." *Behavior Therapy*.

Walker, H. M., R. H. Mattson, and N. K. Buckley. 1968. "Special Class Placement as a Treatment Alternative for Deviant Behavior in Children." In *Classroom Intervention*, ed. E. Haughton, G. Patterson, and H. Walker. Eugene: University of Oregon Press.

Walter, H. I., and S. K. Gilmore. 1973. "Placebo Versus Social Learning Effects in Parent Training Procedures Designed to Alter the Behavior of Aggressive Boys." *Behavior Research and Therapy* 4:361-77.

Weeks, A. H. 1962. "The High Field Project and Its Success." In *The Sociology of Punishment and Correction*, ed. N. Johnston, L. Sairtz, and S. Wolfgang, pp. 203-12. New York: John Wiley.

Weiner, E., and E. Gallistet. 1961. "Prediction of Outstanding Performance, Delinquency, and Emotional Disturbance from Childhood Evaluations." *Child Development* 32:255.

West, D. J., and D. T. Farrington. 1973. *Who Becomes Delinquent?* Second report of the Cambridge Study in Delinquent Development. New York: Crane, Russek.

Wiltz, N. A., and G. R. Patterson. 1974. "An Evaluation of Parent Training Procedures Designed to Alter Inappropriate Aggressive Behavior of Boys." *Behavior Therapy* 5:215-21.

Wolff, S. 1967. "Behavioural Characteristics of Primary School Children Referred to a Psychiatric Department." *British Journal of Psychiatry* 113:885–93.

Wolfgang, M. E., Robert M. Figlio, and T. Sellin. 1973. *Delinquency in a Birth Cohort*. Chicago: University of Chicago Press.

Zeilberger, J., J. Sampen, and H. Sloane. 1968. "Modification of the Child's Problem Behavior in the Home with the Mother as Therapist." *Journal of Applied Behavior Analysis* 1:47–53.

REPLICABILITY OF FINDINGS:
COMMENTS ON DR. PATTERSON'S PAPER

Leonard D. Eron

It is reassuring that Patterson and his associates, on one hand, and my colleagues and I, on the other, have over the years been obtaining similar kinds of findings, even though we have approached our subject matter from different points of view. My colleagues and I have come from a more Hull-Spence-Robert Sears tradition, using large-scale interview techniques with parents as informants, at the same time relying on laboratory studies with ANOVA-type designs in analog situations. Patterson and his associates have come from a Skinnerian, single-case, methodological orientation, but have actually worked with families, fashioning individual training programs based on careful behavioral assessment done in situ. However, our results have been strikingly similar.

For example, Patterson has found that punishment doesn't work with problem children. "Parental punishment," he says, "seemed to accelerate on-going coercive behavior." We also found that, in general, the more a child was punished for aggressive behavior, the more aggressive the child was—at least there was a moderately high correlation between parental punishment for aggression and aggressive behavior that persisted over a ten-year period. But the relation between punishment and aggression is not simple. From our earlier work (Eron, Walder, and Lefkowitz 1971) we can surmise that the effects of contingent response (punishment) on aggression are complicated and mediated by other variables. For example, in an early study we found that punishment reduced aggressive behavior only for certain boys who were strongly identified with their fathers. When high identification was not present, punishment, especially physical punishment, was positively and strongly associated with aggression. Finally, our longitudinal data (Lefkowitz, Eron, Walder and Huesmann 1977) indicate that moderate punishment by parents in the long run produced less-aggressive children than either no punishment or harsh punishment. One implication of this finding for child rearing is that punishment, when used in moderation, seems to be effective in diminishing aggressive behavior. However, when harsh punishment is used, particularly with children who weakly identify with their parents, aggression is heightened—probably as a result of modeling. At the same time, permissiveness, as indicated by no punishment, is equally deleterious, according to our data.

Experimental work done in my laboratory as well as in Patterson's indicates that low-aggressive children—or nonproblem children, as he designates them—respond to punishment in a way that parents anticipate when they punish—that is, the punished child tends not to repeat the behavior for which punishment is administered. With the high-aggressive child or the problem child, the reverse is true. The more such a child is punished, the more aggressive he or she becomes.

It seems that the low-aggressive child has been more effectively socialized to inhibit aggressive responding because parental punishment is more salient. The effectiveness of punishment would be at least in part due to the parents' giving of rewards for other, nonaggressive behaviors. On the other hand, the highly aggressive child has somehow failed to find sufficient reward in low-aggressive responding. Such a child may be so accustomed to punishment as to be unable to see any utility in conforming to the expressed wishes of adults when punishment is the most likely outcome regardless of behavior, and when no rewards are given to make compliance worthwhile. The parent may even be inadvertently providing rewards for aggression. Child aggression may also be fostered when the parent does not seem to care enough to punish undesired behaviors, let alone provide other positive contingencies. In the absence of discriminable rewards, instrumental goals that might more often require aggressive responding would tend to be more gratifying. All parents presumably have the capacity to reward or punish, but it is thought that parents of low-aggressive children have been more successful in teaching nonaggressive behavior. Not only have they employed punishment techniques but, more important, they also have given contingent positive reinforcement for desirable behaviors. The curvilinear relation mentioned before between parental punishment and aggression is understandable if parents of low-aggression children also make use of rewards for good behavior that, when achieved, would decrease the necessity of punishment.

Patterson and his colleagues have produced compelling evidence of how environmental contingencies may facilitate aggressive responding in all children, and he has demonstrated how reinforcement by peers is especially effective in instating and maintaining aggressive behavior. Thus, the child might be strongly reinforced by peers for aggressive behavior while the parents make frequent use of punishment to control behavior in the home. If reward for aggression from peers is so much more a determinant of aggressive responding than is parental punishment, then perhaps parents should find better strategies for controlling their children's behavior. Rewards for appropriate behaviors may prove to be much more effective in reducing aggressive responses at home or in school than any amount of punishment short of physical impairment.

This simple orientation of seeking sources of reward was overlooked in early studies of child aggression, which instead emphasized the assumption that inhibition of aggressive responses would be a necessary consequence of pairing responses with aversive stimulation. A. Bandura and R. Walters (1963) took notice, and wrote: "The development of aggression inhibition through the strengthening of incompatible positive responses ... has been entirely ignored, despite the fact that the social control of aggression is probably achieved to a greater extent on this basis than by means of aversive stimulation" (p. 130).

Even now there is a lack of research that attempts to demonstrate the potential of reinforcing nonaggressive behaviors as a means of reducing aggression. Field experiments or behavior modification cases that Patterson recounts are examples of present work that illustrates the effectiveness of this reinforcement technique, though the effect of reinforcing nonaggressive responding has not yet been successfully demonstrated in the controlled conditions of the laboratory for subjects who are classified as high or low in aggression.

A study completed by one of my students, Rosemary Smith (1977), indicates that eight-year-old children preselected as high-aggressive, when placed in an aggressive machine situation with a target who has been established as a source of reward for nonaggressive behavior, are significantly less aggressive than high-aggressive children with a target that is not a source of reward.

Patterson briefly traces the heady history of behavior modification from the mid-1960s through its development into the social engineering of the 1970s and notes the increasing emphasis during this period on observation as a primary assessment tool for measuring behavior change and the concomitant loss of faith in the validity and reliability of parental descriptions of behavior. However, it is interesting that in our own studies, my colleagues and I have depended heavily on ratings of behavior by parents, both their own behavior and that of their children, and have arrived at findings that are not discrepant with those of Patterson and his group. The reason is perhaps that we have not relied much on global rating of behavior and behavior change, but have instead focused on specific behaviors and contingencies. Parents can be good observers and good reporters when the investigators have gone about their business properly, devising sophisticated scales and questionnaires for parents to respond to. Certainly Patterson has himself demonstrated that parents can be trained to observe and report behavior so as to carry out various behavior modification procedures. It was also a positive experience for an old-fashioned trait psychologist like me to learn that environmental, contingency-bound theorists like Patterson have had to come to terms with the stability of behavior over time and across situations.

My colleagues and I have found reasonably high, positive correlations between aggressive behavior at age 8 and aggressive behavior at age 19; we have found high agreement between self-ratings of aggressive behavior and peer ratings of this behavior; in a series of factor analyses done on measures taken at age 8 and again at age 19, we have derived one major factor of aggression that encompasses different types of aggression (whether physical, verbal, or indirect), different objects of aggression (whether adult or peer), and different provocation levels; we have obtained high correlations between paper-and-pencil measures of aggression and aggressive behavior measured in an overt situation; children who are rated as aggressive in school by their teachers and peers tend, except in unusual instances, to be rated as aggressive at home by their parents. It is also interesting that adolescents who were rated as aggressive witnessed aggressive acts and were victims of such acts significantly more often than those rated as non-aggressive. Thus, aggression, at least as measured in our subjects, seems to be a trait reflected in consistent behavior over a wide range of situations—or, one might say, it is a response class composed of behaviors whose common feature is its irritating or injurious effect on another person.

I was especially pleased that Patterson, in reanalyzing our data, came to the same conclusions that we did—even though he does not say so in so many words: Aggression is a trait; it is a well-learned behavior, a way of interacting with other persons, a way of solving problems that is learned very early in life, is learned very well, and, perhaps because it is so successful, generalizes to many situations. On the other hand, there are a number of other reasons why some children respond with a very narrow band of behaviors, all aggressive. Among these reasons are low intelligence, which limits the range of subtle or oblique behaviors a child can learn, and differential reinforcement, which constricts a child to learning a limited number of ways of interacting with other persons.

Thus, when I say aggression is a trait, I do not mean that it is necessarily genetically determined or that it is invariant and cannot be changed or unlearned. Patterson has certainly demonstrated that this behavior can be changed, even though it has traitlike characteristics. It is just very difficult to change; and I think it is much too optimistic to believe that behaviors, which have taken many years and many successful trials to establish, can be permanently eliminated with a few lessons in child management skills. I know Patterson does not want to give the impression that all this is easy. He and his colleagues undoubt-edly work very hard with each family and spend many hours before accomplishing stable behavior change in a single child. How much more efficient it would be if we could encourage and establish appropriate learning environments in the first place, before the child has developed these "coercive behaviors" that finally force the parent to seek professional help.

My own research findings have convinced me that there are two areas in which changes should be made if we want to reduce aggressive behavior in the first place. One is in the models of adult behavior that are furnished the developing child; another is the sex-typed socialization to which children in our society are subjected. I found consideration of both these factors conspicuously absent in Patterson's description of what he does to diminish coercive behaviors in his young clients after these behaviors have been established.

One of the most striking findings in our ten-year longitudinal study was the lasting effect of the models of aggression to which the child is exposed in the formative years. Children of parents who display aggressive behaviors are themselves aggressive when they grow to adulthood. However, parents are not the only models of behavior to which the child is exposed. Especially important are the models seen on the television screen. As we have indicated, the youngster who is continually exposed to violent heroes on television comes to think violence is part of everyday life—the way to solve problems, to acquire desired goods, to relieve frustration. The more realistic youngsters believe television to be, the more aggressive they are. To counteract this effect, children can be taught early to distinguish accurately between reality and fantasy, their own and that of others, and how to use fantasy constructively in the solution of problems. Of course, a more direct way to diminish the problem is to persuade the networks to reduce the amount of violence in programming. We will not go into ways in which this can be done; suffice it to say that apparently various pressure groups, which have been formed as a result of the publicity given research findings in this area, are beginning to have some influence and the amount of violence to which children are exposed on television screens and in films will be controlled, as it always has been in many European countries.

The other area where preventive measures can be taken—but that will be much more difficult—is to change practices in socialization of traditional sex-typed behaviors. We are faced with the fact that males display more aggressive behaviors than do females—no matter how aggression is measured or observed, males always score higher. In fact, Patterson, at least in the examples of his work that he has given us, seems only to treat boys. Don't girls have problems in "coercive behaviors"? And if not, why not? In our own work we found that boys always scored higher than did girls, but this is not so for all girls—there are some girls who seem to have been socialized like boys, who are as aggressive as boys. Thus, although there may be conditions—organismically normal ones like sex differences in testosterone—that are implicated in aggressive behavior, this behavior is not necessarily immutable. Just as some females can learn to be aggressive, so males can learn not to be aggressive. The significant variables are the values and expectations a society holds for the expression of aggressive behavior in one sex rather than another and the rewards it provides when that behavior is expressed.

The differential effect of television violence on aggressive behavior of boys and girls is a case in point. Girls who watch violent programs tend to be less aggressive than girls who don't watch. The relation is not as strong as is the positive one for boys, but it is there. Why should there be this differential effect of television violence on boys and girls? First, boys are often encouraged and reinforced in the direct and overt expression of aggression. On the other hand, girls are trained not to behave aggressively in a direct manner, and nonaggressive behaviors are reinforced. Thus, for girls viewing television violence may actually be a positively sanctioned social activity in which aggressive girls may express aggression vicariously, since they cannot do so directly in social interactions. The direct avenues for expression of aggressive behavior—such as fighting, wrestling, pummeling, and war games—are open to boys and discouraged for girls.

Two related findings are the significant positive relation for girls between aggression and masculine interest patterns as measured by the masculinity-femininity scale of the MMPI and the significant positive relation between aggression scores for girls and the extent to which they watch contact sports on television. Both of these scores reflect attitudes and behaviors that are normative for boys. For boys, however, there was no relation between viewing contact sports on television and aggression, nor was there a relation for boys between masculinity on the masculinity-femininity scale and aggression. It is very probable that the reason for lack of relation to aggression among boys lies in the minimal variability on the other two variables. Most boys watch contact sports and also endorse the attitudes and interests comprising the masculinity items on the masculinity-femininity scale. Both peer and adult cultures encourage and reinforce direct rather than vicarious participation by boys in contact sports, but make little provision for participation by girls. For boys, knowledge of these sports and activities is virtually peer-mandated, and is required for peer acceptance and popularity. Low-aggressive boys, medium-aggressive boys, and high-aggressive boys all watch contact sports. However, these results indicate that when females are aggressive, some of their interests and activities are similar to those of the male group.

In addition to these explanations, one other factor may play a role in the differential effect of television violence on boys and girls. It has been proposed that girls have been conditioned to express aggression only in a few acceptable forms. One of these would be fantasy. It is now suggested that girls more clearly see television as fantasy, and thus can express their aggressions through viewing television violence. Boys, on the other hand, see television as more realistic; therefore, the modeling effect dominates for them.

What support can we marshal for this theory? It is well-known that young girls have greater verbal fluency, read better, and are better able to fantasize than are boys. Research by J. Singer (1973) has revealed that children can relieve aggression by viewing aggressive acts *if* they have been trained to distinguish reality from fantasy. S. Feshbach (1972) has shown that the labeling of violence as fantasy produced in a Hollywood studio led to significantly less subsequent aggressiveness than when the same dramatic material was identified as a newsreel. Thus, if our theorizing is correct, one would expect girls to be better able than boys to distinguish reality from fantasy in television programs. Data we collected in grade 13 confirm this. Girls think television is significantly less realistic than do boys. Given this finding, one can check some other implications of this theory. Assuming that girls who think television is realistic would be poor fantasizers, one would expect to find them in the higher aggression groups; this is exactly the case. The more aggressive girls are at both age 8 and age 19, the more realistic they think television programs are. Finally, we note that girls who see themselves as masculine in grade 13—that is, who obtain high scores on scale 5 of the MMPI, tend to perceive television as more realistic and to be more aggressive in situations where their peers can see them. There is a moderate correlation between masculinity in girls and perceiving television as realistic, and also between masculinity in girls and aggression.

What are the implications of these findings for the reduction of aggressive behavior in males? I think it is obvious that boys should be socialized more like girls. This is where women's liberationists have it all wrong. Rather than insisting that little girls should be treated like boys and given exactly the same opportunities for participation in athletic events and all other aspects of life, it should be the other way around. Boys should be socialized as girls traditionally have been. Perhaps the level of individual aggression in society will be reduced when male adolescents and young adults, as a result of socialization, subscribe to the same standards of behavior that have traditionally been encouraged for women.

REFERENCES

Bandura, A., and R. Walters. 1973. *Social Learning and Personality Development.* New York: Holt, Rinehart and Winston.

Eron, L. D., L. O. Walder, and M. M. Lefkowitz. 1971. *Learning of Aggression in Children.* Boston: Little, Brown.

Feshbach, S. 1972. "Reality and Fantasy in Filmed Violence." In *Television and Social Behavior,* ed. J. P. Murray, E. A. Rubinstein, and G. A. Comstock, II, pp. 318–45. Washington, D.C.: U.S. Government Printing Office.

Lefkowitz, M. M., L. D. Eron, L. O. Walder, and L. R. Huesmann. 1977. *Growing Up to Be Violent.* New York: Pergamon.

Singer, J. 1973. *The Child's World of Make Believe.* New York: Academic Press.

Smith, R. K. 1977. "Effects of Two Target Strategies upon Aggressive Responding in Children." M.A. thesis, University of Illinois at Chicago Circle.

6

FUNCTIONS OF EMOTIONAL AND COGNITIVE MECHANISMS IN THE REGULATION OF AGGRESSIVE BEHAVIOR

Adam Frączek

In this paper I should like to discuss several issues regarding the nature and functioning of the regulating mechanisms of aggression within a more general framework of mechanisms regulating human behavior. The information and contentions presented will be arranged according to various premises and assumptions.

METHODOLOGICAL ASSUMPTIONS

Even a general look at the empirical data and psychological considerations on aggression is enough to assure us that this phenomenon is far from simple. Aggression has many forms (including expressive, angry, instrumental, goal-centered, asocial, and prosocial) and a wide range of specific manifestations (Buss 1961; Feshbach 1964, 1970, 1974; Frączek 1975; Rule 1974). Various types and manifestations of aggression are distinguished by using different criteria, such as function, form, and level of organization and complexity. In effect there are many mutually incomparable psychological definitions of aggression, and this terminological ambiguity has even led to attempts to introduce other concepts such as agonistic behavior. This lack of terminological and definitional precision reflects the complexity of the problem of aggression rather than the intellectual impotence of psychologists or other specialists. Seeing, then, that we are confronted with a phenomenon that is complex per se, we should not expect to find one simple psychological mechanism responsible for aggressive behavior.

Thus, if we are to reach a fuller understanding of interpersonal aggression, we must take into account the multifaceted determination of this phenomenon. This methodological postulate underlying the psychological analysis of aggression has two aspects. First, by multifaceted determination of aggressive behavior in human beings we mean that such behavior is the result of interaction of individual characteristics with features of the situation currently affecting the individual. Such interaction can be analyzed from a developmental point of view or at a particular moment in time.

Second, by multifaceted determination of aggression we mean that the psychological mechanisms of such behavior cannot be limited to one, simple, unidimensional process or elementary structure. Even if we reduced our interest in aggression to the form that is called impulsive aggression (Berkowitz 1974), we should still not be able to limit ourselves to emotional-drive mechanisms alone. We must assume that even simple aggressive acts are regulated by various psychological processes and structures and that the final action is the outcome of the interaction of those mechanisms. Further, different elements of psychological mechanisms regulate different forms of aggressive behavior performing different functions (such as expressive, impulsive, goal-centered aggression).

LEVELS OF COMPLEXITY AND ORGANIZATION

Other important postulates underlying the analysis of the mechanisms of aggression arise from the evident, though rarely appreciated, observation that human aggressive behavior varies as to level of complexity and organization, and takes place in various time perspectives. If we take these criteria into account, human behavior can be described in terms of reaction, action, or activity—that is, it can be characterized and explained on three different levels. This differentiation is based on the general theory of action developed by T. Tomaszewski (1963; 1975) as well as on conceptions developed by Soviet psychologists (Leontiew 1975).

Generally speaking, by reactions we mean simple responses to external or internal stimulation that are very limited in time perspective. With respect to aggression, an animal's response to a simple painful stimulus is definitely reactive (Ulrich and Symannek 1969). Probably slapping a child who has sharply tugged one's ear also falls under this category. Some, though not all, of the examples of "impulsive" aggression given by Berkowitz (1974) are also reactive types of behavior.

The concept of action reflects a higher level of behavioral organization and complexity, and usually greater duration as well (Tomaszewski 1963, 1975). One of the essential features of action is goal-centeredness, related principally to anticipation both of the final effect to be achieved and the behavior leading to this effect. Hence, when describing aggressive actions, we should include the starting point, the elements or operations of which they consist, factors initiating and blocking actions, and finally their results. Aggressive actions, of special interest here, appear in the context of interpersonal situations, and thus are social in nature (Frączek 1973, 1975). And finally, by activity we usually mean certain fields of human action related to social roles and tasks. Such a classification of human functioning is based mainly on culturally defined patterns of tasks and goals that people should pursue, and their attitude toward such normative patterns. It is noteworthy that in the behavioral sciences we seldom find the term "aggressive activity" denoting long-term organization of individual behavior and the social qualification of such behavior; instead, such terms as "destructive activity" or "asocial (or antisocial) activity" are more frequently used.

When aggressive behavior is described as reaction, action, or activity, the question of the psychological mechanisms mediating such behavior acquires different meaning and scope. I must agree with Berkowitz (1974) that ". . . Perhaps because strong emotions result in an increased utilization of only the central cues in the immediate situation, anger arousal can lead to impulsive aggressive responses which, for a short time at least, may be relatively free of cognitive mediated inhibitions against aggression." (p. 161). Whether cognitive processes were absent in the instigation of anger in emotional response to specific stimulation is another question. On the other hand, I can fully agree with Feshbach (1974) that "The standards of conduct which constitute the basis of aggressive motivation have the same theoretical properties as other internalized norms of behavior. They serve as frame of reference for the evaluation and guidance of behavior. They also provide a structure which energizes the organism into action . . ." (p. 182). Further, ". . . The most obvious source of the standards producing aggressive motivation are explicit cultural norms" (p. 183). Both explanations are probably true, but they have to do with different types of aggression and take into account completely different elements of the mechanisms regulating human behavior.

It follows from the previous discussion about the complexity of the phenomenon called aggression and the need for multidimensional analysis of its underlying determinants and mechanisms, that current theories predominant in the psychology of aggression do not fulfill these requirements. Those theories that have their roots in the frustration-aggression hypothesis (Dollard et al. 1939), despite many transformations and additions, still focus on the emotional and motivational determinants of aggression. In these approaches cognitive mechanisms are treated mainly as the source of blocking of emotional readiness to aggression.

Social learning theory (Bandura 1973, 1976), on the other hand, stresses the situational and social determinants of aggression. Emotional and motivational processes are treated as consequences of operations with which the individual is confronted, and cognitive mechanisms regulate his behavior to the extent that they are the source of internal, symbolic reinforcement. Hence, when we discuss the meaning of emotional and motivational mechanisms and cognitive mechanisms in the regulation of aggression, we find it necessary to seek a different formulation theorem than that provided by these theories.

EMOTIONAL REGULATION OF AGGRESSION

Emotional processes participate in the regulation of human relations with the environment for three reasons:

1. They affect the organism's energy resources, and thus determine the dynamics and, to a certain extent, the level of organization of behavior.
2. They determine the direction of behavior, depending on whether the emotional process is positive or negative.
3. They determine, to a greater or lesser extent, specific forms of behavior related to the qualitative features of the emotional process (Reykowski 1975).

Aspects of Emotional Regulation

The activational aspect of emotion is usually described as ranging from complete lack of activation (as in deep relaxation) to extremely strong arousal (as in "pathological intoxication"), the latter usually leading to complete disorganization of purposeful behavior and loss of rational control of action. Many laws describing the conditions affecting the level of emotional arousal and the consequences of changes in the level of such arousal have been developed, including the Yerkes-Dodson law (Young 1961). The level of emotional arousal can undoubtedly affect the dynamics of aggressive behavior. However, there are many disputes as to whether aggression can be aggravated by nonspecific emotional arousal or whether such arousal must have a specific sign or content (Berkowitz 1962, 1969; Geen and O'Neal 1969; Geen and Powers 1971).

The directional dimension of emotion ranges from negative (unpleasant, unsatisfactory) to positive (pleasant, satisfactory). Apart from their subjective aspect—that is, unpleasant or pleasant feelings—emotions differing in direction affect behavior differently. Positive emotions lead to actions sustaining the pleasant state or to the tendency to keep in touch with stimuli and situations that are the source of such emotions. Negative emotions, on the other hand, evoke actions intended to remove or even destroy the stimuli or situations leading to them, and cause the interruption of behavior producing such emotions. This statement is one of the well-established truths of contemporary psychology, as well as one of the basic axioms of learning theory (Hilgard and Marquis 1940; Cofer and Appley 1964), and a fundamental assumption of behavioral therapy (Yates 1975).

The qualitative aspect of the emotional process is related both to the individual's conscious feelings, more or less verbalized, and to specific forms of behavior. Thus, for instance, curiosity stimulates various exploratory actions; anxiety and fear lead to various forms of withdrawal and escape; anger and irritation are said to evoke attack and reactive forms of aggression (Reykowski

1975a). According to the classical frustration-aggression theory, frustration leads to anger, which is synonymous with stimulation of aggression, whereas anxiety, caused mainly by anticipation of punishment, is the main factor blocking stimulation of aggression (Dollard et al. 1939). However, this relationship was found to be much more complex, and hence more recent theories use the much more enigmatic term "emotional readiness to aggression" to designate those emotional processes that may lead to aggressive reactions (Berkowitz 1962, 1969, 1974).

Sources of Emotional Mechanisms

The development of emotional direction (pleasure vs. displeasure) as well as specific emotional content is a complex process. This process, as well as further statements regarding the emotional regulation of aggressive behavior, can be analyzed within the framework of what we know about the sources and determinants of emotions.

Emotional processes are aroused in several ways:

1. When the organism is affected by primal emotogenic stimuli—that is, factors that naturally evoke emotional reactions
2. By secondary emotogenic stimuli—that is, factors that have acquired emotogenic properties through conditioning
3. By relations between expectations and incoming information (Reykowski 1968, 1975a).

Primary emotogenic stimuli are mainly connected with sensory stimulation and the features of emotions thus evoked—that is, their intensity, direction, and content depend upon the intensity of the stimulus and, most of all, on its biological significance. Thus, stimuli signaling the possibility of need gratification evoke positive emotions, whereas stimuli signaling lack of need gratification evoke negative emotions. Gratification or frustration of biological needs is also connected with different levels of activation and positive or negative emotions. The consequences of the individual's own reactions (positive or negative reinforcement) are also a primary source of emotions. Thus various painful, alimentary, or sexual stimuli, as well as sudden changes of stimulation or frustration, can be treated as primal emotogenic stimuli able to evoke emotional arousal unconditionally. Such arousal can, in certain situations, take the form of expressive behavior or goal-centered, though impulsive, aggressive reactions (Feshbach 1964; Berkowitz 1962, 1969, 1974). However, we would contend that this mechanism plays no significant role in the regulation of interpersonal aggressive actions.

Secondary emotogenic stimuli develop through classical or instrumental conditioning (Pavlov 1927; Skinner 1953), and comprise all those neutral factors that have become associated with primary emotogenic stimuli in the course of experience. This area of investigation into the emotional regulation of behavior, including the utilization of the principles of conditioning in the modification of maladjustive behavior, has a very long and widespread tradition (Watson 1930; Wolpe 1958). In more recent modifications attention is paid not so much to the fact that practically any of a virtually infinite number of factors can become a source of emotional arousal as to the fact that the learning of emotional meaning is social in character, and can take place indirectly or symbolically as well as through vicarious reinforcement (Bandura 1969, 1973).

Secondary and indirectly mediated emotogenic stimuli regulate aggressive behavior by modifying the level of activation and determining the direction and content of emotion. Studies by W. Ciarkowska (Gajda-Ciarkowska 1971; Frączek 1974) have revealed that the intensity of goal-centered aggressive behavior changes when a positively or negatively emotionally charged stimulus appears. Negative emotogenic stimuli associated in previous actions with aversive situations increase the intensity of punishments, whereas positive emotogenic stimuli associated in the past with positive reinforcement decrease the intensity of punishment conveyed to the partner. In other words, even in cases where aggressive behavior is not initially generated by emotional mechanisms, but proceeds in response to the requirements and organization of the situation with which the individual is confronted, the introduction of secondary emotogenic stimuli of a given direction (positive or negative) affects the dynamics of the action. Unfortunately, the content of the emotional reactions to the conditioned stimuli was not controlled in these studies. It can be inferred from the types of reinforcement used during conditioning (electric shocks bordering on pain vs. cigarettes for subjects to whom they had considerable value) that in the first case anxiety was reinforced and in the second, hope or general satisfaction. This would mean that the intensity of aggression increases not only in response to specific emotions like anger or irritation but also, to a certain extent, in response to negative emotional arousal, usually in association with the blocking of aggression. In turn, an increase in activation following positive emotional arousal led to reduction of aggression; thus the dynamics of aggression cannot be regarded as a simple function of increased activation.

Emotional Reactivity

Another problem is the question of what determines individual differences in emotional reactivity and emotional conditioning. According to the Pavlovian tradition, the strength of the response of the organism to a stimulus is a function not only of the properties of the stimulus itself and of former experience, but also of the functional properties of the nervous system. Such parameters of the excitatory and inhibitory processes taking place in the nervous system as strength, mobility, and equilibrium were presumed to determine individual differences in reactivity and conditioning (Strelau 1975). H. J. Eysenck (1960), who has elaborated on this approach on the basis of his own investigations, introduced the personality dimensions of neuroticism and extra introversion. Neuroticism, in the sense used by Eysenck, is connected with the intensity of emotional reactions, the susceptibility to disorganization of behavior and emotional instability, whereas the extra/introversion dimension is associated with the speed of conditioning and the durability of reactions, including conditioned emotional reactions. According, on the other hand, to the concept of temperament developed by J. Strelau, where temperament is understood as a characteristic formal property of behavior, individual differences in reactivity reflect different levels of stimulation requirement.

There have been very few empirical studies on the degree to which the properties mentioned above affect the dynamics of aggression, although it is not difficult to foresee that they should determine the intensity of at least reactive forms of aggression. Our own studies (Frączek and Ciarkowska 1974) have revealed that the level of neuroticism is not related to task-oriented aggression consistent with the requirements of the situation—or, if it is, the relationship is too small to be detected by our current measuring procedures. A different regularity is found, on the other hand, for aggression appearing in response to frustration or a negative conditional stimulus: the level of aggression regulated to a large extent by negative emotions correlates positively with the level of neuroticism.

Transformations of Emotional Mechanisms

Developmental changes in emotions are not limited to the transformation of primary emotional stimuli into secondary and mediated stimulants of emotion. The basic structures through which certain stimuli, situations, or events acquire signal properties are also transformed. Generally speaking, new systems of needs develop as a result of connections between basic needs and the objects and behavior able to satisfy them. This outlook is generally accepted in various theories of personality, and it has developed from the psychoanalytic theory of cathetic object formation and its regulating properties (Freud 1920; Murray 1938; Maslow 1954). Just as primary needs are natural sources of emotion, so secondary needs are supposed to generate emotional processes and specific stimuli, situations, or events associated with the satisfaction of these needs become important sources of emotional reactions.

The above assumption has several consequences for our discussion on the regulating role of emotions in aggressive behavior. First, transformations in the sphere of emotional regulation may lead to the development of a relatively autonomous need for aggression—that is, a need that is satisfied through harming other people and in which positive emotional satisfaction can be gained through observing other people's pain and suffering. In this case we would speak of personally motivated aggressive reactions (Feshbach 1970). A. Bandura and

R. H. Walters' (1959) study on the role of emotional rejection in the development of asocial aggressiveness in boys illustrates this regularity well. R. Hartman's (1969) observations of the aggravation of aggressive behavior through watching others suffer suggests how this mechanism may operate.

By way of digression we may mention that such a need for aggression may, for lack of other possibilities, be satisfied vicariously (for instance, in fantasy or through identification with observed aggressive behavior), leading, in effect, to reduction of manifest aggressive behavior. This does not, of course, mean that mechanisms alternative to the need for aggression develop spontaneously, and I do not think the term "catharsis" (Feshbach and Singer 1971) is correct here.

Second, the developing secondary needs may be in conflict with each other. The idea that motivational conflicts lead to tension, introduced by psychoanalysis and developed by dynamic personality theories, has been substantially supported in both experimental studies and clinical observations (Dollard and Miller 1950; Frączek and Kofta 1975). Enhanced emotional tension, however, is one of the components of emotional readiness for aggression rather than the sole and sufficient prerequisite of aggressive behavior.

COGNITIVE REGULATION OF AGGRESSION

I have already mentioned that emotions can be generated by relations between the individual's expectations and incoming information. In this case emotions are evoked by cognitive operations and are connected with the individual's cognitive structures. I shall discuss this matter further, paying attention to various aspects of cognitive regulation of aggressive actions. I shall not try to present a theory explaining the phenomenon of aggression within the convention of the "cognitive" approach to the analysis of behavior. Rather, I shall try to show the typical cognitive processes and structures that affect various parameters of aggression, basing the discussion on selected empirical data and more general observations. Moreover, I should like to show the various phases of development of aggressive behavior in which different cognitive mechanisms participate.

The expression "cognitive regulators of behavior" is usually used to denote the psychological processes and structures connected with intake, coding, generating, and evaluation of information (Sheerer 1962; Kozielecki 1975; Tomaszewski 1975). Such regulation includes, in particular, sensory-motor and semantic perception, accumulation and organization of external information and personal experience, elaboration of concepts and generation of ideas, processes of understanding and anticipation, and decisional processes. Cognitive structures—that is, systems of information about the world and oneself accumulated after many transformations by the individual—also participate in cognitive regulation (Reykowski 1976). Information accumulated in the course of individual experience leads, generally speaking, to the development of an image of reality and a self-image. These images comprise attitudes, sets, beliefs, and value systems that not only determine the selection of incoming information but also participate actively in the regulation of behavior. The problem of cognitive regulation of behavior also includes speech and the role of consciousness in human activity (Tomaszewski 1975).

Cognitive processes and structures participate in the regulation of aggression in the following ways:

1. They mediate the development of emotional readiness to aggression.
2. They generate emotional and motivational processes that stimulate or block aggression.
3. They generate nonemotional motivation to act aggressively or control aggression.
4. They participate in the programming and control of the dynamics and structure of aggressive actions (Geller 1975).

For the sake of formality, we may mention that the proposed method analyzing the role of cognitive mechanisms in aggression is purely heuristic.

The mediating role of cognitive mechanisms in the regulation of simple forms of aggressive behavior was shown first and foremost in the many studies by L. Berkowitz and his collaborators (Berkowitz 1974). So-called cues that range from simple physical stimuli to complex scenes of physical combat or verbal attack watched on the screen, generally increase the level of punishment of the partner with whom a subject is interacting in the laboratory. Without detailing the various restrictions on this generalization (Frączek and Macaulay 1971), we may assume that the cues must first of all be registered and, second, must be given specific emotional and signal meaning. The registering and decoding of cues involve not only elementary cognitive processes but also more complex structures enabling comparison of incoming stimulation with past experience.

Before the informational meaning of a cue is interpreted, such processes as differentiation, comparison and—in the case of complicated stimulation patterns of human interaction—comprehension of intention or evaluation must operate. I shall not take any definitive standpoint here on the often-discussed question of whether these cues affect the intensity of aggressive reactions through enhancement or lowering of the level of already existing emotional readiness to aggression; through facilitation and enhancement or decrease of general activation; or because they contain information about the permissibility or nonpermissibility of given forms of behavior (Berkowitz 1974; Bandura 1973). Simple aggressive reactions are always mediated to a certain extent by the individual's cognitive activity. The processes taking place in such situations and the interfering cognitive structures differ in complexity and degree of awareness. When I speak here of awareness, I mean the ability of the individual to verbalize the emotional meaning of the situational cue. This ability probably also affects very strongly the dynamics of reactive forms of aggression.

Another area of investigation into the issues discussed here concerns the cognitive mechanisms responsible for the development of emotional processes that have specific direction and content. The now-classic study by S. Schachter and J. E. Singer (1962) revealed that emotional direction and content are formed as a result of nondifferentiated arousal and its interpretation. The basis for such interpretation is information about other people's behavior and the specific meaning ascribed to it. Berkowitz et al. (1969), in their reanalysis of this experiment, pointed out that the subjects' own behavior can also be interpreted, thus leading to the formation of emotion. According to Berkowitz, the experimental subjects first undertake a certain form of activity and then, in their evaluation of the effects of this activity, claim their anger is the basic cause of their reactions. It is not important in this analysis to decide which of the previous hypotheses is more justified, but I wish to draw attention to the fact that cognitive mechanisms can probably participate in the regulation of aggression both at the initiation of such reactions and at points later in the process. The mediating role of cognitive mechanisms in the development of emotional readiness for aggression can also operate according to more complex patterns than those discussed thus far. One of the important mechanisms in such regulation is undoubtedly feedback obtained by the subject in regard to the effects of the activity performed (Baron 1971a, 1971b). This mode of regulation of aggression operates on a different, more complex level than the formation of an emotional readiness to aggression, although it indirectly affects elementary emotional processes and codetermines emotional direction and content.

DISSONANCE AND NORMS AS A SOURCE OF MOTIVATION FOR AGGRESSION

In those studies that are concerned with the sources of emotional processes, attention is paid to the fact that emotional processes form in response to specific relations between expectations and information. It is usually assumed that positive emotions appear when information is consistent with expectations and that dissonance causes negative emotions (Reykowski 1975). According to certain cognitive theories, this is the basic mechanism of behavior (Heider 1958; Festinger 1957).

The thesis that operations occurring in cognitive processes and structures produce emotions requires some comment, particularly in regard to facilitating understanding of the cognitive mechanisms of regulating aggression. First, consonance or dissonance (the term used for conflict in the cognitive sphere) may be associated with two or more currently incoming elements of information that may differ in complexity; relations between a relatively stable cognitive structure formed in the course of development (such as image of reality, belief, or set) and incoming information related to the same area; or relations between various relatively stable cognitive structures, such as elements of the value system. This differentiation is important insofar as it enables us to determine whether and to what extent tension is caused by some external situation or by internal structures developed through accumulation and organization of information.

Second, conflicts in the cognitive sphere are more liable to increase the general tension than independently to generate emotions of unambiguous content. A similar regularity can be found in conflicts between emotions or between needs developed through transformation of emotogenic needs (Reykowski 1973). Secondary interpretation of arousal or the recognition of the meaning of the factor classified by the subject as the source of tension is the basis for aggression-provoking emotions or emotions blocking external expression of aggression. A number of models and studies specify the conditions and mechanisms of aggression in response to threat; this problem has been discussed in detail particularly in studies of psychological stress and stress control (Lazarus 1966; Frączek and Kofta 1975). In my opinion a considerable amount of interpersonal aggression is initiated and controlled by this mechanism. Cognitive processes and structures play a significant part in this mechanism, since they determine whether emotional motivation for aggression will appear and what properties it will have.

Another source of interpersonal aggression, complementary to that discussed above, is the norms, principles, and values registered in the cognitive structures, compelling the subject to attack and destroy the environment in certain situations. This issue has been discussed at length by Feshbach (1974), who shows that internalized norms and standards of conduct determine the degree and type of aggression manifested in specific situations—for instance, in response to attack. According to Feshbach (1964, 1974), the internalization of such a norm, now of historical value but once obligatory, as "an eye for an eye" or "a tooth for a tooth," ". . . defines the infliction of injury as the appropriate response to be made to the experience of injury. The norm of retaliation, then, according to this view, can provide one source of aggressive motivation." Thus, the development of aggression in ontogeny consists not only in the forming of behavior patterns or individual motivation but also in the acquisition and internalization of standards, rules, and norms determining when, how, and to whom one should behave aggressively, as well as under what circumstances one ought to refrain from aggression.

We must analyze the development and functioning of such norms within the framework of the determinants and mechanisms ruling the moral and cognitive development of the individual. Of course, as Feshbach (1974) points out, while the content of internalized standards of regulation and their position in the system of regulating mechanisms depend on social experience, the ability to perceive, understand, and assimilate socially developed norms depends on the level of cognitive functioning of the developing individual. It is possible that certain defects in socialization, resulting from lack of internalization of social norms and standards of behavior, are caused by too early or too late confrontation with social demands.

Standards associated with self-image and self-esteem play a role in the regulation of aggression similar to that of moral norms and standards of conduct (Reykowski 1973, 1975). We can learn from the psychological knowledge concerning socialization and its determinants (Thompson 1971) how these norms and standards, instigating or blocking various forms of interpersonal aggression, develop. Nonemotional motivation toward interpersonal aggression is also analyzed in discussions on delinquent subcultures and the factors causing particular individuals to acquire aggressive subcultural norms (Wolfgang and Ferracuti 1967; Kosewski 1973; Malak 1975).

PROGRAMMING AND CONTROL OF AGGRESSION

Cognitive mechanisms participate in the programming and control of aggression through modification of the intensity and features of actions in response to various external demands and internal norms or standards of conduct, and through planning and selecting those types and forms of aggressive behavior that are optimal for the goals the individual means to achieve. Feedback concerning the consequences of the individual's own behavior and anticipation of its effects are particularly important in this process. Aggression, like other forms of interpersonal behavior, can be more or less elastic; and this elasticity probably depends to a large extent on the participation of higher-order cognitive mechanisms in the control of behavior.

The role of cognitive mechanisms in determining the intensity of aggression, depending on external circumstances, has been shown in many empirical studies. Thus, for example, the intensity of punishment of a partner in the laboratory depends on the relations between the age, sex, and physical fitness of the partner and of the aggressor (Buss 1966). These features of the victim of aggression activate internalized norms and, hence, regulate the dynamics of behavior. The intensity of retaliatory forms of aggression also depends on convictions regarding the degree to which given behavior deserves retaliation and the magnitude of retaliation that will effectively reduce undesirable behavior. Incidentally, general beliefs as to the effectiveness of punishment in the modification of aggression differ substantially from scientific findings or even common-sense analysis of generally available information.

The dynamics of aggression, especially the choice of particular types or forms, is also determined by knowledge concerning harmful or painful types of behavior. The probability that one person will use a knife to stab another or a pistol to shoot an enemy is greater if that person has seen such things happen or at least knows that such behavior is possible (Bandura 1969, 1973). On the other hand, awareness of the tragic results of using such weapons and anxiety associated with such awareness can lead to the selection of less drastic forms of aggression. To some extent, knowledge of possible forms of aggressive behavior and their outcomes makes possible the control of interpersonal aggression, at least in others if not in oneself.

The characteristic features of interpersonal aggression are determined by feedback on its consequences and anticipation of its outcome. The significance of this type of cognitive regulation of aggression is well illustrated in the studies of the effect on further aggressive behavior of observing pain signals in the victim of one's own attack (Baron 1971a, 1971b; Buss 1966; Buss and Brock 1963; Geen 1970; Tilker 1970; Eliasz 1975). Many interesting regularities have been found in these studies. As a rule, observation of the victim's pain usually leads to reduction of secondary aggression, both that determined by negative emotions and task-oriented aggression. It has also been found that the closer the relationship between the aggressor and the victim, the more observation of pain inhibits further aggression; observed pain has especially strong inhibitory effects when the victim is perceived as similar to "self." I may add that perception of others as similar to self implicitly inhibits interpersonal aggression against people thus perceived, even when the aggressor does not observe signs of pain (Kość 1975).

Several mechanisms underlie the inhibition of aggression in response to observed pain signals. Signs of pain inform the aggressor that the activity has been effective if the aggression was intentional (Berkowitz 1974) or has led to undesirable effects if it was incidental. In the first case the action has reached its goal and there is no need to continue it; in the second case the action will be modified or interrupted as inadequate. Observation of pain signals may also lead to the actualization of norms according to which aggression is immoral and socially harmful. The emotional component produced by observing pain in the victim of one's aggression is an important, and often the only, factor enabling anticipation of the consequences of one's aggressive behavior. It signals the possibility of punishment or restrictions, or leads to feelings of guilt.

There are, on the other hand, several occasions on which observation of pain signals and the anticipation of negative consequences of one's aggression aggravate rather than inhibit interpersonal aggression. The analysis of real-life situations (such as lynchings, pacification of Vietnamese villages, fights among gangs) and laboratory investigations (Buss 1966; Kwiatkowska 1975) leads to the conclusion that observation of pain signals may intensify aggression if the aggressor is convinced that the aggression is an essential and effective way of achieving the desired goals and that it is morally justified. Such factors as diffusion of responsibility, the feeling that one's behavior is anonymous, and slackening of outer or inner control also limit or diminish the anticipatory mechanisms that block aggression. Hence, aggression under such circumstances is especially intensive and brutal (Bandura et al. 1975; Bandura 1973; Zimbardo 1969).

REFERENCES

Bandura, A. 1976. "Social Learning Analysis of Aggression." In *Analysis of Delinquency and Aggression*, ed. E. Ribes-Inesta and A. Bandura. Hillsdale, Ca.: LEA Publishers.

———. 1973. *Aggression. A Social Learning Analysis*. Englewood Cliffs, N.J.: Prentice-Hall.

———. 1969. *Principles of Behavior Modification*. New York: Holt, Rinehart and Winston.

———, B. Underwood, and M. E. Fromson. 1975. "Disinhibition of Aggression Through Diffusion of Responsibility and Dehumanization of Victims." *Journal of Research in Personality* 9:253–69.

Bandura, A., and R. H. Walters. 1959. *Adolescent Aggression*. New York: Ronald Press.

Baron, R. A. 1971b. "Aggression as a Function of Magnitude of Victim's Pain Cues, Level of Prior Anger Arousal and Aggressor-Victim Similarity." *Journal of Personality and Social Psychology* 18:48–54.

———. 1971a. "Magnitude of Victim's Pain Cues and Level of Prior Anger Arousal as Determinants of Adult Aggressive Behavior." *Journal of Personality and Social Psychology* 17: 236–43.

Berkowitz, L. 1974. "Some Determinants of Impulsive Aggression." In *Determinants and Origins of Aggressive Behavior*, ed. W. W. Hartup and J. DeWit. The Hague: Mouton.

———. 1962. *Aggression: A Social Psychological Analysis*. New York: McGraw-Hill.

———, ed. 1969. *Roots of Aggression. A Re-examination of the Frustration-Aggression Hypothesis*. New York: Atherton Press.

———, J. P. Lepinski, and E. J. Angulo. 1969. "Awareness of Own Anger Level and Subsequent Aggression." *Journal of Personality and Social Psychology* 11: 293–300.

Buss, A. H. 1966. "Instrumentality of Aggression, Feedback and Frustration as Determinants of Physical Aggression." *Journal of Personality and Social Psychology* 3, no. 3: 153–62.

———. 1961. *The Psychology of Aggression*. New York: John Wiley.

———, and T. Brock. 1963. "Repression and Guilt in Relation to Aggression." *Journal of Abnormal and Social Psychology* 66, no. 4: 345–60.

Ciarkowska, W. 1975. "Wpływ specyficznej stymulacji emocjonalnej oraz cech osobowości na intensywność zachowania agresywnego" (The influence of specific emotional stimulation and personality traits on the intensity of aggressive behavior). In *Z zagadnień psychologii agresji* (Problems of psychology of aggression), ed. A. Frączek. Warsaw: Wydawnictwo PIPS.

Cofer, C. N., and M. H. Appley. 1964. *Motivation: Theory and Research.* New York: John Wiley.

Dollard, J., and N. E. Miller. 1950. *Personality and Psychotherapy. An Analysis in Terms of Learning, Thinking and Culture.* New York: McGraw-Hill.

Dollard, J., et al. 1939. *Frustration and Aggression.* New Haven: Yale University Press.

Eliasz, H. 1975. "Znaczenie obserwowania bólu doznawanego przez 'ofiarę' dla regulacji agresywnego zachowania się" (Significance of observation of the victim's "pain" as a regulator in aggressive behavior). In *Z zagadnień psychologii agresji* (Problems of psychology of aggression), ed. A. Frączek. Warsaw: Wydawnictwo PIPS.

Eysenck, H. J. 1960. *The Structure of Human Personality.* London: Methuen.

Feshbach, N. D. 1974. "The Relationship of Child-Rearing Factors to Children's Aggression, Empathy and Related Positive and Negative Social Behaviors." In *Determinants and Origins of Aggressive Behavior*, ed. W. W. Hartup and J. DeWit, pp. 427–36. The Hague: Mouton.

Feshbach, S. 1974. "Cognitive Processes in the Development and Regulation of Aggression." In *Determinants and Origins of Aggressive Behavior*, ed. W. W. Hartup and J. DeWit, pp. 167–92. The Hague: Mouton.

———. 1970. "Aggression." In *Carmichael's Manual of Child Psychology*, ed. P. H. Mussen. New York: John Wiley.

———. 1964. "The Function of Aggression and the Regulation of Aggressive Drive." *Psychological Review* 71: 257–72.

———, and R. D. Singer. 1974. *Television and Aggression.* San Francisco: Jossey-Bass.

Festinger, L. 1958. "The Motivating Effect of Cognitive Dissonance." In *Assessment of Human Motives*, ed. G. Lindzey. New York: Reinhart.

——. 1957. *A Theory of Cognitive Dissonance*. Evanston, Ill.: Row, Peterson.

Frączek, A. 1975. "Mechanizmy regulacyjne czynności agresywnych" (Mechanisms of aggressive behavior). In *Studia nad teoria czynności ludzkich* (Study of the theory of human actions), ed. I. Kurcz and J. Reykowski. Warsaw: PWN.

——. 1974. "Informational Role of Situation as a Determinant of Aggressive Behavior." In *Determinants and Origins of Aggressive Behavior*, ed. W. W. Hartup and J. DeWit, pp. 225–32. The Hague: Mouton.

——. 1973. "Problems of the Psychological Theory of Aggression." *Polish Psychological Bulletin* 4: 91–96.

——, and W. Ciarkowska. 1974. "The Dynamics of Aggressive Behavior in Relation to Neuroticism, Extroversion and Introversion." Warsaw. (Mimeographed.)

Frączek, A., and M. Kofta. 1975. "Frustracja i stress psychologiczny" (Frustration and psychological stress). In *Psychologia* (Psychology), ed. T. Tomaszewski. Warsaw: PWN.

Frączek, A., and J. Macaulay. 1971. "Some Personality Factors in Reaction to Aggressive Stimuli." *Journal of Personality* 39: 163–77.

Freud, S. 1920. *Beyond the Pleasure Principle*. New York: International Psychoanalytic Press.

Gajda-Ciarkowska, W. 1971. "Znaczenie emocjonalne bodzca jako czynnik modyfikujacy zachowanie agresywne" (Emotional meaning of stimulus as a determinant of aggressive behavior). Master's thesis, University of Warsaw.

Geen, R. G. 1970. "Perceived Suffering of the Victim as an Inhibitor of Attack-Induced Aggression." *Journal of Social Psychology* 81: 209–15.

——, and E. L. O'Neal. 1969. "Activation of Cue-Elicited Aggression by General Arousal." *Journal of Personality and Social Psychology* 11: 289–92.

Geen, R. G., and P. C. Powers. 1971. "Shock and Noise as Instigation Stimuli in Human Aggression." *Psychological Reports* 28: 983–85.

Geller, S. 1975. "Funkcje mechanizmow poznawczych w regulacji agresji" (The function of cognitive mechanisms in the regulation of aggression). In *Z zagadnień psychologii agresji* (Problems of psychology of aggression), ed. A. Frączek. Warsaw: Wydawnictwo PIPS.

Hartman, R. 1969. "Influence of Symbolically Modeled Aggression and Pain Cues on Aggressive Behavior." *Journal of Personality and Social Psychology* 11, no. 3: 280–88.

Heider, F. 1958. *The Psychology of Interpersonal Relations*. New York: John Wiley.

Hilgard, E. R., and D. G. Marquis. 1940. *Conditioning and Learning*. New York: Appleton-Century-Crofts.

Kosć, Z. 1975. "Podobieństwo 'agresora' do 'ofiary' a natężenie czynności agresywnej" (The "aggressor's" resemblance to the "victim" and the intensity of the aggressive behavior). In *Z zagadnień psychologii agresji* (Problems of psychology of aggression), ed. A. Frączek. Warsaw: Wydawnictwo PIPS.

Kosewski, M. 1973. "Funkcje agresji w spolecznosci zamknietego zakladu karnego" (Functions of aggression within the community of the closed penal institutions). *Psychologia wychowawcza* (Educational psychology) 26, no. 3: 332–43.

Kozielecki, J. 1975. "Czynnosc podejmowania decyzji" (Action of making decisions). In *Psychologia* (Psychology), ed. T. Tomaszewski. Warsaw: PWN.

Kwiatkowska, A. 1975. "Antycypacja skutkow agresji jako czynnik regulajacy czynnosci agresywne" (Anticipation of effects of one's own aggression as a determinant of aggressive behavior). Master's thesis, University of Warsaw.

Lazarus, R. S. 1966. *Psychological Stress and the Coping Process*. New York: McGraw-Hill.

Leontiew, A. N. 1975. *Dejatjelnost, soznanie, licznost* (Action, cognition, personality). Moscow: Politizdat.

Malak, B. 1975. "Wlasnosci osobowosci a rodzaj uczestnictwa w podkulturze zakladu poprawczego" (Personality dispositions and the manner of participation in the juvenile delinquent subculture). In *Z zagadnień psychologii agresji* (Problems of psychology of aggression), ed. A. Frączek. Warsaw: Wydawnictwo PIPS.

Maslow, A. H. 1954. *Motivation and Personality*. New York: Harper.

Murray, H. A. 1938. *Explorations in Personality*. New York: John Wiley.

Pavlov, I. P. 1927. *Conditioned Reflexes*. London: Oxford University Press.

Reykowski, J. 1976. "Presocial Orientation and Self-Structure." In *Studies on the Mechanisms of Presocial Behavior*, ed. J. Reykowski. Warsaw: Warsaw University Press.

———. 1975. "Position of Self-Structure in a Cognitive System and Presocial Orientation." *Dialectics and Humanism* 4: 19–30.

Rule, B. G. 1974. "The Hostile and Instrumental Function of Human Aggression." In *Determinants of Aggressive Behavior*, ed. J. de Wit and W. W. Hartup. The Hague: Mouton.

Schachter, S., and J. E. Singer. 1962. "Cognitive, Social, and Psychological Determinants of Emotional State." *Psychological Review* 69: 379–99.

Sheerer, M. 1962. "Cognition-Theory, Research, Promise." In *Papers Read at the Martin Sheerer Memorial Meetings on Cognitive Psychology*, ed. C. Sheerer. London: Harper and Row.

Skinner, B. F. 1953. *Science and Human Behavior*. New York: Macmillan.

Strelau, J. 1975. "Temperament." In *Psychologia* (Psychology), ed. T. Tomaszewski. Warsaw: PWN.

Thompson, G. G., ed. 1971. *Social Development and Personality*. New York: John Wiley.

Tilker, H. A. 1970. "Socially Responsible Behavior as a Function of Observer Responsibility and Victim Feedback." *Journal of Personality and Social Psychology* 14, no. 1: 95–100.

Tomaszewski, T. 1975. "Podstawowe formy organizacji i regulacji zachowania" (The basic forms of organization and regulation of behavior). In *Psychologia* (Psychology), ed. T. Tomaszewski. Warsaw: PWN.

———. 1963. *Wstep do psychologii* (Introduction to psychology). Warsaw: PWN.

Ulrich, R., and B. Symannek. 1969. "Pain as a Stimulus for Aggression." In *Aggressive Behavior*, ed. S. Garatini and E. B. Sigg. Amsterdam: Excerpta Medica.

Watson, J. B. 1930. *Behaviorism*, rev. ed. New York: W. W. Norton.

Wolfgang, M. E., and F. Ferracuti. 1967. *The Subculture of Violence*. London: Tavistock.

Wolpe, J. 1958. *Psychotherapy by Reciprocal Inhibition*. Stanford: Stanford University Press.

Yates, A. J. 1975. *Theory and Practice in Behavior Therapy*. New York: John Wiley.

Young, P. T. 1961. *Motivation and Emotion*. New York: John Wiley.

Zimbardo, P. G. 1969. "The Human Choice: Individuation, Reason and Order Versus Deindividuation, Impulse and Chaos." *Nebraska Symposium on Motivation* XVII, ed. M. Jones. Lincoln: University of Nebraska Press.

7

INTRINSIC MOTIVATION AND INTRINSIC INHIBITION OF AGGRESSIVE BEHAVIOR

Janusz Reykowski

Studies on the control of aggressive behavior over a rather long period of time traditionally were based on the assumption that the basic way of controlling aggressive tendencies is an appropriately directed aversive stimulation. Such a control may consist of a counterconditioning through fear of the internalization of social norms prohibiting or restricting aggression, with the effects that aggressive intentions arouse anxiety and that a possible realization of an aggressive act produces a feeling of guilt. Fear, anxiety, and the feeling of guilt act like externally applied bridles to secure and maintain control of aggression, whatever its source may be.

The theory of social learning enriched this repertoire by introducing the principle of modeling. Thanks to modeling a human being can be convinced, without having to experience a specific, direct learning experience, that aggression leads to negative consequences (is punished) or that it is ineffective. An individual also has a chance to learn nonaggressive ways of solving problems that previously were solved aggressively (Bandura 1969, 1971).

Studies of aggression's cognitive regulators have pointed to two other types of factors that can control aggression. One line of research indicates that signal stimuli constitute one category of such factors. The presence of signals possessing aggressive connotations can, as follows from the studies carried out by L. Berkowitz, facilitate aggressive reactions (Berkowitz 1973); studies of these phenomena have also been conducted in Warsaw by A. Frączek. It was found that the intensity of an aggressive behavior may undergo a change depending on whether, in a particular situation, signals formerly associated with frustration experiences, or actions that had an aggressive meaning, appear or do not appear (Frączek 1973, 1975a). A collaborator of A. Frączek's also found that the presence of signals associated with an emotionally positive experience may weaken aggression (Ciarkowska 1975).

S. Feshbach (1973) has drawn our attention to another group of aggression regulators. He has presented arguments supporting the thesis that the regulation of aggression depends on specific cognitive standards that regulate when, to whom, and how much of an aggressive payoff should be made. The control of aggression is merely an appropriate formation of standards that play a mediating role in the generation of aggressive behaviors.

The diverse conceptions of controlling aggression are not simply describing different but mutually supplementary mechanisms. On the contrary, adherents of some of these conceptions are inclined to believe that recommendations implied in other conceptions are not only ineffective but bring about effects opposite to what had been intended. For instance, punishment for an act of aggression is, according to some of them, the best way of enhancing it (Bandura 1971); a discharge of aggression (real or vicarious) has not a cathartic effect but, on the contrary, maintains aggressive behaviors (Bandura 1971; Berkowitz 1973).

The ways of controlling aggression cannot be discussed, however, without taking into account the fact that phenomena described by the term "aggressive behavior" may have different causes and different mechanisms. In this connection it is highly probable that the particular regulators of aggression described in psychological literature will not have a uniform effect on different kinds of aggression.

Several kinds of aggression can be discerned. Feshbach (1964) mentions hostile aggression and instrumental aggression, and divides the latter into a kind guided by a personal motivation and another kind in which the aim is to gain something for someone else (or for society). Frączek (1975a, b) draws one's attention to a similar phenomenon when he speaks of task-oriented aggression, an example of which is an aggressive behavior instigated by an experimental situation according to Milgram's paradigm.

Still another kind of aggression may depend upon the intrinsic rewarding value of aggressive acts and upon the effects of aggressive behavior; this phenomenon was described by Zimbardo (1969). This is a particularly dangerous kind of aggression—"for the pleasure of it." One can avoid hostile aggression by taking care not to provoke the particular aggressor, and one can avoid instrumental aggression by giving the aggressor whatever is wanted or by complying with the requirements whose violation instigates the aggression. None of these things, however, will satisfy the aggressor who acts aggressively for the pleasure of doing so—the more the victim suffers, the more satisfaction the aggressor gets. If the victim does not suffer much, the aggressor is inclined to intensify the attack.

One can expect hostile aggression to be controlled by external circumstances that stimulate aggressive acts, and instrumental aggression by external factors that reward these aggressive behaviors. In both instances the regulation of aggression depends in a large measure (though not exclusively) upon external events; it also depends on norms taken over from the society that both prohibit aggression and demand it under certain conditions. Both kinds of aggression are also dependent upon models and means of aggressive actions supplied by the society.

A question arises: What factors can control intrinsically motivated aggression—that is, aggression that comes into being on the basis of the mechanism of anticipation of satisfaction from the act of aggression?

I think that on the basis of the data available thus far, one may venture a hypothesis that besides the factors intrinsically stimulating to aggression there are intrinsic factors blocking aggression. Such factors may be sought among the mechanisms of the prosocial motivation. Later I will discuss the characteristics of what have been described here as factors intrinsically stimulating aggression and the characteristics of the prosocial motivation as a mechanism blocking aggression.

INTRINSIC MOTIVATION TO AGGRESSION

In spite of numerous efforts, especially by psychoanalytically oriented investigators and by ethologists (Lorenz 1966), to demonstrate that in man, as in animals, there is an innate drive to aggression, it seems that no sufficient empirical grounds exist to make such a theory acceptable (Bandura 1971). However, I believe that there are grounds for supposing that specific temperamental traits and developmental circumstances lead to the formation of mechanisms through which aggressive behavior and its consequences become a category of sought-after rewards. Moreover, one cannot exclude the possibility that they acquire the properties of needs—that is, a deficit of these rewards may elicit increasing discomfort as the period of deprivation lengthens, and this state of discomfort may be eliminated through the performance of appropriate acts.* I look for the factors that lead to the formation of one's self-structure.

In the 1950s a thesis was formulated that a deficiency, as much as an excess, of stimulation is an aversive phenomenon and that an organism behaves in such a way as to receive an optimum amount of stimulation. Such a view, contrary to the previously widespread belief that animals and humans alike tend toward the reduction of drives (toward the avoidance of stimulation), was explicitly formulated by D. O. Hebb (1955), who cited experiments on sensory deprivation (Bexton et al. 1954) as an obvious argument against the traditional conceptions. Analyzing similar phenomena, C. Leuba (1955) drew attention to the fact that human beings learn to act in such a way as to receive stimulation in an amount proportional to the actual demand: they learn acts, therefore, that either restrain or increase the incoming stimulation. Also, data collected by other authors indicate that humans learn to behave in a manner that enhances stimu-

---

*According to B. F. Skinner (1953), a distinguishing characteristic of a drive is the existence of the operation of a deprivation and a satiation. This criterion is applied here to the concept of need, since the notion of drive is interpreted differently by many authors.

lation, as is shown in the notion of "diversive exploration" in D. E. Berlyne (1965) and other data cited by that author (Berlyne 1967). There is a list of findings to support the view that a deficiency of stimulation may be a source of very strong negative emotions.

The facts presented above show, therefore, that the "mental apparatus" functions correctly when it maintains arousal within specified limits, which is possible when it is appropriately stimulated—just as the human organism can function correctly only when it maintains the temperature of the body on an appropriate level, and this depends on the quantity of heat received from the environment and generated by the body itself. This can be expressed differently in the statement that the organism tends to maintain an optimum arousal level and, in connection with this level, frequently exhibits a demand for stimulation.

The optimum level of arousal and the amount of stimulation required for the maintenance of this level are likely to be different at different times in the same person, and different in different persons. As regards the intraindividual changeability, various factors influence the demand for stimulation, including state of health, secretion of the hormones, fatigue, stimulating or depressant drugs (Leuba 1955), and (especially) habituation. To put it another way, we may expect that the total stimulation to which a person is subjected over a certain period of time determines that individual's adaptation level; therefore, the same stimuli that at one time acted as strongly stimulating ones and maintained the arousal of the subject on an optimal level may, at a different time, lose their stimulating capacity (Helson 1959, 1966). Conversely, spending a long time in a situation devoid of stimuli or in which their effects are very limited may enhance sensitivity, and thus stimuli that formerly were regarded as very weak and of no consequence may begin to arouse interest. For instance, after some time spent in a stimulus-impoverished environment, subjects were inclined to read old stock exchange reports with interest. Rodents kept a long time in isolation exhibit a number of symptoms of enhanced sensitivity to stimuli: their exploratory activities are reduced, their response to pain rises, their sexual activity diminishes (Valzelli 1973).

There are also grounds for supposing that permanent differences exist among humans with respect to the demand for stimulation. This variable has been investigated in various contexts in the laboratory of J. Strelau in Warsaw. Strelau is of the opinion that the demand for stimulation depends on a relatively permanent property of a human being: psychological reactivity (Strelau 1974). The notion of psychological reactivity, which is linked to the theory of the "types of the nervous system" developed by Pavlov and his successors (Teplov 1961; Nebylicyn 1966; Strelau 1972), concerns the hypothetical property of the entire process of reception, on which depend the sensitivity threshold and (connected with it) the efficiency threshold. This property, investigated by Strelau and his collaborators by means of a specially constructed inventory (Strelau 1972), exhibits stability over long periods of time—the test-retest correlation coefficient after an interval of one year amounted to as much as .69 (Strelau unpublished data).

Persons differing with respect to psychological reactivity also display characteristic differences in diverse spheres of behavior. It has been ascertained, for instance, that among persons whose professions entail a risk of strong physical stress (such as pilots) or social stress (such as lawyers) there is a larger proportion of individuals with low psychological reactivity than in professions where either of those stresses are low (such as librarians) (Eliasz 1974a, b). It also was found that people of a given profession who differ with respect to psychological reactivity differ in the style of their work: persons with a high degree of psychological reactivity pay more attention to preparatory and auxiliary actions, so as to avoid any unexpected situations, while persons with a low psychological reactivity rely on improvisational tactics and, as a consequence, are obliged to cope with surprising situations (Strelau 1975). Persons differing in psychological reactivity also differ in the style of self-regulation in a manner analogous to that described above. Data gathered in Strelau's laboratory indicate that people with a low degree of psychological reactivity—and, therefore, have considerable demand for stimulation—exhibit interest in stress-generating situations.

How can one explain the differences in psychological reactivity? We cannot exclude the role of genetic factors. Strelau cites a number of observations in support of the thesis that reactivity as a temperamental trait may be inherited (Strelau 1975). It seems likely that an important role is also played by the quantity of stimulation to which an individual is exposed in the course of development. It is possible that people who live in environments rich in stimulation gradually increase their adaptation level and, consequently, continuously lower their psychological reactivity. Such a hypothesis, however, ought to be verified, since it is not known whether experience could permanently determine such a temperamental property as psychological reactivity. In favor of such a supposition one may cite observations showing that the demand for stimulation among men brought up in a relatively poor and monotonous environment (as in a village far from population centers) may be much lower than that of men accustomed to life in a big city.

What kind of consequences can one expect from a heightened threshold of sensitivity to stimulation? From the description given above, it would follow that for people whose need for stimulation is rather high, an ordinary quantity of stimulation attainable under normal conditions may prove to be insufficient. Therefore, such people will seek situations that could increase their stimulation. High stimulation is associated with strong physical stimuli, sudden changes in situations, very complex situations, and affectively toned physical stimuli (Pieron 1950). With regard to the principal issue that this paper addresses, of particular importance is the high stimulating value of kinesthetic stimuli connected with the performance of strong, violent movements. Apart from the above, all kinds of situations signaling dangers, physical as well as social, carry a strong charge of stimulation; for this reason situations that are risky (such as violation of social norms) can have a strong stimulating effect.

In light of the above description, it is obvious that aggressive behavior can be a source of strong stimulation. This stimulation is generated by one's own actions (when aggression consists of a physical attack) and by the facts that aggression carries danger with it, that it very often brings about a violation of norms, and that the effect of an aggressive behavior sometimes manifests itself in a sudden change in the physical state of an object (a shattering or breaking). To this one should add the expression of pain and fear, the sight of blood and wounds, cries, and so on. It seems that even imagined acts of aggression and their imagined effects, such as physical and mental sufferings of a victim, can have a strong stimulating value.

People who are stimulation-hungry are likely to regard aggression favorably. When one takes this possibility into account, an alternative, integrating interpretation of a good deal of existing data becomes possible. For instance, the statement made by S. Schachter that "habitual criminals" (sociopaths) show a very low level of anxiety (Schachter and Latane 1964) could be interpreted as a consequence of a great demand for stimulation in this category of persons. (See data concerning a negative correlation between the level of psychological reactivity and the level of anxiety) (Strelau 1975). One can interpret similarly the results of B. Hutchings (1973), who, studying criminality of adopted children and their adoptive and biological parents in Denmark, concluded that "Hereditary effect is in the direction of being more important than the environmental." If hereditary factors determine in some measure the level of psychological reactivity, then it is quite possible that a very low level of this reactivity (strong demand for stimulation) in fathers and sons is propitious to the learning of antisocial behaviors (as particularly gratifying).

Thus, the analysis presented above suggests that aggressive behaviors can be a learned technique to compensate for a stimulation deficiency. Such a deficiency may be an incidental phenomenon. For instance, the provocative factors may at times heighten the adaptation level, and this may facilitate aggressive actions.* It is highly probable that such a role can be played by frustration and stress. A similar influence can be exerted by factors that create sexual arousal (Bandura 1971) and by participating in a competition, both for those who lose and for those who win (Bandura 1971).

It should be added that an increase in psychological reactivity may lead to an increment in aggressive behaviors—but, as one can assume, on an entirely different basis: it is not aggression for pleasure, but a defensive aggression; it is

---

*It is worth noting that there is an analogy between the demand for stimulation and the sexual need: the latter can increase under the influence of deprivation as well as under sexual provocation; the same stimuli that arouse one are at the same time the stimuli sought under the influence of the arousal.

a reaction to an excess of stimulation and serves as a means of diminishing it. People who are characterized by high psychological reactivity will not, therefore, look for an occasion on which they can behave aggressively, but can become aggressive in response to a stimulation that—for them—is too strong. This could explain the aggressiveness of mice and rats kept in isolation (Valzelli 1973).

Thus, aggression can be reactive or operant. The present considerations concern the latter type—that is, the instances when people actively look for circumstances in which they can realize aggressive acts, like the mice examined by the Finnish investigator Kirsti Lagerspetz, which, when aroused to aggression, actively searched for a victim to attack (Berkowitz 1965). It is exactly in circumstances like this that aggression and its outcome gain the value of an intrinsic reward.

The analysis presented above explained the intrinsic motivation to aggression as a phenomenon depending on the properties and the functional condition of the primary regulating mechanism—the mechanism that mediates optimum arousal. It seems, however, that this is not the only origin of this form of aggressive motivation. In my opinion, it can also arise in a rather different way: in connection with the formation of a higher regulating structure—that is, of the cognitive network, and, within this network, of a specific mechanism: self-structure.

Considering the cognitive network as a particular kind of registration of experience in the human mind, one can regard self-structure as a subsystem of that network formed in consequence of the differentiation and integration of three kinds of information:

1. Information concerning the state (physical and mental) of the subject, distinguished from information concerning the state of external objects; thus, self-structure provides the basis for discerning between self and nonself.

2. Information concerning the outcomes of one's own actions, discerned from information about the results of other people's actions and of the actions of natural forces; the formation of the self-structure thus becomes the basis of the experience of control of events (discerning between the external and the internal locus of control of events) (Rotter 1966).

3. Information about one's value in comparison with the value of other social and physical objects; this is the foundation for the formation of self-esteem (Reykowski 1975, 1976a, b).

Self-structure, therefore, is an instrument of orientation through which the basic differentiations are made (Piaget 1966): in me; in the outside world controlled by me; in the outside world controlled by outside forces—raising (lowering) my value, raising (lowering) the value of others. The self-structure is also a source of a powerful motivation: toward the maintenance of one's own separateness and identity; toward the maintenance and increase of one's control over the environment (an increase of such control is the source of rewarding experiences, while its loss is experienced as a strongly punitive event); toward the maintenance, protection, and increase of self-esteem. Appropriate information has gratifying or punitive value. The source of motivation lies in the discrepancy between anticipations originating in the relevant regions of the cognitive network and information coming from the outside world or generated from within the system. An individual learns those forms of behavior that can ensure the supply of desirable information, and learns to remove discrepancies that can occur.*

Aggressive behaviors may prove to be a good means of gaining a confirmation or an increase of control. This is an experience known to babies who find that their temper tantrums can be an effective means of controlling their parents. Aggression can prove to be a particularly easy way of coping with problems of control because an aggressive activity, should it prove to be effective, supplies quick and clear signals confirming one's power and competence. The simplest act of destruction is a confirmation of one's strength and prowess. The ability to vanquish an adversary, to humiliate that person, to make the opponent do things the aggressor wants done and that are obviously against the will of the loser constitute direct and unquestionable information confirming one's control.

Aggressive behaviors are also a convenient means of protecting, strengthening, and enhancing one's self-esteem. In view of the fact that the evaluation of one's worth depends on the comparison between one's own position and the positions occupied by other people, one's self-esteem may increase either when one's own position is heightened or when the position of others is lowered. The achievement of the latter objective is served very well by aggressive behavior. Even symbolic aggression, consisting in the utterance of contemptuous opinions to a person who has gained some success, may diminish a distress caused by the relative lowering of one's own status. Still more satisfaction could be derived from actions that cause the lucky adversary actually to be degraded. Manifestations of humiliation and pain are signals confirming one's own supremacy that can also strengthen one's feeling of worth (Feshbach 1964).†

The ease with which aggression can be used to solve the problems of control and self-esteem, and the direct effects it produces, may facilitate its learning in the early stages of the formation of the self-structure. This fact can explain some of the manifestations of unprovoked aggressiveness among children. But there are other means of solving problems connected with the sphere

---

*An individual can also show preferences for a certain, but not very high, level of discrepancy (Hebb 1955; Hunt 1965). This is probably due to the stimulating influence of the discrepancy, and depends on the demand for stimulation.

†Still another form of engaging one's feelings of self-esteem as a mechanism stimulating aggressive behaviors is being analyzed by S. Feshbach. He points out that in many, if not most, cultures appropriate revenge is necessary for maintaining one's self-esteem.

166 / Janusz Reykowski

of "self." In what kinds of situations does an individual prefer aggressive solutions? It seems that there are circumstances that favor the consolidation of aggressive coping techniques.

First of all, one should expect an important part to be played by the magnitude of the demand for confirmatory information (with respect to control or self-esteem). This magnitude will be a function of the level of uncertainty of one's own power and competence, and of self-esteem. This uncertainty may have its source in either unfavorable circumstances during socialization—the degree of one's certainty about one's own worth seems to depend in a large measure on the way in which one was valued by parents (Rogers 1959)—or in various physical or psychological defects of the subject. Likewise, a low social position, being at a disadvantage, and belonging to a group of uncertain status are factors conducive to a feeling of uncertainty with respect to self-esteem (Bettelheim and Janowitz 1950; Greenblum and Pearlin 1953).

Uncertainty concerning one's control of events and the anxiety connected with this uncertainty may pertain to a small or large scope of phenomena. It may apply to some particular area. In such a case the acts directed at confirming control will be focused on that particular area; for instance, one could try to overcome a fear of pain by inflicting pain on oneself or on others; the fear of wounds and blood, by inflicting wounds or observation of mutilated people; the fear of death, by causing death. I should add, however, that the examples mentioned above are manifestations of very primitive, magic forms of gaining control, based on a simple reversal of fear-generating situations (I am afraid, and therefore, contrary to what I feel, I act as if I am not afraid).

In the second place, the choice of aggressive reactions as a technique of coping with the problems of control and self-esteem depends also on resources that are available to the subject, such as physical strength, the subject's social position, and social and intellectual competence. In addition, the subject has to have an occasion for learning aggressive forms of behavior. If no such possibility is available, aggressive intentions may stop at the symbolic level and remain in the sphere of fantasy.

In the third place, the choice of aggressive reactions will be more probable if the individual has no possibility of mastering other techniques of coping with the problems of self-esteem and of control—for instance, the individual never came in contact with nonaggressive models or never learned the ego shields necessary for delaying gratification (Barron 1953). This pattern is illustrated by the results of studies by H. Toch of people who readily resort to violence (criminals as well as policemen): "High sensitivity to embarrassing treatment is usually combined with deficient skill for resolving disputes and restoring self-esteem by verbal means" (Bandura 1971).

All three kinds of factors mentioned above may be observed in children who bully their peers. D. Olweus (1973), in his studies of bullying behavior, found that the following were true of a typical bully:

1. He had a negative attitude toward his father and felt less liked by his parents than other children. Considering the role that acceptance by parents has on the child's self-esteem, such a feeling strongly suggests that the bully has a problem in this area.

2. He was physically stronger than other boys (thus, gaining supremacy over them was very easy). It is worth adding that the victims were recruited, as a rule, among boys who were weaker than others.

3. His school achievements were average or lower than average; therefore, the possibilities of raising his self-esteem through success in school were limited.

The analysis presented above indicates that under certain conditions aggression may become a convenient means of solving personal problems involving one's ego.* Frequent and effective performance of this role can lead to the behavior's becoming an important factor in the individual's psychological balance. Aggression may occur as a permanent means of solving these problems, or it can appear from time to time, whenever anxiety concerning self-esteem or control is aroused—or whenever "suitable objects" emerge—that is, persons who can be attacked with impunity.

Thus, when we ask why aggression arouses so much interest among human beings and why they are so fascinated by violence and brute force, we should not forget that we deal here with a form of behavior that is strongly linked to very important problems of the individual: the means of maintaining an optimal "stimulation" (of the same importance to the "mental apparatus" as optimal temperature is to the organism) and maintaining balance in the self-structure, which is the central mechanism for the integration of human actions.

INTRINSIC FACTORS INHIBITING AGGRESSION

Ethologists, when they compare intraspecific aggression (animal and human), draw attention to the fact that species endowed by nature with dangerous instruments of attack, such as fangs, claws, powerful beaks, or horns, develop techniques of blocking aggression. It is sufficient for a wolf losing a fight with another wolf to uncover its neck to the adversary to make the latter stop the offensive action (Lorenz 1966). Humans, who lack such dangerous instruments, also, according to ethologists, have no innate mechanisms to block acts of aggression. In a fight between humans, the uncovering of a weak spot or the

---

*In the present considerations I concentrated on the problems of control and self-esteem, but aggressive behavior is also possible for confirming one's identity, if the self-image comprises convictions concerning aggressive behavior (for instance, as part of a masculine role). Attention to this aspect of aggressive motivation is drawn in the analysis presented by S. Feshbach (1973).

assumption of a humble posture may not very often save the life of the loser. When one considers that the human being compensated for the absence of biologically developed instruments of combat with an excess of instruments necessary to gratify wants, it becomes evident that he is now a truly dangerous being to other members of the species. Given the circumstances, the lack of innate mechanisms blocking agression must be made up for by an appropriate system of external means of control.

Is it true, though, that humans do not possess any intrinsic, "natural" means of controlling their aggressive acts? This is open to doubt. When one takes into account how propitious conditions for the development of aggression can be found among human beings, it seems strange that on the whole, its intensity and frequency are not greater and that, by and large, it is not a dominant characteristic of human behavior. In this context it is worth mentioning that in research concerning behavior of children from the United States, India, the Philippines, Japan, Mexico, and Kenya, it was found that only about 10 percent of the observed behavioral acts (registered at five-minute intervals) were aggressive, and, of those, only half were unprovoked operant aggressions. The differences among the cultures, though quite considerable, kept within the limits of 3.4 percent to 7.9 percent (Lambert 1973). Among adults, acts of aggression undoubtedly occur even less frequently. What inhibits them? Is it the fear of punishment? It seems that a number of quite different factors play an important role.

Aggression and Empathy

It has long been supposed that an expression of emotion can elicit a similar emotional reaction in the onlooker; W. McDougall (1920) called this phenomenon a "sympathetic induction" and thought that it is an innate property of the human being. Current observations and experimental data indicate that the suffering of another person may evoke a strong aversive reaction in the onlooker. In the research work on obedience carried out by S. Milgram (1963), 35 percent of the subjects refused to apply strong shocks to their partners, reacting with violent emotions to their (pretended) sufferings. Those who submitted to orders and applied maximum shocks were, on the whole, greatly perturbed. Those examined in an analogous experimental situation by H. A. Tilker (1970) reacted with greater distress, the clearer the signals of pain from their partners (personally unknown to them). In this experiment the reactions of persons who witnessed other people's pain at times assumed extreme intensity and were manifested in such acts as snapping wires off the apparatus and physically menacing the experimenter.

It was also found that sufferings of another person, whether observed or imagined, caused an increase in general arousal as manifested in the GSR (Bandura 1969), in shortened reaction time (Geer and Jarmecky 1973), and in various expressive reactions (Piliavin and Piliavin in press). The increase of the arousal may be observed in the very early stages of ontogeny, as shown in the examination of the phenomenon of reflexive crying (Simner 1971).

Could one say that the above data support the view that there is an innate sensitivity to signals of emotions in other people and/or an innate tendency to respond by sympathetic arousal? The question appears to be more complex than that. Current arguments and data support the thesis that manifested emotions evoke emotional arousal in the onlooker. Such arousal can attain a high degree of intensity. It can acquire the characteristics of an empathic reaction—that is, "experiencing of emotion similar to that of another person as a consequence of perceiving feelings of the other person" (Feshbach and Roe 1968). This reaction can be learned through the association of relief felt by the subject when the distress of the other person ceases (or the association of the subject's own joy with the joy of another person). An empirical demonstration of this suggested learning process has been presented by Aronfreed (1970); a fuller description of the development of empathy, in which cognitive mechanisms are considered, is given in Hoffman (1975).

The expression of pain by another person has, as a rule, an unconditional negative stimulus value (as other strong stimuli do), particularly when it appears suddenly (Piliavin and Piliavin in press). For this reason the individual tends to learn those acts that interrupt the inflow of strong stimuli and to avoid behaviors that are likely to evoke them, including one's own aggression. As the above data and other investigations indicate (Eliasz 1975), manifestations of suffering may block an aggressive action, but do not invariably do so. D. P. Hartmann (1964), for example, found that boys from reformatories who saw a film showing the sufferings of a boy attacked by another child of the same age subsequently applied stronger electric shock to a partner if they themselves had previously been victims of a (verbal) aggression. However, if they had not been attacked, then the witnessing of another person's pain caused a diminution of the shocks (in comparison with a control group to whom the film was not shown) (Eliasz 1975). In contrast, Baron (1971) found that the stronger the pain of the "victim," the weaker the aggression, regardless of whether the subjects were previously attacked by their "victims."

It is probable that the sight of suffering and distress of the victim can effectively block aggression, and block it the more strongly, the clearer, and the more evident its manifestations; yet, as Hartman's data indicate, their relationship must be qualified. The aggressor should not be excessively aroused. In the case of excessive arousal, one can expect an opposite effect—in a state of fury, ecstasy, rage, or the "euphoria of victory," pain (of another person as much as one's own) may become a desirable stimulus.*

---

*Perhaps such an extreme arousal is not necessary to produce this effect. The outcomes of several experiments demonstrate that the mere repetition of aggressive acts

Investigations concerning sensitivity to suffering show in a rather systematic way that this sensitivity is modified by certain factors. Thus, the subject's personal responsibility for what the partner is experiencing increases sensitivity to the latter's state (Tilker 1970) and increases the effort to reduce the suffering (the reaction time is shortened) (Geer and Jarmecky 1973); on the other hand, deindividuating factors, such as the distribution of responsibility or anonymity, are conducive to an increase in the intensity of aggressive reactions (Zimbardo 1969; Bandura, Underwood, and Fromson 1975). The findings indicate the role played in the control of aggression by the self-structure.

Self-Structure and the Control of Aggression

According to the assumption previously presented, I consider the self-structure as a part of the cognitive network (Harvey, Hunt, and Schroder 1961; Reykowski in press). The cognitive network is understood here as a multidimensional space representing the physical, social, and temporal organization of external events. We assume that objects or situations that are represented by the cognitive structures may be placed in the cognitive network at different distances from each other. One may suppose that through the systemic interrelations within the network, the active state of one structure may influence the state of other structures and that the smaller the psychological distance between the structures, the stronger this influence will be. The rules governing this influence may be described according to the principles of generalization, with the assumption that we are dealing with "selective generalization" (Ivanov-Smolenski 1954; Krasnogorski 1954). In Soviet laboratories in the 1950s a number of studies were carried out on this form of generalization (Svarc' 1954; Volkova 1953). In the American literature the notion in usage had been "mediated generalization" (Cofer and Foley 1942).

From this structural model one may derive the hypothesis that events concerning people whose representations in the cognitive network are placed "near" the self-structure may evoke a motivational state in the subject similar to what would have been created if the subject had been directly submitted to the influence of such events. Perceived similarity is a manifestation of psychological distance. In our laboratory a number of experiments have demonstrated that the perceiving of others as similar to the self is conducive to actions for their benefit. The magnitude of the motivation to act for the benefit of others (Karylowski 1976; Smoleńska 1975), and the readiness to help others or to

---

enhanced their intensity (Bandura, Underwood, and Fromson 1975; Hewitt 1973; Zimbardo 1969).

make sacrifices for them (Reykowski 1976), depend upon the perceived similarity between the self and others.

Results of investigations carried out in other laboratories point to similar phenomena. Norma Feshbach and Kiki Roe found that the accuracy in identification and sharing of emotional reactions "is systematically related to the similarity between the child and stimulus person" (Feshbach and Roe 1968). H. Tajfel (1974) observed a readiness to prefer the interests of a person whom the subject classified as belonging to the same category as the subject. Observations indicating the role of similarity (or of psychological distance) are related by A. Bandura (1969) and E. Stotland (1969). If the state of the object "similar to the self" may create motivation, stimulating one to act for that object's benefit (an allocentric motivation), then it should be expected that such a motivation could be aroused if the object suffered harm or is in danger of being harmed, including a harm inflicted by the subject's own action. Such a motivation, therefore, could block an aggressive act.

There are facts supporting such a supposition. J. Karyłowski, in one of his investigations, found that the severity of the punishment proposed for persons who had committed a crime is inversely correlated with the perceived similarity of such persons to the subject's self (when the subject has a positive self-image) (Karyłowski 1976). H. Kaufman and A. M. Marcus (1965) found that a person categorized as belonging to the same group (of students) as the subject is treated with more indulgence when transgressing the law than a person who does not belong to the same category. Z. Kość (1975), in the laboratory of A. Frączek, found that subjects applied weaker shocks to persons whom they perceived as similar to themselves, with respect to personality traits, than to persons perceived as dissimilar.

However, there are also findings in which the similarity manipulation produced no effect (Baron 1971). The differences between investigations in which similarity exerted an influence on aggression and those in which similarity had no influence are of considerable interest. In the first case aggression was "task-oriented": a person who had committed an infraction had to be punished, or punishment had to be used as an aid in teaching a person (Karyłowski 1976; Kaufman and Marcus 1965; Kość 1975). In the second case there was not only a task aggression but also a "hostile" one—it had been provoked by previous aggressive behavior of the partner (Baron 1971; Hendrick and Taylor 1971). One may well suppose that the blocking influence of similarity could have been canceled out by the previous strong arousal to aggression.

Should one conclude, therefore, that for a person strongly aroused to aggression it would make no difference at all whether the attacked person is or is not similar to the "self" of the aggressor? In order to be able to answer that question, one has to take into consideration the influence of at least three variables: the magnitude of the arousal to aggression, the degree of perceived similarity, and the magnitude of the harm suffered by the victim. These variables were not controlled in the course of the experiments mentioned here.

It seems that sensitivity to the "state of similar persons" may be an effective means of blocking (or weakening) aggression within certain specified groups. The scope of the effectiveness would depend upon the gradient of the generalization, and this in turn would depend on the self-definition of the subject and on the properties of the cognitive network (Koziełecki 1976); the structural characteristics of the network may favor a sharp differentiation between "we" and "they" (or "I" and "they") or, on the contrary, may facilitate the perception of similarity among a rather wide range of social objects.

Depending on the organization of the cognitive network, various categories of people might be placed outside one area of similarity—such as people who are different ethnically or nationally, who belong to a different social class, or who are different in color. The state of such people will not arouse any feelings of sympathy and, therefore, they are good candidates for the role of scapegoat.

It seems also that persons who perceive themselves as strangers, as not similar to anybody, as not "belonging" are characterized by a very steep gradient of generalization in relation to the "self." In such people the mechanism of blocking aggression in consequence of similarity may not work at all.*

It should be added here that the phenomenon of blocking aggression against similar persons is sometimes interpreted differently from the explanation offered here. In particular, it has been suggested that positive attitudes toward similar persons are due to the rewarding role of the similarity. However, there are arguments that can be advanced against this hypothesis (Hendrick and Taylor 1971). Unfortunately, space limitations do not permit a detailed discussion of this question.

COGNITIVE NETWORK AS THE SOURCE OF THE AUTONOMOUS SYSTEM OF VALUES

The natural consequence of the development of the cognitive network is a gradual building up of the representations of the objects of the physical and social environment. In their development these representations attain a lower or higher degree of stability; an elementary example of such stable organizations is presented by the phenomenon of "object constancy" (Hebb 1949; Kohler 1959; Piaget 1966). An important property of such stable organizations is their tendency to maintain an internal balance. The maintenance of the balance in cognitive organization may be achieved either by appropriate transformation of incoming information assimilation (Piaget 1966) or by introducing changes in the environment (Festinger 1958).

---

*There is probably nothing accidental in the fact that the most brutal are usually formations of the janissary type—that is, nationally or ethnically foreign in relation to the countries in which they are called upon to perform their police functions.

A simple example of the behavioral consequences of the tendency to maintain a balance in the cognitive system is the behavior of a small rhesus observed by H. F. Harlow (Harlow and Harlow 1962). This monkey was brought up under the "care" of a surrogate "cloth mother" whose wooden head was not painted. Other monkeys had cloth mothers whose heads showed outlines of a face. When, after a period of some months, the cloth mother of our rhesus had its head changed to one with an outline of a face, the little monkey reacted negatively to this change and persistently turned its cloth mother's head to the unpainted side. This phenomenon did not occur in the other monkeys.

The above observation seems to illustrate a certain very general principle: cognitive organizations representing objects of the environment comprise standards representing the normal state of these objects. When this normal state is disturbed to a considerable degree, a negative reaction is evoked, leading to a motivation to return the object to its normal state.*

The magnitude of this kind of motivation will depend, as one may suppose, upon the degree to which a given representation has been built up, on its position in the cognitive network of the subject, and on the magnitude of the discrepancy between the standards and the actual (or possible) state. Thus, in accordance with the assumptions adopted here, the maintenance of the balance of important cognitive structures is a source of a motivation that is not derived from other, personal motives. One can, therefore, speak here of an autonomous motivation, recognizing the fact that objects whose state releases this motivation have their autonomous value.

An arousal of the motivation to act for the benefit of objects other than the "self" does not ensure an appropriate action. Whether a behavior will take place will depend on other factors (see the model presented by S. Schwartz 1976).

Motivation that originates in a state (needs, interests) of external objects may be blocked by a rival motivation. The main source of the rival motivation is the self-structure. Hence, it may be expected that a concentration on one's self might inhibit action for the benefit of others (Berkowitz 1970).

Taking the above model into consideration, one may expect that the magnitude of a motivation to act for the benefit of a specified person should depend on the degree of the integration of the representation of that person with other components of the cognitive network of the subject. Empirical arguments in support of this thesis have been supplied by J. Czapiński (1976), who found that a subject acting for the benefit of two companions devotes more effort to the one whose representation is better integrated with other elements of the subject's cognitive network. It also may be expected that the readiness for

---

*I believe that two kinds of standards may appear in humans: that of a normal state and that of an ideal state. I shall omit this particular differentiation here (Reykowski 1975).

prosocial actions will depend on the position of the self-structure in the cognitive network. In the investigations carried out by T. Szustrowa (1972) and J. Kowalczewska (1972), a curvilinear relationship was found between the level of self-acceptance and the readiness to perform prosocial actions.

Not only acting for the benefit of others, but also perceiving the needs of others, depends upon the state of the self-structure. Both a stable dispositional focus on one's own person and an experimentally evoked focus diminish the ability to perceive the needs of others. (Note: this ability also diminishes when the subject concentrates on a task.) On the other hand, when concentration on the self is experimentally lowered, sensitivity to the needs of others increases (Jarymowicz 1977). A similar effect is produced by activation of representation of objects other than the self (Feldman 1976).

So far I have been trying to show that there are grounds to suppose that needs and interests of other people may be a source of an autonomous motivation (if such people are adequately represented in the cognitive network of the subject and if the self-structure, neither functionally nor dispositionally, occupies a dominant position). Such a motivation is obviously antagonistic to aggression and, therefore, should block its development. Unfortunately, I know of no empirical data that bear directly on this hypothesis.

Yet this hypothesis has important implications. It indicates, for instance, that factors favoring the attribution of an excessive importance to one's self—such as an individualistic upbringing—or factors that excessively degrade the self may diminish the potential blocking influence exerted on aggression by the state of external social objects. For this implication there is confirmatory evidence in the research carried out by M. Szostak (1976).

CONCLUDING REMARKS

In this paper I have attempted to demonstrate that aggressive motivation in its proactive form (the operant aggression) may have in the human personality "its own soil" in which it can grow easily. In some instances, when conditions of the "soil" are particularly favorable, it may grow very luxuriantly. To make such an assertion there is no need to assume an existence of innate instincts or aggressive drives; on the contrary, the hypothesis of an innate aggressive drive seems quite unnecessary.

I have considered here two mechanisms governing the intrinsic motivation to aggression: the mechanism based upon the demand for stimulation and the mechanism based upon the maintenance of a balance in the self-structure. The first of these has its basis in emotional structures, the second in cognitive structures. Both mediate aggressive acts performed for the pleasure of inflicting harm, which provides inherent satisfaction. At the same time one finds that the very mechanisms that provide the basis for an aggressive motivation may also provide the basis for a prosocial motivation, blocking or impeding aggression.*

The emotional sources of the motivation to aggression can also generate antagonistic motives based upon emotional empathy. On the cognitive level, the development of the self-structure and a counterpart to egocentric motives occurs through the representation of external social objects and the motivation aroused by their needs. Though a high concentration on the self may diminish a sensitivity to the needs of others, nevertheless, in the self-structure, through the phenomena of generalization, forces blocking aggression may originate. Thus, our data show that the mechanism of similarity has a greater impact on the behavior of egocentric persons.

It seems that, in light of the above, one can suppose that the regulation of aggression is based on the principles of negative feedback ensured by mechanisms that are formed during the natural course of the development of the personality. In consequence, one may expect that a stronger arousal to aggression will be accompanied by a stronger arousal of the blocking mechanisms, so that in everyday behavior oscillation, rather than some unitary pattern (aggressive or prosocial), should prevail. The existence of such a feedback should, as a rule, halt more serious acts of aggression. But this obviously is not the case. Observations of life supply enough evidence for the fact that aggression can sometimes reach a very high degree of intensity with no blocking forces operating. I believe that certain factors disturb the equilibrium and favor aggressive behavior. It seems that such factors actually did exist, and do exist, in the culture. Rules formulated by a given society ordering violence and murder (such rules can be found even in the Bible) and social methods of training that try to extinguish the sensitivity to other people's pain, to subdue sympathy, to develop ruthlessness (in other words, to develop "masculine" traits) are important factors disturbing the equilibrium of mechanisms that serve to control aggressive motivation; the balance of these regulating mechanisms may also be disturbed by certain elements of the mass culture and by certain ideologies.

I think, therefore, that the key question concerning the control of aggression is the question of factors that lead to the corrosion of the intrinsic forces blocking aggression in human beings.

---

*A. Frączek (1975) pointed out the role of the prosocial motivation as a factor blocking aggression.

REFERENCES

Aronfreed, J. 1970. "The Socialization of Altruistic and Sympathetic Behavior: Some Theoretical and Experimental Analyses." In *Altruism and Helping Behavior*, ed. J. Macaulay and L. Berkowitz. New York: Academic Press.

Bandura, A. 1969. *Principles of Behavior Modification*. New York: Holt, Rinehart and Winston.

————. 1973. "Social Learning Theory of Aggression." In *Control of Aggression*, ed. J. Knutson. Chicago: Aldine.

————, B. Underwood, and M. E. Fromson. 1975. "Disinhibition of Aggression Through Diffusion of Responsibility and Dehumanization of Victim." *Journal of Research in Personality* 9: 253–69.

Baron, R. A. 1971. "Magnitude of Victim's Pain Cues and Level of Prior Anger Arousal as Determinants of Adult Aggressive Behavior." *Journal of Personality and Social Psychology* 17, no. 3: 236–44.

Barron, F. 1953. "An Ego-Strength Scale Which Predicts Response to Psychotherapy." *Journal of Consulting Psychology* 12: 327–33.

Berkowitz, L. 1970. In *Altruism and Helping Behavior*, ed. J. Macaulay and L. Berkowitz. New York: Academic Press.

————. 1973. "Some Determinants of Impulsive Aggression." Paper delivered at Conference on Determinants and Origins of Aggression, Monte Carlo.

————. 1965. "Some Aspects of Observed Aggression." *Journal of Personality and Social Psychology* 2: 359–69.

Berlyne, D. E. 1967. "Arousal and Reinforcement." In *Nebraska Symposium on Motivation*, ed. D. Levine. Lincoln: University of Nebraska Press.

————. 1969. *Struktura i kierunek myślenia*. Warsaw: PWN. Translation of *Structure and Direction in Thinking*. New York: John Wiley, 1965.

Bettelheim, B., and J. J. Janowitz. 1950. *Dynamics of Prejudice*. New York: Harper.

Bexton, W. H., W. Heron, and T. H. Scott. 1954. "Effects of Decreased Variation in the Sensory Environment." *Canadian Journal of Psychology* 8: 70–76.

Ciarkowska, W. 1975. "Wpływ specyficznej stymulacji emocjonalnej orza cech osobowości na intensywność zachowania agresywnego." In *Z zagadnień psychologii agresji*, ed A. Frączek. Warsaw: Wydawnictwo PIPS.

Cofer, C. N., and J. Foley. 1942. "Mediated Generalization and the Interpretation of Verbal Behavior." *Psychological Review* 49: 513–40.

Czapiński, J. 1976. "Strukturalne własnosci reprezentacji poznawczej obiektów społecznych a gotowość do działania tych obiektów." *Studia psychologiczne* 15.

Eliasz, A. 1974a. "Aktyvność (reaktywna i sprawcza) a wybór sytuacji o różnym stopniu stymulacji." In *Rola cech temperamentalnych w działaniu*, ed. J. Strelau. Wrocław: Ossolineum.

———. 1974b. *Temperament a osobowość.* Wrocław: Ossolineum.

Eliasz, H. 1975. "Znaczenie obserwowania bólu doznawanego przez 'ofiarę' dla regulacji agresywnego zachowania się." In *Z zagadnien psychologii agresji*, ed. A. Frączek. Warsaw: Wydawnictwo PIPS.

Feldman, R. 1976. "Behavior Patterns of Antisocial Children in 'Prosocial' and 'Antisocial' Peer Groups." Paper for XXI International Congress of Psychology, Paris.

Feshbach, N. D., and K. Roe. 1968. "Empathy in Six- and Seven-Year-Olds." *Child Development* 39, no. 1: 133–45.

Feshbach, S. 1964. "The Function of Aggression and the Regulation of Aggressive Drive." *Psychological Review* 71: 257–72.

———. 1973. "The Development and Regulation of Aggression: Some Research Gaps and a Proposed Cognitive Approach." Paper delivered at Conference on Determinants and Origins of Aggression, Monte Carlo.

Festinger, L. 1958. "The Motivating Effect of Cognitive Dissonance." In *Assessment of Human Motives*, ed. G. Lindzey. New York: Reinhard.

Frączek, A. 1973. "Informational Role of Situation as a Determinant of Aggressive Behavior." Paper delivered at Conference on Determinants and Origins of Aggression, Monte Carlo.

———. 1975a. "Agresja—psychologicsny punkt widzenia." In *Z zagadnien psychologii agresji*, ed. A. Frączek. Warsaw: Wydawnictwo PIPS.

———. 1975b. "Mechanizmy regulacyjne czynności agresywnych." In *Studia nad teoria czynności ludzkich*, ed. I. Kurcz and J. Reykowski. Warsaw: PWN.

Geer, J. H., and L. Jarmecky. 1973. "The Effect of Being Responsible for Reducing Another's Pain on Subject's Response and Arousal." *Journal of Personality and Social Psychology* 26, no. 2: 232–37.

Greenblum, J., and L. J. Pearlin. 1953. "Vertical Mobility and Prejudice." In *Class, Status, and Power*, ed. R. Bendix and S. Lipset. Glencoe, Ill.: Free Press.

Harlow, H. F., and M. K. Harlow. 1962. "Social Deprivation in Monkeys." *Scientific American* 207: 137–46.

Hartman, D. P. 1964. "Influence of Symbolically Modeled Instrumental Aggression and Pain Cues on Aggressive Behavior." *Journal of Personality and Social Psychology* 1: 281.

Harvey, O. J., D. E. Hunt, and H. M. Schroder. 1961. *Conceptual Systems and Personality Organization*. New York: John Wiley.

Hebb, D. O. 1949. *The Organization of Behavior*. New York: John Wiley.

———. 1955. "Drives and C.N.S." *Psychological Review* 62: 243–54.

Helson, H. 1959. "Adaptation Level Theory." In *Psychology: A Study of Science*, ed. S. Koch, vol. I, study 1. New York: McGraw-Hill.

———. 1966. "Some Problems in Motivation from the Point of View of the Theory of Adaptation Level." In *Nebraska Symposium on Motivation*, ed. D. Levine. Lincoln: University of Nebraska Press.

Hendrick, C., and S. P. Taylor. 1971. "Effects of Belief Similarity and Aggression." *Journal of Personality and Social Psychology* 17, no. 3: 342–50.

Hewitt, L. S. 1973. "Who Will Be the Target of Displaced Aggression?" Paper delivered at Conference on Determinants and Origins of Aggression, Monte Carlo.

Hunt, J. McV. 1965. "Intrinsic Motivation and Its Role in Psychological Development." In *Nebraska Symposium on Motivation*, ed. D. Levine. Lincoln: University of Nebraska Press.

Iwanow-Smoleński, A. G. 1954. *Zagadnienia wyższych ozynności nerwowych*. Warsaw: PZWL. Translated from Russian.

Jarymowicz, M. 1977. "Modification of Self-Esteem and Increment of Prosocial Sensitivity." *Polish Psychological Bulletin* no. 1.

———, and J. Rogala. 1976. "Wgląd we własny egocentryzm a umiejętność destrzegania problemów innych ludzi." *Studia psychologiczne* 15.

Karyłowski, J. 1975. *Z badań nad mechanizmami pozytywnych ustosunkowań interpersonalnych*. Wrocław: Ossolineum.

————. 1976. "Evaluation of Others' Acts as Function of Self-Other Similarity and Self-Esteem." In *Studies on the Mechanisms of Prosocial Behavior*. Warsaw: Warsaw University Press.

Kaufman, H., and A. M. Marcus. 1965. "Aggression as a Function of Similarity Between Aggressor and Victim." *Perceptual and Motor Skills* 20: 1013-20.

Kohler, W. 1959. *Gestalt Psychology*. New York: Mentor Books.

Koi, I. S. 1967. Sociologija licnosti. Moscow: Izd. Politicheskoj Literatury.

Kość, Z. 1975. "Podobieństwo 'agresora' do 'ofiary' a natężenie czynności agresywnej." In *Z zagadnień psychologii agresji*, ed. A. Frączek. Warsaw: Wydawnictwo PIPS.

Kowalozewska, J. 1972. "Zaleśnośc między postawami wobec 'ja' i nastawieniami wobec innych a tendencją do podejmowania zachowań allocentrycznych." Master's thesis, University of Warsaw.

Kozielecki, J. 1976. "Elementy teorii samowiedzy." *Psychologia wychowawcza* no. 1: 1-32.

Krasnogorski, N. I. 1954. *Trudy po izuchenij vysshej nervnoj dejatelnosti*. Vol. I. Moscow: Medgiz.

Lambert, W. 1973. "Promise and Problems of Cross-Cultural Exploration of Children's Aggressive Strategies." Paper delivered at Conference on Determinants and Origins of Aggression, Monte Carlo.

Leuba, C. 1955. "Toward Some Integration of Learning Theories: The Concept of Optimal Stimulation." *Psychological Reports* 1: 27-33.

Lorenz, K. 1966. *On Aggression*. New York: Harcourt, Brace, and World.

Łukaszewski, W. 1974. *Osobowość, struktura i funkcje regulacyjne*. Warsaw: PWN.

Malowska, H. 1965. "Poczucie zagrożenia a stosunek do innych." *Studia socjologiczne* no. 2.

McDougall, W. 1920. *The Group Mind*. New York: Putnam's.

Milgram, S. 1963. "Behavioral Study of Obedience." *Journal of Personality and Social Psychology* 67, no. 4: 371-78.

Nebylicyn, V. D. 1966. *Osnovnye svojstva nervnoj sistemy cheloveka*. Moscow: Prosveshchenie.

Obuchowski, K. 1970. *Kody orientacji i struktura procesów emocjonalnych*. Warsaw: PWN.

Olweus, D. 1973. "Personality and Aggression: Some Central Issues and Related Research." Paper delivered at Conference on Determinants and Origins of Aggression, Monte Carlo.

Pavlov, I. P. 1952. *20 lat badań wyższych czynności nerwowych (zachowania się) zwierząt*. Warsaw: PZWL.

Piaget, J. 1966. *Studia z psychologii dziecka*. Warsaw: PWN. Translated from French.

Pieron, H. 1950. "Sensory Affectivity." In *Feelings and Emotions*, ed. M. L. Reymert. New York: McGraw-Hill.

Piliavin, J. A., and I. M. Piliavin. In press. "The Good Samaritan: Why Does He Help?" In *Positive Forms of Social Behavior*, ed. L. Wispe. Cambridge, Mass.: Harvard University Press.

Reykowski, J. 1975. "Position of Self-Structure in a Cognitive System and Prosocial Orientation." *Dialectics and Humanism* no. 4: 19–30.

———. 1976a. "Nastawienia egocentryczne i nastawienia prospołeczne." In *Osobowość a społeczne zachowanie się ludzi*, ed. J. Reykowski. Warsaw: KiW.

———. 1976b. "Prosocial Orientation and Self-Structure." In *Studies on the Mechanisms of Prosocial Behavior*, ed. J. Reykowski. Warsaw: Warsaw University Press.

———. In press. "Cognitive Development and Prosocial Behavior." *Polish Psychological Bulletin*.

Ribinshejn, S. L. 1973. *Problemy obshchej psikhologij*. Moscow: Izd. Pedagogika.

Rogers, C. 1959. "A Theory of Therapy, Personality and Interpersonal Relationships as Developed in the Client-Centered Framework." In *Psychology: A Study of Science*, vol. III, study 1. New York: McGraw-Hill.

Rotter, J. B. 1966. "Generalized Expectancies for Internal vs. External Control of Reinforcement." *Psychological Monographs* 80, no. 609.

Schachter, S., and B. Latane. 1964. "Crime, Cognition, and the Autonomic Nervous System." In *Nebraska Symposium on Motivation*, ed. D. Levine. Lincoln: University of Nebraska Press.

Schwartz, S. H. 1973. "Normative Explanations of Helping Behavior." *Journal of Experimental Psychology* 9, no. 4:349–64.

Shvare, L. A. 1954. "K voprosu o vzajmodejstvie pervoj i vtoroj signalnykh sistem." *Izvestija Akademii pedagogicheskikh nauk RSFSR.*

Simner, M. L. 1971. "Newborn's Response to the Cry of Another Infant." *Developmental Psychology* 5: 136–50.

Skinner, B. F. 1953. *Science and Human Behavior.* New York: Macmillan.

Smolenska, M. Z. 1975. "Self-Other Similarity and Allo-Egocentric Behavior of Gifted Adolescents." In *Studies on the Mechanisms of Prosocial Behavior*, ed. J. Reykowski. Warsaw: Warsaw University Press.

Stotland, E. 1969. "Exploratory Investigations of Empathy." In *Advances in Experimental Social Psychology*, ed. L. Berkowitz. New York: Academic Press.

Strelau, J. 1972. "A Diagnosis of Temperament by Nonexperimental Techniques." *Polish Psychological Bulletin* 3, no. 2: 98–105.

———. 1974. "Założenia teoretyczne psychologii temperamentu." In *Rola cech temperamentalnych w działaniu*, ed. J. Strelau. Wrocław: Ossolineum.

———. 1975. "Reactivity and Activity Style in Selected Occupations." *Polish Psychological Bulletin* 6, no. 4.

Svarc', L. A. 1954. "K voprosu o vzajmodejstvie pervoj i vtoroj signal'nyx sistem." *Izvestija Akademii pedagogicheskikh nauk RSFSR.*

Szostak, M. 1976. "Cognitive Functioning, Self-Attitude and Aggressiveness in Receptive and Prosocial Individuals." In *Studies on the Mechanisms of Prosocial Behavior*, ed. J. Reykowski. Warsaw: Warsaw University Press.

Szustrowa, T. 1972. "Zdolność do działamia na rzecz celów pozaosobistych a niektóre właściwości rodzinnego treningu wychowawczego." *Zeszyty naukowe U.W.* 1.

Tajfel, H. 1974. "Intergroup Behavior, Social Comparison and Social Change." In *Katz-Newcomb Lectures.* Ann Arbor: University of Michigan Press.

Teplov, B. M. 1961. *Problemy individualnykh rakhlicij.* Moscow: NPN RSFSR.

Tilker, H. A. 1970. "Socially Responsible Behavior as a Function of Observer Responsibility and Victim Feedback." *Journal of Personality and Social Psychology* 14, no. 2: 95–101.

Valzelli, L. 1973. "Aggressiveness by Isolation in Rodents." Paper delivered at Conference on Determinants and Origins of Aggression, Monte Carlo.

Volkova, S. L. 1953. "O nekotory k osobennostjakh obrazovanija uslovnykh refleksov rechevye razdrazhitelja u detej." *Fiziologicheskij zhurnal* no. 5.

Zimbardo, P. G. 1969. "The Human Choice: Individuation, Reason and Order Versus Deindividuation, Impulse and Chaos." In *Nebraska Symposium on Motivation*, ed. W. J. Arnold and D. Levine. Lincoln: University of Nebraska Press.

8

AGGRESSION AND VIOLENCE: CRIME AND SOCIAL CONTROL

Marvin E. Wolfgang

In the sociology of crime and criminality, emphasis is placed on cultural and group forces that produce actors who represent forms of deviance from the dominant value, or moral demand, system. The individual offender is not ignored, but is simply clustered with other individuals alike in attributes deemed theoretically or statistically meaningful. The offender's "uniqueness" is retained by the improbability of identity with everyone else on several attributes or variables. Hence, the researchers resort to means, medians, modes, probability theory, inferential statistics, and mathematical models for analyzing predominant patterns and regularities of behavior. Biological and psychological factors are not ignored; but when a monodisciplinary perspective is used by sociologists, the biopsychological is suspended, postponed, or dismissed after consideration. Biological needs and psychological drives may be declared uniformly distributed, and hence of no utility in explaining one form of behavior relative to another. They may be seen as differential endowments of personalities that help to assign, for example, a label of mental incapacity to a group of individuals, some of whom have also violated the criminal codes. But neither the biology of many individuals nor the psychology of many personalities helps to explain the overwhelming involvement in crime of men over women, slums over suburbs, youth over age, urban over rural areas. It is this latter set of macroscopic regularities to which the sociological perspective addresses itself.

DEFINITION AND CULTURAL DIMENSIONS OF VIOLENCE

Violence is difficult to define and is often distinguished from aggression. Aggression may be the more comprehensive and generic term, and has been most extensively explored by psychologists in and out of laboratories. Types of aggression have been differentiated on the basis of the kinds of stimulus situations that elicit destructive behavior. Kenneth Moyer (1971, ch. 3), among many others, has defined and described several classes of aggression that are not mutually exclusive: predatory, intermale, fear-induced, irritable, territorial defense, maternal, and instrumental.

The 13 task force volumes of the National Commission on the Causes and Prevention of Violence struggled with the terms "aggression" and "violence" in 1968 and 1969. Here I shall concentrate on violence as a subset of aggression and shall refer to the intentional use of physical force on another person, or noxious physical stimuli invoked by one person against another. The physical force may be viewed as assaultive, designed to cause pain or injury as an end in itself, sometimes referred to as "expressive violence," or as the use of pain or injury or physical restraint as a coercive threat or punishment to induce another person or persons to carry out some act, commonly called "instrumental violence." Violence may also be legitimate (a parent spanking a child, a police officer forcefully arresting a suspect, a soldier killing an enemy during war) or illegitimate (criminal homicide, forcible rape, aggravated assault). More particularly, I shall concentrate on illegitimate violence, but behind illegitimate violence are cultural dimensions that involve the acceptance of violence.

There is no society that does not have in its normative system some elements of acceptable limits to violence in some form (see Wolfgang 1970, pp. 12–15). Thus, the use of physical force by parents to restrain and punish children is permissible, tolerated, encouraged, and is thereby part of the normative process by which every society regulates its child rearing. There are, of course, varying degrees of parental force expected and used in different cultures and times, and there are upper limits vaguely defined as excessive and brutal. The battered child syndrome is an increasingly recorded phenomenon in society.

The point is, however, that our norms approve or permit parents to apply force for their own purposes against the child. The application of force is a form of violence, and may be used consciously to discipline the child to the limits of permitted behavior, to reduce the domestic noise level, to express parental disapproval, and even unconsciously as a displacement for aggression meant for other targets. This model of parent-child interaction is a universal feature of all human societies. The model is one that the child comes to ingest: that superior force is power permitting manipulation of others, and can be a functional tool for securing a superior position over others, for obtaining desires and ends.

The violence in which the child engages is but an expressed extension of this basic model. The use of physical restraint and force is not a feature only of lower-class families, although studies have shown that its persistent use, and more frequent use over a longer span of childhood, is more common in that social class. The substitution by middle-class parents of withdrawal of rights and affection, of deprivation of liberty, and of other techniques is designed to replace the need for force. And these substitutions constitute an effort to socialize the child to respect other forms of social control. They are also ways of masking the supreme means of control, physical force.

Violence and the threat of violence form the ultimate weapons of any society for maintaining itself against external and internal attacks. All societies finally resort to violence to solve problems that arise from such attacks. War is aggressive force between nations, and is legitimized within each. The recognition of relativity in the moral judgments about violence is quite clear in the case of war. When the thirteen colonies joined together in the eighteenth century to sever ties from Great Britain, they called the action "revolution" and good, in historical retrospect, despite the violence it engendered. When, in the nineteenth century, some states sought to divide the nation, the action was called "civil war" and bad, and the bloodshed was lamented. The Nazis gave justice to American bombs and enlisted a generation of youth to react violently to violence. There are other international conflicts in which nations have been involved and for which the label of legitimacy has been seriously questioned by substantial numbers within their own territories. When this happens, a society becomes more conscious of the process of socializing its youth to accept violence as a mode of response, as a collective problem-solving mechanism. When war is glorified in a nation's history and is included as part of the child's educational materials, a moral judgment about the legitimacy of violence is firmly made.

Socialization means changing the individual into a personality; it is the process of cultural transmission, of relaying through the social funnel of family and friends a set of beliefs, attitudes, values, speech, and habits. When the frontline instruments of war become part of the physical features of a child's life space—when cannons, rifles, grenades, and soldiers are moved from real battlefields to the mind of the child and the world of the playroom, and are among the objects touched and manipulated by the child—then some set of values associated with the legitimacy and recognition of the superiority of violent activity is transmitted. What is not empirically clear is the extent to which such transmission is later translated into violence by the child, as a child, youth, or adult. As a legislator, parent, police officer, or in any other role, the adult is still the carrier of attitudes related to that play activity, unless contrary values have intervened.

Social scientists, psychologists, and psychiatrists have often stressed the importance of the theme of masculinity in American culture and the effect that this image of the strong masculine role has had on child rearing and the general socialization process. The middle-class boy today has some difficulty if he seeks to match himself to the old masculine model, and he may become neurotic and insecure. Among the lower classes, says W. B. Miller (1958), the continuity of the physically assertive male is still one of the "focal concerns." The desire to prove one's masculinity, added to the desire to become a successful male adult member of the lower-class culture, requires adolescent "rehearsal" of the toughness, heavy drinking, and quick, aggressive response to certain stimuli that are characteristic of the lower-class adult male. Such rehearsal involves activities that are not necessarily delinquent but often involve participation in conduct that is defined as delinquent by the representatives of the middle-class dominant culture.

There are many other culture items that contribute to a general aura of violence. Violence in the mass media, automobile advertising that promotes aggressive driving—"Drive it like you hate it, it's cheaper than psychiatry"—and the possession of 100 million guns in the civilian population, a higher gun-to-population ratio than anywhere else in the world, must make a difference. Research gives evidence to these claims (see Wolfgang 1970, pp. 16-19).

FAMILY AND YOUTH CRIMINAL VIOLENCE

Family Violence

Some data on crimes of violence are ordinarily found in official police statistics. Despite limitations, the Uniform Crime Reports offer base-line data. These are police reports from all over the country submitted to the FBI and reported annually in the Department of Justice's *Crime in the United States*, the latest of which appeared in 1974. The only family information offered concerns criminal homicide, which has had an amazing stability of frequency distributions since 1930, when police statistics were first collected on a national basis. Of the 15,910 homicides in 1970, for example, 12.1 percent were spouse killing spouse; and of the 20,600 homicides in 1974, 12.1 percent were in the same category. In the latter year, in addition, 2.7 percent involved a parent killing a child, 8 percent "other relative killings," and 6.2 "romantic triangle and lovers' quarrels." Murder within the family made up approximately one-fourth of all the murder offenses, and half of the family killings involved spouse killing spouse. In these murders the wife was the victim in 52 percent of the incidents and the husband in 48 percent. Fifty percent of the victims were black, 48 percent white, and the remaining were of other races (U.S. Department of Justice 1974, p. 19).

In a study entitled *Patterns in Criminal Homicide* (1958), I examined 588 homicides in Philadelphia to obtain more detailed information about family criminal violence. Of the 136 victims who had a familial relationship to their slayers, there were 100 husbands or wives, 9 sons, 8 daughters, 3 mothers, 3 brothers, 2 fathers, 1 sister, and 10 other types of associations. Of the 100 marital relationships, 53 wives were slain by their husbands and 47 husbands by their wives. Significantly, the number of wives homicidally assaulted by their husbands constituted 41 percent of all women who were killed, whereas husbands homicidally assaulted by their wives made up only 11 percent of all men who were killed.

When a man was killed by a woman, he was most likely to be killed by his wife. Of 75 black males slain by black females, 40 (53 percent) were husbands slain by their mates; and of 9 white males killed by white females, 7 were slain by their mates.

When a woman committed homicide, she was more likely to kill her husband than a husband was to kill his wife. Of 89 black female offenders (for whom a victim-offender relationship had been identified), 40 (45 percent) killed their husband; and of 15 white female offenders, 7 killed their husband. On the other hand, of 321 black male offenders, only 40 (12 percent) killed their wife; and of 118 white male offenders, only 13 (11 percent) killed their wife.

All told, when the 105 identified female offenders committed homicide, they killed their husbands in 45 percent of the cases; but when the 445 identified male offenders committed homicide, they killed their wives in only 12 percent of the cases.

More recent data were collected by the National Commission on the Causes and Prevention of Violence in 1968-69 in a representative sampling of 17 major cities in the United States. In these cities combined, 15.8 percent of homicides involved husband-wife slayings, 2.0 percent children killing a parent, 3.9 percent parent killing a child, 1.4 brother-sister slayings, and 1.6 percent "other family" (Mulvihill, Tumin, and Curtis 1969, p. 287).

Perhaps more so within love and intimate relationships we may say that life's dreams are filled with episodes of potential violence. Love and hate are intertwined, so that one can both love and kill the object of desire. Othello's love for Desdemona was involved in his killing her when he said:

Be thus when thou art dead, and I will kill thee
And love thee after . . . I must weep,
But they are cruel tears. This sorrow's heavenly;
It strikes where it doth love (V.1.18–22).

Aggravated assult is a Uniform Crime Report category that refers to physical injury of a grievous character, inflicted with a gun, knife, or similar weapon. In the 17-city survey, 14 percent of all aggravated assaults were between family members, half of them husband-wife assults (Mulvihill, Tumin, and Curtis 1969, pp. 298-99). Sex-race relationships similar to homicide occur in aggravated assaults. When the victim of aggravated assault is a female, the relationship is more likely to be husband-wife than when a male is a victim. When a mate is assulted, the husband is the offender in about three-fourths of the cases. The difference between an aggravated assault and a homicide may be little more than speedy communication to the police, rapid transportation to a hospital, and the degree and speed of medical care applied to a serious injury.

The National Commission survey also noted the weapons used in spouse slayings and assults. Guns were used in half the cases of homicide, while knives, blunt instruments, and fists were more common in assaults not ending in death. The weapon, rather than the intention or motive, makes more of a difference between serious injury and death. The rates and proportions of family assaults and slayings in cross-cultural studies (Curtis 1974, pp. 51-56)—from primitive African societies to comparisons between Jews and non-Jews in Israel, the Soviet Union, Canada, England, Denmark, and Japan—reveal similar or slightly higher intrafamilial violence. In Japan infanticide rates are higher, and wherever the family is a more dominant social institution, the proportion of homicides is higher within the primary group of the family.

Even so, the incidence of homicide in the family is highest in the lower socioeconomic class. And it is in this lower-class structure that the use of physical assaultive behavior is a more common reaction to social interaction.

Child and Youth Violence

The true extent of child violence is little known, if not unknowable. Neither official public records of the police and juvenile courts, nor the files of child guidance clinics and private physicians—not nationally collected—yield adequate or valid indexes of the total amount of violence among children. Individual research projects may give hints about racial, sexual, age, and other differentials, but these studies do not inform us about the volume of violence in this age group. From what data we do have, even time series are suspect because of changes in reportability, recoding, and the increases in social control agencies that are concerned with such issues. However, using the rubric of "the best available scientific evidence," we seek to piece segmental information and findings together to form a Weberian *Verstehen*, a meaningful whole, while trying to avoid an ideological or theoretical adversary position in defense of a particular thesis.

Studies in criminology refer to what is known as "hidden delinquency" or the "dark figures" of crime. Most of these studies ask junior high school and high school children in anonymous questionnaires whether they have committed various offenses, how often, and approximately when.

The increasingly methodologically refined studies of hidden delinquency have not clearly and consistently reported a significant reduction in the disparity among social classes for crimes of violence. The incidence and frequency of crimes of violence appear to remain considerably higher among boys from lower social classes when the appropriate questions are asked about these offenses over specific periods of time. In their study of delinquents, Leon Fannin and Marshall Clinard reported:

> One of the more important of the tests was a comparison of the frequency with which reported and unreported robberies and assaults were committed by members of the two class levels (middle and lower). The vast majority of all lower class delinquents, 84 percent, had committed at least one such offense compared to 28 percent of the middle class (probability less than 0.01); 28 percent of the lower and eight percent of the middle class had committed 10 or

more violent offenses. Class level was also related to the frequency of fighting with other boys. Lower class delinquents fought singly and in groups significantly more often (probability less than 0.05) than middle class delinquents, with 20 percent of them averaging five or more fights per month compared to 4.0 percent (1974, p. 211).

Official data on child violence may also be found in the Uniform Crime Reports published by the Department of Justice. However, we know something about offenders only when there are arrests, and only about 20 percent of the more serious crimes known result in arrest; of the crimes of violence—homicide, forcible rape, robbery, aggravated assult—about 45 percent result in arrest. Whether it is easier for the police to arrest juvenile than adult suspects is still debatable, but generally believed to be the case (see Sellin and Wolfgang 1964).

Arrest statistics for 1974 show a continuing increase in juvenile violence. For index crimes (violence and theft), 19 percent of all persons arrested were under age 15 and 45 percent were under 18 (U.S. Department of Justice 1974, p. 45). Juveniles are arrested three times more often for property crimes than assault crimes, but still account for 12.5 percent of all persons arrested for violent crimes. Increases in violent crime have been greatest for this young age group. Between 1960 and 1974 national arrests for violence among persons 18 years and older increased 126 percent, but among persons under 18 years of age they increased 254 percent (U.S. Department of Justice 1974, p. 182).

In a study of criminal homicide covering 1948-1952 in Philadelphia, the rate of offenders per 100,000 population for both races reached a peak in the age group 20-24 (12.6), but the age group 15-19 was not far behind, with a rate of 9.4. Males in the younger group were seven times more homicidal (22.7) than females (3.1). But it was younger black males who most dramatically, and with statistical significance, exceeded any other race-sex-age group. The peak age for black males was 20-24, with a rate of 93, compared with white males at 8.2. For black males 15-19, the rate was next highest (79.2), compared with white males (4.6), black females (2.9), and white females (0.4) (Wolfgang 1958, p. 66).

A similar study of rape in Philadelphia over a two-year period showed similar racial differences, but the group 15-19 represented the highest rate for both races (Amir 1971, p. 52). The overall rape rate per 100,000 population for all ages was 180, but for the peak age group 15-19 was nearly 800. Black males in this population had a rate of 2,656 and white males 162.

The National Commission on the Causes and Prevention of Violence presented data that covered ten years, based on the national sample from 17 major cities. Combining the crimes of homicide, forcible rape, robbery, and aggravated assult, the rate of crimes per 100,000 population for all ages 10 and over was 189, but for ages 15-17 the rate was 408 and even for children aged 10-14 it was 123, nearly as high as the rate for all ages 25 and over (127). In fact, the greatest percentage increase in all crimes of violence was for children aged 10-14. For this group the increase from 1958 to 1967 was 222 percent, compared with 103 percent for ages 15-17 and 66 percent for all ages. In short, violent crimes committed by children have been increasing between three and four times faster than violence in general (Mulvihill, Tumin, and Curtis 1969, p. 169).

It should be pointed out that the general rise in crimes of violence in the United States has been to a considerable extent due to the sheer increase of children and youth in the general population, a function of the high fertility rates in the late 1940s and the 1950s. Since 1964 there has been a rapid rise in the 10-24 age group, and probably as much as 20 percent of the rise in violent crime can be attributed to the youthful bulge in the age pyramid. The National Commission on Violence carefully documented a 12 percent attribution to this young group for the rise in violent crime between 1950 and 1965 (Mulvihill, Tumin, and Curtis 1969, pp. 145-52).

We should note, however, a reduction in overall rates of violent crime between 1975 and 1990, if for no other reason than a population diminution in the violence-prone age groups of children and youth (unpublished projections from the Hudson Institute). Youths aged 14-24 represented 27 million (15 percent) of the total U.S. population in 1960, 19.7 percent in 1970, and 21 percent in 1975, but should drop to 16 percent by 1990. Even with continued higher rates of fertility among black families, black children and youth were 6 million (3 percent) of the nation's population in 1973, and will drop to 5.8 million (2.4 percent) by 1990.

VIOLENT CRIME IN A BIRTH COHORT

New kinds of evidence about juvenile crime are being analyzed by the Center for Studies in Criminology and Criminal Law at the University of Pennsylvania (see Wolfgang, Figlio, and Sellin 1972). The data constitute a unique collection of information in the United States about a birth cohort of boys born in 1945. Approximately 10,000 males who were born in that year and who resided in Philadelphia at least from ages 10 to 18 have been analyzed in various ways. Using school records, offense reports from the police, and some Selective Service information for military service, the center has, among other things, followed the delinquency careers of those boys in the cohort who ever had any contact with the police. Comparisons have been made between delinquents and nondelinquents on a wide range of variables, thus yielding findings that are not cross-sectional or tied to a single calendar year. The entire universe of cases is under review, not merely a group that happened to be processed at a given time by a juvenile court or some other agency. Computing a birth-cohort rate of delinquency, as well as providing analyses of the dynamic flow of boys through their juvenile court years, has been possible. The time analysis uses a stochastic model for tracing delinquency of the cohort, and includes such facts as time intervals between offenses, offense type, race, social class, and seriousness of the offenses.

Some of the findings from this Philadelphia study are particularly pertinent for more understanding about youth and crimes of violence. Of the total birth cohort of 9,946 boys born in 1945, about 85 percent were born in Philadelphia and about 95 percent went through the Philadelphia school system from first grade. Of the entire cohort 3,475 (35 percent) were delinquent, meaning that they had at least one contact with the police. Of the 7,043 white subjects, 2,017 (28.64 percent) were delinquent. It is a dramatic and disturbing fact that just slightly more than half of all nonwhite boys born in the same year were delinquent. This higher proportion of nonwhite delinquents constitutes one of the major statistical dichotomies running throughout the analysis of the cohort, and particularly of the delinquent subset.

Of special significance is the fact that only 627 boys were classified as chronic offenders or heavy repeaters, meaning that they committed (or were arrested for) five or more offenses during their juvenile court ages. These chronic offenders represent only 6.3 percent of the entire birth cohort and 18 percent of the delinquent cohort. Yet they were responsible for 5,305 delinquencies, which is 52 percent of all the delinquencies committed by the entire cohort.

Chronic offenders are heavily represented among those who commit violent offenses. Of the 815 personal attacks (homicide, rape, aggravated and simple assault), 450 (53 percent) were committed by chronic offenders; of the 2,257 property offenses, 1,397 (62 percent) were by chronic offenders; and of 193 robberies, 135 (71 percent) were by chronic offenders. Of all violent offenses committed by nonwhites, 70 percent were committed by chronic delinquents; of all violent acts committed by whites, 45 percent were performed by chronic offenders. Clearly, these boys represent what is often referred to as the "hard core" delinquents. That such a high proportion of offenses—particularly serious acts of violence—is committed by a relatively small number of offenders is a fact that loudly claims attention for a social action policy of intervention.

Besides crude rates of delinquency, the birth cohort study also scores seriousness of offenses. Derived from an earlier study of psychophysical scaling by Thorsten Sellin and Marvin Wolfgang, entitled *The Measurement of Delinquency* (1964; see also Newman 1976), these scores denote relative mathematical weights of the gravity of different crimes. The scores represent a ratio scale such that a murder is generally more than twice as serious as rape; an aggravated assault, depending on the medical treatment necessary, may be two or three times more serious than theft of an automobile; and so on. The scale has been replicated in over a dozen cities and countries, and has proved useful in cohort analysis. Each offense in the penal code committed by members of the cohort was scored. This process permitted us to assign cumulative scores to the biography of each offender, and to average seriousness by race, socioeconomic status, age, and other variables.

A further refinement shows the types of physical injury committed by each racial group. The frequency distributions and the weighted rates show that more serious forms of harm are committed by nonwhites. No whites were responsible for the 14 homicides. The modal weighted rate (WR) for nonwhites is to cause victims to be hospitalized (although the modal number is in the "minor harm" category). The WR and number for white offenders is for minor harm. By using the WR, based on the judgmental scale of the gravity of crime, the 14 homicides represent more social harm to the community during the juvenile lifespan (WR = 125.4) of nonwhite boys than the combined 456 acts of physical injury committed by white boys during their juvenile years (WR = 119.3). The same can be said about the 59 acts of violence committed by nonwhites that resulted in hospitalization of the victims (WR = 142.3).

In short, if juveniles are to be delinquent, a major thrust of social action programs might be to cause a change in the character rather than in the absolute reduction of delinquent behavior. It could also be argued that concentration of social action programs on a 10 percent reduction of white index offenses (N = 1,400; WR = 483.63) would have a greater social payoff than a 10 percent reduction of nonwhite nonindex offenses (N = 3,343; WR = 382.45). To inculcate values against harm, in body or property, to others is obviously the major means to reduce the seriousness of delinquency, among both whites and nonwhites. We are simply faced with the fact that more social harm is committed by nonwhites, and the resources and energies of efforts to reduce social harm should be employed among nonwhite youths, especially the very young.

An examination of age-specific rates, especially weighted rates, by race clearly reveals that the incidence of nonwhite offenses at young ages is equal to or greater than that of whites at later ages. For example, the average crude rate per 1,000 nonwhites aged 7–10 (83.32) is higher than the rate for whites between 14 and 15 years of age (72.24). In fact, for the single year when nonwhites in this cohort were 16 years old, their weighted rate of delinquency (633.49) was higher than the rates for whites accumulated over their entire juvenile careers (587.84). It may be said that nonwhites in their sixteenth year inflict more social harm, through delinquency, on the community than do all whites from age 7 to age 18. The incidence (weighted) of nonwhites at age 11 (112.80) is just slightly less than that for whites at age 15 (120.79) or 17 (122.50), a striking indication of the relatively high rate of delinquency at a very youthful age among nonwhites. Another way of pointing out this fact is to draw attention to the greatest weighted rate difference between whites and nonwhites, which is at ages seven through ten. Here the average weighted rate for nonwhites (83.32) is 11.4 times greater than the rate for whites (7.33). At age 11, nonwhites have a weighted rate 6.3 times higher than whites; thereafter the difference fluctuates, dropping to a low of 3.6 times higher for nonwhites at age 15.

THE SUBCULTURE OF VIOLENCE

The forces that generate conditions conducive to violent crime are strongest in urban communities. Cities, with large populations, greater wealth, more commercial establishments, and more products of technology, also provide more frequent opportunities for theft and greater chance of violence. Victims are depersonalized, property is insured, consumer goods in more abundance are vividly displayed and are more portable.

Urban life is commonly characterized by population density, spatial mobility, ethnic and class heterogeneity, reduced family functions, and greater anonymity. When, on a scale, these traits are found in high degree, and when they are combined with poverty, physical deterioration, low education, residence in industrial and commercial centers, unemployment or unskilled labor, economic dependency, marital instability or breakup, poor or absent male models for young boys, overcrowding, lack of legitimate opportunities to make a better life, the absence of positive anticriminal behavior patterns, higher frequency of organic diseases, and a cultural minority state of inferiority, it is generally assumed that social-psychological mechanisms leading to deviation, crime, and violence are more likely to emerge.

All of this is not meant to obscure the fact that poverty also exists in small towns and rural areas. But when multiplied by congested thousands and transmitted over generations, poverty, as Oscar Lewis has claimed, becomes a culture. The expectations of social intercourse change, and irritable, frustrated parents often become neglectful and aggressive. The children inherit a "subculture of violence" where physically aggressive responses are either expected or required by all those sharing not only the tenement's plumbing but also its system of values (Wolfgang and Ferracuti 1967). Ready access and resort to weapons in this milieu may be essential for protection against others who respond in similarly violent ways. Carrying a knife or some other protective device becomes a common symbol of willingness to participate in violence, to expect violence, and to be ready for its retaliation.

A subculture of violence is not the product of cities alone. The thugs of India, the *vendetta barbaricina* in Sardinia, and the *mafioso* in Sicily have existed for a long time. But the contemporary American city has the major accoutrements not only for the genesis but also for the highly accelerated development of this subculture, and it is from this subculture that most violent crimes come.

There is a conflict of value systems. That is, there is a conflict between a prevailing culture value and some subcultural entity. But commission of homicide by actors from the subculture at variance with the prevailing culture cannot be adequately explained in terms of frustration due to failure to attain normative goals of the latter, in terms of inability to succeed with normative procedures (means) for attaining those goals, or in terms of the individual psychological condition of anomie.

The highest rates of homicide occur among a relatively homogeneous subcultural group in any large community. Similar prevalent rates can be found in some rural areas. The value system of this group, we contend, constitutes a subculture of violence. From a psychological viewpoint, we might hypothesize that the greater the degree of integration of the individual into this subculture, the higher the possibility of violent behavior in a variety of situations. From the sociological side, there should be a direct relationship between rates of homicide and the extent to which the subculture of violence represents a cluster of values around the theme of violence.

1. *No subculture can be totally different from or totally in conflict with the society of which it is a part.* A subculture of violence is not entirely an expression of violence, for there must be interlocking value elements shared with the dominant culture. It should not be necessary to contend that violent aggression is the predominant mode of expression in order to show that the value system is set apart as subcultural. When violence occurs in the dominant culture, it is usually legitimized, but most often is vicarious and a part of fantasy. Moreover, subcultural variations may be viewed as quantitative and relative. The extent of difference from the larger culture and the degree of intensity, which violence as a subcultural theme may possess, are variables that can and should be measured by known social-psychological techniques (Shelley and Toch 1962). At present we are required to rely almost entirely upon expressions of violence in various forms of conduct—parent-child relationships, parental discipline, domestic quarrels, street fights, delinquent gang conflicts, criminal records of assaultive behavior, criminal homicides, and so on—but the number of psychometrically oriented studies in criminology is steadily increasing in both quantity and sophistication, and from them a reliable differential psychology of homicides should emerge to match current sociological research.

2. *Establishing the existence of a subculture of violence does not require that the actors sharing in these basic value elements express violence in all situations.* The normative system designates that in some types of social interaction a violent and physically aggressive response is either expected or required of all members sharing that system of values. That the actors' behavior expectations occur in more than one situation is obvious. There are various circumstances in which homicide occurs, and the history of past aggressive crimes in high proportions, among both the victims and the offenders, attests to the multisituational character of the use of violence and to its interpersonal characteristics. (Wolfgang [1958] showed that 65 percent of the offenders and 47 percent of the arrests of those offenders were for aggravated assults. Here, then, is a situation in homicide often not unlike that of combat, in which two persons committed to the value of violence come together and in which chance often dictates the identity of the slayer and of the slain.) But, obviously, persons living in a subculture designated as one of violence cannot and do not engage in violence continuously; otherwise normal social functioning would be virtually

impossible. I am merely suggesting, for example, that ready access to weapons in this milieu may become essential for protection against others who respond in similarly violent ways in certain situations, and that the carrying of knives or other protective devices becomes a common symbol of willingness to participate in violence, to expect violence, and to be ready for its retaliation (see Schultz 1962).

3. *The potential resort or willingness to resort to violence in a variety of situations emphasizes the penetrating and diffuse character of this culture theme.* The number and kinds of situations in which an individual uses violence may be viewed as an index of the extent to which the values associated with violence have been assimilated. This index should also be reflected by quantitative differences in various psychological dimensions, from differential perception of violent stimuli to different value expressions in questionnaire-type instruments. The range of violence expected is rarely made explicit for all situations to which an individual may be exposed. Overt violence may even occasionally be a chance result of events. But clearly this range and variability of behavioral expression of aggression suggests the importance of psychological dimensions in measuring adherence to a subculture of violence.

4. *The subcultural ethos of violence may be shared by all ages in a subsociety, but this ethos is most prominent in a limited age group, ranging from late adolescence to middle age.* I am not suggesting that all members of a particular ethnic, sex, or age group share in common the use of potential threats of violence, but merely that the known empirical distribution of conduct, which expresses the sharing of this violent theme, shows greatest localization, incidence, and frequency in limited subgroups and reflects differences in learning about violence as a problem-solving mechanism.

5. *The development of favorable attitudes toward, and the use of, violence in a subculture usually involve learned behavior and a process of differential learning, association, or identification* (Sutherland and Cressey 1955; Glaser 1956). Not all persons exposed—even equally exposed—to a subculture of violence absorb and share the values in equal portions. Differential personality variables must be considered in an integrated social-psychological approach to an understanding of the subcultural aspects of violence. I have taken the position that aggression is a learned response, socially facilitated and integrated as a habit, in more or less permanent form, among the personality characteristics of the aggressor. Aggression, from a psychological standpoint, has been defined by A. H. Buss (1961) as "the delivery of noxious stimuli in an inter-personal context." Aggression seems to possess two major classes of reinforcers: the pain and injury inflicted upon the victim and the extrinsic rewards. Both are present in a subculture of violence, and their mechanism of action is facilitated by the social support that the aggressor receives in the group. The relationship among aggression, anger, and hostility is complicated by the habit characteristics of the first, the drive state of the second, and the attitudinal interpretative nature of the third. Obviously, the immediacy and the short temporal sequence of anger,

with its autonomic components, make it difficult to study a criminal population that is some distance removed from the anger-provoked event. Hostility, although amenable to easier assessment, does not give a clear indication or measure of physical attack because of its predominantly verbal aspects. However, it may dispose one to or prepare one for aggression.

6. *Aggression, in its physical manifest form, remains the most criminologically relevant aspect in a study of violent assaultive behavior.* If violent aggression is a habit and possesses permanent or quasi-permanent personality trait characteristics, it should be amenable to psychological assessment through appropriate diagnostic techniques. Among the several alternative diagnostic methodologies, those based on a perceptual approach seem able, according to the existing literature (Hankoff 1964), to elicit signs and symptoms of behavioral aggression, demonstrating the existence of this "habit" and/or trait in the personality of the subject being tested. Obviously, the same set of techniques being used to diagnose the trait of aggression can be used to assess the presence of major psychopathology, which might, in a restricted number of cases, have caused "aggressive behavior" outside, or in spite of, any cultural or subcultural allegiance.

7. *The use of violence in a subculture is not necessarily viewed as illicit conduct, and the users therefore do not have to deal with feelings of guilt about their aggression.* Violence can become a part of the life-style, the theme of solving difficult problems or problem situations. It should be stressed that the problems and situations to which I refer arise mostly within the subculture, for violence is used mostly between persons and groups who themselves rely upon the same supportive values and norms. A carrier and user of violence will not be burdened by conscious guilt, then, because generally such an individual is not attacking the representatives of the nonviolent culture, and because the recipient of this violence may be described by similar class, status, occupational, residential, age, and other attribute categories that characterize the subuniverse of the collectivity sharing in the subculture of violence. Even law-abiding members of the local subculture area may not view various illegal expressions of violence as menacing or immoral. Furthermore, when the attacked see their assaulters as agents of the same kind of aggression they themselves represent, violent retaliation is readily legitimized by a situationally specific rationale, as well as by the generally normative supports for violence.

This proposition of a subculture of violence suggests that violence is learned behavior and that if violence is not a way of life, it nonetheless is normal, not individual pathological behavior. And the greater the degree of commitment to the subcultural values, the less the freedom and the fewer the alternative responses the individual has to cope with social encounters. Homicide, rape, and aggravated assault historically have been predominantly intragroup crimes—within the family, among friends and acquaintances, neighbors, and the intimate social network. More physical mobility and more intergroup interactions have increased the number of victims outside the subculture, the number of victims who are strangers to the offenders—and, consequently, have promoted wide public fear of random assaults and victimization.

THE SOCIOPSYCHIC DIMENSION

My colleague from the University of Rome, Franco Ferracuti, and I have used the "subculture of violence" thesis to explain crimes of violence in Sardinia and to examine the social-psychological basis of similar crimes in a Puerto Rican population (Ferracuti, Lazzari, and Wolfgang 1970; Ferracuti and Wolfgang 1973). But physical punishment and general aggressivity are also variables that enter into a more intrapsychic interpretation of the violent child. For example, Pentti Hellsten and Olavi Katila (1965) examined homicides committed by persons under 15 years of age in Finland from 1935 to 1962. The family histories and personalities of five young murderers were considered. In all the cases the authors tried to find common specific traits that could explain the malignant development. In every instance relations between the parents were disturbed. The fathers, in particular, were not able to be objects of affection and identification for their sons. In comparison with their wives they were weak and withdrawing, overshadowed by their spouses. All four mothers and the one stepmother were superficial in their emotional life—emotionally cold, egotistic, incapable of deep affection or compassion for other people. In the cases in which the father fell victim to the son, the mother had displayed lack of respect toward the husband and had impressed his insignificance on the boy. In addition, the mothers had displayed undisguised aggressivity toward their husbands, so that, in one case, the mother became the actual murderer and in another case condoned the murder.

In 1971, Douglas Sargent reported a hypothesis that sometimes the violent child who kills is acting as the unwitting agent of an adult, usually the parent, who unconsciously prompts the child to kill so that the adult can vicariously enjoy the benefits of the act. He develops two corollary hypotheses: first, that the adult plays upon latent hostility the child feels for the victim; second, that the child's susceptibility to, and readiness to act upon, the unconscious prompting of the adult rests upon the child's immature ego and the presence of a special emotional bond between child and adult. Five cases are presented to demonstrate the relationship between a child's homicide and an adult's desire for the results of that crime.

Jane Watson Duncan and Glen M. Duncan (1971) also report that a history of parental brutality is a major criterion for assessing an adolescent's potential for homicidal behavior within the family. They examined five cases of adolescent homicide against parents and showed the progressive deterioration of the interpersonal relationships with the parent-victim. Moreover, Robert Sadoff (1971) examined two cases of parricide (one matricide, one patricide) having similar psychodynamics. The cruel and unusual relationship between victim and murderer is striking. The bond that existed between parent and child was dramatically ambivalent, one of fear and hatred on the one hand, and inexplicable loyalty and yearning on the other. In both cases the predictability of violence was high, and relatives and friends had warned the families of impending explosion if the relationships did not change. These cases indicate that a bizarre neurotic relationship exists between victim and assassin, in which the parent-victim mistreats the child excessively and pushes the child to the point of explosive violence. Because of a strong attachment to one of the parents, the child is unable to leave voluntarily without such explosion. A sense of relief, rather than remorse or guilt, is felt following the parricide, a circumstance that leads to a feeling of freedom from the abnormal relationship. In the two cases a borderline or schizoid personality preceded the acute psychotic deterioration at the time of the killing, and the psychosis was most likely acute paranoid schizophrenic reaction that remitted spontaneously. Also, in both cases an altered state of consciousness existed at the time of the killing, with resultant later amnesia regarding the episode.

This last example appears not to be derivable from, or generated by, a subculture of violence, and thereby shows the more extreme and statistical (as well as normative) aberrance of child violence. Here is violence related to acute psychosis rather than to precipitating forces in the subcultural value system, long ingested into the personality of the culture carrier.

Other evidence about the social dynamics of family structure buttresses this proposition of a subculture of violence where physically assaultive behavior is not uncommon. So prevalent is family violence and the literature on this topic, that in 1974 the National Institute of Mental Health published an elaborate bibliography entitled *Violence at Home* (Lystad 1974). In addition to homicides and aggravated assaults, John O'Brien (1971) reports, for example, spontaneous mention of overt violence in 24 of 150 interviews of divorce-prone families, and George Levinger (1966) found physical abuse a factor in divorce in 20 percent of middle-class and 40 percent of working-class families. A national survey (Mulvihill, Tumin, and Curtis 1969) revealed that one in four men and one in six women approved of slapping a wife under certain circumstances, but lower education and social class were closely correlated. Richard Gelles' exploratory study (1974) reported that violence was a regular and patterned occurrence in 20 percent of families. Uri Bronfenbrenner (1958), Melvin Kohn (1969), Suzanne Steinmetz and Murray Straus (1973), and Lawrence Kohlberg (1964) are only a few among many researchers in social psychology and social psychiatry who report more use of physical punishment and violence among working-class parents than among middle-class parents. This is not to say that middle-class families do not experience violence; but their violence appears to be less publicly visible, less frequent, more restrained, and less lethal. Gelles, in his paper on violence and pregnancy (1975) does not indicate the social class of the 80 families interviewed, but the inference can be drawn that most were of lower socioeconomic status. Violence, he says, occurred during pregnancy in about one-quarter of the families reporting violence. Sexual frustration, a family transitional state of stress and tension, biochemical changes in the wife making her more critical of the husband, and defenselessness of the wife are among the factors he says contribute to assaults on pregnant women. He says: ". . . locating a family where a pregnant wife has been assaulted could serve as an indicator of this family's use of physical aggression as a response to stress and the likelihood of future occurrences of violence toward children" (1975, p. 84). Such a commentary leads to questions about public policy concerned with family crisis intervention, which is still more discussed than implemented and researched.

SOCIAL AND PSYCHOLOGICAL ELEMENTS OF CONTROL

Dispersal of the Subculture of Violence

Violence in the family is partly a reflection of violent expressions in the culture in general. But serious crimes within the family are most commonly related to subcultural values that minimally do not much inhibit physical responses or that maximally condone and encourage them.

The residential propinquity of the actors in a subculture of violence has been noted. Breaking up this propinquity, dispersing the members who share intense commitment to the violence value, could cause a break in the intergenerational and intragenerational communication of this value system. Dispersion can be done in many ways, and does not necessarily imply massive population shifts, although urban renewal, slum clearance, and housing projects are feasible methods. Renewal programs that simply shift the location of the subculture from one part of a city to another do not destroy it. In order to distribute the subculture so that it dissipates, the scattered units should be small. Housing projects and neighborhood areas should be microcosms of the social hierarchy and value system of the central dominant culture. It is in homogeneity that the subculture has strength and durability. (Some of these same notions have been presented by Richard Cloward and Lloyd Ohlin [1960] in their brief discussion of controlling the conflict subculture, and by Peter McHugh [1964] in his paper on breaking up the inmate culture in prison before resocialization can begin.)

Before one set of values can replace another, before the subculture of violence can be substituted by the establishment of nonviolence, the former must be disrupted, dispersed, disorganized. The resocialization, relearning process takes place best when the old socialization and old learning are forgotten or denied validity. Moreover, as Kenneth Moyer, a physiological psychologist, said: "Since the sensitivity of the neural substrate for certain types of aggressive behavior appears to be sensitized by frustration, it should be possible, at least in part, to reduce aggressive behavior by changing the environment to reduce frustration and deprivation" (1971, p. 83). Once the subculture is disintegrated by dispersion of its members, aggressive attitudes are not supported by like-minded companions, and violent behavior is not regularly on display to encourage imitation and repetition.

Murray Straus (1974) has written eloquently about aggression in families, especially about the notion of "leveling," in the sense of giving free expression to one's aggressive feelings in the natural family setting (in therapy referred to as the "ventilationist" approach). He argues compellingly and convincingly against it, and suggests instead that "the greater the degree of intellectualization the lesser the amount of physical aggression" (1974, p. 27). The "rationality of middle class life" and the "rules of civility" that have evolved through the ages in the name of humanism are viewed as significant elements in the reduction of family violence.

Emergency Domestic Quarrel Teams: Family Crisis Intervention

The usual caveat about domestic homicides and the capacity of the police to do much about them appears in almost every annual report from the Department of Justice: ". . . police are powerless to prevent a large number of these crimes. . . . The significant fact emerges that most murders are committed by relatives of the victim or persons acquainted with the victim. It follows, therefore, that criminal homicide is, to a major extent, a national social problem beyond police prevention" (1971, p. 9).

But new rationales and new empirical evidence suggest rejection of this assertion. Some time ago I wrote about this issue as follows:

> A particularly intriguing innovation suggested as a special function of community centers is the "emergency domestic quarrel team" of specialists. With a staff of sufficient size and training to provide twenty-four-hour service on call, the team is viewed as capable of offering rapid social intervention, quick decisions and accelerated resolutions to families caught in a conflict crisis. Traditionally, the police are called into service when domestic quarrels erupt into public complaints. The police are trained principally to interrupt fights in verbal or physical form. Their chief function is to prevent assault and battery at the moment of arrival, to arrest assaulters on complaint, and then to go about their business of patrolling their sector. It is well known that some of the most potentially dangerous calls police officers act upon are reports of domestic quarrels. About one-fifth of all policemen killed on duty are those who responded to "disturbance" calls which include family quarrels.

The suggestion of an emergency domestic quarrel team is meant to include the police as part of the group, primarily to protect the team itself from violent attack. After the initial danger has subsided, the police could withdraw, leaving the team of psychological and social work specialists to talk with the family, to suggest the best solution to the immediate problem, and work out a program for a more enduring resolution.

It should be kept in mind that a relatively high proportion of criminal homicides are classified as emerging from domestic quarrels. These are acts usually committed indoors, not normally subject to observation by patrolmen on the street, and therefore considered virtually unpredictable and unpreventable. An emergency domestic quarrel team might, therefore, function from a community center as an effective homicide-prevention measure. Intervening in earlier stages of physically aggressive strife in the family, the team could conceivably thwart the progression of family violence to the point of homicidal attack. The strategies for resolving domestic conflict are details too specific to pursue further here, but, clearly, experience would accumulate to provide increasing sophistication. In addition to information shared in an adequate referral system, these teams would soon develop expertise in handling many difficult family situations. It should be further noted that twice as many homicides among blacks as among whites are known to develop from quarrels within the family, usually between husbands and wives. These are almost invariably lower class, poor black families. The emergency teams to which we refer would operate out of centers often located in areas with high concentrations of the black poor.

Various indices to measure the success of these teams can easily be imagined. Keeping in mind our focus on crimes of violence, one index of the value of emergency intervention could be changing rates of domestic homicides and aggravated assaults. Perhaps even rate changes in general throughout an ecological area would be influenced. After all, an unresolved family conflict may cause some family members to displace their cumulative aggressivity on close friends, neighborhood acquaintances, or even strangers. For we do not know the number of homicides and aggravated assaults recorded by the police as due to altercations which may have had their genesis in a hostile exchange in the family (Wolfgang and Ferracuti 1967, pp. 301–02).

Stimulated by the work of Morton Bard (1969), a family crisis intervention unit was established in New York City some years ago. The research design and findings were inconclusive, although Bard did report that training police officers for handling family disputes appeared to be related to the fact that no homicides occurred in any of the 962 families previously seen by the unit, that family assaults were fewer, and there were no injuries to any officer in the unit (Bard and Berkowitz 1969; see also Bard and Zacker 1971).

New data yield empirical support for the hypothesis that family homicides might be reduced if more intensive, focal attention were given to domestic disturbance police calls. Data were collected, under support from the Police Foundation, on homicides and aggravated assaults occurring in Kansas City, Missouri, during 1970 and 1971 (see Wilt and Bannon 1974). In one-fourth of the homicides and one-third of the aggravated assaults, either the victim or the suspect had an arrest for a disturbance or assult within two years of the homicide or assault in question. Even more striking is the fact that about 90 percent of the homicide victims and suspects had previous disturbance calls to their address, with about 50 percent of them having five or more calls. The same was true for assault victims and suspects. Unfortunately, in most of these previous disturbance calls, the police did nothing more than prevent immediate physical injury; there were few arrests or convictions. The family members were asked whether, if charges were not brought, they expected to repeat their disturbance behavior; two-thirds said "yes." Apparently subsequent disturbances often result in family homicide. The best set of variables to predict a future domestic killing or aggravated assault includes the presence of a gun, a history of previous disturbance calls, and the presence of alcohol. Moreover, when physical force was used in a family disturbance, known threats to do so had preceded it in eight out of ten cases.

The study in Kansas City is a complex and elaborate one. My major reason for mentioning it is to suggest that with appropriate intervention counseling, and referral and treatment of family disturbance calls, there is a probability of reducing not only domestic homicide but family violence in general.

Increasing Affection and the Repertoire of Response

James Prescott (1975) has synthesized cultural and laboratory studies of punitiveness, repression, and violence. In a compelling argument for more freedom of pleasurable physical expression and less repression of sexual behavior, Prescott links crimes of violence, physically aggressive behavior in general, child abuse, and homicide with deprivation of physical affection and repression of adolescent sexual behavior. In rather strong declarative terms he asserts:

> I am now convinced that the deprivation of physical sensory pleasure is the principal root cause of violence. Laboratory experiments with animals show that pleasure and violence have a reciprocal relationship. That is, the presence of one inhibits the other. A raging violent animal will abruptly calm down when electrodes stimulate the pleasure centers of its brain. Likewise, stimulating the violence centers in the brain can terminate the animal's sensual pleasure and peaceful behavior. . . . Among human beings, a pleasure-prone personality rarely displays violence or aggressive behaviors, and a violent personality has little ability to tolerate, experience, or enjoy sensuously

pleasing activities. As either violence or pleasure goes up, the other goes down (Prescott 1975, p. 11).

Moyer (1971, p. 122) summarizes the concept of reciprocal inhibition in neural systems that underlie certain hostile and affiliative tendencies, and points out the common experience that one does not have both affiliative and hostile tendencies toward the same stimulus at the same time. "It seems highly likely, in fact," he says, "that the neural substrates for hostility and affiliation are reciprocally inhibiting. When the tendencies to one are physiologically blocked, the result is an *increase* in the display of its counterpart" (1971, p. 126).

Aggression control of the internal environment, as well as the external, is possible through drugs, hormone therapy, and direct stimulation of brain systems that inhibit aggressive tendencies. But I have emphasized behavioral alteration of the external environment, partly because I am a sociologist and partly because the macro forces appear to be more capable of effecting a greater reduction of criminally violent behavior.

Sensory deprivation, lack of affection in infancy and adolescence, and sexual repression and punitiveness are forms of reduced alternatives and expressions of freedom. It may be noteworthy that Sheldon and Eleanor Glueck (1950) found a similar relation between lack of affection by the mother, erratic supervision by the father, and delinquency among boys. I would add further that the psychological and sociological ingredients of the subculture of violence are characterized by physical punishments and a variety of sensory and cultural deprivations, thus reducing alternative behaviors and pleasurable responses, promoting promiscuity (but not affection and bonds of intimacy), restricting the mobility of the mind, and thereby reducing individual freedom.

Sociologically, a subculture-of-violence thesis may be used to explain much of the violence generated by a value system geared to a ready response of physical assault on ritually acknowledged cues (see West and Wiles 1974). When the repertoire of response is limited to relatively inarticulate capacities, when physical punishment of children is common practice, when the rational civility of middle-class values of respect for person and property are undeveloped or missing, when parental affection for and caring supervision of children are absent, the major modal categories of violent behavior are more likely to emerge in expressions that violate both codified law and dominant communal norms.

Affection and firm supervision of children cannot be legislated. Teachers and significant others cannot, by administrative fiat, become kind and gentle. But activities can be promoted in the home and school to socialize children— even those from a subculture of violence—into nonviolence, to desensitize them to linguistic and behavioral cues that evoke violence. Pleasurable rewards and lucid, certain, but not severe sanctions promote the greatest probability of nonviolent conformity to social rules of conduct. If, as Prescott, Moyer, and others claim, pleasure and violence are antitheses, the message is as old as it is clear, and is buttressed by evidence from all the healing arts and behavioral sciences: Give the infant, child, adolescent, and adult affection, recognition, and reward for being alive and unharming to others; offer freedom from excessive restraints, pleasures for the body, and a broad repertoire of verbal articulating ways to respond to stimuli in all forms of social interaction.

REFERENCES

Amir, Menachim. 1971. *Patterns in Forcible Rape.* Chicago: University of Chicago Press.

Bard, Morton. 1969. "Family Intervention Police Teams as a Community Mental Health Resource." *Journal of Criminal Law, Criminology and Police Science* 60, no. 2: 247–50.

———, and Bernard Berkowitz. 1969. "Family Disturbance as a Police Function." In *Law Enforcement, Science and Technology*, ed. S. Cohn, II. Chicago: IIT Research Institute.

Bard, Morton, and Joseph Zacker. 1971. "The Prevention of Family Violence: Dilemmas of Community Intervention." *Journal of Marriage and the Family* 33, no. 4: 677–82.

Bronfenbrenner, Uri. 1958. "Socialization and Social Class Through Time and Space." In *Readings in Social Psychology*, ed. E. E. Maccoby, T. M. Newcomb, and E. L. Hartley, pp. 400–25. Third ed. New York: Holt, Rinehart and Winston.

Buss, A. H. 1961. *The Psychology of Aggression.* New York: John Wiley.

Cloward, Richard A., and Lloyd Ohlin. 1960. *Delinquency and Opportunity: A Theory of Delinquent Gangs.* Glencoe, Ill.: Free Press.

Curtis, Lynn A. 1974. *Criminal Violence.* Lexington, Mass.: D. C. Heath.

Duncan, Jane W., and Glen M. Duncan. 1971. "Murder in the Family: A Study of Some Homicidal Adolescents." *American Journal of Psychiatry* 127, no. 11: 74–78.

Fannin, Leon F., and Marshall B. Clinard. 1965. "Differences in the Conception of Self as a Male Among Lower and Middle Class Delinquents." *Social Problems* 13 (Fall): 205–14.

Ferracuti, Franco, Renato Lazzari, and Marvin Wolfgang. 1970. *Violence in Sardinia.* Rome: Mario Bulzoni.

Ferracuti, Franco, and Marvin Wolfgang. 1973. *Psychological Testing of the Subculture of Violence.* Rome: Mario Bulzoni.

Gelles, Richard. 1974. *The Violent Home: A Study of Physical Aggression Between Husbands and Wives*. Beverly Hills, Calif.: Sage.

———. 1975. "Violence and Pregnancy: A Note on the Extent of the Problem and Needed Services." *Family Coordinator* (January): 81–86.

Glaser, Daniel. 1956. "Criminality Theories and Behavioral Images." *American Journal of Sociology* 5: 433–44.

Glueck, Sheldon, and Eleanor Glueck. 1950. *Unraveling Juvenile Delinquency*. New York: Commonwealth Fund.

Hankoff, Leon D. 1954. "Prevention of Violence." Paper read at annual meeting of Association for the Psychiatric Treatment of Offenders, New York.

Hellsten, Pentti, and Olavi Katila. 1965. "Murder and Other Homicide by Children Under Fifteen in Finland." *Psychiatric Quarterly Supplement* 39, no. 1: 54–74.

Kohlberg, Lawrence. 1964. "The Development of Moral Character and Moral Ideology." In *Review of Child Development Research*, ed. Lois W. Hoffman and Martin L. Hoffman, I, 383–433. New York: Russell Sage Foundation.

Kohn, Melvin L. 1969. *Class and Conformity: A Study in Values*. Homewood, Ill.: Dorsey.

Levinger, George. 1966. "Sources of Marital Dissatisfaction Among Applicants for Divorce." *American Journal of Orthopsychiatry* 26: 803–07.

Lystad, Mary, ed. 1974. *An Annotated Bibliography: Violence at Home*. Rockville, Md.: National Institute of Mental Health.

McHugh, Peter. 1964. "Social Requisites of Radical Individual Change." Paper presented at annual meeting of American Sociological Association, Montreal.

Miller, Walter B. 1958. "Lower Class Culture as a Generating Milieu of Gang Delinquency." *Journal of Social Issues* 14: 5–19.

Moyer, Kenneth E. 1971. "Kinds of Aggression and Their Physiological Bases." In Moyer, *The Physiology of Hostility*, pp. 25–51. Chicago: Markham.

Mulvihill, Donald J., Melvin M. Tumin, and Lynn A. Curtis. 1969. *Crimes of Violence*. Washington, D.C.: U.S. Government Printing Office.

Newman, Graeme R. 1976. *Comparative Deviance: Perception and Law in Six Cultures*. New York: Elsevier.

O'Brien, John, 1971. "Violence in Divorce-Prone Families." *Journal of Marriage and the Family* 33: 692–98.

Prescott, James W. 1975. "Body Pleasure and the Origins of Violence." *Bulletin of the Atomic Scientists* (November): 10–20.

Sadoff, Robert L. 1971. "Clinic Observations on Parricide." *Psychiatric Quarterly* 45, no. 1: 65–69.

Sargent, Douglas. 1971. "Children Who Kill—a Family Conspiracy?" In *Theory and Practice of Family Psychiatry*, ed. John G. Howells. New York: Brunner/Mazel.

Schultz, L. G. 1962. "Why the Negro Carries Weapons." *Journal of Criminal Law, Criminology and Police Science* 53: 476–83.

Sellin, Thorsten, and Marvin E. Wolfgang. 1964. *The Measurement of Delinquency*. New York: John Wiley.

Shelley, E. L. V., and H. Toch. 1962. "The Perception of Violence as an Indicator of Adjustment in Institutionalized Offenders." *Journal of Criminal Law, Criminology and Police Science* 53: 463–69.

Steinmetz, Suzanne, and Murray A. Straus. 1973. "The Family as Cradle of Violence." *Society* (formerly *Transaction*) 10: 50–58.

Straus, Murray A. 1974. "Leveling, Civility, and Violence in the Family." *Journal of Marriage and the Family* 36: 13–29.

Sutherland, Edward, and Donald Cressey. 1955. *Principles of Criminology*. Philadelphia: Lippincott.

U.S. Department of Justice. 1974. *Crime in the United States*. Washington, D.C.: U.S. Government Printing Office.

West, D. J., and P. Wiles. 1974. *Research on Violence*. Bibliographical Series no. 6. Cambridge: Cambridge University Press. With bibliography by Cheryl Stanwood.

Wilt, G. Marie, and James Bannon. 1974. "A Comprehensive Analysis of Conflict-Motivated Homicides and Assaults, Detroit, 1972–1973." Submitted to Police Foundation, Washington, D.C.

Wolfgang, Marvin. 1958. *Patterns in Criminal Homicide*. Philadelphia: University of Pennsylvania Press.

———. 1970. *Youth and Violence*. Washington, D.C.: U.S. Department of Health, Education, and Welfare.

——, and Franco Ferracuti. 1967. *The Subculture of Violence*. London: Tavistock and New York: Barnes and Noble.

Wolfgang, Marvin, Robert M. Figlio, and Thorsten Sellin. 1972. *Delinquency in a Birth Cohort*. Chicago: University of Chicago Press.

9

THE PRISON AS AN AGGRESSIVE SOCIAL ORGANIZATION

Marek Kosewski

SOCIAL REGRESSION TOWARD AGGRESSION

The present paper focuses upon the mechanisms by which people enter into relations that result in the formation of groups, or social organizations at large, marked by aggressive acts of the members. Such associations will be called aggressive social organizations.

Let us consider a number of features illustrating the functioning of groups composed of aggressive individuals. The most characteristic intragroup norm is expressed in the principle that the weaker and less aggressive individual is dominated by the stronger and more aggressive one (see Czapów and Manturzewski 1960; Yablonsky 1962). Physical domination is the basis for differentiation in social status and social role within the group. In particular, the role of the leader implies supreme fighting competence. By accepting this state of affairs, the group members contribute to the emergence of a definite social expectation: the higher a member's social status, the more aggressive that person's behavior must be.

The differentiation of group roles and of status in the group on the basis of physical domination and fighting competence is a typical feature of highly organized animal communities. We might therefore say that human groups that are organized on this pattern have suffered a primitivization of social organization: they have regressed to a more primitive development stage, one marked by physical coercion as the differentiating factor of group role and status.

Requests for reprints should be sent to Marek Kosewski, Psychology Department, Institute of Social Prevention and Research, Warsaw University, ul. Podchorążych 20, 00-721 Warsaw, Poland.

Are there any other similarities in the functioning of animal communities and violent gangs that would indicate the social primitivization of the latter? To find an answer to this question, let us examine the ways by which an individual advances in social status within the gang.

A high status in the gang is acquired primarily through fights with other gang members; this circumstance prejudges the functional role of intragroup aggression, which serves to promote an individual's social status. While also instrumental in raising the individual's prestige within the group, extragroup aggression is but an auxiliary, rather than an essential, tool in the striving to attain high status in the group. The seemingly irrational aggression described by Yablonsky (1962) occurred in the presence of other members of the violent gang, and it seems reasonable to assume that its aim was to raise the aggressor's prestige among his companions. Approached from this angle, we could scarcely speak of irrational aggression but, rather, of well-motivated, goal-directed behavior. Incidentally, the typical hoodlum never attacks anyone is isolation, and it need not be fear that prevents him from doing so; it is, rather, the fact that such an attack would not be noticed by his companions, and hence could bring only bodily harm.

The typical unprovoked, incidental act of aggression has much in common, as far as social function is concerned, with what students of animal social life have called "attack for flattery." Observed in monkey groups, such attacks involve sudden, unprovoked aggression against the nearest animal, the sole function of which appears to be the promotion of the aggressor's social status in the pack (Kawamura 1967).

A great many, if not the vast majority of, aggressive attacks occurring in violent gangs are directed at other group members or at members of other gangs. This is evidenced by the intensity of fights between rival juvenile gangs striving to win control over a particular area, or between gangs invading each other's territory. Trespassing on the territory controlled by a gang exposes the trespasser—whether another gang or a member of such a gang—to attack, in analogy to the "territorial aggression" observed among animals.

These similarities in the social functioning of highly organized animal groups and violence-based human groups entitle us to speak of the primitivization of human social behavior and its regression to an evolutionarily earlier stage. Such a formulation does not preclude the presence of rather essential differences between animals and human organizations of this kind. Evidently, human organizations function with reference to supreme values that serve to integrate and organize a group. It does not require much imagination to think of groups counting violence, fighting, and aggression among their crucial norms or values. Initially forming the underlying principle of behavior, aggression can separate itself from its original goal—the attainment of status in the group—to become a self-contained value and a criterion by which members of the group judge themselves and their fellow members. Functioning in this way, the group tends to evolve its own "ideology." When such an ideology has come to encompass a number of groups, we speak of the emergence of a subculture of violence, in extension of the meaning assigned to this term by M. E. Wolfgang and F. Ferracuti (1967).

We have noted a number of similarities between the social organization described above and the organization and social functioning of the higher organized animals. Considering that human social organizations are based, as a rule, on such values as education, profession, intelligence, or income, and that physical domination and violence are the basic differentiating factors of social status in animal communities, it seems reasonable to describe the emergence among humans of groups based on violence as a regression in the formation and functioning of communities. On the understanding that violence implies aggression, we are tempted to refer to the pertinent phenomenon as social regression toward aggression, and to the outcome of this process as an aggressive social organization.

In the concluding part of this paper the reader will find some hypotheses concerning the conditions that favor the formation of specific kinds of aggressive social organizations. With this aim in mind, let us now examine a social organization based on aggression in some detail. Studies conducted in Poland and in other countries indicate that the informal organization developed by prison inmates through reliance on the norms of the traditional prison subculture— known as the inmates' "other life"—has a number of important traits in common with the aggressive social organization.

THE PRISON COMMUNITY AND ITS FUNCTIONING

There are two reasons why attention is paid in this paper to the social processes observed in the prison community. By approaching this community as an aggressive social organization, I hope to establish how the norm of aggressive behavior, developed within a social group or community, affects the entire range of the individual's social functioning. It has to be realized that this norm is not autonomous, and that mutual aggression among members of an aggressive social organization is not the only rule regulating their social conduct. Any social organization is based, in its functioning, on a particular set of principles, which are the product of the conditions in which people live and of the cultural values and personality traits of these people.

On studying the penitentiary and criminological literature from a number of countries, I find a marked convergence and similarity in the processes and events observed in the penitentiaries, despite variations in local conditions.

What are the reasons for the far-reaching similarity of developments recorded behind prison walls? For one, all penitentiaries reveal some common features, primarily isolation, rigor, and discipline. There is further the similarity of attitudes of the larger society toward the convicts across a great many countries: rejection, distrust, and lower status resulting from the serving of a sentence. Also of considerable importance is the architecture of the traditional prison and the paramilitary organization of the prison guards. Placed in similar conditions, prisoners are bound to be exposed to similar processes as members of a prison community.

The Prison Community

Students of prison life tend to overlook the fact that the prison community does not consist of the inmates alone. They customarily stress the prisoners' code of conduct—norms handed down by oral tradition—next to prison mores and inmate roles, as well as prison slang and songs. The resulting system is often referred to as the prison subculture.

Along with the informal organization that imposes definite requirements on the inmates—and also, as argued below, on prison officials—there is the formal organization of a prison, which comprises prison guards and the administrative personnel. This social group is governed primarily by what is laid down in writing, in the form of legal and statutory regulations; these regulations determine the internal structure of the group and specify the rules by which its members are guided in treating the inmates and in their mutual relations.

It goes without saying that the injunctions imposed on the inmates by the prison authorities are usually at odds with the inmate community's requirements: the prison official is obliged to obtain information about the inmates, but the inmates are obliged to withhold such information; the prison official is supposed to educate the inmates, which implies the latter's collaboration, while the inmates are committed to refrain from all collaboration with the administration; and so on. The same can be said of the requirements facing the guards: those imposed by the formal system are at odds with those enforced by the inmates' informal organization. Should this mean that inmates and guards are incessantly at war? Quite the contrary; the prison tends to function smoothly, aside from sporadic riots and other collective acts of disobedience on the part of the inmates.

Combined with the realization that guards and inmates pursue contradictory goals, the smooth functioning of prison suggests that through long practice and tradition certain rules of conduct have developed in the prison that have to be observed by both guards and inmates. These principles that govern the functioning of the prison community exhibit several features:

1. They are acceptable to either group by being compatible with both the written norms of conduct and the unwritten mores of either group.

2. They are instrumental in promoting a cause of importance to either group, even though each group may have an entirely different reason (motivation) to support the given cause. For instance, discipline and some kind of a rule of law are in the interest of both the inmates and the guards, though for different reasons.

3. They are of sufficient importance to either group so as to prove stronger than the desire to observe the norms of conduct ideally prescribed by the otherwise clashing rules of the two groups. In other words, in some cases the principles in question must impose limitations on the realization of "ideal" group duties.

4. In order to safeguard the smooth functioning of the entire system, these principles cannot contradict each other. They complement each other, or imply each other, or mutually restrict their interpretation and applicability so as to prevent a clash between two principles.

The present analysis of the functioning of the prison community starts with an evaluation of the deprivations suffered as a result of being placed in prison. I shall adhere in this respect to the classification of inmate deprivations offered by G. M. Sykes (1958). There are also Polish studies in agreement with Sykes's proposition (Waligóra 1966; Jarzębowska-Baziak 1972; Górski 1972).

There is every reason to subscribe to another assumption by Sykes (Sykes and Messinger 1960): that the norms and rules of conduct developed by inmates are meant to alleviate the deprivations they suffer in prison.

The principles governing the functioning of the prison community, as specified below, apply to the traditional penitentiary, or one that imposes all five types of deprivations described by Sykes (1958).

My investigations, which led to the formulation of the principles listed below, were conducted among young adult convicts (up to 25 years of age) in Poland, and as such they apply directly to this kind of prison community.

The Principles of Interpersonal Relations

The Principle of Violence

Violence, or physical domination, is the basic factor that determines the domination and submission relations obtaining among prisoners and between prisoners and prison officials.

From the moment of incarceration on, the inmate is exposed to violence in the prison. This fact prejudges submission to prison officials. The convict's refusal to follow an order—say, to leave the cell—is countered with physical force; the most severe punishment of the Polish prison, sleeping on a bed of boards, amounts to a physical deprivation. The application of violence by prison officials is subject to strict regulations and is in no way arbitrary, but this does not affect the essence of the deprivation imposed on the inmate.

The principle of violence applies broadly to the prisoner's relations with other inmates, as evidenced by a number of studies. According to Sykes (1958), the conflict is afflicted by both psychological and material deprivations. From the frustration-aggression theory it follows that such deprivations usually result in an upsurge of aggressive tendencies, which may be channeled by the development of a suitable system or a framework for aggression.

Forming a principle of behavior, aggression can be easily diverted toward the fellow inmate by a mechanism known in psychology as the displacement of aggression (Berkowitz 1962). Aggressive attacks on prison guards occur fairly rarely, being committed, as a rule, by inexperienced individuals who have had no time nor possibility to adjust to prison conditions (Fox 1954, 1958). The mature and experienced inmate prefers to avoid conflicts with the prison authorities, and the inmate code in fact recommends the avoidance of trouble. For it is not only punishment that deters inmates from directing their aggression against prison officials. The inmate's social status in the prison hierarchy depends primarily on the use of violence in relation to fellow inmates; nothing short of such aggression is instrumental in elevating the inmate's social status. Intelligent prisoners who know how to muster support from their fellow inmates are able to acquire a high status in the prison community. The same can be said of well-known criminals, such as professionals with long records. But this is important only in determining the level at which physical confrontation may take place. The question of rule over the cell or cellblock will eventually be decided by a fight between the present leader and a rival.

It has to be borne in mind that in the specific conditions of the prison community, where the individual is largely deprived of all customary tokens of social status—property, clothing, and professional standing—sheer force aligned with aggressiveness is the most easily available and easily perceived instrument of stratification. The adoption of this manner of winning social status in the inmate collectivity is also promoted strongly by the inmates' preincarceration records; many of them were members of violent gangs before being taken into custody.

One particular effect of the principle of violence is the presence in the prison community of the "scapegoat" as an inmate category upon whom the aggression of the other inmates is centered. There is considerable evidence to show that through the diversion of inmates' aggressive tendencies toward individuals branded as punks, rats, or square Johns, the leaders are shielded against their fellow inmates' enmity.

Greatly intensified by the frustrating prison conditions and channeled by the leaders upon lower-status members of the inmate community, aggression—as prescribed by the inmate code of conduct—is instrumental in developing social stratification among prisoners. By determining the relationships obtaining in the inmate collectivity, the principle of violence helps to alleviate the psychological deprivations suffered by the prisoners.

This last statement calls for some elaboration. By employing aggression, the prisoner can play the classical role of the male, displaying brute force, and can also satisfy sexual needs by bullying a fellow inmate into submission, or by sheer violence. The resultant stratification endows some of the group members with power of a particular scope, and provides them with opportunities to make decisions and issue orders, thus meeting their need for independence and autonomy and compensating for their formal status as absolutely submissive and docile subordinates in relation to the prison officials.

By providing a social stratification among the inmates with reference to force and aggressiveness, aggression enables each prisoner to define his own value on a fairly subtle scale. It offers a simple tool that can be used to effect shifts along this scale toward a higher status and, hence, also a higher self-esteem. Originally threatened by society's rejection, the convict's self-image is boosted effectively by promotion in the prison hierarchy, especially since the progressive institutionalization of the inmates in the prison community gradually increases the significance of the norms and standards obtaining behind prison walls.

Thus we come to the conclusion that the principle of violence serves to alleviate the deprivations, listed by Sykes (1958), that are imposed on the prisoner by loss of autonomy and heterosexual relations, and also lessens the feeling of rejection by the larger society and the ensuing threat to self-image.

The Principle of Exploitation

The social hierarchy formed on the principle of violence in the prison community imposes an internal order involving specific relations between inmates with reference to unwritten mutual rights and duties. The first and foremost right is that of exploitation of the lower-status inmate by the higher-status inmate, along with the corresponding duty of the former to serve the latter in return for protection and assistance against outward threat.

Thus, interpersonal relations in the prison, covering both relations among inmates and between inmates and guards, are based directly on the benefits each party can derive from such relations.

The tendency for such interpersonal relations to develop in the prison community shall be referred to as the principle of exploitation. To forestall misunderstanding, let me make it clear at this point that there are certain limitations to the rule: the term "tendency" implies that there may be exceptions, in that relations between a particular inmate and a guard, or between two particular inmates, may not be based on this rule.

A further limitation concerns the scope of relations among inmates based on the principle of exploitation. Not every member of the prison elite is able to have any lower-status inmate as a subordinate on account of the former's status. The exploitation-based bonds are a product of the personal relationship between two inmates or a number of inmates. Alternatively, relations between two people may be fully balanced, in that both parties need each other to the same extent, rendering approximately equal services to one another. This means that the leader participating in such a relationship need not apply coercion to obtain the other's submission: the need for protection and security can be so strong under prison conditions that the subordinated individual may be interested in maintaining this kind of relationship.

This leads us to the function of interpersonal relations based on the principle of exploitation. While suggestive of the opposite, subordinate relations do meet the need for security. The hierarchy elaborated in this way introduces a certain order in the inmate community; relations between convicts are subject to definite norms from which ensue their rights and duties, including the right of exploitation, but also protection of the exploited from an attack by an aggressive fellow inmate. The weaker partner in such a relationship is faced with a vicious circle: whereas submission diminishes the threats one is exposed to by his submission, it also lowers one's status in the eyes of the collectivity and thus exposes him to attack from criminals dedicated to the principle of violence.

The other function of the principle of exploitation and of interpersonal relations based on this principle is to satisfy the inmates' material needs. In this sense the principle of exploitation amounts to the material exponent of the principle of violence, supplementing in some ways the functions of the latter. Relations between inmates and guards also are based on mutual exploitation. In the traditional prison opposing ideologies have developed, on the strength of which the inmates regard the guards as treacherous hacks and the guards look upon the inmates as cows. While both written and unwritten rules prohibit close relations between the two parties, the practical functioning of the prison leads to frequent violations of these rules.

Leaving aside the case of the informer, who is held in contempt by both parties, there are always some "good guys" on either side, between whom closer relations exist. Based on the principle of exploitation, such relationships are tolerated by both parties; the prison authorities show tolerance so long as these relations do not trespass a certain limit, being used to obtain information on the "other life" of the prison—for the purpose of maintaining order and discipline. Prisoners tolerate them, too, so long as they do not endanger the informal structure and the functioning of the inmate community, and provided they have no overtones of friendship and solidarity. Such relationships are thus justified by the benefit the inmate is able to derive from them. Generally speaking, both parties admit the possibility of mutual manipulation—whether the object is the guard or the inmate—aimed at securing specific benefits. A truly close relationship would endanger the homogeneity of the entire system and of the traditional status quo.

The Principles of Intergroup Relations

The Principle of Relative Solidarity

Solidarity in resisting and opposing the other party, the prevalent type of cohesion in prison, develops in either the inmate community or the guard community whenever one group feels threatened by the other.

This formulation implies that both the inmate group and the guard group have an internal structure like any other social group—that is, that members of the group, while performing specific roles, align themselves into various subgroups, and that these subgroups are linked by ties of mutual dependence, rivalry, or subordination, so that the entire group has a low degree of cohesion. This pattern of relationships between subgroups is subject to change; the degree of cohesion is bound to increase whenever one of the groups (in this case, inmates or guards) is exposed to danger generated by the presence or functioning of the other group. The principle of relative solidarity implies that the essence of cohesion and solidarity consists in the sense of integrity of each group. Either group reveals solidarity only in opposing the other group (hence the term "relative solidarity"). The inmates' cohesion and solidarity vis-a-vis the prison system and its representatives come into evidence only when the inmates themselves are exposed to threat or deprivation by the system.

In this sense one might say that the inmates' solidarity is but an outcome of the deprivations they suffer in the prison system.

The Principle of the Status Quo

Both prisoners and guards seek to maintain the status quo in the structure and functioning of the entire prison community.

The inmates' solidarity vis-a-vis the prison and its representatives is severely limited by another principle, the need to maintain the status quo in the relationships between the formal and the informal organizations of the prison. The fact that inmates and guards alike have been functioning together for so long, and have produced a stereotype of sufficient stability to resist various reform projects, shows that the two groups are linked by a substantial area of mutual understanding and common interests. Let us inspect some dimensions of this area, particularly those where the interest of the formal organization coincides with the interest of the prisoners' informal organization (see Sykes and Messinger 1960; McCorkle 1962).

First, just as the guards are concerned with the prevention of crimes and infractions among inmates, so the inmates are interested in keeping criminality, usually directed at members of the community, down to a certain level. The basis for this kind of attitude is the desire to avoid excessive tensions that might split the inmate community if the victimized inmates should turn to the prison authorities for help. A single complaint might suffice to have the leader of a cell or cellblock transferred to another area, where he would have to start building up his status from scratch. In effect, the leaders have reasons to restrain their subordinate inmates from committing grave offenses or infractions; in this way they work toward the same ends as the prison authorities.

Second, not all activities imposed on the inmates by the authorities are unattractive: sports, movies, and cultural pursuits are in fact a kind of reward conditional upon a minimum of order and discipline. At the same time the cell-block officer is unable to manage the collectivity of 100 or 200 unorganized inmates without delegating part of his power to some inmates and their leaders; in fact, precisely this helps him to maintain tidiness and discipline in the cell-block. But having secured the cooperation and good will of the inmates, the cell-block officer is bound to repay these services of the influential inmates by shutting his eyes to minor infractions or by issuing positive evaluations of conduct that ensure them privileges. In effect, the formal prison organization collaborates extensively with the informal organization in pursuit of the same goals, though in each case the motivation is different.

Third, the hierarchical system in the inmate community, together with the various inmate roles, especially those that involve interaction with the guards (that is, inmates delegated to jobs of some authority), develops in close correspondence to the prison staff structure. Since the delegated inmates are those who enjoy the confidence of a particular officer, any change in the formal structure of the prison is bound to bring about changes, or at least uncertainty, in the informal organization.

The net result is that both parties have a common goal in the preservation of the status quo and of the principles of functioning of the entire prison community.

It has been stated before that the informal structure developed by the inmates is designed to alleviate the deprivations they suffer. The limits set to this goal are due not only to the objective physical conditions, but primarily to what the prison administration informally endorsed at the outset. The minimal goals pursued by the prison administration comprise peace, discipline, and order. The inmates, on the other hand, are primarily interested in alleviating at least some of the hardships they endure by preserving the principle of violence and the principle of exploitation, both of which contribute to such alleviation. The interests of the two parties are the same up to a certain point, and this informal settlement is heeded by either side, forming the principle of the status quo.

The Principles of the Prison Community's Functioning in Relation to the Norms of the Inmate Code

The principles that govern the functioning of the prison community raise a number of problems. One is the relation of these principles to the norms specified by the prisoners' informal code of conduct. In general the principles are superior to the code norms, and as such they determine the practical interpretation of the latter. There is no clash between the two; the code norms in fact reflect the principles that govern the functioning of the prison community. The principle of relative solidarity can be traced in the norms that prohibit the inmate from informing or collaborating with the prison authorities. The principle of violence reappears in the injunctions "be tough and brave" and "don't let a guy insult you." The principle of exploitation is contained in the norms that refer to sly dogs and pigeons. The status quo principle cannot be easily related to any particular norm of the inmate code, but its effect is evident in the formulation of certain norms.

What is significant is that the inmate code norms contain bans on definite conduct toward the prison official—bans on informing, asking for help, collaboration—as stipulated by the postulates of enmity and contempt. None of them, however, demands that a "big wheeler" be tough on the guards by applying either physical or verbal aggression. And precisely this banned behavior would seem consistent with the tough attitude, except that it would have disastrous consequences for peace and order, jeopardizing all attempts at maintaining discipline, and hence would endanger the minimal goals pursued by the prison authorities, as well as infringe on the status quo obtaining in the relations between inmates and guards. It is likewise obvious that members of the "elite" as a rule avoid open conflict with prison officials.

FACTORS CONTRIBUTING TO THE FORMATION OF SOCIAL ORGANIZATIONS BASED ON VIOLENCE AND AGGRESSION IN PRISON

The discussion of violence and aggression makes one aware of some of the conditions that are conducive to the formation of aggressive social organizations. All the aggression-based social organizations discussed so far have been formed by criminals: violent juvenile gangs or criminals in prison. Attention has been paid to young people ranging in age from under 17 to 25. But the formation of aggression-based social organizations seems also to be typical of juvenile delinquents confined in correctional institutions, as evidenced by S. Jedlewski (1966) in his study of the informal organization of juveniles confined to reformatories.

Criminals who build up the aggressive organization of the prison either have a record of confinement in correctional institutions or have been active in violent gangs. By this line of reasoning one could point convincingly to the vicious circle of cause and effect, and not be far from the truth. There is no denying that one of the sources of the aggressiveness observed in the social behavior of criminals is the norm of aggressive behavior and violence in relations with other people, a norm acquired rather early in life.

Without rejecting this finding, let us turn our attention to those elements of the prison milieu that seem to be conducive to the formation of aggressive social organizations. Investigating the mechanism by which the informal social ties formed among prisoners develop into informal organizations, one cannot fail to derive several corollaries from available sociological and pschological evidence.

For the functioning of an informal organization in a penitentiary, the inmates of that institution must exhibit a modicum of common goals and aims, common norms and values, and an articulated social structure involving well-differentiated social ranks and roles.

Suppose a new penitentiary is gradually being filled with convicts. There is no informal organization in the prison, to start with. For simplicity's sake let us further suppose that the newly arrived inmates do not know each other, and hence cannot import a previously formed social structure. Let us now examine the ways in which an informal inmate organization might develop and what its ultimate structure would be.

The prison in question is of the conventional type, so the deprivations suffered by the inmates would be of the type discussed earlier. Placed in such conditions, the inmates would visualize their common aim as resisting the oppressive situation, in an effort to alleviate the deprivations imposed on them.

From the very start a social barrier tends to build up between inmates and prison officials. The roles of official and inmate are clearly delineated from the outset. This differentiation comprises differences in social status, in rights and privileges, in dress, and in many other areas. If we add to this the psychologically obvious tendency among inmates to view the prison staff as responsible for the deprivations associated with confinement, there can be no doubt that a sense of identity and of enmity toward the officials is bound to develop in the inmates.

In a situation where prisoners remain together for long periods, experience a sense of identity as a collectivity, and possess a minimum of common aims, a social structure is bound to develop through the operation of group processes. The norms and values developed in the group become the basis for the differentiation in social roles and social ranks among its members. What would be the norms in the case under consideration and how would the social ranks and roles become differentiated?

Any group is apt to develop some norms and values that serve to integrate it; what norms and values these are, depends largely on the personality of the people composing the group and on the aims of the group. In this case the group is composed of criminals, people who have internalized too few socially approved norms and values. In their case the differentiation in social status inside the group cannot proceed on the basis of such criteria as education or professional or social standing, which differentiate people in the larger society. All the prisoners bring into their confinement is their experience won in peer groups and criminal gangs, and in this the use of violence figures prominently.

The fact that the norm of violence becomes particularly important in jail seems to be due to two factors implied by the prison conditions. For one, the deprivations imposed by the confinement are a source of frustration, which tends to generate aggression. Another circumstance increases the inmates' susceptibility to aggression, and their tendency to behave aggressively. If we assume that among prison inmates there is a tendency to differentiate social roles and ranks on the basis of a specific need or demand for such differentiation and for the development of a power hierarchy, then this demand can be met most fully by physical domination. As it is, violence meets two essential conditions: it serves to differentiate between individuals with considerable precision and clarity, and it permits the necessary mobility in the power structure.

There is, further, the important function of violence consisting in the alleviation of the deprivations suffered by inmates. The principle of violence and aggression molds interpersonal relations in the inmate community, and as such is also functional in terms of the goals of inmate activities.

Hence there are two factors that favor the development among inmates of an informal organization based on aggression.

First, the inmates' past records and experiences are brought to the prison. Being short of internalized norms and values of a prosocial character, convicts have nothing with which to replace the unavoidable norm of violence as a regulator of social relations in the prison community.

Second, the specific conditions of the prison cause violence and aggression to become the overriding principle of social functioning. By adopting the principle of violence, the inmates seek to adjust to a difficult situation full of deprivations. An experiment conducted by C. Haney, C. Banks, and P. Zimbardo (1973) suggests that the social regression toward aggression, resulting in the formation of a social organization based on violence, is a kind of defensive reaction that enables the inmates to preserve their psychological integrity. In the "experimental prison" established by these authors and filled with volunteer undergraduates as both inmates and guards, the "inmates" developed profound emotional disturbances in a matter of days. The reason may have well been their inability (arising from a number of factors) to develop an informal organization based on violence.

EMPIRICAL DATA

The research results reported below are based on a random sample of 122 young-adult prisoners and are related to predictions derived from the principle of violence. The empirical verification of the operational hypotheses ensuing from the remaining three principles of prison community function, by means of quantitative techniques, is now in progress.

Hypothesis 1

To verify the hypothesis that long-term prisoners are more aggressive than short-term prisoners, two prisoner subgroups were isolated, on the basis of their prison records, from among the sample of young first offenders (N = 122) studied by the author.

Subgroup 1, short-term prisoners, consisted of 25 inmates, none of whom had served more than four months both in the penitentiary and under arrest (average imprisonment 3.3 months).

Subgroup 2, of long-term prisoners, consisted of 23 inmates who had served from 11 to 14 months (average term 12.2 months) at the time of investigation.

Table 9.1 presents the essential data concerning age and type of offense committed by each subgroup. A chi-square test showed that the difference between the two in the type-of-offense distribution is insignificant.

TABLE 9.1

Age and Type of Offense: Short-Term and Long-Term Prisoners

Subgroup	Mean Age	No. Who Committed Aggressive Crimes	No. Who Committed Nonaggressive Crimes	Total
Short-term (up to 4 mos.)	19.1	15	10	25
Long-term (11– 14 mos.)	18.6	13	10	23
Total		28	20	48

Source: Compiled by the author.

Table 9.2 presents the scores on the Buss-Durkee Inventory of the long- and short-term prisoners. This evidence supports my claim that prisoners who had served a longer term were more aggressive than those who had served a shorter term. An average difference of nine months in the length of time in prison (or under arrest) produces significant differences on the scale of physical attack (I) and a distinct increase in hostility (V and VI) and negativism (IV). The duration of imprisonment does not affect the tendency to verbal hostility (VII), which in any case is fairly strong in young-adult offenders. The subgroups do not differ significantly in the sum for scales I to VII (the test of overall aggressiveness). Thus, whereas the subgroups do not differ in overall aggressiveness, they do differ in the structure of aggressive behavior and the longer prison terms affect the various manifestations of aggression in different ways. The hypothesis postulating an influence on the term of imprisonment on a prisoner's aggressiveness should therefore be reformulated in the following way: Young-adult first offenders show a stronger tendency toward the use of violence in relation to fellow inmates and more hostility and negativism when they remain in prison for a longer term.

TABLE 9.2

Mean Scores on Buss-Durkee Inventory: Short-Term and Long-Term Prisoners

Subgroup	I Attack	II Indirect Aggression	III Irritability	IV Negativism	V Resentment	VI Suspiciousness	VII Verbal Hostility	VIII Guilt	Sum of I-VII
Short-term	10.1	8.1	10.9	3.8	7.0	8.7	13.2	10.9	61.8
Long-term	13.2	8.6	10.2	4.7	9.3	12.2	13.7	12.8	72.2
F-Ratio of Variance	1.34	1.99	1.21	1.32	1.07	1.01	1.17	1.43	1.63
Level of Significance of T-Test	0.01	–	–	0.05	0.01	0.01	–	0.09	–

Source: Compiled by the author.

In the case of recidivists the duration of imprisonment is bound to be less significant, since the extension of the prison term by a few months over the earlier term of a dozen or so months (on the average) does not add much to the imprisonment record of the convicts. Consequently, the correlations between the term served and aggressiveness should be different for the group of first offenders and the group of recidivists. The actual findings are shown in Table 9.3. The association between aggressiveness and term of imprisonment is indeed less pronounced for recidivists, whose correlation coefficients are statistically nonsignificant, than for first offenders.

Hypothesis 2

To test the hypothesis that higher-status inmates are more aggressive than lower-status inmates, three 30-member groups of young-adult prisoners were studied by Janusz Krawczenko (1968).

The first group comprised "tough guys" or "big wheelers" who commanded considerable authority among their fellow inmates and were the ringleaders of the prison's "second life." Their identification presented considerable problems, and called for consultation with the prison psychologist and prison officials, the analysis of personal files (notably regarding offenses in prison), and, on many occasions, interviews with fellow inmates.

The second group comprised prisoners discriminated against by the prison community—"punks," "rats," and others—who were frequent victims of aggression. This group could be easily identified, since in most cases its members eventually turn to the prison administration for help. The selection procedure was basically the same as with the previous group.

The third group comprised young-adult offenders drawn randomly from the prison population.

With this kind of selection the highest average status will be in the first group, the lowest in the second group, and that of the third group will be somewhere between the other two.

As can be seen from Table 9.4, members of the prison elite differ from the average prisoners (the third group) only in the use of violence.

For Scale VII the F-ratio of the variance in the random group to the variance in the high-status group amounts to 3.42 and is significant at the 0.02 level. But since the differences between the means were based merely on Student's t (a nonparametric test could not be employed because of the unavailability of the data obtained four years earlier), the significance of the difference on scale VII between these two groups can be regarded only as a hypothesis derived from the difference between means.

The high-status group differs from the low-status group on three scales: attack, irritability, and verbal hostility, and in the sum of scales I to VII, which reflects overall aggressiveness. It will be noted that only the scale of attack does

TABLE 9.3

Correlations between Duration of Imprisonment and Aggressiveness Measured on Buss-Durkee Inventory

Group	I Attack	II Indirect Aggression	III Irrita-bility	IV Nega-tivism	V Resent-ment	VI Suspicious-ness	VII Verbal Hostility	VIII Guilt	Sum of I-VII
Young-adult first offenders (N = 122)	0.45†	0.07	0.18*	0.29†	0.31†	0.33†	0.09	0.09	0.025
Young-adult recidivists (N = 35)	0.10	0.32	0.12	0.09	0.10	0.15	0.08	0.17	0.13

*significant at .05 level.
†significant at .01 level.
Source: Compiled by the author.

TABLE 9.4

Buss-Durkee Index Mean Scores of High-Status, Low-Status, and Randomly Selected Prisoners

Group	I Attack	II Indirect Aggression	III Irrita- bility	IV Nega- tivism	V Resent- ment	VI Suspicious- ness	VII Verbal Hostility	VIII Guilt	Sum of I–VII
High- status	16.1	8.7	15.2	6.7	9.6	9.9	18.8	11.4	85.0
Low- status	10.6	7.8	11.3	5.5	8.0	10.5	13.7	14.7	67.4
Random sample	13.2	8.9	15.1	6.1	10.3	11.1	14.9	12.5	79.6

Source: Compiled by the author.

actually differentiate all three groups from one another. In this way the experiment has confirmed that a prisoner's informal status is a function of aggressiveness, and notably of the inclination to apply violence.

Up to this point aggressiveness as measured by the Buss-Durkee Inventory has been treated as the dependent variable, whereas recidivism, duration of imprisonment, and other factors have been viewed as independent variables. Such a methodological orientation prejudges the interpretation of the data. For example, the finding that "tough guys" are more aggressive than other prisoners does not tell us whether the more aggressive prisoners are as a rule "tough guys." To tackle this particular problem, we have to reorient our investigation.

Hypothesis 3

The third hypothesis is that aggressive prisoners tend to possess a high status in the informal structure of the penitentiary. From among the random sample of 122 young-adult prisoners, two groups were isolated on the basis of their scores on scales I to VII of the Buss-Durkee Inventory: one scoring above 80 (over $M + 0.72$ s.d.) and the other scoring below 54 (below $M - 0.72$ s.d.). The first of these groups will be called aggressive ($N = 32$); the second, nonaggressive ($N = 32$)..

These groups did not differ significantly in terms of social or occupational structure and level of education. The average prison sentences were 32.27 and 26.68 months, respectively. The difference in the mean duration of imprisonment (8.35 months for the aggressive and 5.52 months for the nonaggressive) did not reach statistical significance ($t = 1.31$ versus the required $t = 2.04$ at the 0.05 level of significance).

On the evidence of data from the personal files and the opinions issued by the prison officials, each subject was assigned to one of three categories: the elite ("tough guys"); the intermediate stratum (representing a majority of the prison community); and the lower stratum (the "punks" and others whose informal status is the lowest).

TABLE 9.5

Aggressiveness as a Function of Informal Status

Group	Elite	Intermediate Stratum	Lower Stratum	N
Aggressive	12	14	6	32
Nonagressive	4	14	12	30
Total	16	28	18	62

Note: $Chi^2 = 6.22$ is significant ($df = 2$) at the 0.05 level.
Source: Compiled by the author.

As can be seen from Table 9.5, aggressive prisoners have a higher status in the prison community than nonaggressive inmates. Confronting this finding with the earlier evidence that a prisoner's aggressiveness increases with informal status, we find aggressiveness and status to be strongly interdependent. Aggressive prisoners hold a high informal status, and the high-status inmates are more aggressive than the others.

These results support squarely the hypothesis that social relations between prisoners are based on the principle of violence. The same evidence confirms the initial suggestion that the informal organization of the prison is based on violence.

REFERENCES

Berkowitz, L. 1962. *Aggression: A Social-Psychological Analysis.* New York: McGraw-Hill.

Czapów, C., and S. Manturzewski. 1960. *Dangerous Streets.* Warsaw: KiW. In Polish.

Fox, V. 1954. "The Frustration-Aggression Hypothesis in Corrections." *Quarterly Journal of the Florida Academy of Sciences* 17, no. 3 (Sept.): 140–46.

———. 1958. "Analysis of Prison Disciplinary Problems." *Journal of Criminal Law, Criminology, and Police Science* (Nov.–Dec.): 329–36.

Górski, J. 1972. "An Analysis of Resocialization Potential of Internal Prison Regulations." Ph.D. dissertation, Faculty of Psychology and Pedagogy, Warsaw University. In Polish.

Haney, C., C. Banks, and P. Zimbardo. 1973. "Interpersonal Dynamics in a Simulated Prison." Department of Psychology, Stanford University. Mimeographed.

Jarzębowska-Baziak, B. 1972. *Resocialization in Correctional Institution for Young Adults.* Warsaw: Wydawnictwo Prawnicze. In Polish.

Jedlewski, S. 1966. *The Pedagogical Analysis of Disciplinary and Isolatory System in Resocialization of Juveniles.* Wrocław: Ossolineum. In Polish.

Kawamura, S. 1967. "Aggression as Studied in Troops of Japanese Monkeys." In *Aggression and Defense*, ed. C. P. Clemente and D. B. Lindsley. Berkeley and Los Angeles: University of California Press.

McCorkle, L. W. 1962. "Guard-Inmate Relationships in Prison." In *The Sociology of Punishment and Correction*, ed. N. Johnston, L. Savitz, and M. E. Wolfgang. New York: John Wiley.

Sykes, G. M. 1958. *The Society of Captives.* Princeton: Princeton University Press.

——, and S. L. Messinger. 1960. "Inmate Social System." In *Theoretical Studies in the Social Organization of the Prison.* Social Science Research Council Pamphlet no. 15, pp. 5–11, 14–19. New York: the Council.

Waligóra, H. 1966. "Psychological Mechanisms of Self-Mutilation." In *Self-Mutilations Among Prisoners,* ed. J. Machalski. Warsaw: Wyd. OBP Min. Sprawiedliwości. In Polish.

Wolfgang, M. E., and F. Ferracuti. 1967. *The Subculture of Violence.* London: Tavistock.

Yablonsky, L. 1962. *The Violent Gang.* New York: Macmillan.

10

AIMS AND TECHNIQUES OF INTERVENTION IN JUVENILE DELINQUENT SUBCULTURES

Sepp Schindler

The general expectation is that juveniles can find their own way in society, but in reality many have more or less serious conflicts with the law and legal authorities. Social integration is not a problem only of juveniles, but primarily the problem of adults. Throughout the history of human society, adults have been frightened by the behavior of young people showing a lack of respect toward them, inconsistency of behavior, and new forms of behavior. This was reported by Socrates and in a medieval town chronicle. Today there are similar opinions all over the world. This, of course, does not mean that all young people become delinquent, but expresses the belief among adults that things are going wrong. Young people become deviant.

This feeling, stated by the majority of adults in a society, is reflected in the way the authorities deal with deviant youngsters. Thus it is understandable that the most important aim is to socialize the young people—and in this sense socialization means changing their behavior. This, of course, involves rather repressive ways of dealing with the problem, in which control and institutional education predominate. Juveniles cannot accept this kind of policy, and so their behavior shows their feelings against the official institutions and people representing them. To make a long story short, it could be said that this method produces security for the adults and continuity in the development of a society in which the minimum of change is provided. The aim is to satisfy the expectations of the adults.

The question arises whether another way of dealing with this problem is possible. This new approach is based on educational traditions concerned with the needs of pupils. It is manifested in works of Johann Heinrich Pestalozzi, Don Bosco, Father Flanagan, and Makarenko—with differences, of course, in what they define as basic needs.

The psychoanalytic tradition, based on consideration and experience, is represented in the works of August Aichhorn (1925) and Fritz Fedl (1951). The common basis for this approach is the recognition of certain deficiencies in the development of deviant young people—for example, a lack of early experiences, especially emotional ones (Bowlby 1951; Spitz 1945) and/or a lack of acceptance by others (Erikson 1950). At the end of the long developmental process the youngster reveals a disturbed attitude toward the self and is barely able to cope with other people.

The whole problem appears far more complex. It should be stressed that what we are dealing with is not a one-way process. Other people—society—do not trust the delinquent, and thus it becomes a vicious circle. Repressive aims, based on strong control, fail to provide any effective changes in the relationship between juveniles and adults. On the contrary, they reinforce the youngster's feeling of being different, deviant (Matza 1969). And it is precisely because of this feeling that the youngster behaves in a different way and, because of the different behavior, is not accepted by those who are more or less integrated into the society. On the other hand, juveniles in the same difficult situation would gladly accept the newcomers, and in this way a subculture would develop. C. Czapów and S. Mantuszewski (1960) have described such a subculture and the intention of juveniles not to be what the adults are.

Some years ago in Vienna there was a youth club in a district known for its high percentage of delinquent juveniles. The club was organized in order to reach these delinquents, but this was never said to the youngsters. The behavior in this youth club was nearly the same as in other clubs. Juveniles were coming to meet each other, to dance, and to discuss their problems. The question was whether the target group actually participated. Consultation with the juvenile court showed that more than half of these juveniles had previously been sentenced. The same phenomenon of participation was later found in contacts with most, but not all, of the delinquents. If the delinquents are taken as normal people, they tend to behave as normal people do. This leads to the policy of helping juveniles to solve their problems themselves; they, and not the social workers, have the full responsibility for their behavior. Thus the situation and the type of interaction are changed, although change may create problems for traditional social workers.

What are the consequences of such a policy? First of all, juveniles should have as much freedom as possible and, second, as much help as necessary. The most important thing is neither institution nor organization, but personal contact with another human being. The organization has only to provide this contact. This is a very serious matter, and the most important aim to be realized: it is the basic principle of the Austrian probation system (*Bewährungshilfe*).

The organization of the probation system tends to be informal. In general, probation officers must know their charges, help them, and advise them. Whatever they do, it must be done with a therapeutic approach. Probation officers must be aware of their own feelings—even hostile ones—toward the youngsters for whom they are responsible. Therefore special meetings have been organized where individual supervision and group sessions give the opportunity to express these feelings freely. Finally, it is necessary to have a situation as free from fear as possible. This is obtained through the independence of the system from the judge and, as much as possible, of the single probation officer from the hierarchy of the organization. Also, the possibility of understanding one's own professional role is provided by training and mutual contacts with juveniles. Such a flexible system can guarantee that the probation officer is in contact with the changing problems of juveniles as they relate to changes in the probation officer's own development and social situation. In such a way individualization becomes possible.

The question arises as to the efficiency of such a complicated system and the methods for its implementation. Ten years after the first experiences with this method, it could be shown that serious crimes could be reduced by half when compared with an untreated group (Schindler 1967). More recently efforts have been made by Pilgram and Steinart (1973) and by Hinsch (1974) to analyze the effects of this treatment. Most differences reported were significant at the 1 percent level, and at least at the 5 percent level. First, there was a difference between institutionalized treatment and the conditional sentence of probation with and without a probation officer. All groups were comparable with respect to criminal records, life history, and length of sentence. The results show that among the institutionalized juveniles only 25 percent were without further criminal records during the following five years, while in the probation group the figure was 55 percent, and in the group of juveniles with conditional sentences, 71 percent had no further criminal record. These findings underline the low success rates of institutionalization.

Probation service proves most successful in cases where the criminal record is of greater importance and/or the school/work record of the delinquent is inadequate. It is also the most effective measure if the family situation of the juvenile is seriously disturbed. In the case of a relatively normal family situation, crimes of lesser importance, and a relatively good labor situation, conditional sentence itself, without any further measures, proves to be most effective. In this case recidivism increases if the young people are put under the care of a probation officer. This shows clearly that the relation between the cause of delinquent behavior—the social situation and the personality—on the one hand, and the sentence—the legal measures—on the other hand, has to be recognized.

Another study shows that for the probation officer it is easier to establish rapport with a juvenile if the officer can define the relevant problems, especially family problems, and if a correspondence exists with the juvenile's own definition of the problem. In other words, help is acceptable and efficient only when a problem really exists and some common perception of the problem is shared. In this case the formal beginning of the personal relation between probation officer and juvenile is not so important. Measures of simple control are not effective at all. Moreover, the results obtained in this study show clearly that the probation officer is most effective when showing acceptance and help, as opposed to control and prohibition. It is of no importance whether parents are accepting or prohibiting. Still, young probation officers and officers with less experience—these are similar but not the same—have more success when operating in the same direction as parents. Older probation officers can be most successful by being accepting even when acting against parents. Most juveniles expect formal social control to be prohibiting and repressive, and to act against their needs. The probation officer must be careful that this does not become a reality; in this way the officer can define the situation adequately and find an agreement with the youngsters so as to fulfill their needs within socially accepted limits. It has also been shown that after a five-year period, the special school and work situation of young people who had been on probation was better than that of juveniles who had been in institutions or without official help.

What do these findings mean for the regulation of aggression? First of all, the repressive reaction to crime and aggression can make this kind of behavior far more intense than it was before punishment. Second, the major influences of the justice system upon human development are more effective when applied with care, understanding, and discrimination. Otherwise there is a strong probability of creating a persistent criminal subculture.

REFERENCES

Aichhorn, A. 1969. *Wayward Youth*. Bern: Huber.

Bowlby, J. 1951. "Maternal Care and Mental Health." Geneva: WHO Monograph 2.

Czapów, Mantuszewski, St. 1960. *Niebezpieczne Ulice*. Warsaw.

Erikson, E. H. 1963. *Childhood and Society*. New York: Norton.

Hinsch, J. 1974. "Langfristige Effekte Jugendgerichtlicher Maßnahmen auf das Sozialverhalten junger Erwachsener." Phil. Diss., Wien.

Matza, D. 1969. *Becoming deviant*. Abweichendes Verhalten, Heisalbar.

Pilgram, A., and H. Steinert. 1973. "Über die Wirkungsmechanismen von Sozialarbeit und die organisaterische Bewältigung der Gegenübertregungsprobleme des Bewährungshelfers." In Biermann, G. Jb.d.Psychohygiene, Bd. 1, Reinhard München, 90–106.

Redl, F. 1955. *Our troubles with defiant youth, children*. Washington.

———, and D. Wineman. 1951. *Children Who Hate*. Glencoe, Ill.: Free Press.

Rosenmayr, L., H. Strotzka, and H. Firnberg. 1968. *Gefährdung und Resozialisierung Jugendlicher*. Wien: Europa-Verlag.

Schilder, E. 1976. "Strafvollzug in Freiheit, Die Entwicklung der bedingten Ver-Urteilung und der Bewährungshilfe in Österreich." In *Festschrift für Christian Broda*. Wien: Europa-Verlag.

Schindler, S. 1967. "Bewährungshilfe und Anstaltseinweisung als Mittel der Strafenpolitik bei Jugendlichen." *Österr. Juristenzeitung* 22: 205-08.

————. 1968. *Jugendkriminalität*. Wien: Österr. Bundesverlag.

Spitz, R. 1945. *Hospitalism, The Psychoanalytic Study of the Child* 1. 53-74, and 2 (1946), 113-17.

11

EMPATHY TRAINING:
A FIELD STUDY IN AFFECTIVE
EDUCATION

Norma Deitch Feshbach

The main focus of this presentation is to report on the progress of a field study, in which children are being trained to develop empathic skills, currently being carried out in several Los Angeles schools. This investigation is part of a broader training program, codirected by Seymour Feshbach and myself, in which training procedures and curricula are being developed for use with children in the upper elementary grades. The major purpose of the procedures and the project is to foster personal growth in the children while enhancing the development of positive social behaviors. Specifically, the objectives of our overall training project are threefold: first, to develop empathy and fantasy training procedures to be used with preadolescents in a variety of settings, especially public schools, for the purpose of reducing aggression and antisocial behaviors and fostering prosocial values and behaviors; second, to further theoretical understanding of the psychological properties of empathy and fantasy, particularly in regard to their role in the regulation of aggressive behaviors and the mediation of positive, prosocial values and actions; third, to develop specific curricula to be used in schools and other settings to implement affective educational goals related to the regulation of aggression and other social actions (Feshbach and Feshbach 1975).

The context of this current endeavor is a long-standing interest in and concern with the theoretical properties of empathy (N. Feshbach 1975a, 1978; Feshbach and Feshbach 1969; Feshbach and Roe 1968), and in the social problems posed by aggression and violence in our society, especially in the schools (S. Feshbach 1970; Feshbach and Feshbach 1971). In recent years there have been a number of major inquiries concerned with the incidence and causes of

---

The Empathy and Fantasy project is supported by National Science Foundation Grant BNS 76-01261.

aggression and violence. One of the striking and depressing aspects of this major social and clinical problem is the degree to which young people are involved. A major theoretical and social question is how to reduce, modify, or regulate these aggressive and violent behaviors in young children—whether they occur in the home, school, or community—without incurring adverse side effects in the process. In view of our background and interest in the process of empathy, as well as our general orientation toward the use of positive socialization practices in child training, including the regulation of aggression, it is not surprising that one of the strategies we selected focuses on procedures designed to enhance empathic behaviors in children.

CONCEPTIONS AND DEFINITIONS

Traditionally, when the question of empathy has been raised, it has been in the context of counseling and psychotherapy (Rogers 1957; Rogers and Truax 1967). In a similar vein, educational interest in this construct has tended to focus on empathy as a dispositional attribute enhancing the teacher's understanding of a student's behavior, very much in the sense that empathy has been posited to facilitate understanding and communication with the client. However, the recent upsurge of research interest and activity in the study of children's empathic behavior is a reflection of a broader contemporary orientation toward children's social development (Chandler in press; Deutsch 1974; N. Feshbach 1978; Hoffman 1975; Smither 1978). Perhaps one attraction of the concept of empathy is that it is related to the cognitive, affective, and social domains of the child's repertoire. Also, empathy may have an appeal because of its humanistic salience. By its very definition it is an interpersonal phenomenon denoting a model of social interaction and social relationship. It has connotations of human bonding, shared experiences, human compassion, and personal intimacy. Some expansive writers have even attributed to empathy a key function of group survival. At the very least it can be considered as having an important role in social communication and in the quality of group interaction.

Given the recency of extensive research interest in children's empathy, it is not surprising that a considerable hiatus exists between the broad social and humanistic properties ascribed to empathy and its current theoretical and empirical status (Shantz 1975). We are still enmeshed in definitional controversies and ambiguities that primarily revolve around the degree of cognitive complexity and emotional involvement entailed in the empathic response. While time constraints do not allow a detailed and complete review of the varied conceptions of empathy and their correlated methodologies, a brief summary of alternative conceptual orientations is relevant to an understanding of our experimental strategies.

One of the earliest references to the concept of empathy appeared in the writings of the German psychologist Theodore Lipps, who labeled the phenomenon *Einfühling*, the literal translation of which is "feeling into another" (Katz 1963). Perhaps the most critical aspect of this historical note is the emphasis given to the vicarious sharing of an affective experience, an emphasis that continues to be represented in major contemporary approaches to the understanding of empathic behavior. The importance of the affective dimension of empathy is evident in the writings and conceptions of W. McDougall (1908), H. S. Sullivan (1953), and Sigmund Freud (1950), as well as in the thinking of more contemporary investigators (Aronfreed 1968; Berger 1962; N. Feshbach 1975a, b, 1976a, 1978). While the individual conceptions vary in explanation and description, especially with regard to whether a cognitive component is implicated in the process, there is a critical thread common to all these affective approaches. The unifying concept that distinguishes them from the more cognitive approaches is the requirement of an affective correspondence between the emotional experience of the observer and the observed. This emphasis on the affective component, which goes beyond the mere understanding of the emotional experiences of the other, emphasizing an affective experience in the observer as a requisite for empathy, is consistent with the conceptualization guiding our project. The latter recognizes that while an empathic response may be contingent upon cognitive skills, it is not equivalent or synonymous with cognitive behavior.

A variety of formulations fall under the general rubric of cognitive and social cognitive approaches to empathy. An early conception of empathy in predominantly cognitive terms appeared in the writings of George Mead (1934). A critical element in his theorizing was that empathy was acquired or learned through role-taking and imitation, a proposition that is represented in contemporary cognitive approaches, most notably in those formulations derived from Piagetian theory (Chandler and Greenspan 1972; Chandler in press). Within this latter framework it is posited that the child's comprehension and understanding of the social environment, while initially immature and egocentric, develop into a more mature cognitive state characterized by the ability to assume the perspective of other individuals. Being able to view the world visually, cognitively, and socially from the perspective of others is contingent upon the development of role-taking skills, which appears to be related to the child's ability to infer the perceptual activities and experiences of another person (Flavell, Botkin, Fry, Wright, and Jarvis 1968). The child who is egocentric, who still has not developed the ability to decenter, is said to be deficient in role-taking skills (Chandler, Greenspan, and Barenboim 1974). Thus the Piagetian concept of decentering has been extended to role-taking activity, but not role-taking in the classic social-role sense of the term. Rather, role-taking is considered as the antithesis of egocentric activity, and refers to the ability to take the position or perspective of another person, a view highly similar to the definition originally offered by Mead (1934) and currently subscribed to by L. Kohlberg (1969).

It is assumed that until the age of six, the child is egocentric and does not distinguish his or her own view of social situations from other possible views

(Selman and Byrne 1974). It is further suggested that from approximately six to ten years of age, the ability accurately to infer the other's intentions, feelings, and thoughts develops, as well as the ability to understand that another person can also infer the child's thoughts. This ability to accurately infer the intentions of others and reciprocally share perspectives is considered genuine empathy by M. J. Chandler (1974). This and other approaches, while varying in the complexity of the assumed mediating process or cognitive activity, essentially view it as equivalent to some form of social cognition. However, when empathy is defined solely in cognitive terms, it appears to have little theoretical utility beyond that contributed by the cognitive functions themselves.

The three-component conceptual model (N. Feshbach 1975, 1976b, 1978; N. Feshbach and Kuchenbecker 1974) that has guided and evolved from the research efforts upon which our present project is based, views empathy in children as a shared emotional response that the child experiences on perceiving another person's emotional reaction. Empathy is conceptualized as having significant cognitive and affective components. At the cognitive level, early rudimentary manifestations of empathy are dependent upon a discriminative skill: the ability to discriminate affective states of others. For example, for a child to react empathically to sadness or joy or some other feeling in another person, the child must be able to identify the relevant affective cues that discriminate these emotional states from each other and from a neutral affective state. This response reflects an elementary form of social comprehension. A second cognitive factor influencing empathy, reflecting a more advanced level of cognitive competence, or social comprehension, is the ability to assume the perspective and role of another person. It is as though the observing child is viewing the situation in the same way as the child who is actually experiencing the situation. Emotional responsiveness is posited as a third component; that is, the observing child must be able to experience the negative or positive emotion that is being witnessed in order to be able to share that emotion. Each of these three factors—discrimination of affective cues, other-person role perspective, and affective responsiveness—important components of empathy, provided us with the conceptual basis and rationale for the design and development of the training exercises used in our field study.

FUNCTIONS OF EMPATHY

While the basis for the construction of the curriculum derives from the question of what empathy is, the question of what empathy does provides the rationale, theory, and empirical basis for the project itself. The question of what empathy does raises a different set of issues and changes the focus from the components of empathy to the functions of empathy. An analysis of the functions of empathy, especially in children, suggests a broad network of possible mediating effects that might include increased self-awareness, social understanding, greater emotional competence, heightened compassion, caring and related behaviors, enhanced communication skills, and greater cohesion among the cognitive, affective, and interpersonal aspects of the child's behaviors— this latter function is the main focus of this paper and the field project.

While the literature relative to each of the possible developmental effects of empathy has not been extensive, and the findings in some cases are ambiguous, in general the research indicates that empathy is likely to have a positive effect on the child's personal and social adjustment (N. Feshbach 1975, 1976a). This appears to be especially the case in reviewing the data on the relationship between empathy and aggression. In a number of separate investigations carried out within and outside of our laboratory, with children and adults, a consistent inverse relationship between empathy and aggression has been obtained (Feshbach and Feshbach 1969; Huckabay 1972; Mehrabian and Epstein 1972; N. Feshbach 1976b). In addition, there is already some preliminary evidence that training in empathy or empathy-related skills, such as role-playing behavior and perspective-taking, holds considerable promise for reducing aggressive or antisocial behaviors and promoting social adjustment and social perspective skills (Chandler, Greenspan, and Barenboim 1974; Spivak and Shure 1974; Staub 1971; Van Lieshout, Leckie, and Smits-Van Sonsheek 1978; Pitkänen 1974).

Whether one emphasizes the cognitive or the affective components of empathic behavior, the enhancement of empathy should result in a reduction in aggressive behaviors and in the facilitation of more constructive forms of social interaction. The cognitive components of empathy—the ability to identify emotion in other people, and especially the ability to see situations from the perspective of another person—can be expected to lead to greater social understanding. A child with such ability who wants to play with an attractive toy is less likely to react aggressively to the attempts of the peer to play with the desired toy than a child who lacks this understanding. Also, it appears that empathy facilitates behaviors that are incompatible with aggression. In a number of investigations of such prosocial behaviors as altruism, sharing, and generosity, empathy is postulated to be a key mediating mechanism (Hoffman 1975; Staub 1971). Closely related to this mediating role of empathy in facilitating prosocial behaviors are its conflict-resolving properties. The ability to assume another person's perspective and to understand the feeling of the other person is presumed to be a key element in conflict reduction. Reducing conflict also reduces conflict-related behaviors, particularly aggression. In addition, perceiving a situation from another's perspective as well as from one's own should promote prosocial, mutually satisfactory solutions to potential conflict situations.

From my point of view, the affective component of empathy has a very special relationship to the regulation of aggression. Aggressive behavior is a social response that has the defining characteristic of inflicting injury upon persons or objects, causing pain and distress. The observation of these aversive behaviors should elicit distress responses in an empathic observer even if the observer is the instigator of the aggressive act. The painful consequences of an aggressive act, through the vicarious affective response of empathy, may be expected to function as inhibitors of the instigator's aggressive tendencies, thus contributing to an inverse relationship between empathy and aggression.

RATIONALE OF THE STUDY

Therein lies the rationale for the study. The goal is to modify, and possibly eliminate, aggressive behavior. But our plan is to accomplish this not by focusing on aggression per se, but through enhancing the child's empathic skills. Thus a major underlying assumption of this study is that youngsters who are considered to be aggressive, acting-out individuals have limited empathic skills or do not use these types of skills in a wide range of situations. We further assume that these cognitive and cognitive/affective behaviors can be trained through prescribed intervention procedures that evolved from a conceptual model of empathy and social understanding.

METHOD

We are now in the third phase of the Empathy Training Study. The initial phase, to which we refer as the preparatory phase, lasted almost a year and was spent in the development of training procedures and measures. During the second phase we carried out the pilot experiment. The pilot study was actually a fully designed study that was so designated because we carried it out in one school and had decided beforehand to use the data obtained as a basis for refining the training procedures. Indeed, on the basis of the findings, which were significant and consistent with the experimental hypotheses, changes were made in the experimental procedures. The third phase of the project, the study proper, is now in progress in two schools in the Los Angeles area.

TRAINING EXERCISES

One of the first major tasks was the conceptual articulation and production of the curriculum for two empathy training programs and for a problem-solving control training program. Three sets of materials, each consisting of 30 hours of exercises and activities, were devised. They were designed for elementary school children in grades 3 to 5, for use in small groups of 4 to 6 children. Each activity lasts from 20 to 50 minutes. Efforts were made to include a variety of tasks and to have the materials presented in an interesting and engaging manner. Activities include problem-solving games, story telling, listening to and making tape recordings, simple written exercises, group discussion, and more active tasks, such as acting out words, phrases, and stories. Several exercises involve videotaping children's enactments and replaying them for discussion.

For the first empathy training condition, called "affective-cognitive," activities were derived from the three-component model of empathy described above. The model states that a truly empathic response to another human being requires identifying the other's emotional state (affect identification), understanding the situation in which the other person is involved from that person's point of view (perspective-taking), and experiencing in oneself the emotions felt by the other person (emotional responsiveness). To increase skill in affect identification, children are asked to identify the emotions conveyed in photographs of facial expressions, tape recordings of affect-laden conversations, and videotaped pantomimes of emotional situations. In addition, the children themselves role-play in a wide range of games and situations in which they act out and guess feelings.

To foster children's ability to assume the perspective of another person, training exercises include a variety of games and activities that become progressively more difficult. Early in the training program the children are asked to experience and imagine various visual perspectives ("What would the world look like to you if you were as tall as Wilt Chamberlain—or as small as a cat?"). They are asked to imagine the preferences and behavior of different kinds of people ("What birthday present would make each member of your family happiest?" "What would your teacher [your older brother, your best friend, a policeman] do if he found a lost child in a department store?"). Children listen to stories, then recount them from the point of view of each character. Numerous later sessions are devoted to role-playing: each child plays a part in a scene, then switches roles and plays the parts of other characters, thus experiencing several perspectives on the same interaction. Children will often be shown videotapes of their enactments to gain an outside perspective of themselves and the situations enacted. Discussion following role-playing sessions includes identification of the feelings experienced by the characters enacted.

Exercises designed for affective-cognitive training are characterized by a general focus on the experience and expression of emotions. Children participate in numerous open (but nonthreatening) discussions of many aspects of emotion.

By contrast, for our second Empathy Training Program condition, designated as "cognitive training," we devised exercises that would focus on the same process but would have a nonaffective content. Thus, exercises in this condition focus on the nonemotional aspects of social interaction, discrimination of social cues that contain information about the thoughts, intentions, and probable future behavior of others; discussion centers on intentionality, motivation, and problem solving, rather than on emotion.

In most cases the exercises or activities are structurally identical and involve similar stimuli, with the specific focus of the discussion being different. For example, one exercise involves listening to and discussing a story: all experimental groups hear the same story, but the groups focusing on cognitive skills discuss the problems presented in the story and the various solutions and alternatives available to the characters, taking into account the different points of view.

The groups focusing on cognitive and affective skills include a discussion of the characters' feelings and reasons for their feelings, in addition to the comprehension points discussed with the cognitive groups. The control groups hear a different story that deals with science or science fiction. There are some activities, however, in which the training stimulus is varied for the different conditions. For example, when the groups focusing on both affective and cognitive skills act out emotions as a form of charades (such as happy, sad, proud, embarrassed, scared), the groups focusing on the cognitive skills act out various people they know (grandmother, father, baby sister). Discussions in both groups emphasize recognizing the cues they use to identify the various actions. The control activity for that exercise is a science discovery project requiring identification of properties of various "mystery powders," and is not intended to parallel the experimental groups directly.

The activities designed for "problem-solving control training" are intended to improve the students' problem-solving skills in nonsocial settings. A large proportion of the exercises focus on discovery learning through science experiments involving interesting chemical reactions and work with solutions of different densities and solubilities. A number of the exercises are games of logic, using attribute blocks and other commercial games. Spatial relations and physical perspective skills are developed through graphing activities and mapping projects. Here, too, wherever possible, control exercises are very similar to the experimental group exercises in format, with only the content varying. For instance, if the experimental groups play the game "Concentration" in order to match facial expressions (happy to happy, angry to angry) of the individuals portrayed on the game cards, the control group plays "Concentration" but matches shapes printed on the cards.

Each of our exercises has an objective in terms of both the specific component of empathy addressed and the specific skill intended to be engendered in the child. The procedure for each exercise is spelled out so that group leader, teacher, graduate student, or any designated trainer can carry it out with the children by following the instructions. At this stage of the project, the exercises have been revised twice, the most significant modifications introduced as a result of the pilot study. The changes were made on the basis of information provided by all the participants: group leaders, observers, research staff, and the children. As a result of this evaluation, efforts were made to make the activities more effective and more involving by eliminating and by changing the exercises and their sequence. The findings of the study proper will determine whether they will be ready for dissemination for the classroom teacher.

THE PILOT EXPERIMENT

The pilot experiment was conducted at an elementary school consisting of 65 percent black, 14 percent Chicano, and 19 percent Anglo children. The study sample included 60 children in the third, fourth, and fifth grades, of whom 30 were girls and 30 were boys. The ethnic distribution was representative of the school population. The school had been identified by the Los Angeles Unified School District administrative staff as one with a high number of reported crimes. It was also ranked in the lower half of the district on an assessment of family income and property in comparison with other Los Angeles schools.

The children were selected for participation in the study on the basis of teacher ratings of their aggressive behavior, and were assigned scores of high, medium, or low aggression. Two-thirds of the sample selected were from the group identified as high aggressives; the rest were from the medium and low groups. Each group had six children, was composed of four high-aggressive children, was mixed racially, and included three boys and three girls.

The research design included two experimental conditions designed to develop empathy and one participating control condition, with two groups of six children for each condition. In addition to the participating subjects, there was an additional sample of 24 nonparticipating controls who were pretested and posttested but did not take part in any other activities. Subjects were assigned at random to these experimental and control conditions, with the constraints regarding level of aggression, sex, and ethnicity noted above. Each experimental and control group met with a trained "instructor" or group leader for one hour, three times a week, for ten weeks. The project had been assigned a regular classroom in the school, which was used for the duration of the study. To control for instructor effects, every group met with three different instructors, and each instructor worked with three or four different groups.

As indicated previously, the empathy training conditions were distinguished by differing emphasis on the theoretical components of the construct of empathy. One condition focused exclusively on the cognitive skills necessary for empathic behavior, while the other focused on both the affective and the cognitive skills required. The groups focusing primarily on the cognitive skills emphasized causes of the behavior of others, while the groups focusing on both cognitive and affective solutions emphasized the feelings involved in the problems or situations as well. The activities for the control condition generally involved nonsocial problem solving tasks and discovery science projects.

A number of measures were administered before and after the ten-week experimental period. These included teacher ratings of aggressive and prosocial behaviors (Adelman and Feshbach 1973), student self-ratings of aggression and prosocial behaviors (Adelman and Feshbach 1973), spatial perspective-taking (Finney 1977)—this measure yields an "other perspective," or correct response, and "Ego Perspective" score—WISC Vocabulary and Comprehension (Wechsler 1974), Wide Range Ready Achievement (WRAT) (Jastak, Jastak, and Bijou 1965), three TAT-type cards, a role-taking measure (Walker 1977), and a Use of Social Information measure (Cutrona and Feshbach 1978). In addition, the children in the study were rated by their teachers for two days each week during the course of the ten-week period. Also, behavior observations were obtained for each child in the training groups during each training session.

The task of measure selection and development was of critical importance in this project, and should be further elaborated. But first, a brief summary of the highlights of the pilot data and the changes we effected in the study as a consequence of our findings are in order. Perhaps the most striking and encouraging finding is the pattern of change in the teachers' ratings of aggression. The greatest decrement in aggression is manifested by the "affective-cognitive" group and the least difference is manifested by the nonparticipating controls, this difference being statistically significant. When an individual analysis was carried out on those subjects who displayed the most positive changes in behavior after empathy training, we found that half of the subjects in the experimental groups showed considerable change on both the aggressive and the prosocial behavior. Of the eight experimental subjects who showed the greatest positive behavior change, six improved dramatically on spatial perspective-taking, particularly in their lowered tendency to make egocentric responses. Four subjects showed marked improvement in their ability to assume the social role of another person. Perhaps most surprising, two subjects showed improvement on the WISC-R vocabulary subtest of more than two standard deviations.

Changes in Procedure

In spite of or because of the heartening findings from the pilot data, a number of changes were implemented. The major change made after the pilot study was the decision to eliminate one of the empathy training variations, that of cognitive training. We found that the children did not enjoy the cognitive training exercises as much as the affective-cognitive ones. Consequently, any subsequent difference in treatment effects on aggression could be attributed to the difference in liking. (As a not so incidental note, the children found the participating control exercises to be the most fun. Empathy training is hard work, both for the children and for the group leaders.) In addition, during the cognitive training session the children frequently would spontaneously introduce affective comments, and trainer efforts to avoid these elements appeared artificial and restrictive. It was felt that from a methodological standpoint it would be more desirable to increase the number of subjects in the affective-cognitive empathy training groups, permitting more systematic analysis of predispositional variables, than to retain the cognitive training condition.

A number of other procedural modifications were introduced. Improvements in the empathy curriculum have already been discussed. Other, more minor changes were initiated. For example, we decided to assign one trainer to a particular group. Finally, we made a number of changes and additions in regard to the battery of our dependent outcome measure.

Measures

The project entails a series of different measures. One set is designed to assess the dynamics of the training process itself, and involves the continuous monitoring of each child at each training session on a variety of aggressive, prosocial, and attentional scales by highly trained but naive observers. Another set of measures is included to assess the effects or outcome of the training program on the children's level of aggression, prosocial behavior, and achievement skills. A third set of measures has been developed in connection with this project to provide information on the effects of the training on the mediating processes of empathy and social understanding. This latter set of measures includes an affective matching test, an emotional responsiveness measure, an audio-video empathy measure, and a role-taking measure. Each of these four new measures corresponds to the conceptual model of empathic behavior that has guided the study and the curriculum. The effort involved in the design and development of these new measures has rivaled the energy and time expended for the entire project. Similarly, a full report of the procedures, analysis, and findings of the study (Feshbach, Powell, Hoffman, Last, and Cohen 1978) carried out as a basis for the development of these first three instruments would be too extensive to be presented here. Suffice it to say that in order to provide appropriate affective stimuli for the measures—stimuli that would be age-, sex-, and ethnic-group-appropriate—it was decided to conduct a study to determine situations that have emotional impact for children. A survey of such situations for children from five to eleven years of age was undertaken in the Los Angeles school district. A total of 240 children from five schools were interviewed over a period of several months. The sample consisted of equal numbers of boys and girls from kindergarten, second, third, fourth, and sixth grades. It was drawn from five schools, four of which were lower-middle socioeconomic status and one of which was upper-middle socioeconomic status. Four ethnic groups were included: Anglos, Asians, blacks, and Chicanos.

The children were questioned about situations that respectively aroused each of the following emotions: sadness, anger, fear, happiness, pride, embarrassment, surprise, disgust. Responses that were normative across sex and ethnicity and the ages we were working with were then used in developing the empathy measures.

THE EMPATHY TRAINING STUDY

The participants in our new empathy training program are 98 third and fourth graders. These children attend two middle-class elementary schools in the Los Angeles City Unified School District. A third of our sample (and the school itself) is made up of minority children.

Criterion measures designed to select children who would participate in the study included a teacher rating of social behavior in the classroom (the Social Interaction Inventory) and a modified peer evaluation of interpersonal functioning (the Class Play) (Walker 1977). The sample of children selected received the battery of tests that was used in the pilot study, as well as modifications of the Sears self-concept measure and the Rothenberg measure of social sensitivity (Walker 1977), and the new tasks created to assess the components of empathy (Feshbach, Powell, Hoffman, Last, and Cohen 1978).

Following the pretest period, the children were randomly assigned to treatment groups. Each participating group has six members; four children in each group have scores above the mean of both criterion measures of aggression and two children have scores below the mean. Four of the members are boys and the other two are girls. Apart from these restrictions, all members were randomly assigned. Of the twelve groups, eight are receiving training in empathy skills and four are receiving control exercises designed to enhance problem-solving skills. The remaining 24 children in the sample are nonparticipating controls.

The children who have been assigned to groups meet for thrice-weekly sessions lasting 45 minutes each. The training phase is ten weeks, and will be followed by a period of posttesting. Throughout the implementation of the training exercises, the children's teachers are completing daily behavior rating forms twice weekly on each child in the study. At the completion of the training phase the criterion measures will be readministered. In addition, a follow-up assessment will be carried out six months later.

A POINT OF VIEW

It is anticipated that the findings yielded by these evaluations will be consistent with those obtained in the pilot study. The demonstration that participation in empathy training results in less aggression and more positive social behaviors is, of course, of central interest. Of equal interest is the relationship between changes in the several components of empathic behavior and changes in these major social behavior outcome variables—that is, it is important to determine the processes mediating the effects of the training curriculum. Implicit in this statement is the view that both curriculum development and evaluation efforts require a theoretical substructure. This point has been made before, and is particularly apropos when considering affective, personal, and social educational objectives (Bloom 1976). In the case of this project, the development of curriculum was based upon an explicit theoretical model and research findings bearing on the process and correlates of empathy (N. Feshbach 1975, 1976a, 1978). Similarly, the outcome variables also were theoretically linked (N. Feshbach 1978; Feshbach and Feshbach 1969), as were the measures selected and developed to assess these variables (Feshbach, Powell, Hoffman,

Last, and Cohen 1978). In a very real sense this project reflects the intimate relationship between developmental psychology and curriculum innovation. Also evident is the reciprocal interplay between laboratory studies and field investigations, between basic research and applied research, and between educational evaluation and experimental procedures.

The most significant dialectic represented here, intrinsic to the conception and implementation of this experimental program, is the relationship between affect and cognition. It is too often assumed that the affective and cognitive domains are separate, orthogonal systems. Thus, the goals of humanistic or affective education are frequently interpreted as unrelated or even contrary to academic goals. However, there is a substantial body of theory and research, including psychoanalytic theory, attribution theory, and Piagetian theory, that indicates that the development of cognitive skills and affective skills is reciprocally and intricately interrelated.

This is not to imply that all learning involves affect or that all cognitive and affective changes are inevitably and mutually dependent. But at a broad and basic level they are closely connected—to each other and to social behavior. The association among affect, cognition, and social behavior is especially epitomized in the construct of empathy. It is hoped that the empirical data from the empathy part of the project will confirm this theoretical assumption and propel us into the next stage of our field study, which deals with the psychological and educational realities of another psychological process, that of fantasy.

REFERENCES

Adelman, H., and S. Feshbach. 1973. "Early Identification of Educational and Mental Health Problems." Paper presented at meeting of American Psychological Association, Montreal.

Aronfreed, J. 1968. *Conduct and Conscience: The Socialization of Internalized Control over Behavior.* New York: Academic Press.

Berger, S. M. 1962. "Conditioning Through Vicarious Instigation." *Psychological Review* 69, no. 5: 450–66.

Bloom, B. S. 1976. *Human Characteristics and Social Learning.* New York: McGraw-Hill.

Chandler, M. J. 1973. "Egocentrism and Antisocial Behavior: The Assessment and Training of Social Perspective-Taking Skills." *Developmental Psychology* 9, no. 3: 326–32.

———. 1974. "Accurate and Accidental Empathy." Paper read at Symposium on the Concept of Empathy: Bond Between Cognition and Social Behavior, at annual conference of American Psychological Association, New Orleans.

———, and S. Greenspan. 1972. "Ersatz Egocentrism: A Reply to H. Borke." *Developmental Psychology* 7, no. 2: 104–06.

———, and C. Barenboim. 1973. "Judgements of Intentionality in Response to Videotaped and Verbally Presented Moral Dilemmas: The Medium Is the Message." *Child Development* 44: 315–20.

———. 1974. "The Assessment and Training of Role-Taking and Referential Communication Skills in Institutionalized Emotionally Disturbed Children." *Developmental Psychology* 10, no. 4: 546–53.

Cutrona, C., and S. Feshbach. In press. "Cognitive and Behavioral Correlates of Children's Differential Use of Social Information."

Deutsch, F. 1974. "Observational and Sociometric Measures of Peer Popularity and Their Relationship to Egocentric Communication in Female Preschoolers." *Developmental Psychology* 60: 745–47.

Feshbach, N. D. 1975a. "Empathy in Children: Some Theoretical and Empirical Considerations." *Counseling Psychologist* 4, no. 2: 25–30.

———. 1975b. "The Relationship of Child-Rearing Factors in Children's Aggression, Empathy and Related Positive and Negative Social Behaviors." In *Determinants and Origins of Aggressive Behavior*, ed. J. DeWit and W. W. Hartup, pp. 427–36. The Hague: Mouton.

———. 1976a. "Empathy and the Regulation of Aggression in Children." In Abstract Guide. XXI International Congress of Psychology, July, p. 55.

———. 1976b. "Empathy in Children: A Special Ingredient of Social Development." Invited address to Western Psychological Association, Los Angeles.

———. 1978. "Studies on Empathic Behavior in Children." In *Progress in Experimental Personality Research*, vol. VIII, ed. B. A. Maher, pp. 1–47. New York: Academic Press.

———, and S. Feshbach. 1969. "The Relationship Between Empathy and Aggression in Two Age Groups." *Developmental Psychology* 1: 102–07.

———. 1971. "Children's Aggression." *Young Children* 26, no. 6: 364–77.

Feshbach, N., and S. Kuchenbecker. 1974. "A Three Component Model of Empathy." Paper read at Symposium on the Concept of Empathy: Bond Between Cognition and Social Behavior, annual meeting of American Psychological Association, New Orleans.

Feshbach, N., M. Powell, M. Hoffman, U. Last, and R. Cohen. 1978. "Developmental Study of Children's Reports of Emotional Arousing Situations." Mimeographed.

Feshbach, N., and K. Roe. 1968. "Empathy in Six and Seven Year Olds." *Child Development* 39: 133–45.

Feshbach, S. 1970. "Aggression." In *Carmichael's Manual of Child Psychology*, ed. P. H. Mussen, pp. 159–259. New York: John Wiley.

———, and N. Feshbach. 1975. "Effects of Fantasy and Empathy Training on Aggression." Grant proposal submitted to National Science Foundation, Grant BSN 76 01262.

Finney, J. 1977. "Developmental Changes in Perspective Taking." Paper presented at American Psychological Association, San Francisco.

Flavell, J. H., P. T. Botkin, C. L. Fry, J. W. Wright, and P. E. Jarvis. 1968. *The Development of Role-Taking and Communication Skills in Children*. New York: John Wiley.

Freud, S. 1950. *Group Psychology and the Analysis of the Ego*, trans. J. Strachey. New York: Bantam Books.

Hoffman, M. L. 1975. "Developmental Synthesis of Affect and Cognition and Its Implications for Altruistic Motivation." *Developmental Psychology* 11, no. 5: 607–22.

Huckabay, L. M. 1972. "A Developmental Study of the Relationship of Negative Moral-Social Behaviors to Empathy, to Positive Social Behaviors and to Cognitive Moral Judgement." *Science and Direct Patient Care II, Proceedings of Fifth Annual Nurse Scientist Conference*. Denver.

Jastak, J., S. Jastak, and S. Bijou. 1965. *Wide Range Achievement Test*. Newark, Delaware: Guidance Corp.

Katz, R. L. 1963. *Empathy: Its Nature and Uses*. London: Free Press of Glencoe.

Kohlberg, L. 1969. "State and Sequences: The Cognitive Development Approach to Socialization." In *Handbook of Socialization Theory and Research*, ed. D. Goslin. Chicago: Rand McNally.

Mead, G. H. 1934. *Mind, Self, and Society*. Chicago: University of Chicago Press.

Mehrabian, A., and N. Epstein. 1972. "A Measure of Emotional Empathy." *Journal of Personality* 40, no. 4: 525–43.

McDougall, W. 1908. *An Introduction to Social Psychology*. London: Methuen.

Pitkänen, L. 1974. "Nonaggressive Patterns of Coping with Thwarting Situations as Alternatives to Aggression." Paper presented at biennial meeting of International Society for Research on Aggression.

Rogers, C. R. 1957. "The Necessary and Sufficient Conditions of Therapeutic Personality Change." *Journal of Consulting Psychology* 21: 95–103.

——, and C. B. Truax. 1967. "The Therapeutic Conditions Antecedent to Change: A Theoretical View." In *The Therapeutic Relationship and Its Impact: A Study of Psychotherapy with Schizophrenics*, ed. C. R. Rogers. Madison: University of Wisconsin Press.

Shantz, C. U. 1975. "The Development of Social Cognition." In *Review of Child Development Research*, vol. V, ed. E. M. Hetherington. Chicago: University of Chicago Press.

Selman, R. L., and D. F. Byrne. 1974. "A Structural-Developmental Analysis of Levels of Role-Taking in Middle Childhood." *Child Development* 34: 803–06.

Smither, S. 1978. "A Developmental Reconsideration of Empathy." *Human Development* 20, no. 6: 1–37.

Spivak, G., and M. Shure. 1974. *Social Adjustment of Young Children*. San Francisco: Jossey-Bass.

Staub, E. 1971. "The Use of Role-Playing and Induction in Children's Learning of Helping and Sharing Behavior." *Child Development* 42: 805–16.

Sullivan, H. S. 1953. *The Interpersonal Theory of Psychiatry*. New York: Norton.

Van Lieshout, C. F. M., G. Leckie, and B. Smits-Van Sonsheek. 1973. "The Effect of a Social Perspective Taking Training on Empathy and Role-Taking Ability of Pre-School Children." Paper presented at the biennial meeting of the International Society of Behavioral Development, Ann Arbor, Michigan, August, 1973.

Walker, A. 1977. "Social Competence in Middle Childhood: Conceptions and Characteristics." Ph.D. dissertation, UCLA.

Wechsler, D. 1974. *Manual for the Wechsler Intelligence Scale for Children— Revised*. New York: Psychological Corp.

12

SELF-CONTROL AS A PREREQUISITE FOR CONSTRUCTIVE BEHAVIOR

Lea Pitkänen-Pulkkinen

The great differences between the methods that have been used in attempting to regulate aggressive behavior correspond to the differences between underlying theoretical explanations of aggression. And not only do the methodological implications of known biological, physical, and social interpretations of aggression differ, but so does the faith in the possibilities of aggression control. In this paper I shall offer a further frame of reference, which represents a kind of social-cognitive approach to the appearance and control of aggression.

The starting point of my approach was a descriptive model (Figure 12.1) portraying aggressive and nonaggressive patterns of behavior linked to the expression and control of impulses.

The model has two main dimensions that define four patterns of behavior in thwarting situations that may become generalized in more permanent personal styles of coping with new stimulus situations. According to the model, there is not one, but in principle three, different alternatives to aggression. One is anxiety, which the analytically oriented have claimed as an alternative to aggression if aggression is suppressed. A second is submission, which the trait theorists have held to be the opposite of aggression. A further alternative can be distinguished, in which the individual is active with regard to the situation, as in aggression, but chooses a course of action for solving the problem that takes into account the parties involved and considers the possible consequences.

The vertical axis of the model, "Number of Overt Responses," indicates the frequency of the responses that tend to actively modify the stimulus condition and to eliminate the threat. The horizontal axis, "Strength of Self-Control," refers to one's capacity to evaluate the consequences of one's own behavior consciously and to regulate it on this basis, while still being sufficiently able to express and satisfy needs without causing harm to other members of society.

The underlying assumptions of the model are as follows. The primary effect of a thwarting stimulus on an organism is activating, which is revealed as

FIGURE 12.1

Aggressive and Nonaggressive Patterns of Behavior

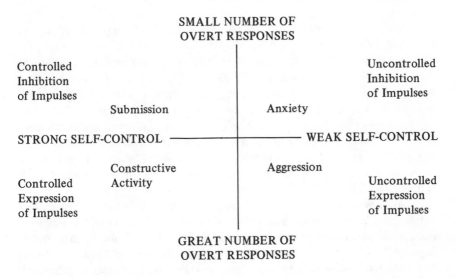

SMALL NUMBER OF
OVERT RESPONSES

Controlled Inhibition of Impulses — Uncontrolled Inhibition of Impulses

Submission — Anxiety

STRONG SELF-CONTROL ——————— WEAK SELF-CONTROL

Constructive Activity — Aggression

Controlled Expression of Impulses — Uncontrolled Expression of Impulses

GREAT NUMBER OF
OVERT RESPONSES

Source: Pitkänen 1969.

both emotional and behavioral reactions. The individual has an unlearned disposition to defend against thwarting stimuli. This can be called an approach tendency, which means an attempt to eliminate a thwarting stimulus by delivering noxious stimuli to another individual (Buss 1961). If approach is prevented by the threat of counteraggression, the feelings of fear and anxiety give rise to an avoidance tendency. An avoidance indicates a kind of control of aggression but depends on external factors, such as threat of punishment.

These two tendencies, aggressive approach and fearful avoidance, are not sufficient to cover the variations characteristic of the responses of human beings to thwarting stimulus situations. In humans the response tendencies are complicated by cognitive processes. The individual is able consciously to appraise the stimulus situations encountered and to decide between the ways of coping with them. The criteria used are more internalized than an external threat. This capacity is reflected in the strength of an individual's self-control. At first, when self-control is weak, external controllers influence behavior to a greater degree. As self-control develops, one learns not to act in opposition to approved behavior patterns even when no punisher is present. This is a gradual process by which one takes the primary responsibility for one's own behavior. In all societies there are social requirements to which the developing child must accommodate, and thus the child must frequently abandon ways of reacting that earlier led directly to rewards.

DEVELOPMENT OF SELF-CONTROL

Various learning processes are possible in the development of self-control. First, the influences of models on the development of self-control have been demonstrated in the strengthening of inhibitions of responses and resistance to temptation (Bandura and Walters 1963), self-imposed delay of reward (Bandura and Mischel 1965), and learning empathy and altruism (Test and Bryan 1969). Second, the various forms of direct reinforcement and punishment influence the development of self-control—for example, self-imposed delay of gratification and altruism (Grandal, Preston, and Rabson 1960; Aronfreed and Reber 1965; Dolan and Adelberg 1967). Third, some theorists have resorted to mediational concepts to bridge the gap between external and internal control, as reviewed by B. McLaughlin (1971).

According to J. Aronfreed (1968), self-control is achieved because self-critical responses are associated with external punishment in such a way as to make their occurrence contiguous to the attentuation of anxiety. Aronfreed's explanation of self-control is based on the acquisition of self-critical responses that have acquired secondary reinforcement value and that mediate behavior in the absence of agents of punishment. Other theorists have given anxiety a less central role and have stressed the importance of complex cognitive processes that mediate self-control behavior. A. Bandura's (1969, 1973) theory of observational learning emphasizes internal representational responses that mediate overt behavior. These mediational responses convey information to the observer about the characteristics of appropriate responses and permit the observer to make judgments as to whether a given response should be performed. They thereby mediate the form that behavior takes and allow for self-control in the absence of agents of punishment.

Other kinds of mediating processes have been suggested by S. Schachter (1964) and R. S. Lazarus (1966), who have noticed that emotional behavior depends upon the interpretation of internal reactions. This is based on the observation and appraisal of situational cues. For example, a frustrating situation can be judged as either arbitrary or meaningful, and accordingly one's own emotional state as warranting either anger or even amusement. Situational clues in a frustrating situation as determinants of subsequent behavior have been stressed by L. Berkowitz (1969). Children can be trained in the appraisal of the situation they encounter. In the study by S. Mallick and B. R. McCandless (1966) children lost a cash prize because of another child's clumsiness. Those children who had the clumsiness reinterpreted by being told that the other child was "sleepy and upset" showed less aggression than did the other children.

In the appraisal, cognitive mediating processes in the form of verbal activity are highly significant. Verbal behavior is important to the control of behavior in other respects as well. L. S. Vygotsky (1962) has assumed that the internalization of language is central to one's regulation of one's own activity. The regulation takes place through "inner speech." A. R. Luria (1969) distinguishes different stages in the development of verbal regulation of behavior. "The first stage during which the speech of the child itself plays a regulating role in the organization of motor reactions is a stage in which the regulating role is accomplished by the nonspecific impulse influence of speech. Only at 4½ to 5 years is organization controlled by the selective, semantic side of the speech system" (p. 159).

The possibilities for classifying and evaluating behavior increase with conceptual development. The individual learns to define the various possibilities for solving a problem situation, to judge their consequences, and to make a choice. Depending on the consequences of the chosen behavior, one then either praises or criticizes oneself. Thus verbal self-control consists of the process of choosing a course of action and an internal evaluation of the success of the choice made. This, according to D. Meichenbaum (1973), is furthered by verbal guidance of activity.

The methods that parents use for rearing their children can be evaluated on the basis of the kinds of learning processes to which they appeal. Aronfreed (1968) divides child-rearing methods into sensitization and induction. Through sensitization techniques the child learns that transgressions will be punished, but does not acquire internal standards that would guide behavior. Aggression toward parents is punished, but toward peers it may be encouraged. Induction techniques of discipline include the communication of reasons for the undesirability of certain behaviors, the pointing out to children of the consequences their behavior has for others, and the use of withdrawal of affection to motivate the child to adhere to the verbalized standards or values. Induction methods are likely to produce internal control of behavior. M. L. Hoffman and H. D. Saltzstein (1967) have, however, demonstrated the difference between withdrawal of affection, as dependency-producing, and the induction proper that stresses the consequences behavior has for others, thus arousing feelings of empathy. As a verbal method, induction consciously uses cognitive mediating processes in the development of self-control.

MANIFESTATIONS OF SELF-CONTROL

The manifestations of self-control include resistance to temptation, self-imposed delay of gratification, self-reinforcement, self-criticism, and moral behavior (McLaughlin 1971). L. Kohlberg (1969) has stated that self-chosen moral principles represent the highest degree of moral behavior: "These abstract ethical principles are universal principles of justice, of reciprocity and equality of human rights, and of respect for the dignity of human beings as individuals."

In moral development either inhibition of behavior or learning desirable, prosocial behavior can be stressed. The latter is represented by altruism and empathy. Empathy consists of a cognitive component—the capacity to view events from the standpoint of others—and an emotional component—the capacity to experience others' emotions vicariously (Mehrabian and Epstein 1971; Staub 1971). The autonomy of altruism has been viewed in various ways. According to Aronfreed (1968), empathy is the prerequisite of altruism, since one must be able to empathize with others in order to predict the consequences of one's own behavior, on which Aronfreed claims altruism is based. D. Rosenhahn (1973), R. Leeds (1963), and J. Macaulay and L. Berkowitz (1970) believe altruism is autonomous

Empathic and altruistic people have been observed to be adjusting, nonaggressive, patient, and flexible (Dymond 1950; Feshbach and Feshbach 1969; Greif and Hogan 1973). Empathy and altruism have also been shown to increase with age (Macaulay and Berkowitz 1970), as do the inhibitory aspects of self-control—depending, certainly, on learning experiences.

According to my descriptive model, strong self-control may manifest itself both in an overtly active and in a passive way, as may weak self-control. The differences between these two types of approach and avoidance tendencies and their histories are clear. The basic patterns of behavior, described in terms of expression versus inhibition of impulses and self-control, are as follows (see Figure 12.1):

1. Uncontrolled expression of impulses. The goal of action in a thwarting situation is to eliminate the threat immediately. This is done by delivering noxious stimuli to another organism, for which reason the response is defined as aggressive. Looking only after one's own interests, without consideration for the suffering of others, is characteristic of aggressive behavior. Aggressive models and failures in the internalization of social standards in the process of socialization lead the individual to persist in this primitive method of coping.

2. Uncontrolled inhibition of impulses. In thwarting stimulus situations, an individual's responses are characterized by avoidance behavior, in fear of external threat. For those social skills one lacks, one has no response habits enabling one to eliminate the thwarting stimulus nonaggressively. Activation aroused by the stimulus is bound to the individual's emotions: fear and anxiety about an inability to defend oneself. Inability to solve social problems may be a result of a deficiency in one's own resources (such as physical weakness) or of one's upbringing, which has encouraged simple avoidance responses.

3. Controlled inhibition of impulses. An individual tends to block awareness of emotional arousal by means of cognitive appraisal of the situation. The norms and standards are highly internalized and action is motivated by a need for approval, a consequence of strong dependency on authority figures. Any defensive initiation might threaten this relationship, and therefore an individual tends to submit. As a consequence of deliberateness, an individual has few conflicts with others, and aggressive habits remain weak. Consequently, the develop-

ment is contrary to that in the behavior defined as aggressive: aggressive behavior creates new conflicts and tends to provoke new aggression.

4. Controlled expression of impulses. Activation aroused by aggression stimuli is controlled through cognitive appraisal of the situation and is displayed in neutral forms. The norms and standards are highly internalized, and action is motivated by a desire to behave in a socially acceptable manner. An individual's initiative is not blocked by excessive dependency on authority figures; on the contrary, activeness is encouraged. The person considers alternative ways of coping with thwarting situations, and aims at peaceful settlement of controversies and at eliminating aversive stimuli with feelings of empathy toward the other parties involved. Aggressive behavior may occur, but with consideration and in situations in which it is not compatible with socially acceptable behavior. Therefore this type of activeness or approach tendency is called constructive.

VALIDATION OF THE MODEL

To validate the two-dimensional descriptive system, several factor analyses of peer and teacher ratings were carried out (Pitkänen 1969). The factor structures were mutually consistent, as revealed by transformation analyses. The first two factors could be identified as the main dimensions of the model. They accounted for more than 70 percent of the total variance of the ratings.

By choosing groups representative of each of the four behavior patterns in their extreme forms, and by studying behavior stability in these groups, a high degree of stability was observed in typical behavior after periods of one (Pitkänen 1973) and six years (Aalto et al. 1975). These follow-up studies were based on peer ratings. In 1968 the subjects (N = 369) were 8-year-olds from 12 school classes. Six years later, in 1974, they were spread into 60 classes. Peer ratings were made in every class. The behavioral patterns, surprisingly, remained the same in spite of changes of teachers and classmates: in only 3 percent had the self-control improved from weak to strong, so as to cause a change from the aggressive or anxious extreme group to that of the constructive or submissive. A corresponding change toward weakening self-control had taken place in 15 percent.

The original classification of the subjects into the extreme groups was made on the basis of factor scores of 33 rating variables. In the follow-up studies only eight items were used, one for each category of the model in Figure 12.1. The items used were of the type "Which of your classmates are energetic, always on the go, and often in contact with others?" This item indicates a great number of overt responses. The aggressive also have weak self-control. Therefore they have to be scored high on the item "Which are impulsive, lack concentration, and change moods?" and high, of course, in their typical pattern of behavior: "Which are aggressive, say naughty things, and attack without reason?" The other groups can be formed correspondingly, by looking at the scores on the

FIGURE 12.2

Background Factors of Aggressive and Nonaggressive Behavior Patterns: Schematic Illustration of Three Discriminators

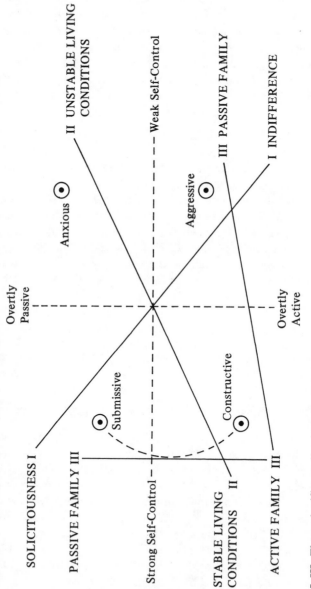

I-III   Three significant discriminators
        Subject groups
----   Main dimensions of the model of aggression and nonaggression

Source: Compiled by the author.

questions concerning the two main dimensions and at the scores on the alternative behavior patterns (Pitkänen-Pulkkinen and Pitkänen 1976).

In studying the growth environments of the groups representing various behavior styles, in connection with the follow-up study over six years, essential differences were observed in them on the basis of the subjects' and their parents' interview, which shed light on the development and stability of patterns (Aalto et al. 1975).

Nine principal components could be extracted from the several hundred interview variables (Hurme 1976). Figure 12.2 shows schematically the results of a discriminant analysis based on the factor scores. The groups were significantly distinguished by three discriminators.

The first discriminator, "Indifference Versus Solicitousness," distinguished the aggressive from the other groups. The discriminator consisted mainly of a laissez-faire versus caring attitude toward the child. Inadequate upbringing of the aggressive child was often the case in broken homes and unstable housing conditions. If the father lived at home, he seldom had a regular day job. He either worked varying shifts or stayed at home, incapacitated for work. The fathers of this group abused alcohol more than in the other groups. The parents of the aggressive children were the youngest in this population, and first-born children were overrepresented in the aggressive group. Corporal punishment and nagging were used more than verbal guidance in raising the children. Obviously the young parents had been unable to offer the children an emotionally and physically stable home and mature care. In contrast, the opposite extreme group, the submissive, had perhaps overresponsible parents who took care of their numerous children in a solicitous manner. The parents were older than those of the other groups, partly because of the late birth order of the submissive children. Common to both groups was a passive family atmosphere in terms of scant family interaction and the lack of guidance of models in activities outside the family.

The second discriminator, "Unstable Versus Stable Living Conditions," distinguished the anxious from the rest. Instability included several changes of residence, school, and day nursery. Many parents had divorced. The mothers mostly worked varying shifts which added further to instability of family life. The number of children was small, which meant small support from siblings in the parents' absence. Obviously, the unstable growth environment, with changing or deficient human contacts, had produced feelings of insecurity in the children. The anxious differed from the other introverted group, the submissive, in this respect particularly; the submissive had lived in quite stable conditions and in large families. Common to these groups was protective caring for children and an inward-oriented, passive family atmosphere. In spite of the difficulties parents had in looking after their children in the anxious group, they did take care of them, in contrast with the parents of the aggressive group, who were not interested in their children. Unstable living conditions were common to both groups representing weak self-control.

The constructive group had lived in stable conditions. The family atmosphere had been active, which meant abundant family interaction in terms of talking and shared activities. The parents had interests outside the home and they systematically encouraged the children's hobbies—for example, playing musical instruments—and had shown interest in their schoolwork. The parents had not overprotected their children or been indifferent. Obviously, the atmosphere had been what is called "democratic," and at the same time both outward- and family-oriented.

Social class differences, measured in terms of income or level of schooling, are small in Finland. This may be one reason for the fact that the groups did not differ in this respect. More significant for children's social-emotional development is the psychological climate. It proved to be as possible to love a child in poor conditions as in wealthy ones. The same was true of ignoring family life. The groups did not differ even in mothers' employment. Some 70–80 percent of mothers were employed in each group. More important than this was the regularity of working hours and the stability of day care. These conditions were the worst in the anxious group.

The follow-up study provided firm support for the descriptive model of aggressive and nonaggressive patterns of behavior, and for the hypotheses concerning the development of each pattern. Weak self-control was typical of the young people who had lived in unstable conditons that had not advanced the internalization of social standards. The parents were younger than average and unable to offer the child a permanent home, stable day care, and mature care at home. The parents' irregular work, abuse of alcohol, and emotional problems, reflected in a high number of divorces, were marked. The family atmosphere was passive in terms of talking, shared activities, and extrafamilial interests. The clear difference between the aggressive and anxious groups was in the indifference of the parents toward their children. In the aggressive group, upbringing was based mainly on informal socialization by peers and mass culture. Free-time activities or academic achievements were not supported or supervised; the child was left alone in the streets with friends. The results on aggression correspond to many previous findings (Olofsson 1973; Malewska and Peyre 1970; Kärrby 1971; McCord et al. 1963; Eron et al. 1971).

Strong self-control was typical of those who had lived in stable and child-oriented conditions. The parents had looked after their children well, showing interest in and supervising their activities. As to the methods of child rearing, the study provided evidence for the relationship between sensitization techniques and weak self-control and, correspondingly, induction techniques and strong self-control. Overprotection of the submissive and the resulting strong dependency on authority figures confirmed Hoffman and Saltzstein's (1967) idea of the complex effects of Aronfreed's induction techniques. Verbal guidance in the induction proper was most obvious in the rearing of the constructive group. Verbal advice and reasons for expectations were given more than punishments. According to Hoffman (1970), the induction method, in which the child's attention is directed to the feelings of others and the consequences of one's behavior for others, is most effective in training the child to control impulses with empathy. Since the parents of the constructive group had not overprotected their children, they had let them become independent. Activeness in regard to new situations was furthered by the lively family interaction that was at the same time both outward- and family-oriented.

The implications of the results on the significance of the strength of an individual's internal control for the destructive versus constructive quality of behavior were in accordance with my original hypotheses, as well as the effects of external control on the quantity of overt behavior. Eight years of research had produced such abundant confirmatory evidence for the model that there was reason to experiment with its application to the regulation of aggression.

In the modifications of behavior, the problem of values implicit in the expected change arises. Concerning aggressiveness, cultural values vary and are ambiguous because of various conceptions of the content of aggression. There is another problem worth considering, too. It concerns the methods of behavior modification: the question of in what ways and to what extent the modification of an individual's personal behavior is ethically justified.

In my experiments the problem of values has been approached by regarding constructive activity as an objective of the expected change. Constructive behavior is active in regard to the situation, but maintains positive communication. I consider this sort of activity socially more mature than aggressiveness. Valuing activity more than submission may be a personal choice. There are societies in which submission to existing rules is seen as a necessity for maintaining the system, and therefore submission is set as an important aim of socialization. Submission does not, however, make use of all the resources of the great majority. My concept of democracy presupposes the active participation of all parties involved. In regulating aggression I hold the individual's internal control to be more essential than external control, where development is directed toward strengthening internal control of impulses, not toward the inhibition of impulses.

The ethical questions concerning treatment methods have been approached in my experiments by emphasizing the development of self-control as a target. The aim has not been to force a person to behave in a certain way, but to increase awareness of the alternatives of behavior from which to choose. Flexibility of behavior has also been valued, because it furthers social interaction.

The experiments carried out under my direction to study the possibilities for developing self-control and its effects on observed behavior have concentrated on the influences of a simulation method (Pitkänen 1974) and those of its extension (Heikkinen et al. 1976a), and on the effects of instructing parents in child rearing (Heikkinen et al. 1976b).

FIGURE 12.3

Effects of Simulation Exercises on the Control of Aggressive Behavior

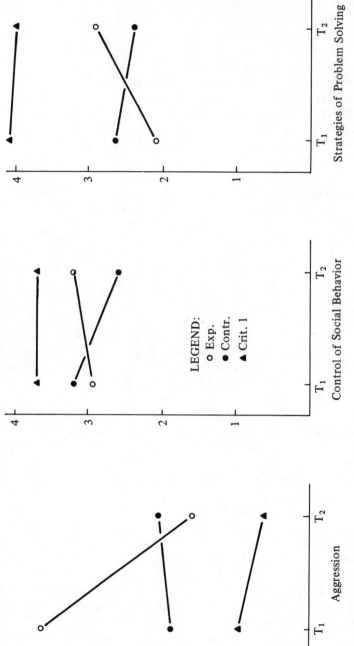

LEGEND:
o Exp.
● Contr.
▲ Crit. 1

Aggression

Control of Social Behavior

Strategies of Problem Solving

Source: Pitkänen 1974.

PROGRAM EXPERIMENTS IN
DEVELOPING SELF-CONTROL

The first experiment was carried out to discover whether it was possible to increase an aggressively behaving individual's awareness of nonaggressive alternatives of behavior through treatment aimed at the cognitive appraisal of a situation (Pitkänen 1974). The subjects consisted of two matched, extremely aggressive groups of eight-year-old boys, and of one criterion group of constructive boys. Videotape recordings of behavior in nine standardized situations were used both in pretest and posttest. Between the pretest and posttest the experimental group was submitted to simulation exercises of eight lessons given over a period of four weeks. Following J. S. Bruner's (1966) three modes of representation, the symbolic level involved creative problem-solving exercises using mental images; the iconic level was based on series of slides depicting the development of a conflict situation; and on the enactive level information was obtained through concrete action in the form of role-playing. The method was promising, since in the aggressive experimental group, aggression decreased and constructive activity increased (Figure 12.3). The criterion group of constructive boys was superior in every measured variable, but the experimental group tended to come near it.

With funding from the Academy of Finland, a further study was carried out under my direction, the purpose of which was to prepare an extended program for the development of self-control in children and test it in day care centers (Heikkinen et al. 1976a). The program consists of 36 teaching units, each lasting 20 minutes. Optimum group size is four to six children, in order that they may be handled individually and that guided discussions may be possible. The program is intended for five- to seven-year-olds. It centers on three main themes that represent important prerequisites to the development of self-control and constructive behavior (Table 12.1).

Activities in the program include picture stories; role-playing; physical games such as the "Millipede," in which the children line up and hold on to the waist of the person in front of them, then walk in step; arts and crafts; and other games. Discussion occupies the central position in the teaching units, where the idea is to connect the material presented with the children's own experiences. Each teaching unit is backed by a selection of books, arts and crafts, music, and games that may be used as additional material.

The goal in developing self-control was constructive activity. A few examples of the manifestations of constructiveness are

- Thinks of others: is able to listen to others, respect others' rights and points of view
- Communication skills: negotiates, speaks in a friendly way, is conciliatory, suggests and accepts compromises
- Is capable of reciprocity—for example, sharing and taking turns, requesting and giving assistance

TABLE 12.1

Main Themes of the Children's Self-Control Development Program
and Topics of Teaching Units

Main Themes	Teaching Unit

Understanding of self and others	acceptance of difference (4 units) includes
	    animals are different
	    people are different
	acceptance of self (4 units) includes
	    the magpie that wanted to be a bullfinch
	    the bunny that mocks its friend the squirrel

Understanding of feelings	facial expressions in different emotions feelings in different situations (2 units)

Understanding of constructive behavior	cooperation (6 units) includes
	    the animal's first day at school
	    the millipede
	    a little child can help, too
	sharing and taking turns (4 units) includes
	    Kari, who always bickered
	    Tommi's new ball
	achievement of goals (5 units) includes
	    it doesn't pay to threaten
	    Kaisa the complainer
	    how I ask nicely
	dealing with anger (4 units)
	    Harri, who learned to think twice
	    a wise person settles arguments first
	thinking of others (6 units)
	    the fifth wheel
	    by accident and on purpose
	    saying you're sorry

Source: Compiled by the author.

- Capacity for teamwork: is responsible, accepts the goals and rules of the group, is flexible
- Control of emotions: avoids arguments and revenge, is able to change means to an end, to replace one end with another and reappraise situations if other person's motives are in sharp conflict with one's own.

One phase of the research studied whether the effects of the program are dependent on the instructor and whether the pretest has some reactive effects on the posttest. No significant effects were noticed.

The pretests and posttests of the experimental and control groups were carried out by means of interviews and observation. In interviews an attempt was made to evaluate the level of the child's self-control. As Figure 12.4 shows, the experimental group's self-control developed significantly from the pretest to the posttest.

In the experimental group 96 percent displayed an increase of more than 10 points toward the strengthening of self-control, whereas in the control group a corresponding variation of only a small percentage occurred (Figure 12.5).

Observation took place in eight arranged situations, on the basis of which it was decided whether the effect of teaching was visible in an increase of constructive behavior. As Figure 12.6 shows, the difference between the experimental and control groups was significant in the posttest but not in the pretest.

FIGURE 12.4

Changes in Self-Control, Based on Interviews

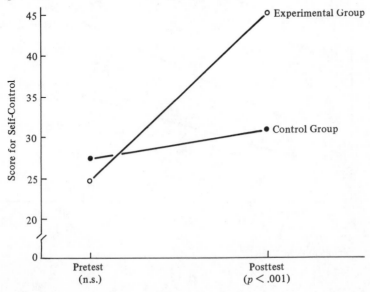

Source: Compiled by the author.

FIGURE 12.5

Individual Change Scores in Self-Control, Based on Interviews

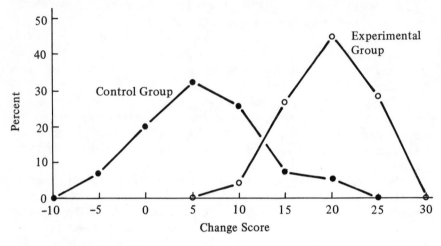

Source: Compiled by the author.

FIGURE 12.6

Changes in Constructive Behavior, Based on Observations

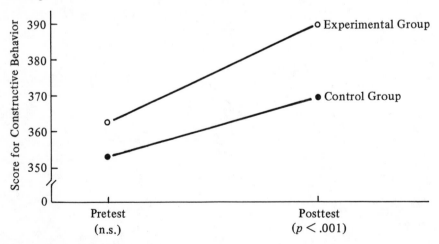

Source: Compiled by the author.

The greatest differences between the experimental and control groups occurred in obeying rules, sharing toys, helpfulness, sympathy with others' happiness and sadness, and ability to deal with anger. In some other aspects, such as playing with others, the control group children also progressed after having spent one or two months in kindergarten. The experiment was made in the autumn.

I understand that this type of program for developing self-control in children may provide some support for family education if given in kindergartens, or it may offer some material to willing parents for stimulating their children's social development. The key to children's self-control is in the family, as was shown in connection with the follow-up study. Despite excellent medical care for mothers and children, at the moment Finland has no family education for future parents. The new network of health center psychologists will provide the possibility for this. Family education could also be included in the curriculum of comprehensive and vocational schools.

To develop material based on research that would be applicable to these purposes, my research group prepared a 20-hour program, each lesson lasting 45 minutes, that concentrated on the elucidation of the above-mentioned factors affecting the child's social development. The program was tested with men and women aged 19 to 28 who were studying metalwork, carpentry, restaurant service, and cartography at a vocational center. They were either unmarried or the parents of very small children. Before the guidance program was presented to the experimental group, the members of both the experimental group and the control group were interviewed. The interviews revealed that the subjects' knowledge of the prerequisites for the development of a child's constructiveness was deficient. Their understanding of systematic child rearing was slight. Instead, trust was placed in the child's own spontaneous activeness and ability to learn through experience. More than half were in favor of physical punishment. Only a few were able to consider causes and effects—for example, the origin of feelings of inferiority—in connection with the stability of day care or the absence of one parent. The majority of those interviewed said they needed information dealing with child rearing.

The aim of the teaching program was to provide information about the prerequisites of self-control and constructive behavior. Approximately 300 slides were prepared for the program, to illustrate the spoken material. The lessons included discussions and note taking. Summaries of the main ideas in each lesson were prepared and given to the students.

In line with the results of the discriminant analysis, the lessons dealt with child-rearing methods, features related to the stability of the growth environment, and family activity. Table 12.2 shows the grouping of the lessons according to these main themes.

The posttest showed an increase in the subjects' understanding of the prerequisites for strong self-control and constructiveness. The experimental group was better able than the control group to apply its knowledge to child-

TABLE 12.2

Main Themes of the Child-Rearing Guidance Program and Topics of the Lessons

Main Themes	Lesson
Child rearing	parents' responsibility "permissive" or guided upbringing consistency of upbringing model learning child-rearing methods moral and norm education
Growth environment	basic security family living conditions parents' work conditions child's day care use of alcohol relations between parents mother as sole provider
Family activity	family atmosphere father's participation in child rearing social skills school attendance friendship use of free time
	Summary

Source: Compiled by the author.

rearing situations described verbally. The experimental group considered the program interesting and useful for all future parents.

SELF-CONTROL AS A GOAL OF EARLY EDUCATION

The development of self-control is more or less explicitly included in the social-emotional goals for early education in most countries. Following Makarenko's principles, in the Soviet Union particular attention is paid to the development of self-control (Bronfenbrenner 1972). General educational goals include helpfulness, friendliness, self-confidence, solidarity, and obedience. These goals of personality development are essential for living in a collective. Compared with my model, they perhaps emphasize submission more than constructive activity. In the German Democratic Republic self-control is sought through physical activity. In Israel's kibbutzes the goals of early education are to a high degree consistent with those in socialist countries.

In the West the development of self-control has not been emphasized as strongly. In the United States more stress is placed on the child's right to grow and develop freely than on teaching self-control. A number of programs for social-emotional development have been prepared to meet the needs of early education. Such a program is D. Dinkmeyer's (1970) Developing Understanding Self and Others (DUSO). The program includes extensive material (illustrated books, cassettes, hand puppets) for daily use over a period of several weeks. This material is very closely bound up in American culture. It has been shown to have positive effects on self-understanding and the ability to work independently (Koval and Hales 1972).

In Sweden several research projects have been started in connection with the arrangement of preschool education, the goal of which is to develop methods of increasing children's capacity for constructive problem solving and democratic cooperation (Stukát and Sverud 1974).

Finnish early education has been influenced both by the socialist countries and by the West. The development of self-control has not been explicitly mentioned among the objectives. Instead, some social skills, such as thinking of others and cooperation, that presuppose strong self-control of behavior have been emphasized. The development of the objectives and methods of social-emotional education in Finland is still in its infancy; as it grows, one would hope for a firmer base in theory than previously.

REFERENCES

Aalto, P., H. Hurskainen, A. Kangas, R. Kanto, A Mönkkönen, and A. Seila. 1975. "Aggression Risk Groups." Master's thesis, University of Jyväskylä. In Finnish.

Aronfreed, J. 1968. *Conduct and Conscience*. New York: Academic Press.

———, and A. Reber. 1965. "Internalized Behavioral Suppression and the Timing of Social Punishment." *Journal of Personality and Social Psychology* 1: 3–16.

Bandura, A. 1969. "Social-Learning Theory of Identificatory Processes." In *Handbook of Socialization Theory and Research*, ed. D. A. Goslin, pp. 213–62. Chicago: Rand McNally.

———. 1973. *Aggression: a Social Learning Analysis*. Englewood Cliffs, N.J.: Prentice-Hall.

——, and W. Mischel. 1965. "Modification of Self-Imposed Delay of Reward Through Exposure to Live and Symbolic Models." *Journal of Personality and Social Psychology* 2: 698–705.

Bandura, A., and R. H. Walters. 1963. *Social Learning and Personality Development.* New York: Holt, Rinehart and Winston.

Berkowitz, L. 1969. "The Frustration-Aggression Hypothesis Revised." In *Roots of Aggression*, ed. L. Berkowitz, pp. 1–28. New York: Atherton.

——, J. P. Lepinski, and E. J. Angulo. 1969. "Awareness of Own Anger Level and Subsequent Aggression." *Journal of Personality and Social Psychology* 11: 293–300.

Bronfenbrenner, U. 1972. "Soviet Method of Character Education: Some Implications for Research." In *Readings in Child Behavior and Development*, ed. C. Lavatelli and F. Stendler, pp. 447–56. New York: Harcourt Brace.

Bruner, J. S. 1966. "On Cognitive Growth: I." In *Studies in Cognitive Growth*, pp. 1–29. New York: John Wiley.

Buss, A. H. 1961. *The Psychology of Aggression.* New York: John Wiley.

Dinkmeyer, D. 1970. *Developing Understanding Self and Others.* Manual DUSO D-1. Circle Pines, Minnesota: American Guidance Service.

Dolan, D. J., and K. Adelberg. 1967. "The Learning of Sharing Behavior." *Child Development* 38: 695–700.

Dymond, R. 1950. "Personality and Empathy." *Journal of Counseling Psychology* 14: 343–50.

Eron, L. D., L. O. Walder, and M. M. Lefkowitz. 1971. *Learning of Aggression in Children.* Boston: Little, Brown.

Feshbach, N. D., and S. Feshbach. 1969. "The Relationship Between Empathy and Aggression in Two Age Groups." *Developmental Psychology* 1: 102–07.

Grandal, V., A. Preston, and A. Rabson. 1960. "Maternal Reactions and Development of Independent Achievement Behavior in Young Children." *Child Development* 31: 243–51.

Greif, E., and R. Hogan. 1973. "The Theory and Measurement of Empathy." *Journal of Counseling Psychology* 20: 280–84.

Heikkinen, A., T. Markkanen, and M. Ranta. 1976. "Prevention of Aggression. I. Developing Self-Control in Children." Master's thesis, University of Jyväskylä. In Finnish.

Heikkinen, R.-L., A.-L. Hietaharju, L. Hietahärvi, and A. Karppinen. 1976. "Prevention of Aggression. II. Instruction in Child-Rearing for Parents." Master's thesis, University of Jyväskylä. In Finnish.

Hoffman, M. L. 1970. "Moral Development." In *Carmichael's Manual of Child Psychology*, ed. P. H. Mussen, pp. 261–359. New York: John Wiley.

——, and H. D. Saltzstein. 1967. "Parental Discipline and the Child's Moral Development." *Journal of Personality and Social Psychology* 5: 45–57.

Hurme, H. 1976. *Multidimensional Analysis of the Background Factors of Self-Control: Based on the Material of the Study "Aggression Risk Groups."* *Report of the Department of Psychology, University of Jyväskylä* no. 177. In Finnish.

Kärrby, G. 1971. *Child Rearing and the Development of Moral Structure.* Stockholm: Almqvist and Wiksell.

Kohlberg, L. 1969. "Stage and Sequence: The Cognitive-Developmental Approach to Socialization." In *Handbook of Socialization Theory and Research*, ed. D. A. Goslin, pp. 347–480. Chicago: Rand McNally.

Koval, D., and L. W. Hales. 1972. "The Effects of the DUSO Guidance Program on the Self-Concepts of Primary Children." *Child Study Journal* 2: 57–61.

Lazarus, R. S. 1966. *Psychological Stress and the Coping Process.* New York: McGraw-Hill.

Leeds, R. 1963. "Altruism and Norm of Giving." *Merrill-Palmer Quarterly* 9: 226–32.

Luria, A. R. 1969. "Speech Development and the Formation of Mental Processes." In *A Handbook of Contemporary Soviet Psychology*, ed. M. Cole and I. Maltman, pp. 121–62. New York: Basic Books.

Macaulay, J., and L. Berkowitz, eds. 1970. *Altruism and Helping Behavior.* New York: Academic Press.

McCord, W., J. McCord, and A. Howard. 1961. "Familial Correlates of Aggression in Nondelinquent Male Children." *Journal of Abnormal and Social Psychology* 62: 79–93.

McLaughlin, B. 1971. *Learning and Social Behavior.* New York: Free Press.

Malewska, H., and V. Peyre. 1970. "Economic Development, Mobility of Population and Process of Social Deviation of Youth." *Polish Sociological Bulletin* 1: 94–111.

Mallick, S., and B. R. McCandless. 1966. "A Study of Catharsis of Aggression." *Journal of Personality and Social Psychology* 4: 591-96.

Mehrabian, A., and N. Epstein. 1972. "A Measure of Emotional Empathy." *Journal of Personality* 40: 525-43.

Meichenbaum, D. 1973. "Kognitive Faktoren bei der Verhaltensmodifikation: Veränderung der Selbstgespäche von Klienten." In *Selbstkontrolle*, ed. M. Hartig, pp. 197-213. Munich: Urban und Schwarzenberg.

Olofsson, B. 1973. *Unga lagöverträdare, III, Hem, uppfostran och kamratmiljö: Belysning av interju -och uppföl iningsdata*. Stockholm: SOU.

Pitkänen, L. 1969. *A Descriptive Model of Aggression and Nonaggression with Applications to Children's Behavior*. Jvv. Stud. Educ. Psychol. Soc. Res. 19.

———. 1973. "An Aggression Machine. III: The Stability of the Aggressive and Nonaggressive Patterns of Behaviour." *Scandinavian Journal of Psychology* 14: 75-77.

———. 1974. "The Effect of Simulation Exercises on the Control of Aggressive Behaviour in Children." *Scandinavian Journal of Psychology* 15: 169-77.

Pitkänen-Pulkkinen, L., and M. Pitkänen. 1976. "Social Skills of Aggressive and Nonaggressive Adolescents." *Scandinavian Journal of Psychology* 17: 10-14.

Rosenhahn, D. 1973. "The Kindnesses of Children." In *Preschool Children*, ed. M. C. Smart. New York: Macmillan.

Schacter, S. S., and J. E. Singer. 1967. "Cognitive Social and Physiological Determinants of Emotional States." *Psychological Review* 69: 379-99.

Staub, E. 1971. "The Learning and Unlearning of Aggression: The Role of Anxiety, Empathy, Efficacy and Pro-Social Values." In *The Control of Aggression and Violence*, ed. J. L. Singer, pp. 93-124. New York: Academic Press.

Stukat, K.-G., and K.-A. Sverud. 1974. *Förskoleprojektet: Göteborg. Utbildningsforskningsrapport 11. Skolöverstyrelsen*. Stockholm: Utbildningsförlaget.

Test, M. A., and J. H. Bryan. 1969. "The Effects of Dependency, Models and Reciprocity upon Subsequent Helping Behavior." *Journal of Social Psychology* 78: 205-12.

Vygotsky, L. S. 1962. *Thought and Language*. Cambridge, Mass.: MIT Press.

13

THE REGULATION AND MODIFICATION OF AGGRESSION: COMMONALITIES AND ISSUES

Seymour Feshbach

My goals in this concluding chapter are threefold. The first is to provide an overview of the alternative perspectives on the maintenance and change of aggressive behavior offered by the contributors to this volume. I particularly wish to focus on themes and issues common to several or most of the papers and to note areas of theoretical and empirical contention. The second objective is to consider issues that have been neglected in the research literature, where significant gaps exist in our knowledge of the parameters and consequences entailed in changing aggressive patterns of behavior, and to suggest research areas that appear promising. The third objective is an analysis of the problems of changing aggression in the light of the constraints of social reality. Leaving the laboratory for the world of social policy and decision making poses ethical issues and value and pragmatic considerations that warrant attention and discussion.

ORGANISM-ENVIRONMENT INTERACTION

The various approaches to aggression that have been considered in this volume use different methods (such as hormones and reinforcers) and are addressed to different levels of behavior in animals and humans (such as cognitive structures and social organizations). Consequently, possible areas of disagreement are not sharply joined, nor are areas of consensus very evident. Nevertheless, from an examination of the papers there emerge several themes bearing on some major questions concerning the nature of aggression and its control. One of these themes is the dialectic between dispositional and situational factors. It is almost a banality to refer to the person-environment interaction in accounting for behaviors. Yet it is too easily forgotten or ignored, and most especially when considering aggressive phenomena. Investigators focusing on brain mechanisms and genetic structures sometimes forget that central nervous system processes are strongly influenced by external stimuli or that genes do not function in an environmental vacuum. They may then attribute criminal behaviors to an extra Y chromosome or see violence as largely a function of a malfunction in the amygdala. Sociologists, on the other hand, attentive to the impressive social class, ethnic, religious, age, and national differences in violent behaviors may overlook the substantial variability in aggression within a social group. Poverty, race, and age may be predictors of criminal aggressive acts; but most adolescents, including those from economically disadvantaged and ethnic minority backgrounds, are not criminals.

The significance of the interactive determination of aggression is evident in all of the biologically oriented papers. J. M. R. Delgado points out that the effects of stimulation of the cortex are dependent upon the nature of the stimulus confronting the organism. Stimulation of certain brain areas in the presence of a submissive animal results in an aggressive response, while stimulation of the same brain area in the presence of a dominant animal produces a submissive response. At the same time, external stimulus conditions, such as the presence of a friend versus an enemy, that ordinarily exercise a discriminative function can be overwhelmed with cortical stimulation of areas mediating attack behavior. Delgado finds that although the animals will recognize enemies and friends, an organized aggressive behavior sequence is directed toward friends as well as enemies. These observations reflect a subtle interaction between direct cortical stimulation and environmental parameters such that brain stimulation can eliminate the effects of some environmental influences on aggression while others maintain their potency.

The paper by Kirsti Lagerspetz also presents several illustrations of the interaction between environment and biological structures. She nicely demonstrates, through selective breeding and systematic experimentation, the role of genetic factors in aggression in mice. She shows that when an aggressive strain, her TA mice, are raised by nonaggressive mothers (TWM), aggressive differences consistent with the genetic background still remain. Nevertheless, one can train aggressive animals to behave nonaggressively through defeat. Attacks by partners and the experience of defeat can inhibit the stimulating effects of electric shock on genetically aggressive mice. These data are quite consistent with the observations of Delgado, although the experimental paradigms and species employed are very different. Similarly, one can find a number of examples of dynamic organism-situation interactions in the extensive and systematic series of studies described by Elzbieta Fonberg. Thus lesions in the medial amygdala of cats will eliminate predatory behavior of cats, although the latter will still eat food. With time, the operated-upon cats will hunt mice, but not in the presence of other cats, even submissive ones.

The reinforcing contingencies and norms and values characterizing the situations in which aggression is or is not elicited receive greater emphasis in Gerald Patterson's review of social learning approaches to the management of aggression, in Leonard Eron's discussion of the socialization of sex differences in aggression, and in the sociological contributions by Marvin Wolfgang and Marek Kosewski. Here, too, one can discern indications of the significance of organism-environment interaction, despite the minimal attention given to organism variables. Prisons may breed violence, but they do so in a population already prone to violence. An obvious and important property of reinforcing situations is their correlation with selected organism behavior. Reinforcers do not operate at random, and the "emission" of aggression does not occur randomly. The children who develop aggressive behavior problems have had, by reason of temperament and frustration, a greater likelihood of behaving aggressively. The social environment—family, school, peers—can enhance these responses or discourage them. Patterson has shown how some parents, though intent upon inhibiting aggression, manage to reinforce and exacerbate their child's aggressive behaviors. Wolfgang reports that adolescents contribute disproportionately to the incidence of crime and violence. Why crime is age-related may have both biological and social roots. In any case, the adolescent disposition for social deviation is reinforced by a subculture of violence.

One method of reducing aggressive crime is to break up this subculture through dispersion and social integration. A very different mechanism is through changes in the birth rate. In fact, Wolfgang points out that population studies indicate that in the United States a significant drop will occur in the proportion of adolescents and, as a result, he predicts that a significant drop in aggressive crime rates will take place. This example of alternative modes of intervention anticipates an important proposition that will subsequently be discussed: that it may be possible to reduce aggression through environmental manipulation even if one demonstrates physiological or other dispositional causes, or through manipulation of the organism even if one demonstrates environmental causes.

The papers by Adam Frączek and Janusz Reykowski place the disposition-situation interaction within the broader context of the organization of behaviors and the complex affective and cognitive feedback system that helps regulate the organism's activity. The phenomenon of aggression is analyzed in terms of considerations of personality structure and personality dynamics. And, very much within the European tradition, an effort is made to provide an integrative account of molecular stimulus-response events in terms of more holistic levels of analysis. The chapters by Norma Feshbach and Lea Pitkänen-Pulkkinen offer experimental applications based upon theoretical orientations consistent with the Frączek and Reykowski papers: Both Feshbach and Pitkänen present programs that attempt to modify aggressive behavior through modifying a significant element in the organism's personality structure and organization. In the former instance the objective is to enhance the child's self-control skills. In each instance the organism-environment interaction is altered through augmenting the organism's ability to respond more effectively to situations that frequently elicit aggression.

One implication of a thoroughgoing organism-environment conception of the antecedents of aggression is the recognition that there are many possible strategies that can be employed for altering aggressive behavior. One can intervene at the organism level, modifying physiology through administration of hormones and other chemical agents; reducing feelings of frustration and anger through cognitive restructuring, insight, and enhancement of self-esteem; and fostering alternative responses to aggression through systematic reinforcement and reeducation. In a similar manner one can intervene at the environmental level, changing the socioeconomic circumstances that breed frustration and discontent, modifying ecological factors and cultural resources so as to make aggressive responses less probable (for instance, lowering population density, eliminating weapons, and changing social norms and expectations so that nonaggressive behaviors are valued and encouraged).

Moreover, dispositional (organism) and environment factors are often interconnected; each may reinforce the other and changes in one domain may produce changes in the other. For example, socioeconomic status and other environmental variables may influence diet and exposure to toxic agents and similar factors that can produce biochemical, even morphological, changes in processes and structures that are implicated in aggressive behavior. Even genetic factors linked to aggression can be affected by features of the culture and environment; for instance, social values placed upon aggression may affect the attractiveness of sexual partners and may selectively influence mating practices so that highly aggressive individuals produce more progeny than do less aggressive individuals. Differences at the level of the organism also shape the environment. Individuals who find aggression reinforcing may help foster social arrangements that increase the level of aggression in the society; an example is violent people who selectively promote physical punishment practices that in turn are strong antecedents to aggression. History is replete with instances of individuals who through their own paranoia and hostility have brought about social changes that encourage hostility and aggression in others (for instance, Hitler and the Nazis). The matrix of variables that mediate aggressive behavior is most aptly designated by such overused but, in this instance, appropriate terms as "field" and "system." An alteration of one part of the field can produce perturbations throughout the system.

Conceptualizing aggression in this manner has significant implications for its modification. Thus, although aggressive behavior is multiply determined, one does not have to modify each determinant in order to bring about a major change in the system or field from which aggression and violence emerge. Modification of some components of the system can have far-reaching consequences without directly changing other components. For example, individual aggressive dispositions, socioeconomic inequities and frustration, social attitudes toward violence, and the availability of weapons may all influence the degree of violence manifested in a society. However, a major change in social attitudes toward the use of aggression in solving individual and social conflicts could sharply reduce the incidence of violence even though no direct effort was made to modify the other variables. A marked reduction in access to weapons could have similar consequences, although its effects are not likely to be as striking as those ensuing from a change in social attitudes and values.

The interaction between physiological attributes of the organism and situational attributes of the environment, noted by Delgado, Fonberg, and Lagerspetz, implies that violence and destruction do not inevitably ensue when parts of the cortex mediating aggression and violence are activated. "Murder" is not a property of brain tissue or of neurochemistry. Activation of parts of the brain or stimulation of particular chemical secretions may increase the likelihood of an attack response that will result in the destruction of another human. But, as Delgado's paper so nicely illustrates, the occurrence of an attack when neural structures implicated in aggression are activated depends very much upon features of the organism's environment. Biological language that sometimes appears in popular and even scientific writings, such as "killer instinct," is unfortunately misleading and obscures our understanding of the intricate interactions and processes that give rise to destructive behavior.

INTRINSIC AGGRESSION

A second theme that appears in these papers, not as common as the theme of interaction but sufficiently frequent and significant for special notice, is that of intrinsic aggression. The concept of intrinsic aggression refers to aggressive activity that does not seem to be a function of reinforcers other than the infliction of pain and the performance of the aggressive response itself; that is, the organism's satisfaction appears to be intrinsic to the aggressive act itself. The question of "intrinsic" aggression is fundamental to understanding the phenomenon of aggression and the possibilities of its control and modification. It relates to the issue of an instinctive aggressive drive and to the role of learning and experience in aggressive behavior. Despite the significance of the question of intrinsic aggression, there has been relatively little in the way of systematic analysis and research on this issue. Contrasting positions have largely been based on assumption rather than on empirical evidence. Thus, Freud assumed the existence of an instinctual aggressive drive. The frustration-aggression hypothesis constituted a modification of the Freudian position but nevertheless posited an aggressive drive, in this case linked to the degree and amount of frustration experienced by the organism. It may be that there is a relationship between frustration and aggressive drive. However, as research subsequent to the formulation of the frustration-aggression hypothesis has shown, the relationship between frustration and aggressive behavior is complex and dependent upon other properties of the situation.

There are many responses that organisms make to frustration. At the human level, whether aggression is one of these depends upon such cognitive dimensions of the frustration as the perceived degree of intentionality, justification, and responsibility of the frustrating agent. Even where aggression has been demonstrated to be a consequence of frustration, evidence for an aggressive drive remains ambiguous. The aggressive response may simply be an innate or learned reaction to frustration; removal of the source of frustration, rather than injury to the frustrating agent, may be the primary function of the aggressive response to frustration. The persistence of aggression will then depend upon the persistence of the frustration rather than upon the evocation of an aggressive drive.

The utility of the concept of aggressive drive has come increasingly into question as psychologists and biologists have found it possible to explain a great deal of aggressive behavior without invoking a drive concept. As F. A. Beach (1965) has noted in his studies of sexual behavior in animals, the more that is understood about the sequence of mechanisms mediating sexual behavior, the less necessity there is of invoking a drive or motivation concept. At the human level, aggressive drive or motivation theories have been less popular in recent years, and have given way to explanations in terms of conditioning (Berkowitz 1974), modeling (Bandura 1973), or social reinforcement (Buss 1971; Patterson, Littman, and Bricker 1967). Still, the concept of aggressive drive or some equivalent is not without its adherents. The phenomenon of displaced aggression in birds, and related observations, led Konrad Lorenz (1966) to postulate neural mechanisms by which aggressive tension is temporarily stored. Studies at the human level, indicating that the infliction of pain can be a reinforcer (Feshbach, Stiles, and Bitter 1967), also point to the viability of an aggressive drive or motivation concept.

In considering the issue of an aggressive drive or aggressive motive, it is theoretically useful to distinguish between satisfactions associated with performance of the aggressive response and satisfactions associated with the infliction of injury. At the empirical level it is difficult to separate these two possible sources of reinforcement. The difference lies in whether the organism is motivated to perform an aggressive response, the incidental consequences of which are the infliction of injury, or whether the primary object of the aggressive sequence is injury to some other organism. This difference is expressed in the distinction made between "the desire to hit" or "the desire to hurt" (Feshbach 1964). A motivation "to hit" may arise from the blocking of the expression of angry affect (Feshbach 1964) or from the interruption of an aggressive response sequence (Berkowitz 1964). The point here is that if the motivation is to hit rather than to hurt, one can separate the aggressive response from its injurious consequences—cathartic exercises that provide pillows to beat or punching bags to hit fall into this category. However, if the motivation is to injure, then the form of the response becomes less important. Physical attack can give way to pressing a button that delivers an electric shock, signifies disgrace or humiliation, or results in the explosion of a bomb. For both applied and theoretical reasons, wherever possible, in demonstrating that organisms are motivated to aggress, it is useful to distinguish between the reinforcing properties of the aggressive response per se and the reinforcement that may be associated with the infliction of injury.

The demonstration of aggressive motivation in animals and humans, and the determination of the conditions under which organisms are motivated to inflict injury or behave aggressively, are the first requirements of any theory of aggression that posits an intrinsic aggression component. Several experiments reported in Lagerspetz's and Fonberg's papers bear directly upon this question. The second requirement is an explanation of the antecedents of intrinsic aggression. Is the performance of an aggressive response or the infliction of injury innately satisfying, or are the motivational properties a consequence of learning and experience? Thus R. L. Sears (1958) has proposed that the infliction of injury acquires secondary reinforcing properties through association with a primary reinforcer. Aggression, according to this model, is first elicited by a frustrating or painful stimulus. If the aggressive response is successful in removing the source of discomfort, then injury cues associated with the consequence of aggression, through a process of conditioning, may become associated with the reduction in discomfort and distress and acquire some of the reinforcing, goal qualities of the reduction in an aversive stimulus. This secondary reinforcement model of the acquisition of intrinsic aggression is certainly plausible. However, it remains speculative, in that there is no empirical evidence to support it.

I have proposed elsewhere (Feshbach 1974) a model of the acquisition of aggressive motivation based on the internalization of retaliatory norms. This conception of aggressive motivation—a motive for which the goal response is the infliction of injury—is based upon the observation that much aggressive behavior is formally indistinguishable from punishment, especially physical punishment. A commits an infraction that distresses B, and B responds by retaliating against A—that is, by punishing A in some way. Many of us are socialized, through observation, identification, and direct instruction, to feel uncomfortable until we have successfully retaliated against someone who has hurt or unjustly frustrated us. Much aggressive motivation can be understood in the context of equity theory (Walster, Berscheid, and Walster 1973), with the infliction of pain being the principal method of restoring equity. Here, too, it must be noted that while there is some evidence supporting this punishment model of aggressive motivation, it is largely indirect. In addition, it is possible to view aggression as a form of punishment without invoking drive or motivational properties. Patterson, interestingly, frequently labels parental punishment of an aggressive child as an act of aggression toward the child when physical punishment or verbal abuse is employed. While his social reinforcement model does not directly use motivational concepts, to the extent that the parent is reinforced by the infliction of pain (rather than by the child's conformity response, request for forgiveness, or other reaction following pain infliction), aggressive motivation can be viewed as implementing the parent's punishment behavior.

The "retaliation" or "punishment" model that is proposed to account for aggressive motivation is based on processes such as the internalization of social norms, processes that are largely restricted to the human level. However, data reported in the chapters by Lagerspetz, Fonberg, and Delgado provide compelling evidence of some forms of intrinsic aggression at the animal level. Lagerspetz reports that TA mice will learn a response where the only "reward" is fighting with an opponent. In addition, subsequent to the interruption of a fight, animals will cross an electrified grid, apparently to reach their opponent and resume the fight; that is, the goal of "fighting" is sufficiently strong to overcome the aversive properties of the electric shock. One might reasonably conjecture that the motive in this instance is not the infliction of pain but the performance of an aggressive response. The experimental paradigm—interruption of fighting and then its resumption—is consonant with the assumption of a response-continuation motive.

The cortical stimulation and related experiments described by Fonberg and by Delgado point to the presence in animals of organized sequences of responses that culminate in the attack of another organism. The only "goal" discernible in this sequence of responses appears intrinsic to the aggressive act. In using the term "intrinsic" in this context, I am not referring to the biological or social basis of aggression but, as previously indicated, to the goal of reinforcing properties of the aggressive act and the infliction of pain and injury. The behaviors subsumed by Fonberg under the category of "emotional aggression," to the extent that they entail persistent, directed activity, are a form of intrinsic aggression. One could conceptualize emotional aggression and other types of affective reactions as simply a constellation of autonomic and motor reactions to a particular stimulus situation, without calling upon any notions of goal, motive, drive, or intrinsic satisfaction. While parsimonious and perhaps adequate for mild emotional arousal, this approach does not deal adequately with the consequences of strong emotional arousal. Under such a condition, behavior segments of varying degrees of complexity and organization are initiated. Once under way, the course of these reactions is difficult to modify or shift, and when it is blocked or interrupted, one typically finds evidence of a strong disposition directed toward the completion of the emotional sequence. Thus Fonberg notes that hypothalamically stimulated attack is less dependent on the presence of visual stimuli; when the latter are removed, the attack persists. She also notes that there are strong motor components in the response to hypothalamic stimulation, suggesting that the form of intrinsic aggression involved is response completion rather than pain infliction. The observation that aggressively aroused dogs will direct an aggressive attack toward a stick rather than the experimenter also indicates that the aggressive "goal" is response completion or expression, not the infliction of pain or injury.

Intrinsic aggression is a central theme of Reykowski's paper. Whereas in the animal studies cited by Lagerspetz, by Fonberg, and by Delgado, aggression is a consequence of strong stimulation and the animal is presumably acting so as to decrease the level of stimulation, Reykowski proposes that in humans one major source of the intrinsic motivation of aggressive behavior is the need for stimulation. The intrinsic satisfaction that some individuals find in acts of aggression and destruction is seen to be a consequence of the heightened stimulation associated with such acts. This model of aggression is especially appropriate to those situations in which there is no obvious antecedent painful or frustrating stimulus. It does not even require a target that is disliked. The basic satisfaction is derived from the augmentation of stimulation—primarily from the kinesthetic feedback of strong, violent movements but also from the risks usually inherent in aggressive situations, from sudden changes produced in the physical state of the target, and from the pain and cries of the target. Thus the "need for stimulation" interpretation provides an explanation of both the reinforcing properties of an aggressive action and the reinforcing properties of the infliction of pain and injury.

Reykowski's model of aggression is consistent with one of the major explanations of psychopathic behavior. The "need for stimulation" hypothesis has had considerable heuristic value in the study of psychopaths (Hare 1970), many of whom have been engaged in antisocial aggressive acts. The "lack of stimulation" model, however, does not account for the role of anger and of dislike of a target in intrinsic aggression. To explain this form of intrinsically motivated aggression, Reykowski, and also Frączek, elaborate upon more complex cognitive mechanisms that are implicated in aggressive behaviors, particularly mechanisms directed toward maintenance of self-esteem. These latter analyses reflect the increasing theoretical importance ascribed to the role of cognitive processes in motivation and affect, including aggressive motivation and its relation to the self system (Feshbach 1964). Frączek makes an important distinction between the role of cognitive processes in impulsive aggression and in interpersonal aggression, cognitive factors being much more significant for interpersonal aggression although sometimes entering into impulsive aggressive behaviors. The "direction" of an emotion may be much less important than its intensity in influencing impulsive aggression. However, as Frączek demonstrates in a series of experiments, the direction or cognitive aspect of an affective cue is critical for interpersonal aggression, with positive affective cues reducing and negative affective cues enhancing aggressive behaviors. In summary, the papers by Reykowski and Frączek highlight the role of cognitive mechanisms in determining why we derive satisfaction from aggression against people who injure us and whom we dislike.

ALTERNATIVES TO AGGRESSION

A third theme that is present in many of the papers is the regulation of aggression through the teaching of alternative behaviors and control mechanisms. There are a number of possible suggestions for modifying aggression that could have emerged from these diverse contributions. One might have focused on the reduction of frustration and related aversive conditions fostering aggression, both at the sociological level and at the child-rearing level. Yet even the sociologically oriented papers were concerned with normative conditions that maintain and encourage aggression rather than with the role of poverty, rising expectations, crowding, or anomie. It is of interest that in none of the physiologically oriented papers were biochemical, neurosurgical, or neural stimulation procedures proposed for the alteration of aggressive behaviors. Rather, suggestions concerning control were made in terms of environmental input or emotional conditioning. It is certainly quite possible, even likely, that another group of participants would have proposed different approaches to the management of human aggression. It is of interest, nonetheless, that despite the varying theoretical and methodological orientations represented in the contributions to this volume, there is a fair degree of consensus on how to approach the problem of coping with aggression.

Perhaps contributing to this commonality is the recognition of major ethical and practical obstacles in altering biological functions and in eliminating economic inequities and social injustice. In an important sense, modifying aggression through increasing response alternatives, through enhancing the individual's ability to inhibit and control impulsive expression, and through clarification of and changes in social norms governing aggressive behavior is directed toward conditions affecting the performance of an aggressive response rather than toward the motivation and learned or physiological disposition to aggress. The program described by Sepp Schindler, which has a strong therapeutic component, is perhaps an exception to this generalization. The programs reviewed by Patterson and the suggestions offered by Eron are certainly addressed to the learning of aggression as well as to factors affecting performance. However, it is attention to alternative modes of responding to provocative stimuli and to response control that remains the dominant motif.

Fonberg draws our attention the the possibilities of conditioning positive affect to stimuli that serve as inappropriate targets of aggression. Reykowski and Norma Feshbach discuss the aggressive control functions of empathy, with the latter presenting encouraging outcome data indicating that training the affective-cognitive skills entailed in empathy is one promising approach to the management of aggression. The training program described by Pitkänen, with its greater emphasis on response alternatives to aggression, also holds considerable promise. A particularly attractive feature of the Feshbach and Pitkänen programs is the ease with which they can be incorporated into school curricula. The Wolfgang, Kosewski, and Eron papers, and to some degree the programs reviewed and the model implemented by Patterson, point to the potential utility of altering social norms that maintain aggressive and discourage nonaggressive responses. Thus the "subculture of violence" helps maintain delinquent behaviors. If adolescents in this subculture moved to residential areas in which a subculture of nonviolence prevailed, then one might anticipate a sharp decline in the delinquent behavior of these adolescents. Similarly, modifications in the value structure of the prison hierarchy can bring about changes in the level of violence in the prison. And, as Eron suggests, applying to boys the social norms and expectations that govern aggressive behavior in girls should result in a decline in male aggression to the lower levels exhibited by girls.

None of the proposed programs offers any panacea for the complex problem of aggression and violence in contemporary society. They offer, at best, partial solutions entailing the modification of social norms and values, which will undoubtedly encounter considerable resistance. Nevertheless, it would seem well within the realm of feasibility to implement programs that at the individual level and in limited cultural settings will enhance aggressive controls and expand response alternatives.

SOME RESEARCH QUESTIONS TO BE ADDRESSED

There is much that is not known about aggressive behavior. Each of the individual papers raises as many questions as it resolves; the biochemistry, the neurophysiology, the socialization, the regulation and modification of aggression all pose research questions regarding which there is conflicting evidence and interpretations or that have yet to be explored. However, it is not the objective of this brief section to enumerate areas of research ignorance. Such a task might require a whole volume in and of itself. Rather, the goal is to consider a few examples of research questions that bear upon the regulation of aggression, recognizing that one could cite many more.

In part because this conference was directed toward issues entailed in the regulation of aggression, the participants have largely viewed aggression as a "problem," a behavior that requires modification and regulation. Since aggression in contemporary society is a very real problem, there is a tendency to view aggressive behavior as a biological anachronism, a vestigial behavior tendency that may once have been functional for *Homo sapiens* but now constitutes a liability. This may well be the case; human violence does pose a serious threat to life and to the social fabric. And, along with most behavioral scientists, I believe that it is critical that we sharply reduce the level of aggression in human affairs. However, it is not clear that one would want to reduce all forms of aggression— for instance, the use of aggression for self-defense, for defense of one's group or nation, and for maintaining social control and protection of the community.

One might contend that the socially approved utilization of aggression and force is not equivalent to interpersonal, antisocial acts of violence and destruction. However, quite apart from definitional and value considerations, there is the empirical question of the relationship between the regulation of aggressive behaviors that are socially disapproved and aggressive behaviors that are socially sanctioned. If children are socialized so as to foster better aggression controls and nonaggressive response alternatives, what effects would such socializations have on the capacity to behave aggressively for protective purposes? Presumably societies can foster discriminations between situations in which aggression is appropriate and situations in which it is inappropriate. But there have been few, if any, efforts to determine the effectiveness and limits of such discriminations. Theoretically, it should be easier to establish such discriminations for instances of instrumental, as compared with emotional, aggression. However, as Fonberg notes, it is rare that instrumental aggression does not contain some emotional components. Consequently, inhibition of affective aggression may affect instrumental aggression as well.

Moreover, as has been discussed elsewhere (Feshbach 1974), the socialization of aggression may influence other components of the personality that may be correlated with the constellation of affect and instrumental responses that constitute the aggressive system. Assertion and competitiveness are examples of behavior clusters that are related to aggression. We know very little about the developmental sequence that these behaviors follow, particularly whether aggression inhibition and other aggression controls generalize so that assertion and competitiveness are also inhibited. There is by now a substantial body of data indicating a relationship between the sexual system and the aggressive system such that changes in one influence the other (Malamuth, Feshbach, and Jaffe 1977). One can reasonably anticipate that other systems of behavior will be affected by the process through which aggression is socialized and regulated.

At a more fundamental level we have yet to determine the precise consequences of various mechanisms of aggression control upon the aggressive response itself. We do not know the effects of the inhibition, through fear of punishment, of a strong aggressive response upon subsequent manifestations of aggression. The effective management of anger is also at issue. Systematic comparisons of the consequences of expressing anger, albeit in harmless ways, versus inhibition of angry feelings, versus anger avoidance through conditioning of alternative affective responses have yet to be carried out. There are some data indicating that modification of aggressive reactions to provocations by cognitive restructuring of social norms is less likely to result in conflict and displacement than is modification of aggression through inhibitory fears (Kaufmann and Feshbach 1963a, 1963b). However, these data are at best suggestive, and much more research is needed to address this issue. Given such psychosomatic conditions as hypertension that are believed by some to ensue from the suppression of anger, and given the interpersonal threat posed by displaced aggression, the question of the effects of various methods of controlling and socializing aggression is a critical one.

One additional research question that merits some discussion because it has largely been neglected is the basis for the attraction and interest that aggressive themes and incidents elicit. From prehistoric cave drawings and Egyptian pictographs to the Greek tragedies, the Bible, Shakespeare, and contemporary literature, there is evidence of human preoccupation with aggression and violence. Is this fascination with aggression simply another manifestation of our own aggressive dispositions? Does this involvement in aggressive themes have any functional value—as a process for expressing, understanding, and managing aggressive feelings? Perhaps the attraction to themes of aggression and violence is related to other motivational systems—for example, the need for stimulation that Reykowski has discussed. In this connection the question arises as to why a need for stimulation eventuates in aggressive action and preferences rather than in other types of stimulating events (such as the excitement of achievement, mastery of nature, and other prosocial behaviors). Perhaps, given a need for stimulation, the excitement of violence is much more readily accessible than other forms of stimulation and, as a result, it may be difficult to dissociate aggressive actions and interests from the need for stimulation. At the same time it may be possible to satisfy this need by exposure to vicarious aggressive experiences in literature and drama while establishing sharp discriminations between such vicarious experiences and participation in real aggressive actions. In brief, we may be better able to manage aggression by understanding the bases for its apparent attraction for so many people.

MODIFYING AGGRESSION:
ETHICAL AND PRAGMATIC ISSUES

Ethical and pragmatic issues arise whenever one confronts the task of resolving a behavior or social problem. This is the case whether one is addressing a psychological disorder such as schizophrenia or a social problem such as poverty. These issues become especially acute when one deals with the complex behavior system of aggression, which entails behaviors that need not reflect a psychological disorder or necessarily be detrimental to the interests of society. Revolutions are accomplished through acts of aggression. Whether one opposes the goals of the revolution or rejects the tactics employed is a value issue that involves more than scientific considerations. From certain perspectives the willingness to resist oppressive authority and risk one's life for the sake of a social cause would be taken as positive indicators of the vitality and cohesion of a subgroup and its members.

Issues regarding criminal violence would appear to be more straightforward. There are few who would place a positive ethical value on the use of violence for personal gain or to resolve a personal problem. One might understand the basis for the violent act but not condone it. Even here ethical and social values are not always clear. Vengeance to achieve restitution for an injury or humiliation is accepted in many cultures, and is sanctioned by parts of the Old Testament. The vigilante theme—going outside the law to achieve restitution when it cannot be achieved within the law—is a familiar one in American folklore. However, the dimension that introduces particularly sensitive ethical issues is the relationship between psychopathology and antisocial aggressive behaviors. Some violent acts undoubtedly arise out of an emotional disturbance, and others are precipitated by a neurological disorder. But many acts of aggression and violence are instrumental in nature and are responses to environmental circumstances. Again, while these acts must be controlled and disciplined by society, behavioral and biological scientists need to be conscious of the special concerns and issues that arise when social deviance becomes intertwined with mental illness.

The difficulty of discriminating between violent acts that are cruel and are not primarily a reflection of mental illness elicits several related concerns. First, the biological approach may distract us from the major causes of violence in the society. To quote the Nobel laureate Salvatore E. Luria:

> It is easy to see that such biologizing of crime and aggression serves to make people close their eyes to what crime really is: a social illness, fed by poverty and profit. . . . It is not the expression of a few genes or chromosomes. We biologists and medical scientists should be alert not to let our sciences be dragged into these kinds of sterile pursuits. (1974, pp. 27–28).

One might argue that a social orientation distracts us from the biological antecedents of violent crime. This may be the case, and this is precisely where the ethical issue is joined. Scientists' views concerning the causes and remediation of violent, socially deviant behaviors have important social consequences for the prevention and treatment of such behaviors. One discovers an extra Y chromosome on a gene of a criminal, and forces are set into motion that all too readily bridge the gap between a limited and questionable data base and social policies. The prevailing power structure in any society will tend to attribute social deviations to problems within the individual rather than to problems within the society. For this reason alone, one must be especially cautious in generalizing from laboratory data based upon small, selected samples to the larger social problems presented by aggressive deviant acts.

A related concern stemming from a mental-illness conception of aggression and violence is the danger of the label "mental illness" being used to discredit violent acts that are forms of social protest. Since resistance to constituted authority is often defined as violence, there is the possibility of the psychological and psychiatric professions being used as instruments of the state to insure social conformity. In the American psychiatric literature one can find statements by some leading authorities in which the individual's ability to meet the needs of society, rather than the individual's well-being, is defined as the goal of psychiatric treatment (Brill 1971). Such a view inexorably aligns the mental health profession with the status quo. And it is a view that is highly compatible with the position that violence is primarily a reflection of a brain or emotional disorder.

These caveats and cautions are not intended to hinder scientific efforts to determine the bases of aggression and violence and the mechanisms for regulating and reducing them. Scientists should be free to pursue these research questions and should be encouraged to do so. Human violence is a major social problem causing untold pain and suffering, and threatening the very existence of the species. The analyses of aggression presented in this volume and the programs described for regulating and reducing aggression are modest beginnings. None purports to offer radical solutions. But this is as it should be. It reflects the current state of knowledge and the caution that must be exercised when one explores an amorphous area in which it is difficult to tell where science ends and personal and social values begin.

REFERENCES

Bandura. A. 1973. *Aggression. A Social Learning Analysis*. Englewood Cliffs, New Jersey: Prentice-Hall.

Beach, F. A., ed. 1965. *Sex and Behavior*. New York: John Wiley.

Berkowitz, L. 1964. "Aggressive Cues in Aggressive Behavior and Hostility Catharsis." *Psychological Review* 71: 104–22.

——. 1974. "Some Determinants of Impulsive Aggression: Role of Mediated Associations with Reinforcements for Aggression." *Psychological Review* 81: 165–76.

Brill, N. 1971. "Treatment Goals in Psychiatry." *Psychiatry Digest* 32: 16–21.

Buss, A. H. 1971. "Aggression Pays." In *The Control of Aggression: Aggression and Violence*, ed. J. L. Singer. New York: Academic Press.

Feshbach, S., W. Stiles, and E. Bitter. 1967. "The Reinforcing Effect of Witnessing Aggression." *Journal of Experimental Research in Personality* 2: 133–39.

Hare, R. D. 1970. *Psychopathy, Theory and Research*. New York: John Wiley.

Kagan, J., and H. A. Moss. 1962. *Birth to Maturity*. New York: John Wiley.

Kaufmann, H., and S. Feshbach. 1963a. "Displaced Aggression and Its Modification Through Exposure to Anti-aggressive Communication." *Journal of Abnormal and Social Psychology* 67: 79–83.

——. 1963b. "The Influence of Anti-aggressive Communications upon the Response to Provocation." *Journal of Personality* 31: 428–44.

Lesser, G. 1958. "Application of Guttman's Scaling Method to Aggressive Fantasy in Children." *Educ. Psychol. Measur.* 18: 543–51.

Lorenz, K. 1966. *On Aggression*. New York: Harcourt, Brace and World.

Luria, S. E. 1974. "What Can Biologists Solve?" *New York Review of Books*, Feb. 7.

Patterson, G. R., R. A. Littman, and W. Bricker. 1967. "Assertive Behavior in Children: A Step Toward a Theory of Aggression." *Monogr, soc. res. Child Dev.*, 32 (5 and 6).

Sears, R. L. 1958. "Personality Development in the Family." In *The Child*, ed. J. Seidman, pp. 117–37. New York: Reinhard.

Walster, B., E. Berscheid, and G. W. Walster. 1973. "New Directions in Equity Research." *Journal of Personality and Social Psychology* 25: 151–76.

INDEX

Azrin, N. H., 18, 19, 37

Baenninger, R., 73
Bailey, D. W., 67
Baker, B. L., 99
Balasubramaniam, V., 35
Ballantine, T. H., 35
Bandler, R. J., 27, 31
band of Broca, 40
Bandura, A., 134, 141, 143, 144, 145,
    147, 150, 151, 158, 159, 160, 163,
    166, 168, 170, 170n., 171, 252,
    276
Banks, C., 220
Bannon, James, 202
Bard, Morton, 201, 204
Barenboim, C., 236, 238
Barnard, J., 115
Barnett, S. A., 17
Baron, R. A., 148, 151, 169, 171
Barrera, F., 90
Barron, F., 166
Beach, F. A., 276
Becker, W. C., 118
behavior modification, 142, 259
Bennett, R. M., 78
Benning, J. J., 87
Berger, S. M., 236
Berkowitz, L., 140, 141, 142, 143, 147,
    148, 151, 158, 159, 164, 173, 213,
    252, 254, 276
Berland, R., 91
Berleman, W. C., 95
Berlyne, D. E., 161
Bernal, Martha, 84, 85, 98, 103, 116,
    117, 118
Bernard, B., 31
Berquist, E. H., 16
Berscheid, E., 277
Bettelheim, B., 166
Bexton, W. H., 160
bibliotherapy, 114
Bijou, S., 98, 248
Bitter, E., 276
Block, J., 88
blood pressure, and attack, 31
Bloom, B. S., 245
Bolstad, O. D., 85, 117
Bosco, Don, 229
Botkin, P. T., 236
Bouma, H., 30
Bowlby, J., 230
Bowman, P. H., 87

Bowne, 29
Brain, P. F., 78
brain systems: and aggression, 7, 26–30,
    36; biochemistry/neurohormonal
    aspects, 30–33; and emotions, 6; and
    lesions, malfunctioning, 15ff., 27, 36;
    and predators, 16, 29; and rage, 9, 18,
    26, 33, 56; and sex hormones, 32; and
    social hierarchy, 29–30; and stimula-
    tion and attack, 60–61, 272, 275
Bricker, W., 276
Brill, N., 284
Brock, T., 151
Brodsky, G., 98, 119
Bronfenbrenner, U., 198, 266
Bronson, F. H., 32, 78
Brown, J. L., 18
Brown, R. A., 98
Brudnias, 15
Brügger, M., 26
Bruner, J. S., 261
Bryan, J. H., 252
Buckley, N. K., 118
Buehler, R. E., 90
Burchard, J. D., 90, 97
Burkholder, R., 118
Burns, B., 98
Burov, Y. V., 31
Buss, A. H., 75, 78, 139, 150, 151, 195,
    251, 276
Buss-Durkee Inventory, on prisons, 221,
    226
Byrne, D. F., 237

Cairor, H., 90
Cambridge-Somerville Project, 94–95
carnivores: food deprivation in, 14; and
    hunting, 10
Carpenter, J. A., 78
case method, 95, 96, 132
CASE project, 90, 91
castration, and aggression, 32
catecholamines, and aggression, 31
cats: and aggression, 3, 16-17, 29, 32;
    attack behavior of, 27, 37–40; brain
    functioning of, 272; defensive behavior
    of, 31, 32; learning in, 57; as nonpreda-
    tors, 16; predatory behavior of, 16;
    rage in, 56; shock behavior of, 18
caudate nucleus, 37
Center at Oregon for Research in the Be-
    havioral Education of the Handicapped,
    118

288

Center for Studies in Criminology and Criminal Law, 190
central nervous system, pathway traffic in, 58
cerebrum, and social hierarchy, 62 (*see also* brain systems)
Chamberlain, P., 89
Chandler, M. J., 235, 236, 237, 238
children: acting out of, 83-92; and classroom interventions, 117-20; and culture, 57; empathy in, 238, 239; [training exercises, 239-41; training study, 244-45]; Oregon Social Community Center, 98-117; parent training, 98; punishment of, 277; self-control of, 252-53, 257, 261-66; and social learning, 95-97, 98-117; summary on, 120-21; treatment of; [community-based, 93-95; outside community, 89-92]
child rearing: and self-control, 253, 257, 265; societal regulation, 184 (*see also* children)
chlorodiazapoxide, and defensive-aggressive behavior, 31-32
Christensen, A., 103, 105n., 109, 109n., 111, 115
Christensen, O., 99
Christophersen, E. R., 115, 116
Ciarkowska, W., 145, 158
class, socio-economic: and self-control, 258; and violence, 185-86, 189, 191, 198
classical conditioning, 143 (*see also* Pavlov, I.)
classrooms (*see* school)
Clement, B. W., 85, 109n.
Clemente, C. D., 40
Clinard, Marshall, 188
Cloward, Richard, 199
Cobb, J. A., 117, 118
Cofer, C. N., 142, 170
cognition, 72-74; and aggression, 146-48; and empathy, 236, 246; feedback system in, 273; and self-control, 152, 152-53
Cohen, H., 90, 111
Cohen, R., 244, 245, 246
cohort, birth, violent crime in, 190-92
Conger, J. J., 88
Conger, R. E., 96, 101
Contrera, J. F., 77
corporal punishment, and aggression, 257

cortex, and aggression, 36, 40-41, 272 (*see also* brain systems)
counterconditioning, and norms, 158
Crawley, J. N., 77
Cressey, Donald, 195
crime, and social control: birth cohort, 190-92; child/youth, 188-90; and culture, 183-86; family, 186-88, 200-2; sociopathic dimension, 197-204; subculture of, 193-97, 199-200, 203
Crime in the United States (Department of Justice), 186
culture: and aggression, 168; and violence, 183-86, 193
Curtis, Lynn A., 187, 188, 198
Cutrona, C., 242
Czapiński, J., 173
Czapów, C., 208, 230

Dabrowski, K., 43
Daniel, K., 119
Dart, R., 57
De France, J. F., 30
Delfini, L. F., 84, 85
Delgado, J. M. R., 3, 18, 19, 25, 27, 29, 30, 35, 36, 37, 40, 54-63, 272, 275, 278
delinquency (*see* juvenile delinquency)
Deltman, A. T., 90
Denenberg, V. H., 67
Department of Justice, 186, 189
depressant drugs, and aggression, 161
depression, and aggression, 26
DeRisis, W. J., 90
Desdemona, 187
Desjardins, C., 32, 78
Deutsch, F., 235
Developing Understanding Self and Others (DUSO), 267
Diament, C., 119
diazepam, and social contexts, 62-63
diet, and aggressivity, 34
Dietz, A., 119
Dinitz, J., 95
Dinitz, S., 88
Dinkmeyer, D., 267
displacement, of aggression, 213
"diversive exploration," 161
divorce, and physical abuse, 198
dogs: neurosis in, 26; rape symptoms in, 19, 25; trained attacks by, 10; tranquilized, 42
Dolan, D. J., 252

Fonberg, E. M., 3, 15, 16, 17, 18, 25, 26, 27, 30, 36, 37, 40, 272, 275, 277, 278, 280
Ford, D., 115
Forehand, R., 112
Fox, V., 213
Frączek, Adam, 1–5, 139–51, 158, 159, 171, 175n., 273, 279
F-ratio, 223
Fredericson, E., 32
Freud, Sigmund, 1, 145, 236, 275
Fromson, M. E., 170, 170n.
fructivores, humans as, 10
frustration, and fixation, 26
frustration-aggression hypothesis, 141, 143, 212–13, 275, 280
Fry, C. L., 236
Furness, F. M., 90

Gallistet, E., 87
gangs: ideology in, 209–10; status in, 208–10, 213 (*see also* adolescents)
Geen, R. G., 142, 151
Geer, J. H., 168, 170
Geiger, S. C., 35
Geller, S., 147
Gelles, Richard, 198
generalization: in classroom learning, 118–19; and self-structure, 170, 172
genetics: and aggression, 3, 34, 57–58, 274; and behavior traits, 67; and hunters, survival of, 10 (*see also* heredity)
genotype, and aggression, 71
Gersten, J. C., 87, 88
Giardina, W. J., 31
gibbons, attacks of, 60
Gibbons, S., 83
Gilmore, S. K., 85, 109n., 111, 116, 117
Ginsburg, B. E., 42, 71
Glaser, Daniel, 195
Glavin, J. P., 118
Gloor, P., 35
glucosteroids, adrenal, 32
Glueck, Eleanor, 87, 203
Glueck, Sheldon, 87, 203
goats, neurosis in, 26
Gordon, S. B., 111
Górski, J., 212
Graham, P., 88
Grandal, V., 252
gratification, delayed, 252
Graziano, A. M., 103

Greenblum, J., 166
Greenspan, S., 236, 238
Greenwood, C., 118
Greif, E., 254
guilt: and aggression, 158; and parricide, 198; and violence, 196
Gullion, M. E., 99, 116
guns, in homicides, 187
Guttman scalogram, 83–84

halfway houses, 96, 97
Hales, L., 267
Haney, C., 220
Hanf, C., 98
Hankoff, Leon D., 196
Hare, R. D., 279
Harlow, H. F., 25, 173
Harlow, M. K., 173
Hartman, R., 146
Hartmann, D. P., 169
Harvey, O. J., 170
Hathaway, S. R., 87
Hautojärvi, Sirkka, 75
Havighurst, R. J., 87
Hawkins, N., 98
Hawkins, R. P., 98
Heath, R. G., 33, 37
Hebb, D. O., 160, 165n., 172
Heider, F., 148
Heikkinen, A., 259, 261
Hellsten, Pentti, 197
Helson, H., 161
Heimburger, R. F., 35
Hendrick, C., 171, 172
Hendriks, A. F. C. J., 84, 105, 107, 112
Henry, J. P., 32
heredity, and aggression, 66–71, 80
Herfesty, L. J., 99
Hess, W. R., 26, 56
Hett, G. G., 119
Hewitt, L. S., 170n.
High Field Experiment, 96
Hilgard, E. R., 142
Hilton, S. M., 29
Hinsch, J., 231
hippocampus, electrical activity of, 30
Hoffman, M. L., 169, 235, 238, 244, 245, 253, 258, 259
Hoffmeister, F., 31
Hogan, R., 254
holistic analysis, 273
homeostasis, neurohumoral, 25

Meichenbaum, D., 253
Mempel, E., 35
mesencephalic level, and aggression, 27
Messinger, S. L., 212, 216
metamphetamine, and biting attack, 31–32
Meyer, H. J., 93
mice: aggression in, 31, 66–81, 272; breeding of, 66–67; fighting behavior, 278; hormones, and attack, 32; isolation of, 164
Mickle, W. A., 33
midbrain, and aggression, 26, 30, 40 (*see also* brain systems)
Milgram, S., 159, 168
Miller, N. E., 146
Miller, W. B., 185
Miller, W. C., 88
Milne, D. C., 85, 109*n*.
Mindanao, Philippines, 34
Minnesota Multi-Phasic Personality Inventory (MMPI), 84, 112, 136–37
Mir, D., 18
Mischel, W., 252
Mitchell, S., 85
modeling, parent training in, 101
Monachesi, E., 87
monkeys: aggression of, 29, 37; attack behavior of, 60; cognitive system in, 173; experimental study of, 55; instrumental learned responses, 19; rage points in, 25; social hierarchy in, 61–63
monoamines: and aggression, 31, 32, 33; turnovers in, 25, 26
Montagu, Ashley, 10, 34, 57
Moore, D. R., 89, 115
moral behavior: development of, 96; and self-control, 253
Morris, Desmond, 57
Morris, H. H., 88
Morrison, D. C., 98
motor system, and aggression, 7
Moyer, Kenneth E., 7, 16, 54, 184, 199, 203
Mukai, L. H., 89
Mulvihill, Donald J., 187, 198
Munkvad, I., 31
Munro, B., 101
Murphy, J. T., 30
Murray, H. A., 145
Myer, J. S., 16, 37

Nakao, H., 19, 26
Narabayashi, H., 35
National Commission on the Causes and Prevention of Violence, 1, 184, 187, 189
National Institute of Mental Health, 198
Nemiah, J. C., 36
neurons, action/inhibition of, 58
neurophysiology, of aggression, 54–63; and brain structures, 26–30; electrophysiological correlates, 30; experiments on, 55–57; genetic and environmental determinants, 57–58; mechanisms in, 26–35
neurosis: and acting out, 87; and emotional reaction, 145; and fear, 24, 25; in goats, 26; and motor acts, 26; and parricide, 198; and reinforcement, 25
Newman, Graeme R., 191
Nobylicyn, V. D., 161
noradrenaline: and aggression, 31; and neurochemical turnover, 25
norepinephrine (*see* noradrenaline)
norms, social: and aggression, 148–50, 281; and counterconditioning, 158; in prisons, 212, 219; socialization of, 278
North, J. A., 85
nucleus corporis geniculati medialis, 62
nucleus ventralis posterior lateralis, 61

obedience, and pain infliction, 168
object constancy, 172
object formation, cathetic, 145
O'Brien, John, 198
Ohlin, Lloyd, 199
O'Keeffe, J., 30
O'Leary, K. D., 118, 119
olfactory deprivation, 36 (*see also* sensory deprivation)
Olofsson, B., 258
Olson, D. H., 103
Olweus, D., 86, 88, 166
O'Neal, E. L., 142
Oniani, T. H., 19, 30
Oomura, Y., 30
Oppenheim, A. M., 85
Oregon Research Institute (ORI), 103
Oregon Social Learning Center (OSLC): comparison studies, 116–17; follow-up studies, 112–16; outcome studies, 103–9; process change, 111–12; success in, 109–11

race: and empathy, 244; and violence, 189, 190, 191, 192
rage: and aggression, 17; attack of, 16, 38, 40; and avoidance responses, 25; and brain centers, 18, 26, 33, 35, 40, 56; conditioned, 19; and flight, 18; instigation of, 56; reaction, 56; and subconscious, 43; system in, 9; traits specific to, 7
Ramamurthi, B., 35
Randrup, A., 31
rape, 189, 196
rats: aggression in, 30, 31, 36; castration of, 32; fixation of, 26; frustration of, 26; isolation of, 164; maternal aggression, 32; mankillers, 16; predatory behavior of, 27; shock behavior of, 18; trained attacks of, 13
Raush, H. L., 90
Ray, R. S., 99, 117, 118
Reber, A., 252
Reckless, W. C., 88, 95
Redl, R., 90
Reeves, A. G., 35
reflexive crying, 169
reformatories, in Kansas, 90
Reid, J. B., 84, 96, 98, 99, 101, 104, 105, 107, 109, 112, 117
reinforcement, 25, 112–13; and aggression, 3, 7, 9–26, 134, 271, 277; [and neurosis, 25; pure emotions, 17]; of deviance, 93; and family interaction, 99; and fighting behavior, 75; food acquisition, 15, 16; pain as, 276; secondary, 271, 277; and self-control, 252; vicarious, 144
relative solidarity, principle of, 215–16
Renfrew, W. W., 16
reproducibility coefficient (RQ), 84
retardation: and acting out, 85; and parent training, 113
rewards, intrinsic, 159
Reykowski, Janusz, 3, 142, 143, 146, 148, 149, 150, 158ff., 164, 170, 171, 173n., 273, 278, 279, 280
Rhodes, W. C., 83
ribonucleic acid (RNA), 33
Rivera, G., 101
Roberts, W. W., 16
Robins, L. H., 85, 88, 96
Robins, N. L., 88, 96
Robinson, B. W., 17, 19, 29

Roe, Kiki, 169, 171, 234
Rogers, C., 166, 235
role-playing: and empathy, 236, 238; parent training in, 101; and self-control, 261; skills in, 236
Romaniuk, A., 26
Rosen, P., 84
Rosenhahn, D., 254
Rosenthal, T. L., 118
Rosvold, H. E., 27
Rothenberg measure of social sensitivity, 245
Rotter, J. B., 164
Rule, B. G., 139
Rutter, M., 85

Sabelli, H. C., 31
Sadoff, Robert, 197
Sallows, G., 112
Saltzstein, H., 253, 258
Sampen, J., 98
Sano, K., 35
Sargent, Douglas, 197
Sawa, M., 30
Sawtell, 202
Scarpitti, F. R., 87, 88, 90
Schachter, S., 148, 163, 252
Schelle, J., 98, 109n.
Schindler, Sepp, 4, 229–32, 280
schizophrenia, 198, 283
Schleidt, 81
schools: adjustment problems in, 85, 85n., 86–88, 97; and aggression, 135, 280; attendance rates, 98; classroom intervention, 117–20; and delinquents, 231; empathy in, 244; self-control in, 255; self-esteem in, 167
Schreiner, L. H., 27
Schroder, H. M., 170
Schultz, L. G., 195
Schwade, E. D., 35
Schwartz, S., 173
Schweid, E., 98
Scott, J. P., 17, 67, 143
Sears, R. L., 258, 277
Sears self-concept measure, 245
secondary emotional aggression, 10–17, 151
Selective Service, 190
self-concept, and empathy, 245
self-control, and constructive behavior: developmental aspects, 252–53; and

education, 266–67; manifestations of, 253–55; model of, validation, 255–60; program experiment in, 261–66; training in, 273
self-esteem, 167, 274
self-structure: and aggression, 170–72; and cognitive network, 174
Sellin, Thorsten, 89, 189, 190, 191
Selman, R. L., 237
Sem-Jacobsen, C. W., 35
sensitization techniques, 258
sensory deprivation, 160, 163n., 203
sensort-motor perception, 146
septum, and emotions, 37
Serduchenko, 15
serotonine: and amygdalar neurons, 31; endogenous synthesis of, 31
Seward, J. P., 32
sex chromosomes, 78 (see also genetics)
sex-related aggression, 7, 17
sexuality: and aggression, 7, 17, 75, 163n., 274, 282; competition for, 5; and motivation theory, 276; repression of, 202; and violence, 199
sham rage, 29
Shantz, C. U., 235
Shaw, D. A., 99, 118
Shealy, C. N., 27, 29
Sheard, M. H., 27, 40, 52
Sheerer, M., 146
Shelley, E. L. V., 194
Shemberg, K. M., 115
Shepherd, M., 85, 86
Shure, M., 238
Siegel, A., 40
Simcha-Fagan, O., 87
Simner, M. L., 169
Singer, J. E., 137, 148
Singer, R. D., 146
Skinner, B. F., 1, 132, 143, 160n.
Skinrud, K., 99
Skog, D., 40
sleep, waves in EEG, 40
Sloane, H., 98
Smith, Rosemary, 134
Smither, S., 235
Smits-Van Sonsheek, B., 238
Smoleńska, M. Z., 170
social environment, and aggression, 71–77
social hierarchy, 29–30, 61–63
Social Interaction Inventory, 245

social isolation, 75–77 (see also sensory deprivation)
socialization: and aggression, 281–82; and delinquency, 229; and empathy, 235; and norms, 278; and self-control, 259; sex-typed, 135–38, 272–73; social standards on, 254
social learning theory, 141, 158; on acting-out child, 93; and aggression, 66; and change, 111–12; and child problems, 93–97; for treatment, 115
sociopaths, anxiety in, 163
spatial skills, training for, 241
Spiegel, E. A., 35
Spitz, R., 230
Spivak, G., 238
Sprague, R. L., 118
squirrel monkeys, 30 (see also monkeys)
Stachnik, T. J., 10
status quo, principle of, 216–17
Staub, E., 238, 254
stealing, and coercive behavior, 107
Steinart, H., 231
Steinmetz, Suzanne, 198
Steriade, M., 30
Sterman, M. B., 40
STET daily report, 116
Stiles, W., 276
stimuli, and aggression, 3, 4, 24
stochastic model, on delinquency, 190–91
Storr, A., 57
Stotland, E., 171
Straughan, D. W., 31
Straus, Murray, 198, 200
Strelau, J., 144, 145, 161, 162, 163
Stuart, R., 98
Stukát, K. G., 267
subconscious, and rage, 43
subcultures: of juvenile delinquents, 229–32; of violence, 197–200
substantia innominata, 35
Suchowska, 170
Sullivan, H. S., 236
Summers, T. B., 27
Surgeon General's Scientific Advisory Committee on Television and Social Behavior, 1
Sutherland, Edward, 195
Sverud, K. A., 267
Swedish University of Turku, 66
Sweet, W. H., 35

ABOUT THE
EDITORS AND
CONTRIBUTORS

SEYMOUR FESHBACH, professor and chairman of the Department of Psychology, UCLA, has long been associated with research on aggression. He has conducted studies on the effects of varying methods of aggression control on the displacement of aggression. His research has produced publications on the effects of television violence on aggression, particularly the report of what is generally believed to be the first systematic field experiment on television exposure. Feshbach has also written a number of theoretical papers on aggression.

ADAM FRĄCZEK, professor of special education and of psychology at the Institute of Psychology, University of Warsaw, worked with Leonard Berkowitz, a leading authority on aggression. He also has worked independently in Poland, and has written extensively on problems of aggression and emotion. Presently he directs an active research group in Warsaw.

JOSÉ M. R. DELGADO is currently the director of the Neurological Research Institute at the University of Madrid. His research in the area of brain and behavior is well-known, particularly his work on implantation of electrodes in areas of the cortex that mediate aggressive behavior.

LEONARD D. ERON has carried out an extensive series of investigations addressed to the development of aggressive behavior in children. His paper on the long-term effects of exposure to aggressive television has been particularly influential. He also has been editor of the *Journal of Abnormal Psychology*.

NORMA DEITCH FESHBACH is a developmental psychologist who has carried out pioneering work in the area of children's empathy, and in the relationship of empathy to aggression. She is codirector of the UCLA Bush Foundation Program in Child Development and Social Policy, professor and head of Early Childhood and Developmental Studies in the School of Education, professor of psychology, and president of the Western Psychological Association for the year 1979-80.

ELZBIETA FONBERG is a physiologist whose research on central physiological mechanisms mediating emotional behavior is internationally known. She has been influential by virtue of her research and the many physiological psychologists from the United States and Europe who have studied and worked in her laboratory in Warsaw.

KIRSTI LAGERSPETZ is a Finnish physiological psychologist who has published extensively on physiological and genetic mechanisms mediating agressive behavior in rodents. Her recent work on genetic influences and on the relationship between the sexual and aggressive behavior systems has attracted considerable interest.

MAREK KOSEWSKI is a psychologist at the University of Warsaw, Institute of Social Prevention and Resocialization, whose specialty is criminology. He provides a significant social-psychological and sociological perspective on problems of aggression.

GERALD R. PATTERSON is a clinical psychologist whose analyses of the factors maintaining aggressive behavior in highly aggressive children have resulted in widely cited intervention programs. In recent years he has developed systematic behavioral programs designed to alter interaction patterns in families with aggressive, acting-out children.

JANUSZ REYKOWSKI is a senior professor of psychology at the University of Warsaw. He has made significant contributions to personality theory and to the study of altruism and other prosocial behaviors.

LEA PITKÄNEN-PULKKINEN is a Finnish psychologist who has published extensively in the area of children's aggression. Her recent development of psychoeducational programs designed to modify children's aggressive behaviors has attracted much interest and attention.

SEPP SCHINDLER is a professor of psychology at the University of Salzburg whose specialty is delinquency. He has played a significant role in the development of programs for delinquent youngsters that have been adopted throughout Austria.

MARVIN E. WOLFGANG is a sociologist who is acknowledged to be a leading authority on problems of crime, violence, and delinquency. He played a significant role in the preparation of major public policy statements by presidential commissions on television and violence, and on pornography.